Japanese Colonial Education in Taiwan

Harvard East Asian Series 88
The East Asian Research Center
at Harvard University administers
research projects designed to
further scholarly understanding of
China, Japan, Korea, Vietnam,
Inner Asia, and adjacent areas.

For Maia and Yoshi Tsurumi, Stan and Win Henderson

Copyright © 1977 by the President and Fellows of Harvard College
All rights reserved
Preparation of this volume has been aided by a grant from the
Ford Foundation.
Printed in the United States of America

Library of Congress Cataloging in Publication Data

Tsurumi, E   Patricia, 1938-
  Japanese colonial education in Taiwan, 1895-1945.

  (Harvard EastAsian series; 88)
  Bibliography: p.
  Includes index.
  1. Education—Taiwan—History.   I. Title.   II. Se-
ries.
LA1136.T76   370'.951'249   76-29628
ISBN 0-674-47187-3

Japanese Colonial

Education in

Taiwan, 1895-1945

E. Patricia Tsurumi

Harvard University Press
Cambridge, Massachusetts
and London, England
1977

Preface

Japanese imperialism is an important issue for all serious students of Japan's modern history. What motives lay behind Japan's rise as an imperialist power in the late nineteenth and early twentieth centuries? Who benefited from this phenomenon? Who were the main actors in Japan's imperialist scenario? What influences did the example of the Western powers exert upon the formation of Japanese imperialism? What was the relationship between Japanese nationalism and overseas expansion? How closely related is Japanese overseas expansion after World War II to the prewar imperialism? Surely answers to these and other questions must be found before Japanese imperialism can be understood properly.

Scholars of modern Japan have long recognized this challenge, and there is no scarcity of studies of Japanese imperialism. In the main, these have tended to concentrate upon the relationship between Japan's internal political and economic history and the course of expansion abroad. Such analyses have contributed generously to our understanding of the characteristics of Japanese imperialism and of the nature of modern Japan in all its political, economic, social, cultural, and psychological dimensions.

However, Japan's specific colonial ventures in Asia have commanded less scholarly attention than has the larger imperialist experience. In order to supplement, complement, and perhaps refine somewhat the existing analyses of the dynamics of Japanese imperialism, it is necessary to know a great deal more about Japan's administration of its former overseas territories. Studies of Japanese colonialism are, for the most part, still in an embryonic stage. For instance, in spite of abundant data, the role played by Japan's three major colonies — Taiwan, Korea, and Manchuria — in the ruling country's modern economic development has yet to be delineated. Yet this is a vital issue for all economic historians

concerned with Japan. (I am indebted to Ramon Myers for bringing this to my attention.) Some splendid pioneer work has already
been published in Japan, and Chong-sik Lee's *The Politics of
Korean Nationalism* (1963), a study of some of the consequences
of Japanese rule in Korea, has set high standards for all Western
students of Japanese colonialism for more than a decade. It is
hoped that the present study, in conjunction with others which
focus on Taiwan, Korea, or Manchuria, will help tell the story of
Japan as a colonial power. It is also hoped that this study will be
of use to students of comparative colonialism.

Japan was the only non-Western colonial power before World
War II. Was Japanese colonialism any different from its Western
contemporaries? How much was the Japanese administration of
Taiwan like French, Dutch, British, or American rule in other
parts of Asia?

How closely did the actions of the colonial governments resemble the pattern of governmental initiative in the home islands
established by the Meiji rulers and their successors? Formal schooling was a key tool of the Meiji nation builders. How important
was Japanese education in Taiwan as an instrument of colonial
development? This book is specifically addressed to that question.

Another important concern is the effect of colonization on the
people who are colonized — what it does to their minds as well as
to their bodies. Psychological consequences of colonization are
often among the most difficult to pin down, but they are nonetheless of enormous importance. Among other things, they affect
the colonized and the colonizers' perceptions of themselves, relations between the two in the post-colonial era, and relations
of the two with other nations. Different peoples react differently
to colonial regimes: the contrast between Taiwan and Korea is a
case in point. In this instance the different reactions influence
even current study of the two colonial experiences. The intense
alienation from their Japanese rulers felt by colonized Koreans is
abundantly reflected in contemporary Korean research concerned
with Korea's Japanese period, while many Taiwanese scholars
write in an amazingly detached fashion about their country's
years under Japanese government. As colonial schools and increasing literacy do not affect different peoples equally, neither
do they affect everyone within a given society equally. Although
this study offers more questions than answers in this sphere, it

does seek to draw attention to the ways in which various groups of Taiwanese were influenced by Japanese education.

Japanese and Chinese romanizations in the text and the glossary observe the following principles: where the narrative deals with Taiwan during its Japanese period, the Japanese romanization is generally given first for words that can be read in both Japanese and Chinese, with the Chinese provided in parentheses where relevant, for example, Taihoku (Taipei). Major exceptions to this rule are two: names of Chinese-Taiwanese individuals, and place names of minor localities for which the Japanese readings are unknown. In both cases Chinese readings alone are provided. Japanese readings of Taiwanese place names follow the readings given in Abe Kiyoshi, *Taiwan chimei kenkyū* (1937). When the narrative deals with pre-1895 Taiwan or post-1945 Taiwan, only Chinese romanizations have been given.

In completing this book I have incurred boundless debts. I am deeply grateful to the Canada Council for its generous support. The Canada Council made the research for and the writing of this book possible.

To many individuals I owe an enormous amount. I owe a great deal to Albert Craig and Donald Shively, under whose direction the project first took shape. I am deeply indebted to Mr. Craig for encouragement, intellectual stimulation, common sense, humor, and above all invaluable advice from beginning to end of the study. Special thanks go to George Potter of the Harvard-Yenching Library. In Japan I was aided by the knowledge and kindness of many individuals. I am grateful to them all. In Taiwan too I benefited from the help of scholars and librarians. I will never be able to express adequately my appreciation to the many Taiwanese in different parts of the island who kindly and patiently answered my questions and told me their stories. Their warmth and friendliness made a field trip to Taiwan in 1969 an experience I shall always treasure. Cynthia Flood, who read and criticized the entire manuscript, aided me enormously during the final stages of research and writing. My thanks go to June Belton, Marie Castro, Thora Chinnery, Rachel Cummins, Nancy Grab, and Marianne Jaccobi, through whose herculean efforts the final manuscript took shape. Any work of this nature benefits from the work of other scholars, and the notes acknowledge some of what I owe to others who have studied Taiwan. However, I must acknowledge special gratitude to Ching-chih Chen, for the example his superlative research has set and for the generosity with which he shared his vast knowledge of Taiwan's past. The person to whom I owe most is Yoshihiro Tsurumi, scholar, teacher, critic, calligrapher, friend, magnificent manager of the practicalities of everyday living.

Contents

Tables

Appendix Tables

1 / The Setting

The late nineteenth century in Japan was a period of excitement and change. New ideas circulated, new laws were promulgated, new institutions appeared, as the country's leaders raced to create a modern nation. Modern statehood, they reasoned, would put an end to Japan's humiliating unequal treaties with the Western nations; but their long-range goal was far greater than this. Their aim was nothing less than a Japan capable of matching the industrial, military, and even colonial achievements of Europe and America. Foreign Minister Inoue Kaoru (1835-1915) expressed this aim in 1887: "What we have to do is to transform our empire and our people, and make the empire like the countries of Europe and our people like the people of Europe. To put it differently, we have to establish a new, European-style empire on the edge of Asia."[1] In 1895, a year after serious renegotiation of the unequal treaties had begun, Japan took a significant step toward the establishment of that European-style empire on the edge of Asia when she acquired her first colony. This was the island of Taiwan, which China ceded to Japan after the Sino-Japanese War of 1894-95.

Japan's leaders were painfully aware of their country's position as the first non-European state to join the ranks of the nineteenth-century colonial powers and felt that all eyes in the West were upon them. They were certain that Japanese conduct on the island would be compared to European colonial rule in other parts of the globe. As Gotō Shimpei (1857-1929), the key administrator of Taiwan during its early years as a Japanese colony, recalled a little more than a decade later:

> With regard to the transfer of Formosa, it may be noted that Japan made no preparations whatever for the administration of the island at the time of its acquisition, notwithstanding the fact

1

that, in the case of other nations confronted by a similar occasion, elaborate schemes are generally formulated to meet contingencies connected with the occupation of a new territory. Under these circumstances there was every reason to doubt whether Japan could ever succeed as ruler of the island. Experienced men of other countries, who had practical experience of the difficulties in governing a new territory, were inclined to predict that Japan would, like Sparta of old, certainly fail as a ruler in peace though she might succeed in war.[2]

With all the world watching, Gotō and his colleagues were determined that Taiwan should become a model colony. It was to become a well-regulated, economically productive territory, inhabited by a peaceful, industrious population.

At the time of the Japanese takeover in 1895, Taiwan was anything but a model colony. Chinese imperial government no longer functioned, anti-Japanese sentiment ran high, and administrative chaos prevailed.[3] Troops ruthlessly suppressed opposition to Japanese authority, but the new rulers quickly realized that armed force alone would not consolidate their new territory.[4] Civil institutions would have to be introduced to keep order, to exploit the island's economic resources, and to enlist cooperation from the islanders. Education was to play an important part in these plans.

Education, it was hoped, would secure the cooperation and allegiance of the natives and perhaps eventually would even assimilate them. Schools, like soldiers, would help control the people. "After military conquest, after the violent medicine, a sedative is needed," wrote one of Taiwan's new rulers in 1904.[5] But education was to be much more than the ideological arm of military victory and pacification. Education was seen as an instrument of fundamental social, political, economic, and cultural change; it was to transform a segment of traditional China into an integral part of modern Japan.

This was an ambitious and optimistic program. In the nineteenth century Taiwan was known, among Chinese officials who might have the ill luck to be posted there, as a malaria-ridden hole. Its inhabitants — two and one half million bellicose Chinese settlers and almost 150,000 headhunting aborigines — were considered even less hospitable than the unhealthy physical environment.[6] Taiwan, which was not incorporated into the Chinese empire until the late seventeenth century, had remained a peripheral area remote from the political and cultural heartland of China.

Early History of Taiwan

A green, mountainous oval, Taiwan measures approximately 240 miles from north to south, and 90 miles from east to west at its broadest point. No place on the island is more than fifty miles from the smooth coastline which winds in and out for 708 miles. It lies astride the Tropic of Cancer, and it ranges from a subtropical climate in the north to tropical in the south. Located almost at the point where Southeast Asia becomes East Asia, Taiwan is 695 miles south of Japan and 199 miles north of Luzon, the large northern member of the Philippine archipelago.[7]

Long before the island became Japan's first colony, before it joined the Chinese empire, before the first Chinese migrants crossed the Taiwan Strait, there were Malayo-Polynesian aborigines living there. Modern carbon dating has pinpointed various aborigine cultures at different locations from about 3000 B.C. onward. These headhunting peoples hunted, fished, and practiced primitive farming.

Although the first Chinese settlers probably reached Taiwan in the twelfth century, Chinese immigration never really got under way until the eighteenth century.[8] At first the migrants came mainly from the province of Fukien across the 150 miles of the Taiwan Strait, which separated the island from the Chinese mainland, but soon they were joined by natives of the neighboring province of Kwangtung. The few thousand Chinese settlers opened up farm land, often at the expense of the island's first inhabitants, who either rented ground to the newcomers or had it wrenched from them by force. The immigrants hunted deer, fished in coastal waters, and fought and traded with the aborigines. They moved into aborigine villages and bullied their inhabitants by threatening to cut off their salt supplies. Among these frontiersmen were merchants who traded with China and Japan. Great profits were realized from the trade with Japan in particular, because in that country deer hides, used to make warriors' armor, were in seemingly limitless demand.[9]

Under Dutch Rule

All this was changed by the arrival of the Dutch. From 1624 to 1662, under the Dutch East India Company, Taiwan became an important entrepôt in Holland's worldwide trading network. The company exported sugar, venison, antlers, and rattan to China in exchange for raw silk, silk fabric, porcelain, drugs, and gold. Taiwan became a great distribution center, handling gold, silver, and copper from Japan, spices from Southeast Asia, and Taiwanese sugar bound for China, Japan, Persia, and even Europe. The Dutch East India Company's trade monopoly was backed by well-armed soldiers, so the Chinese could do little but grumble, or try to poach and smuggle.[10]

As in Java, the company was not content to take its trading goods from what it could gain in peaceful exchange with the island's inhabitants.[11] Trading goods were obtained through levies and license fees as the Dutch gained control of more and more Chinese and aborigine settlements. Aborigine villages were compelled to pay tribute, usually deer hides, although the tribes were allowed a great deal of internal self-rule. Chinese settlers were often forced to lease their farms from the company, which claimed sovereignty over all land. From 1645, Chinese who wished to trade with aborigines had to purchase licenses to do so from the Dutch East India Company. The Dutch became moneylenders too, as Chinese merchants sought additional funds to add to their own investments in large-scale sugar and rice cultivation.[12]

Despite Chinese resentment against Dutch taxes and restrictions, immigration from China continued and even increased. Moving in from the coast, settlers fought aborigines for their lands, driving them to the interior and to the east. As the Ming Dynasty (1368-1643) ended, war and chaos on the mainland sent thousands of Chinese across the Taiwan Strait. When the fighting subsided in southeast China about 1648, some of these migrants returned to the continent. But in the 1650s the great Ming loyalist, Cheng Ch'eng-kung (1624-1662), who was known to the Dutch as Koxinga, dug himself in on the Fukien coast to resist the new dynasty's attempts to dislodge him, and another wave of refugees crossed the strait to Taiwan.[13]

For the first decade or so the Dutch welcomed this influx, for they recognized the Chinese as able farmers. Friction between Dutch and Chinese did not disappear, however. A poverty-stricken immigrant who survived the hazardous journey across the strait had to stay alive and find a livelihood, perhaps in a rice or a sugar plantation. If later he moved on to open up farm land on his own, or decided to hunt or fish, such encroachment upon

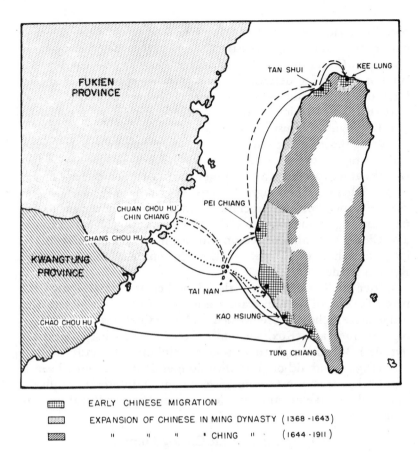

EARLY CHINESE MIGRATION

EXPANSION OF CHINESE IN MING DYNASTY (1368-1643)

" " " · CHING " · (1644-1911)

aborigine prerogatives might cost him his life; yet he had to pay the Dutch for the privilege of attempting these enterprises. Memories of earlier days when Chinese freedom had been restricted only by nature and by aborigines made the Dutch monopoly hard to endure. In September 1652 a large-scale Chinese uprising challenged Dutch control, and the remaining decade of East India Company rule was troubled by Chinese unrest.[14]

The Kingdom of Koxinga

In 1661 Koxinga, frustrated in his fight against the Ch'ing on the mainland, left Fukien province and led his forces to Taiwan. With the help of local Chinese his army landed and after a nine-month siege drove out the Dutch. Although Koxinga died the following summer, his successors maintained Taiwan until 1683 as a base for attack against the Ch'ing who had wrested the Chinese empire from the Ming dynastic line. Refugees from politics and famine in China proper flocked to the kingdom of Koxinga, in spite of the Ch'ing defense policy of moving coastal dwellers inland and forbidding all contact with Taiwan. In fact, it was in part this policy which motivated already displaced peasants to join Koxinga's colonists in Taiwan.

During the long siege Koxinga's followers had experienced critical shortages, for captured Dutch stores were consumed in a few months and expected grain shipments from Fukien did not materialize. Therefore he assigned his men to lands as farmer-soldiers as soon as possible and proclaimed an ambitious program to expand fishing, commerce, and forestry in addition to agriculture. The Ch'ing ban inhibited communication with the Chinese mainland, but ships went freely to the Philippines, Japan, and the Ryukyu islands.[15]

Under the Koxinga family, the island became increasingly Chinese. To obtain administrators and to reinforce loyalty to the Ming cause, schools were opened and examinations were held at regular intervals. (Koxinga himself erected the first Confucian temple.) But although there was a sprinkling of literati among the refugees and although well-to-do merchants had long been a part of the scene, most colonists were poor and illiterate, unlikely to be able to take advantage of educational and cultural institutions.[16]

An Outpost of the Ch'ing Empire

In 1683 Koxinga's twelve-year-old grandson surrendered to the Manchu court, and Taiwan entered the Ch'ing empire as a prefecture of Fukien province. The island was divided into districts (hsien) and subprefectures (*t'ing*) and became part of the regular Ch'ing administrative structure.[17] The supervision of aborigines was handled separately from the regular administration of the settled areas, and as long as the tribes were peaceful they were left to run their own affairs. About ten thousand soldiers supported the civilian officials, who by 1811 were responsible for a population of nearly two million Chinese.[18] Although Ch'ing officials organized local mutual security groups (*pao-chia*) and militia units (*lien-chuang* and *t'uan-lien*) to assist their regular troops, they, like the Dutch, found the Chinese settlers a turbulent lot. From 1696 to 1838 there were twenty-seven major rebellions in

Taiwan prefecture; it became widely known as a place where there was "a small rebellion every three years and a large disturbance every five."[19] Opposition to Ch'ing authority was by no means the only type of disorder. Bloody battles raged among ethnic and subethnic groups of settlers, as rivalry among families, surname groups, local associations, and whole communities found an outlet in private warfare.[20] Chinese and aborigines fought each other too.[21]

Ch'ing policy continued to forbid emigration to the troublesome island until 1760. Only government officials and accredited traders were allowed to leave for Taiwan and they were not permitted to take their families with them; the Chinese government branded as outlaws all unauthorized travelers to the island. For almost a century after the ban was lifted the Manchu court ignored this watery fringe of the empire. It was only when hard pressed by the Western imperialist powers in the middle of the nineteenth century that the Ch'ing began to actively encourage Chinese settlement in Taiwan, as a weapon against foreign encroachment from the south.[22] Although immigration was illegal before 1760, throughout the Ch'ing period Taiwan's Chinese population steadily increased.

The life patterns of most of the Chinese settlers in Taiwan changed little during the two hundred years of Ch'ing rule — they continued to farm, fish, log, and trade as before — but certain developments did take place which had important effects upon the island's later history. Rice was now exported to the mainland, especially to rice-hungry Fukien, while sugar and other agricultural products were sent to Japan and the Philippines as well as to north China. Trade continued to be profitable and Chinese merchants, who during the Dutch period had often been agricultural as well as commercial entrepreneurs, prospered unchallenged until 1858, when American and Russian diplomatic representatives persuaded the Ch'ing to add Taiwan to the list of places open to foreign residence and commerce. During the following decade British firms, already settled in ports on the mainland, became prominent in the tea and camphor business, and by the 1880s Western dealers were handling almost all the sugar exports.[23]

From the earliest times on, a large percentage of the Chinese who came to Taiwan had been single males. During the Dutch period, Koxinga's rule, and up through the eighteenth century, many of these remained seasonal visitors, returning to their homes on the mainland after the growing season was over.[24] Thus it is not surprising that during the early Ch'ing period in particular men still far outnumbered women; the aged and the very young were rather scarce.[25] In many villages and even in some of the towns the patterns of settled family and social life familiar in mainland China were not always possible. Settlers did, however, bring their customs and lifestyles with them when they could. As the Chinese population became larger and more permanent, communities became more and more like those on the mainland.[26] By the nineteenth century, near the administrative centers on the western plains and around the prefectural capital in the south, a small but distinct class of literati had emerged.

To encourage children of this scholar-gentry class to study the Confucian classics, prefectural and district academies were supported by public taxes and by revenue from lands attached to the academies.[27] Since each government academy taught a few dozen privileged pupils at most, private schools and private tutors prepared most of the young hopefuls who planned to sit for the imperial examinations and try for literati rank.[28] "As of 1810 the total literati class probably did not exceed five thousand of a population of roughly two million. Thus the literati comprised less than .5 percent of the population, a ratio much smaller than on the mainland."[29] Although the class was small, it was, like the group on the mainland, extremely important because of its wealth, status, and power.[30] In 1883 over two thousand individuals were reported studying for the examinations.[31]

Taiwan's involvement in the Sino-French War of 1883-85 finally brought this outpost of the empire to Peking's attention. When the war ended in 1885 Liu Ming-ch'uan (1836-96), the able officer who defended Taiwan against a French onslaught during the war, took over the governorship of the island. In 1887 the court raised Taiwan's status: the prefecture of Fukien became a separate province.[32] To prepare Taiwan to protect China against future Western aggression from the south, Liu immediately began a thorough overhaul of its government and society. He introduced fiscal and administrative reforms, initiated new policies for dealing with the aborigines, improved coal mining and shipping, and started to build a railroad and telecommunications network. With defense priorities in mind he remodeled Taipei, the city in the north he chose to be Taiwan's new capital.

He set up a school of Western studies to train foreign language specialists and opened a telegraphy school. Unfortunately for Liu, his innovations brought upon his head the wrath of conservatives at the Peking court. In 1891 he was replaced by a conventional bureaucrat who promptly discontinued his projects.[33]

The Japanese Takeover

This then was the Taiwan that Japan acquired in 1895. Still a frontier region populated by aborigines and unruly Chinese pioneers, the island was nevertheless clearly a part of the Chinese empire. Chinese settlement patterns and customs were identifiable and a small literati class supported schools, teachers, and candidates who sat for the imperial examinations. Agriculture and trade sustained the dominant Chinese, while the aborigines lived as best they could on the fringe of settled and fertile regions.

During the five-month campaign to occupy the island, Japanese troops encountered stiff resistance from segments of the native population—aborigine as well as Chinese—who for a variety of reasons feared and resented the takeover.[34] Japanese soldiers were not able to distinguish easily between rebels and neutral, peaceful villagers, and, with the intention of setting an example to anyone dreaming of joining the guerillas, they killed, burned, and looted indiscriminately, terrorizing the general population. Not surprisingly, this high-handed policy increased the hostility and confusion, and the opposition became even more widespread. For three years the Japanese were surrounded by defiance as swelling bands of Chinese rebels took up banditry, aborigine raids continued, and a sullen populace shunned contact with the invaders whenever possible.[35] Epidemics ravaged the island, killing more Japanese soldiers than military campaigns did. Some conciliatory overtures were made toward influential literati families, but the colony's first two governors-general spent most of their energies trying to restore order among the Taiwanese, as the Japanese called the Chinese settlers,[36] and to contain the aborigines within their mountain strongholds. Officially the colony was divided into three administrative districts but civil government existed on paper only.[37]

Consolidation and Plans for the Future

Under the third governor-general, Kodama Gentarō (1852-1906), who arrived with his chief civilian administrator, Gotō

Shimpei, in 1898, foundations for civil institutions were finally laid. Colonial government structures were nearly all put under the control of a civil administration bureau (*minseibu*) headed by Gotō. A redefinition of military and police jurisdictions severely limited the activities of the army and military police and produced a well-coordinated civil police force which was much more effective in overcoming unrest than earlier forces had been. The headquarters of this police force were, of course, in Gotō's bureau. The confused maze of law courts which had been thrown up hurriedly to deal with offenses against Japanese authority was simplified and clarified. A land survey and population census, far more detailed and thorough than any undertaken in the past, soon provided the new government with vital statistics about the people and territory they had annexed.[38] Educational planning was a fundamental part of these measures to secure civil rule. Not surprisingly, the new colonial rulers drew heavily on the philosophy and experiences of the educational system instituted in Meiji Japan in formulating concepts and programs for Taiwan.

For the rulers of Meiji Japan, education—particularly higher education—was a means toward the acquisition of the Western technological and managerial skills which the would-be nation state needed. They saw elementary schools, especially, as avenues to general acceptance of the new lifestyles and occupations they were introducing in Japanese society. Elementary schools were also expected to forge a unified and loyal nation out of a population with strong regional ties. The loyalty of such a unified Japanese people would of course be to the country's rulers and their goals.

The Meiji educational system therefore included two main components. The upper level consisted of a small number of secondary schools and an even smaller number of institutions of higher learning. Tokyo University was chief among the latter group, which also included specialized colleges and higher technical schools. A few selected elementary school graduates were prepared for entrance to this upper level by middle schools and, in some cases, higher girls' schools. The lower level of the system provided elementary schooling for the 90 percent of the population whose formal education ended at primary school graduation.

Meiji educational planners thus carefully developed the two tracks of schooling which gave "Japanese education its 'dumbbell' configuration: a small corps of highly, even liberally, educated scholars, technicians, and bureaucrats on one end; on the other an entire population trained to basic literacy and economic usefulness and political obedience, up through the primary level; and very little in between."[39] Although with the vast expansion of higher level facilities following World War I about 20 percent of the population received some sort of postprimary schooling, as late as 1945 "there were only 390,000 students enrolled in all institutions of higher education . . . , a figure that represented approximately 5 percent of the appropriate age group."[40]

It was the lower level of the Meiji educational system—the track designed to enlighten, discipline, and indoctrinate the Japanese masses—which served as the model for the Japanese in Taiwan in 1895. Although some felt that some postprimary technical education was needed there, it was a rare mind among the island's new rulers that dared to dream of any Taiwanese joining the empire's highly educated elite.[41] But the need for basic elementary schooling was seen as urgent. Japanese education in Taiwan was to be mainly elementary education; it was to train the Taiwanese for life and work in a new world; and it was above all to make them unquestioningly loyal to Japan. In short, it was to transform a segment of traditional China into an integral part of modern Japan.

How was this to be done? The new Japanese rulers in Taiwan were not favorably impressed by the local gentry's schools and schoolmasters. Perhaps these reminded them all too much of the simple "temple schools" (*tera koya*) of their own not-too-distant past.[42] The kind of education they had in mind was closer in spirit to Liu Ming-ch'uan's short-lived experiments, but it soon became clear that the Japanese planned to introduce modern scientific education to Taiwan on a much more ambitious scale. Their aim was a network of elementary schools for children which would not only usurp the functions of traditional Chinese schools and tutors but would also eventually reach far more youngsters than Chinese classical education ever had.

The Japanese wanted to replace "backward" Chinese learning with the modern, scientific education pursued so enthusiastically in Meiji Japan. But the modern education of contemporary Japan included a significant amount of an East Asian cultural tradition shared with China. This tradition emphasized the written word, the teachings of the Chinese sages, and a range of Confucian values: benevolent rule, loyalty, hierarchical status relations, and family morality. Taiwan's new rulers thought that this common heritage, properly manipulated, would help them to gain the loyalty and cooperation of the colony's people.

But because Chinese classical studies had been associated with Taiwan's past under Chinese rule, many Japanese regarded them with suspicion. Great care was to be taken to lift Confucian morality from its historical context. Where the classical tradition urged loyalty and obedience to one's superiors it was to be strengthened; where it encouraged identification with China it was to be forbidden. Confucian principles, colonial educators thought, could be taught through all-important Japanese language studies, which would emphasize loyalty to Japan as they improved communication between ruled and ruler. Arithmetic, because it was seen as the basis of a scientific training which would equip Taiwanese children for life in a modern society, was also considered an essential subject. Hence the first Japanese schools stressed Japanese language and arithmetic. Other subjects were desirable or expedient but definitely of lesser importance. Decrying the "backwardness" of the island's Chinese schools and teachers, Japanese educators began their attack upon traditional education by concentrating on the children of the literati.

2 / The Groundwork: Gradualism and Separatism

The first assault on the massive problem of educating the Taiwanese gentry's children was led by Izawa Shūji (1851-1917).[1]
Izawa had been sent by the Ministry of Education to the Bridgewater Normal School in Massachusetts in 1875 and had come
back to Japan an enthusiast of Western-style education; he introduced gymnastics and Western music to Japanese schoolchildren.
When Mori Arinori (1847-89) became education minister in 1885
he made Izawa chief of the ministry's textbook bureau, which was
a strategic post in an administration divided on the question of
moral education in the schools.[2]

Like the unconventional and controversial Mori, Izawa believed that all schooling must serve the needs of the state, but he
differed from the education minister on one important issue.
Mori felt that economic realism and operational efficiency required that local governments, private donors, and parents be
heavily involved in financing education; Izawa thought that the
state had an obligation to pay for all public schools.[3] Since Japan
was finding out that nation building was an extremely costly
process, it was no wonder that Izawa had difficulty gaining a sympathetic hearing in government.[4] Education already consumed a
large proportion of the national budget, and other priorities were
considered more important. When Izawa's powerful patron Mori
was assassinated in 1889 his personal position within the ministry
was weakened, and he decided to try to bring pressure upon the
government from outside. In 1890 he therefore organized the
Society for State Education (Kokka kyōiku sha), which for several years campaigned unsuccessfully for the public financing of
education.[5] Disappointed but not despairing, Izawa saw the cession of Taiwan to Japan in 1895 as a second chance for his ideas;
perhaps his vision of "state education," spurned in Japan, could
be realized in the schooling of the Taiwanese.[6]

Early in 1895 Izawa found an opportunity to present a set of detailed proposals for education in Japan's first colony to Rear Admiral Kabayama Sukenori (1837-1922), unofficially recognized as governor-general designate of Taiwan.[7] His proposals were divided into "emergency activities" and "permanent activities."[8] The main object of both was a plentiful supply of Japanese-language teachers, who represented in Izawa's view the most essential ingredient for educational success. "Emergency activities" outlined crash programs to train both Japanese and natives as Japanese-language teachers, and to teach Japanese to natives hoping to become clerks in the colonial administration.[9]

Izawa recommended two main projects for postprimary schooling as "permanent activities": a Japanese-language school, and normal schools for natives. The former was to comprise an education department to train Japanese for service in future elementary and normal schools, and a language department to provide a thorough grounding in Japanese for prospective Taiwanese clerks and interpreters.[10] This department would also offer instruction in native languages for Japanese nationals. The normal schools were to be strictly for natives.[11]

Kabayama must have looked with favor upon the proposals, because Izawa accompanied the rear admiral when he went to take up his duties as the first Japanese governor-general of Taiwan in the late spring of 1895. On May 21 an education bureau (*gakumu bu*) was established in the government general's civil department (*minsei kyoku*), with Izawa as its acting chief. But because of hostility toward the Japanese around the administration's headquarters at Taihoku (the Japanese name for Taipei), the education bureau soon moved to Shisangyan (Chih-shan-yen), a hamlet about three miles north of Taihoku.[12]

Izawa had stumbled across this hamlet one day while exploring the countryside with a Taiwanese interpreter. His interest in the landscape deepened when he learned that the literary talent of its gentry was famous throughout Taiwan. At Shisangyan itself he discovered a ruined temple sheltering a single priest, who told Izawa that formerly a school, much respected by the residents of the district, had existed on the spot.[13] Against the advice of his Taiwanese interpreter — who warned him that the neighborhood was a haunt of bandits — he decided that this was the ideal site for his education bureau and his first school.

A few days later he returned and delivered a two-hour lecture to the local gentry. The themes of his speech were: cession of Taiwan to Japan, submission to the Japanese emperor, and education to make Taiwanese into law-abiding Japanese citizens (*Nihon no ryōmin*). Izawa told his audience about the Japanese emperor and his descent from a ruling dynasty unbroken from time immemorial. Since this powerful monarch, he explained, had taken the mandate of heaven from the Ch'ing emperor, the people of Taiwan owed him all their loyalty. He announced his plans for opening a Japanese-language school at Shisangyan and urged them to send him their children and young men.[14]

Although Izawa's listeners were polite enough, they seemed to receive his claims with some doubt. Nevertheless, the day after his lecture five or six Taiwanese youths arrived at his school and he began Japanese-language classes.[15] Soon he had enough pupils to divide into two groups. He prepared the older ones, who were from 17 to 27 years of age and who were already well versed in classical Chinese, for positions as clerks; younger lads he trained to be Japanese-language teachers. At the same time he directed research carried on by education officers (*kyōkan*), who numbered nine by December of that first year.[16] In addition to the experimental teaching — for that was what the lessons given to the Taiwanese amounted to — Izawa and his men studied local languages, paying particular attention to pedagogical, commercial, and military vocabularies. They also compiled a Japanese language instruction manual, and ambitiously sent a thousand copies to the colony's regional administration offices.[17]

The work of Izawa's team seemed to thrive. By September of 1895 the school had twenty-one pupils, and in October six of these were presented with certificates recognizing their scholastic progress.[18] Formal Japanese schooling complete with graduation ceremonies and diplomas had come to Taiwan — or at least to Shisangyan. At the end of October Izawa returned to Japan to find additional teaching staff, taking with him two Taiwanese pupils as proof of progress made in the colony. He was still away in January 1896 when hostile islanders attacked and killed the six education officers who had remained behind at Shisangyan. In April Izawa returned with new recruits (thirteen education bureau officials and thirty-six teacher trainees) and the Shisangyan school was reopened — although the Japanese who taught there were now fully armed.[19]

The thirty-six trainees were all graduates of Japanese normal schools, but they knew nothing of the local languages. The dominant Taiwanese dialect, which the Japanese knew as Amoy, was difficult because of its eight tones, four more than standard Mandarin Chinese. Thus the first six weeks of the trainees' stay at Shisangyan was spent mastering the simple Taiwanese conversation they would need to hold classes. Izawa closely supervised their studies, which also included music, natural history, hygiene, and military-style gymnastics. Izawa believed in intensive training and kept his recruits too busy to associate with the growing community of Japanese stationed in Taihoku. Other government-general officials dubbed the lonely school at Shisangyan "Izawa's hermitage."[20]

The year 1896 was a good one for both Izawa's emergency proposals and his permanent proposals. In that year Japanese-language training for Taiwanese children and young adults began in earnest as fourteen Japanese-language institutes, modeled on the Shisangyan school, were opened in different parts of the island.[21] These institutes followed the plan Izawa had presented to Kabayama the year before. They offered Taiwanese aged fifteen to thirty, who sought clerical employment with the new regime, a six-month course in Japanese and arithmetic. They provided a four-year program for children aged eight to fifteen who might also be instructed in written Chinese, geography, history, singing, and gymnastics. Instruction in sewing was available for any girls whose parents could be persuaded to enroll them.[22] Groups of teacher trainees came in a steady flow from Tokyo and after about ten weeks' preparation were sent to teach in the Japanese-language institutes or to open new ones.[23] This year saw the beginning of the Japanese Language School, which took over the training of teachers from Japan. It also set up programs in its education department and language department for Taiwanese, who usually entered with a sound literary background in classical Chinese.[24]

During May 1897 Izawa was in Tokyo, seeking support for the estimates in his education budget. Unfortunately for him, the home government was in the process of cutting the subsidy given the Taiwan government general. The colonial government's civil department head, Mizuno Jun—a veteran of the Ministry of Home Affairs—saw that the lion's share of the restricted allotments went to tax collectors, prison wardens, and police superintendents, while Izawa and his bureau had to bear the brunt of the funds' cut. In bitter resentment against Mizuno, his immediate superior, Izawa sent a protest from Tokyo directly to Governor-General Nogi Maresuke (1849-1912), who in October 1896 had replaced Kabayama's successor, Katsura Taro (1847-1913). He then resigned his position as chief of the education bureau.[25]

Izawa was upset because other sections in the colonial budget had been favored over his own, but in fact the entire budget was under attack. After martial law was officially lifted in April 1896, it was no longer possible to hide the cost of running Taiwan in the gigantic military budget appropriated to prosecute the Sino-Japanese War.[26]

The first two years of the Taiwan experiment had dampened much of the original enthusiasm for annexing foreign territory.[27] Taiwan was rife with scandal and jurisdictional confusion among Japanese officialdom, and resistance and rebellion from the native population persisted. The government general raised funds from levies and land, sugar, camphor, exports and imports, and from the revenue on mining and prospecting licenses; but these monies did not amount to more than a fraction of Taiwan's operating costs. The budget of the Taiwan administration for the fiscal year 1896 was 10,610,000 yen, of which only 2,620,000 yen were collected in Taiwan.[28] Although a subsidy of almost seven million yen from the home government had bailed out the 1896 budget, by 1897 a strong current of opinion held that, for a country in the middle of costly industrialization, colonialism was a habit too expensive to support. Consequently, the annual subsidy was reduced by approximately one million yen.[29]

With vociferous public criticism of the government general's failure to quell lawlessness and growing opposition to even a reduced subsidy for Taiwan, it is not surprising that police and penal sections and items aimed at increasing local revenue took precedence over education in the budget. Izawa took the defeat of his education estimates personally, and after his clash with Mizuno he sadly gave up his tight hold over Japanese education in Taiwan. However, he remained as an educational consultant to the Taiwan administration until he was appointed principal of Tokyo Higher Normal School (Tokyo kōtō shihangakkō) in October 1899.[30]

Yet he had mapped out the direction for education in Taiwan. Under the next governor-general, Lieutenant General Kodama Gentarō, Izawa's ideas were to be realized in a system of schools, curricula, pupils, teachers, and administrators. When Kodama and Director of Civil Administration (*minseichōkan*), Gotō Shimpei, arrived in March 1898, sixteen Japanese-language institutes and thirty-six branch institutes were in operation.[31] In October 1897 the Japanese Language School's students and teachers had been able to leave their temporary quarters for spacious new classrooms and dormitories.[32]

The eight years following Gotō's arrival in 1898 saw the development of a large and many-faceted education system in Taiwan. The overall strategy directing the proliferation of new educational forms was aimed at: winning support for the new regime; developing a stratum of Taiwanese sufficiently well educated to service the administrative and clerical apparatus of the colonial government; educating Japanese nationals living in Taiwan; popularizing formal education for girls; producing Taiwanese teachers and medical personnel; and making the island's school system as financially self-sufficient as possible. To these ends, common schools, normal schools, and medical schools were created. Private schools—whether Chinese, Christian, or Japanese—were pressured to shut up shop and move into the public school mainstream. Campaigns were launched to encourage girls to attend school, and a variety of means was used to create local revenue to support the educational system.

The Common Schools

Instead of expanding Japanese language institute facilities, Kodama's administration began to set up what it hoped would be a more permanent type of elementary school, the common school (*kōgakkō*), but in objectives and curriculum the common school was almost identical to Izawa's institute.[33] It had two aims, stated in the Common School Regulations of 1898. The first was to give Taiwanese children a good command of the Japanese language; the second was to teach them ethics and practical knowledge, in order to cultivate in them qualities of Japanese citizenship (*kokumintaru no seikaku*). The six-year common school course consisted of ethics, Japanese language, classical Chinese (composition, reading, calligraphy), arithmetic, music, and gymnastics. It was open to children aged eight to fourteen.[34] In 1904 the school age was extended to include seven-year-olds and sixteen-year-olds; music became elective rather than compulsory; manual arts, agriculture, or commerce were introduced as optional subjects "in accordance with conditions of the locality"; and sewing classes for girls were added.[35] Common schools soon outstripped the language institutes, which were discontinued altogether in 1905. In 1898 seventy-six common schools were accredited; by the end of Kodama's term eight years later, 180 government elementary schools catered to approximately 32,000 pupils.[36]

As Table 1 shows, absenteeism remained a serious problem for the common schools, but it seems to have fallen off somewhat by 1906. In 1898 more than half the students enrolled were absent daily; in 1906, 65.52 percent of the students enrolled were present on an average day. As Gunnar Myrdal has pointed out in *Asian Drama,* such daily attendance rates tell much more than

TABLE 1. Common schools, 1898-1906

Year	Common schools including branch schools	Teachers	Students	Percentage of Taiwanese school-aged population enrolled in common schools	Average daily attendance as percentage of students enrolled
1898	74	247	7,548 boys 290 girls	–	49.32
1899	106	371	9,932 boys 443 girls	2.04	–
1900	126	485	11,759 boys 1,133 girls	2.19	–
1901	136	547	15,298 boys 1,657 girls	2.85	–
1902	154	608	17,492 boys 2,090 girls	3.21	58.51
1903	161	709	19,800 boys 2,469 girls	3.70	59.64
1904	168	676	21,136 boys 2,896 girls	3.85	60.66
1905	167	700	24,398 boys 3,653 girls	4.66	61.82
1906	181	752	28,186 boys 4,095 girls	5.31	65.52

Sources: Yoshino Hidekime, *Taiwan kyōiku shi* (Taihoku, 1927), p. 199; *TKES,* pp. 408-409.

do enrollment figures about how many children were actually going to school.[37]

Officials carefully observed the attendance patterns of common school pupils, recording and evaluating the reasons for absence. Children were often absent on local festival days, but studies conducted in 1899 found three principal causes for frequent absenteeism. First, illness, which was often caused by virtual epidemics of communicable disease; second, idleness; and third, family reasons. This last often meant that parents were not concerned about irregular attendance at the common schools, which they might see simply as places where their children could pick up some Japanese. Such parents might, however, ensure that their children attended Chinese private schools regularly; many pupils were simultaneously enrolled in both school systems.[38] After analyzing the specific causes of absenteeism in various regions, the Japanese sought to remove them. The colonial government's sanitation measures eventually reduced the incidence of illness; gentry families were pressured to cooperate more actively with the new system; educators took pains to see that the common schools offered at least some of the training in the Confucian classics which well-to-do Taiwanese wanted for their sons.

The Japanese claimed that Chinese, an important part of the curriculum of the early common schools, was taught to enable Japanese and literate Taiwanese to communicate. In reality, the inclusion of this subject was central to the attempt to make these schools attractive to the Taiwanese gentry.[39] In the first grade, pupils were taught Chinese from the *Three Character Classic* and the *Classic of Filial Piety*. The following year they studied the *Greater Learning* and the *Doctrine of the Mean,* and third and fourth graders struggled with the *Analects of Confucius.* For four years these classics were taught by a native old-style schoolmaster, in much the same way as at a Chinese private school. Only in the fifth and sixth grades did the children learn to read these works in Japanese fashion.[40]

The Kodama administration recognized the high prestige enjoyed by Chinese learning and maintained a respectful attitude toward it. Governor-General Kodama and Director of Civil Administration Gotō personally honored Taiwanese men of letters. Kodama revived the Ch'ing custom of holding banquets to honor the elderly and sponsored Chinese poetry parties in which both Taiwanese and Japanese trained in the Chinese classics took

part.[41] Not every educated Taiwanese responded to such overtures — especially since the Japanese were asking them to participate in cultural change rather than assuring them that their old
position of cultural dominance would be guaranteed — but a good
many were favorably impressed, and the banquets honoring the
elderly were particularly popular. The governor-general's personal appearance at such functions was greeted enthusiastically.[42]
Similarly, the employment of Taiwanese scholars as Chinese
teachers in common schools encouraged gentry families to send
their sons there, as did the classical Chinese training which these
schools offered.

Although common school courses featured Chinese studies,
this did not mean that Japanese language was neglected. More
attention was devoted to spoken and written Japanese than to any
other subject. Common school textbooks and teaching materials
were compiled and edited by government-general officials and
they, like the teachers themselves, were always on the lookout for
methodology which would improve Japanese language instruction.[43]

Morality was also considered of utmost importance; in addition
to a weekly ethics lesson, morals were to be inculcated during the
teaching of all subjects. Here again the new system's debt to the
pioneer work and thought of Izawa was apparent. He had hoped
that Japanese, geography, history, science, and arithmetic would
eventually replace the Chinese poetry and prose composition so
prominent in the Chinese private schools. Yet he had insisted that
Japanese educators retain the wisdom of Confucius, Mencius,
and other suitable mentors within the Chinese classical tradition.[44] To the Confucian conception of a righteous king ruling
because he possessed a heavenly mandate, Izawa had added the
Japanese notions of imperial virtue and rule by an unbroken
dynasty of emperors. Education officials of the Kodama administration followed his example. Common school teachers were
urged to incorporate as much suitable Confucian morality as possible into the all-important Japanese language classes and indeed
into all areas of the curriculum. In both Chinese and Japanese
language classes Confucian ethics were presented as Japanese
ideals or as universal principles shared by but not unique to the
Chinese people.

The common schools also tried to impart useful, everyday
skills. In arithmetic classes, for instance, pupils mastered the

romanized letters of a local Taiwanese dialect which were printed on bags of sugar produced in Taiwan. Also, probably primarily for merchant children, there were lessons in the letter-writing styles employed in trade with the Chinese mainland.[45] In his diary Izawa had noted that such practical instruction provided incentives for some Taiwanese to send their sons to school, and the common school regulations of 1898 reaffirmed his insistence on practical knowledge.[46] Certainly incentives were necessary: as Table 1 shows, in spite of practical instruction and classical Chinese, the first efforts to gain large numbers of regularly attending pupils were less than successful. A member of the Japanese Diet who visited Taiwan during Kodama's administration complained that "the Formosan Chinese has no higher ambition than to enjoy mere animal pleasures of life . . . If, therefore, you speak to him about his children's education, he at once asks, 'How much extra will it enable them to earn?' Without a satisfactory answer on this point, he is most unwilling to send his children to school."[47] Prosperous landlord and merchant families appear to have been understandably reluctant to support a costly education they had not asked for, and under Kodama and Gotō the Taiwanese were increasingly required to foot the bills of common schooling.

Beyond the Common School

As the Scottish Presbyterian missionary William Campbell observed, youths who had attended common school could find employment as clerks and interpreters in the colonial government.[48] Yet Japanese educators also encouraged those who had been to common school to take up the traditional occupations of Taiwanese landlord or merchant families. Able common school graduates who were dissatisfied with clerkships or familiar local community leadership roles were to be carefully channeled into the two professions which the government general was anxious to popularize among ambitious and able Taiwanese: teaching and medicine.

A major part of Izawa's original education proposals had been normal schools to train Taiwanese as Japanese language teachers. In 1899 three such normal schools were opened: one each in Taihoku, Taichū (Taichung), and Tainan. Their three-year course included ethics, Japanese language, composition, reading, arithmetic, bookkeeping, geography, history, science, calligraphy, music, gymnastics, and pedagogy just as Izawa had planned.

These were all taught in contemporary Japanese normal schools, but such schools in Japan offered English, handicrafts, and agriculture or commerce as well. The science curriculum of normal schools in Japan was organized differently too; natural science was taught as one subject and physics and chemistry as another.[49] Taiwanese aged eighteen to twenty-five who had graduated from a Japanese language institute (common schools had only been in operation a year in 1899) were eligible to apply to a normal school. The entrance requirement was thus a low one—only four completed years of Japanese schooling.[50]

The year they opened, the three normal schools admitted a total of about 150 students.[51] In 1902, when the five-year-old Japanese Language School in Taihoku began a teacher training program for Taiwanese, the normal schools in Taihoku and Taichū were closed. Their facilities and equipment were taken over by the Japanese Language School and their students transferred to that institution. Two years later the normal school in Tainan was also discontinued and its students sent to the Japanese Language School.

Official reasons given for abolishing these three normal schools so soon after their establishment are interesting. The authorities stated that centralization of teacher training was more convenient and that the Japanese Language School's course provided a sufficient supply of Taiwanese teachers. They feared the normal schools would soon produce more Taiwanese teachers than the common schools—believed to be expanding at a satisfactory pace—could absorb. They also claimed that the people in the Tainan area had shown little enthusiasm for education and that there were many extracurricular advantages to be gained from study in the capital.[52]

The policy was to provide only enough teachers to meet the needs of the common schools and to avoid creating or encouraging any general demand for higher education among Taiwanese. Gotō bluntly told his education personnel they must take care to see that Taiwanese did not become educated above their stations in life. He flatly opposed those who favored opening up a wide range of vocational education facilities, arguing against this on budgetary grounds as well as on principle.[53] Mochiji Rokusaburō (1867-1923), chief of education affairs in the government general from 1903 to 1910, was not entirely opposed to vocational training,[54] but he agreed with Gotō on the question of not educating

Taiwanese for employment which would not be made available to them. In his book on early Japanese colonial policy in Taiwan he wrote:

> The aim of ordinary education [in Taiwan] is to educate the children of the middle and upper classes. Thus we see that in Taiwan ordinary education, although called "ordinary education," should really be referred to as "elite education." Today the proportion of [Taiwanese] school-aged children in school does not exceed 10 percent. But in regard to education facilities we must consider what kind of harvest we want to reap. It is indeed regrettable that the production of unemployed intellectuals is so conspicuous in the mother country itself. It is of utmost importance, then, that we take care to see that similar results do not come out of the education facilities in the colony.[55]

As Table 1 illustrates, in 1902, when the common school system was considered to be expanding at a satisfactory rate, the percentage of Taiwanese children enrolled in these schools was 3.21 and the average daily attendance rate was less than 60 percent of those enrolled. The administration did not intend to sponsor a rapid development of elementary school facilities, much less would it permit large numbers to graduate from normal school.

Medicine was the other profession requiring postprimary education that was opened almost immediately to Taiwanese. Only a few could take advantage of medical training, but this restriction resulted as much from the expensive and specialized nature of the field as from colonial policy. Taiwan's modern medical education began in 1897 with a training center attached to the Japanese hospital in Taihoku. In 1899 the Japanese Diet approved a budget of 30,588 yen 53 sen to set up a school to train Taiwanese doctors.[56] The ten first-year and five second-year Taiwanese trainees at the center became the Taiwan Government General Medical School's first students, while seventy newcomers were enrolled in a one-year medical preparatory course. The government general hoped to build up the school to two hundred and fifty students with a yearly output of about fifty graduates.[57] Medical students could apply for government scholarships, but scholarship holders were obliged to work in posts assigned by the administration for a full five years following graduation.

In 1902 a veteran health administrator, Takagi Tomoeda, was appointed principal of the medical school and director of the

Taihoku hospital. Although he gave up his directorship of the hospital in 1907, Takagi remained as principal until 1915 when Horiuchi Tsugo, who had been teaching in the medical school since the day it opened, took over. Thus there was a continuity in the medical school's management unmatched in other areas of the colony's education.[58] Its academic standards were not as high as those of medical colleges (*senmon gakkō*) in Japan, since its graduates spent a total of only eleven years in school (six in common school, one in the preparatory course, and four in the regular course). They did make outstanding contributions to better health and hygiene in Taiwan.[59]

Gotō Shimpei, a medical doctor himself, had experienced a great deal of success as an innovative medical administrator before he accompanied Kodama to Taiwan.[60] He brought with him ambitious sanitation policies and saw that they were rigorously enforced. The colonial government built water works and regional hospitals and required rigid adherence to regulations concerning sewage disposal, water supplies, and drug control. It established and staffed quarantine stations and energetically prosecuted antimalaria and rodent prevention campaigns.[61] The most conspicuous agent of improved sanitation was the heavy-handed colonial police, who made sure all Taiwanese adhered to the new measures, but common school lessons in health and hygiene spread new attitudes and information which reinforced police action.[62] The administration's introduction of Western-style medicine as a prestigious and profitable profession for Taiwanese was crucial to the institution of public medicine as an important means of disease prevention and control.[63] It is generally agreed that whatever else Japanese colonialism did or did not do in Taiwan, it was responsible for a drastic decline in the death rate and a remarkable improvement in general sanitation. Much of the credit for these achievements must go to Taiwanese graduates of the medical school.[64]

There were fewer opportunities for higher education in fields other than teaching or medicine. A handful of Taiwanese received technical training at the experimental stations the Japanese set up to encourage improvements in sugar and other agricultural products, but such openings were rare.[65] Briefly, from 1902 to 1907, a vocational department in the Japanese Language School offered courses in telegraphy and agriculture, and it produced a total of sixty-seven graduates before it was discontinued.[66] Other Taiwanese qualified for employment with the colonial government by graduating from the Japanese Language School's three-year Japanese language course, which became a five-year course in December 1905. From 1897 to 1906 this course admitted 345 entrants and produced 138 graduates. This exceeded by far the number enrolled in the school's native language course for Japanese, which was discontinued in 1901 because of a lack of applicants.[67]

Education for Girls

Few of the pupils in the common schools were girls. Although there are some famous women scholars and poets in Chinese history, it was rare for respectable gentry families to give their daughters a classical education or even to teach them systematically to read and write.[68] In the Confucian scheme, a female offspring eventually married and pursued her career as loyal daughter-in-law, devoted mother, and faithful wife within her husband's family. These roles did not require literacy, much less literary talent. Robert Van Gulik's comment on typical upper-class Chinese attitudes toward female education in earlier times applies also to the late Ch'ing period:

> According to the Confucianist conception, the husband's interest in his wife as a human being was supposed to cease as soon as she had left his bed. One need not wonder, therefore, that as a rule very little was done for the literary education of girls and women; it was thought sufficient if they knew how to please their husband in bed, look after the young children, and perform their household tasks. They were not supposed to share the man's intellectual interests and they were strictly forbidden to meddle with his activities outside the house. Even the young daughters in upper class families were taught only the womanly skills such as weaving and sewing, and looking after the household, they were not taught reading and writing in the regular manner. And although there were not a few girls who learned to read and write by themselves in a haphazard way, the majority of decent women were illiterate. It was, curiously enough, the singing girls who learned elementary reading and writing as part of their professional training.[69]

Before the Japanese takeover, if girls in Taiwan were taught at all they were usually taught at home. Few were ever sent to the private schools which, in addition to preparing some young men for the imperial examinations, transmitted literacy and literary knowledge to a greater number. In 1899 the Japanese found that of a total of 29,941 pupils in 1,707 Chinese private schools only 65 were female.[70] Although government-general officers did their utmost to make girls as well as boys welcome in the new schools, Taiwanese who were willing to send their sons to common school continued to keep their daughters home.

The problem was not a new one for Japanese administrators. Indeed, and for similar reasons, in Japan the elementary school attendance of girls lagged far behind that of their brothers during the first three decades of the Meiji period.

From at least the seventh century, the Japanese had from time to time borrowed extensively from Chinese civilization. During the two and one half centuries preceding the Meiji Restoration of 1868, Chinese cultural influences were particularly strong. Confucianism, albeit a Japanized Confucianism, was the ideology of the samurai class that ruled the country. For samurai men this meant a softening of their stern warrior ethics and also required serious Chinese classical scholarship in order to master Confucian morality and apply it to contemporary political problems. But for samurai women and, because commoners aped their betters, for women of almost all classes, this meant a gradual but drastic reduction in social status, confinement to limited roles, and thorough domination by their menfolk.[71] As in China, the ideal woman's life was declared to be one of selfless obedience first to her father, then to her husband and later, in widowhood, to her son. Some authorities did hold that it was a good idea for samurai women to have a rudimentary knowledge of some of the Chinese classics, because women after all were largely responsible for rearing the children; also, not-so-bright men had been known to be heavily influenced by their wives. But in general, as in China, upper-class girls were not required nor encouraged to master classical Chinese in order to attain the Confucian morality expected of them. Perhaps it was a holdover from their glorious literary past, but upper-class Japanese women were permitted to "acquire some literary skills without losing, and in fact in the process enhancing, their femininity" by studying selected Japanese classics of a less sinicized era.[72] Obedience and sewing were more important parts of a samurai girl's education than either classical Chinese language or Japanese literature. And samurai girls, even when taught their letters, were educated at home; schools were not established for them as they were for samurai boys.

Commoners, on the other hand, did sometimes send their girls to *tera koya* school with boys during the Tokugawa period (1600-1867). By the end of the period, commoner girls who went to school to learn to read and write represented about 10 percent of all Japanese girls, but they were outnumbered four to one by commoner boys who attended school.[73] "This four to one ratio of boys to girls is an average of a wide range of variation. Merchants were perhaps the most likely to be willing to spend money educating their girls, since shopkeepers' wives needed to read and write in order to help in the shop. Even within farming districts there was considerable variation, however."[74] Although education of female commoners in Tokugawa Japan was less rare than in Ch'ing China, the vast majority of the agricultural population felt that schooling was not necessary for farmers' wives. In some areas of the country this feeling was stronger than in others, as Meiji officials found when they tried to increase primary school attendance during the 1870s and 1880s. A survey in 1883 reported that in Okayama prefecture forty girls for every hundred boys attended primary school, compared with twelve girls to every hundred boys in Nagano, although both regions were agricultural.[75]

Why the Meiji government was so intent upon achieving universal elementary school attendance of girls as well as boys remains something of a mystery. In retrospect this seems a farsighted policy, even for leaders determined to change in some important aspects ways of life and thought long held by an entire people, especially considering that these leaders themselves sprang from Confucian Tokugawa society. In the idealistic education code (*gakusei*) of 1872, which made parents responsible for seeing that their "boys and girls without distinction" attended primary school, it was grandly announced that although in the past learning (*gakumon*) had been for the warrior class and not for farmers, artisans, merchants, and women, the situation was now changed.[76] Two decades after the early Meiji enthusiasm for serious academic training for women had subsided (coeducation of male and female students in postprimary educational institutions was prohibited in 1879),[77] the education ministry still struggled with parents reluctant to send their daughters to primary school. An education ministry directive of 1893 suggests that the old idea that because women were responsible for training the young they must not remain ignorant spurred the effort to make sure that girls as well as boys received a primary school education. The directive begins: "There is no difference in need for elementary education between boys and girls. However, girls' education will have a great bearing on the future education [of young children] in the home."[78]

Pressure was applied to parents until more and more of them began to give way. Whereas in 1880 only 21.91 percent of the female population of elementary school age in Japan was in school compared to 58.72 percent of the male population of the same age, during 1895, the year Taiwan was ceded to Japan, 43.87 percent of Japanese girls and 76.65 percent of Japanese boys attended school. By 1900 the percentage increased to 71.73 for girls and 90.55 for boys. Over the following ten years the gap narrowed, and by 1910 the goal of universal primary school attendance was almost reached, with 98.93 percent of the country's boys and 97.38 percent of the country's girls going to school.[79]

Although the government general found Taiwanese familes even more reluctant than Japanese to send their girls to school, the difference was one of degree, not kind. The problem was approached in much the same way as in Japan. Officials encouraged and urged, provided special classes to teach practical and popular skills like sewing, and tried to get respectable Taiwanese women into the schools as teachers in the hope that their presence would make common schools more acceptable places to send girls. Experience in Japan suggested that once large numbers of boys were attending regularly, girls might then appear at school in increasing numbers.

"Higher education" for Taiwanese girls was therefore one area which was unequivocally encouraged. As early as 1897 Izawa had opened an elementary school for Taiwanese girls, which soon included an advanced department of handicrafts. Here sewing, embroidery, flower craft, and knitting were taught to graduates from the six-year common school course and to others considered qualified enough for admittance. Nine of the handicraft department's first group of twelve graduates in 1900 immediately became common school teachers.[80] Many of their successors also went to teach in common schools, since girls were encouraged to enter the department with a teaching career in mind. The department was small, but the school was not much larger. In 1898 there were 46 girls enrolled in the handicraft department and 34 in the elementary course; by 1905 the school, which offered the colony's only public "higher education" for Taiwanese girls, had 160 students, 42 of whom were in the handicraft department.[81] Such minute figures perhaps help explain the government general's eagerness to push female secondary education. It could hardly have been a threat to anyone.

Shobō

Even more than Izawa, Gotō's common school architects sought pupils primarily among gentry and merchant children. They wanted only the brightest and most serious students. Young children from homes that provided leisure for study and respect for learning were considered most desirable, but older children or young adults who already possessed some training in Chinese literature were also welcome. Such students could speedily be trained as clerks and interpreters, although some Japanese educators felt that they were less malleable than their younger siblings. The immediate object was not to teach the unschooled but rather to get Taiwanese out of the Chinese schools and into the common schools. The common schools hoped eventually to enroll young boys before they began attending Chinese schools, but in the meantime they were satisfied if they could lure older pupils away from native schoolmasters.

In order to attract students from the various types of Chinese school, which the Japanese lumped together under the classification *shobō* (*shu-fang*) or "[Chinese] private school,"[82] allowances of fifteen sen a day for older pupils in Japanese language institutes were authorized in 1896.[83] In November 1898 *shobō* were placed under the jurisdiction of the colony's regional administrations, which were instructed to see that hours of instruction were fixed, that only government-general-approved textbooks were used, that *shobō* teachers attended summer schools set up for them by the administration, and that Japanese language and arithmetic were gradually made required subjects.[84] This last injunction proved too ambitious and appears to have been honored more in the breach than in the observance. However, regional authorities were permitted to encourage reform by giving financial aid to *shobō* whose classes, management, and sanitation were outstanding.[85]

Despite efforts to Japanize their curricula and steal their students, Chinese private schools continued to thrive as traditional one-teacher enterprises. When Taiwan was ceded the Ch'ing governmental academies were closed—their function of training candidates for the imperial examinations was now obsolete—and such community schools (*i-hsüeh*) as survived the confusion of the takeover were absorbed in the more numerous private schools.[86] As common schools multiplied, the private schools sometimes provided a supplement rather than an alternative to a Japanese education, even though they were also favored by literati who rejected outright all that Japanese rule stood for. As a contemporary observer noted, "After common school classes are dismissed many pupils go to a *shobō* to master Chinese learning."[87]

Shobō lessons were usually divided into reading, lectures, calligraphy, and composition. Reading was taught in the traditional fashion: the pupil learned to read aloud and memorize a text before he was able to understand its meaning. The teacher demonstrated correct reading of a passage by reading it off to a group of five or six pupils, who repeated the words and phrases after him. Then they returned to their places to repeat the passage over and over until they had memorized it completely, and meanwhile a second group received a similar lesson from the teacher. Later the first group's members appeared individually before the teacher and demonstrated, without looking at the text, how well each could recite it. Later they were asked to write it out from memory.[88] The beginner, like the first grader in common school, usually started with the popular primer, the *Three Character Classic,* which, in 365 alternately rhyming lines of three characters each, disseminated in simple form the basic doctrines of the classics. Having mastered this, he moved on to the Four Books and the Five Classics of the Confucian canon.[89] In his lectures the teacher discussed the text his pupils had been memorizing, explaining in their own Taiwanese dialect the meaning of individual characters, phrases, and sentences and the classical literary style. In calligraphy class, pupils were required to write out passages from a text. Composition assignments included both prose and poetry compositions.[90]

Although control of a thousand or more *shobō* during the early years of Japanese rule was less thorough than the colonial government would have liked, local administrators did use their powers to suspend or dissolve Chinese schools thought to have "unsuitable facilities" or to be teaching anything not in the interests of the government general. Official interference in organization, hours, and curricula complicated the operation of the *shobō* and may well have made them less convenient to some Taiwanese parents. The Japanese policy of inviting esteemed *shobō* teachers and other respected Taiwanese scholars to teach Chinese in the government schools was also aimed at weakening the status of the *shobō*, although not all those invited accepted.[91] The Chinese schools remained formidable rivals to the common schools for many years. But when Kodama's administration ended in 1906, *shobō* had begun to suffer a significant decline in terms of both numbers of schools still operating and numbers of students attending them.[92]

Education for Japanese Nationals

The first Japanese to arrive in Taiwan were soldiers, but before long, families began to accompany civil and military officials, and the authorities began to worry about a growing number of Japanese children. At the end of 1896 two hundred pupils' names were on the rolls of the half dozen private schools which had been set up to meet this need.[93] These were generally temporary and makeshift affairs, soon to be replaced by government schools and teachers.[94] In 1898 the government general restricted the founding of new private schools and placed strict controls on all such existing institutions,[95] and even before this, in 1897, the first government primary school for Japanese children had been established in Taihoku. The following year four additional government primary schools were opened, and in 1899 three more were added.[96] In 1897 separate classrooms for Japanese children who lived in the more remote regions were set up in some language institutes, and this practice continued within the common schools. From 1905 this practice was supported by a system which allotted primary school teachers to the isolated areas that needed them, and by the following year there were fourteen classrooms of this sort in common schools.[97] Because the problem of Japanese children scattered throughout the island continued to plague educators, these classrooms functioned until 1919.[98]

Teachers of the colony's first primary schools had problems. The children came from different parts of Japan and did not speak one common dialect; the Tokyo dialect, designated as the "national language," was predominant only in government-general offices. Yamashina Nobutsugu, a teacher in the first government primary school when it opened in Taihoku, recalled that language difficulties were compounded by the fact that use of a standard national language in all school textbooks was still not universal. "What gradually came to be used in the classroom and on the playing field was what we might now call a kind of Taiwan-style abbreviated Japanese without proper word endings."[99]

School supplies brought by ship from Japan were often slow in arriving, and Yamashina's pupils suffered a chronic shortage of teaching and classroom materials. From their classrooms they could hear the cries of Taiwanese prisoners incarcerated in the nearby prison; from the school gates they constantly witnessed the departure of troop expeditions against defiant islanders. Yamashina worried about the influence of all this brutality upon the young minds in his care. In such an environment, he wondered, how could a teacher give schoolroom lessons in ethics?[100]

Since Izawa had insisted that it was important for the Japanese to learn about the Taiwanese, the first primary school curriculum provided for instruction of Taiwanese languages and culture in the highest grades.[101] With this exception they closely resembled primary schools in Japan in organization, subjects taught, and textbooks used. Like their cousins at home, colonial primary school children spent most of their time studying Japanese, arithmetic, and calligraphy. They also learned drawing, singing, and gymnastics, and in the fifth and sixth grades they studied Japanese history and geography. By 1902, when regulations for Taiwan primary schools were promulgated, the only difference between primary schooling in the colony and the home country was that such schooling was not compulsory for Japanese children in Taiwan.[102]

At this time a large percentage of the Japanese population of primary school age in Taiwan did not attend school. In Japan the Primary School Ordinance of 1900 had made four years of primary schooling mandatory, but during 1900 only 29.5 percent of Taiwan's Japanese children of primary school age (six to fourteen) were enrolled in school, and five years later primary schools and the classrooms for Japanese in common schools accommodated only 72.9 percent of these children.[103] This situation left colonial primary school children still well behind their home country counterparts, 95.6 percent of whom were attending primary school during 1905.[104] But by 1910 Japanese children in the colony had almost closed the gap: their primary school enrollment was only 4.9 percent behind that of children in Japan.[105] Since isolated Japanese children still existed in remote districts, this was an impressive feat. Even without compulsory education the school attendance pattern of Japanese children in Taiwan closely followed that of their counterparts in Japan.

In 1898 a middle school department was opened in the first public school in Taihoku for ten Japanese boys.[106] This department moved to the Japanese Language School in 1902, and five years later it was made a middle school attached to the Japanese Language School. Middle school students were scarce during the first decade of the colony's history. Parents sent their sons home to go to middle school, and adolescent boys left the colony as a matter of course when their fathers' postings there were over.[107] Post-primary schooling for Japanese girls was also provided in a special department of the Taihoku Second Primary School, which was founded in April 1904 with 33 pupils.[108] The following year it was upgraded to a higher girls' school attached to the Japanese Language School.

Izawa's program to train colonial Japanese as teachers for Taiwan's native schools continued to be official policy during the Kodama administration,[109] which aimed to make the colony as self-sufficient as possible. When the Japanese Language School was officially opened in the fall of 1887, its education department already had thirty-one Japanese enrolled.[110] During the years that followed, however, enrollment increased very little, probably because there was a shortage of young Japanese to be trained, and teachers were still brought out from Japan. In spite of the availability of teachers from the ruling country, training Japanese as well as Taiwanese teachers for the common schools continued to be a serious concern of the government general. As in Izawa's time training for the Japanese who were going to teach Taiwanese children included intensive study of the Taiwanese language.[111]

Containment of Private Schools

In addition to trying to attract *shobō* students, Japanese officials also coveted young Taiwanese attending the small number of Christian missionary schools on the island. For several decades before the Japanese arrived, Christian missionaries had been active in Taiwan. Spanish Dominicans came in the 1850s; English Presbyterians carved out an enclave at Tainan during the following decade; George MacKay of the Canadian Presbyterian Church began mission work from Tamsui in the north in 1872.[112]

Western missionaries, although they had commiserated with

their native followers regarding the brutal military methods by which the Japanese first established their authority on the island, often cooperated, sometimes enthusiastically, with the Japanese search for promising pupils and teachers.[113] William Campbell, the Scottish Presbyterian, noted in 1901 that Taiwanese members of his flock recognized the advantages of having their children attend common school:

> Those [Taiwanese Christian] brethren with whom I conferred also admitted that their children obtained many substantial advantages in going to the Government Schools, such as free tuition of a very effective kind, strict, but not severe, control of the pupils in fine airy buildings, instruction on subjects which would really fit them for future work, and opportunity for acquiring a knowledge of the Japanese language they could not get elsewhere. Much stress was laid upon this last-named item; for those converts were shrewd enough to have noted that any well-behaved young man of ordinary ability, who could speak Japanese with fluency, might assure himself of well-paid interpreting or clerical work in any of the Government offices scattered over the Island.[114]

When Taiwan was ceded to Japan, the Dominicans had recently opened a school for girls near Takao (Kaohsiung), and both the Canadian and English Presbyterian missions operated schools which gave young islanders of both sexes a Christian secondary education. The main intent was to prepare converts for church work, but mission school teachers at Tamsui and Tainan taught secular Western-style subjects as well.[115] William Davidson, the United States consul in Taiwan at the turn of the century, reported that in Tainan the secondary school offered "accommodation for forty boys, and the school is always full." He added that another forty boys were being trained in a "theological college" there, and that a girls' school and "an establishment for the training of Bible women" were "under the charge of the ladies attached to the mission."[116] At MacKay's base in Tamsui, in 1900, Oxford College boasted thirty-seven students and the girls' school thirty-four.[117]

No clash occurred between colonial officials and missionaries and their Christian converts over these schools. Although secondary schools run by missionaries came under private school regulations, the Japanese left the two Presbyterian training centers and the small Dominican establishment more or less undisturbed.

They added to their curricula; Japanese language was made mandatory, but religious instruction was allowed. The pupils in these schools were so few that the colonial government could afford to ignore them, especially when doing so courted the good will of the Western missionaries. Smaller and less well-established schools attached to Christian congregations were sometimes disbanded and their pupils invited to attend common schools.[118] The missionaries seem to have regarded this annoyance as more than compensated for by the satisfaction of seeing modern, Western-style Japanese education advance at the expense of the "pagan" Chinese schooling which most of them abhorred.[119]

The three types of private schooling that existed in Taiwan at the beginning of the Japanese regime—the *shobō*, the missionary schools, and the schools for the children of Japanese nationals—all came under steadily intensifying pressure during the first decade of colonial rule. This policy reflected the attitude toward private education that Japanese education authorities had displayed since the Meiji Restoration. The early Meiji government had regarded private schools as second-best makeshift substitutes for the government schools which were to replace them as soon as possible. They were never officially acknowledged as acceptable alternatives to public education. As temporary substitutes for government schools, early Meiji private schools received some recognition for their graduates, but they rarely gained any public financial support.[120] As central government control of public education tightened in the 1880s and 1890s, the regulation of private school affairs became stricter too.

After the Imperial Rescript on Education was promulgated in 1890, education ministry officials and their supporters fought a war of words with Christian private school teachers and principals, who resisted the notion that all Japanese private schools were substitutes for government education. Most of the battles were waged in the columns of contemporary newspapers and magazines, but from time to time individuals connected with private schools defied official policy. Perhaps the most famous act of defiance was the refusal of the Christian educator, Uchimura Kanzō (1861-1930), to bow to the Imperial Rescript on Education at a school ceremony. This and other incidents angered many in the Meiji government, but in the early 1890s the government was not yet prepared to punish offenders. As Inoue Kowashi (1844-95) warned, the relationship of education to religion was a delicate matter which the government had to approach with caution. Inoue, in a paper probably written before he became education minister in 1893, reminded his colleagues that the powerful Western nations, with whom Japan was striving to improve her treaty relations, demanded freedom of religious activity for Christians in Japan. The government took Inoue's advice, although the slowness to move against Christian schools may also have been partly because until the late 1890s it was unclear whether jurisdiction over religious schools belonged to the Ministry of Education or to the Home Ministry. In 1899, the year Britain gave up extraterritoriality in Japan, the Private School Rescript ended the battle.[121]

The rescript banned religious instruction in school and also affected nonreligious private schools. It required private schools to become subcontractors for government-style education. Textbooks and lecture schedules had to have education ministry approval; principals and teachers came under close government supervision. Any teaching against Shinto, Buddhism, the Japanese government, allied governments, or the Japanese people was forbidden. Prohibitions against the discussion of contemporary political affairs were also included. The difference between public and private schooling became primarily one of finance: only the former received government funds.[122]

The Taiwan government general's restrictions on private schools followed a similar script. In 1905 private school regulations for the colony spelled out prohibitions akin to those in Japan's regulations of 1899.[123] Colonial administrators tolerated some of the private schools which predated Japanese rule in Taiwan, but they gave no encouragement to anyone, including Japanese nationals, who sought to open new ones. As noted earlier, Chinese private schools were tolerated partly because of Kodama's policy of respecting traditional learning. In any case it would have been highly impractical to order their dissolution. Numerous and scattered about the island as they were, checking their operations was hard enough; enforcing their abolition would have demanded a great deal of energetic manpower. However, Kodama's government general sent detailed guidelines for their inspection and regulation to the regional authorities in November 1898. Even after this, regional officials received directives concerning the *shobō*, suggesting that the central administration did not think local administrators were supervising these schools carefully enough.[124]

Aims and Achievements of the Period

The actual establishment of the new school system in Taiwan was accompanied throughout by a propaganda campaign, aimed by the administration at the most influential sectors of Taiwanese society. For example, in March 1900 the government general sponsored the founding of the Society for Uplifting Culture (Yōbunkai; *Yang-wen-hui*) in Taihoku. The aim was to win the understanding and cooperation of the literati for the new regime's reform programs including, of course, the new education. To this end, the government general invited all gentry holding the grade of *ling-sheng* or higher according to the Ch'ing examination system to be the guests of honor at the society's eight-day inauguration ceremonies.[125] Those who accepted—and approximately half of the island's top gentry did so[126]—were wined and dined extensively and shown over the colonial government's new buildings and facilities.[127]

Both Kodama and Gotō addressed the Yōbunkai members at the opening meeting on March 15. Although they paid respectful homage to the group's Chinese classical learning they also urged the members to take advantage of the new schooling the Japanese offered. Gotō compared the curriculum of the Chinese private schools with theirs to the disfavor of the former and asked the gentry to stop patronizing Chinese schools. Cultured Taiwanese should not, he implied, be afraid to learn from other civilizations. Japanese schools should be welcomed, said Gotō, not only because of the impeccable mandate possessed by the Japanese imperial family, but also because only with such schools could Taiwan hope to survive the worldwide struggle of nations. It was Japan's new education system, he claimed, that had done so much to enable Japan to meet Western nations on their own ground. Taiwan's future would similarly depend upon her ability to become a land of modern educated people. He urged his listeners to move beyond concentration on their own elitist culture and to concern themselves with the educational needs of the masses.[128]

On March 18 Gotō reiterated this theme at a speech given during the Yōbunkai members' visit to the new hospital in Taihoku's fledgling medical school. Again respectfully acknowledging the erudition of his guests and quoting liberally from the Chinese classics, he urged them to give serious attention to the practical studies introduced by the Japanese. Although the new learning, of which medical science was an important example, represented the scientific and technological knowledge of the West, it was by no means the exclusive property of the West. Japanese, who did not copy directly from the West but instead selected suitable technology from Western learning, had already made Western medical science their own; the Taiwanese could do likewise. Although in China foreigners were scornfully regarded as barbarians, other nations recognized the value of cultural borrowing. In Europe and in Japan, as well as in China, people studied the Chinese classics, so the Chinese of Taiwan should not be afraid to take the useful knowledge the West had to offer.[129]

Taiwanese literati were urged to cooperate with the colony's sanitation policies, which would improve the lives of all islanders, and to send their brightest youths to medical school. Gotō insisted that he did not want to destroy or even to criticize Chinese learning, but only to criticize that frame of mind which excluded all other learning and thus opposed progress. In other words, although the literati would continue to be respected as distinguished bearers of Chinese learning with its valuable moral heritage, they would have to become involved in Gotō's new learning if they wished to retain their positions of intellectual leadership. As Gotō had told the same audience three days earlier, involvement in the new education meant working for the advancement of popular education — supporting the extension of the common school system — as well as seeing that gentry offspring continued to maintain high standards of scholarship. For although the new medical school represented new learning at its highest level, in order to benefit from medical training Taiwanese youngsters would first have to be prepared by practical studies at a lower level.[130]

However, Gotō and other key administrators in the Kodama regime frankly admitted, especially when talking to each other,[131] that many years must pass before common schools could hope to supply anything approaching the universal elementary education rapidly being achieved in Japan. A few advocates of compulsory education for all could be found in the colonial government from the beginning of Japanese rule, but their case had always been flatly rejected on the grounds that enforcement was impossible and the expense undesirable.[132] Common school pupils were expected to remain a small percentage of the islands' school-aged population for years to come.

By the end of the Kodama Gentarō regime in 1906, a two-track system of public education had definitely emerged.[133] On the lowest level, the Taiwanese track consisted of an island-wide network of common schools, while primary schools served Japanese nationals. The former took in 5.31 percent of the Taiwanese school-aged population; the latter, 68.61 percent of the colony's Japanese school-aged children. On the secondary level both tracks centered on the Japanese Language School, although they proceeded separately within that institution. Except for rare openings at experimental stations, the only public secondary education not under the wing of the Japanese Language School was the medical school's course, which had close connections with the hospital in Taihoku.

In the main, the Taiwanese track was Izawa Shūji's plan come to life, but the Kodama-Gotō team had also put their stamp upon it. From 1898 to 1906 education policy was skillfully coordinated with the administration's other policies. For instance, the government general's clarification of land rights and landholding favored the same class of Taiwanese they hoped to attract to the common schools.[134] Sanitation and education policies were especially closely linked.

The common school's Chinese language studies, and to a lesser extent, toleration of the *shobō* were part of Kodama's general policy of accommodating the traditions and customs of the Taiwanese. Gotō considered accommodation of utmost importance if assimilation of the Taiwanese were ever to take place. As he put it, "You do not turn a flounder into a sea bream overnight."[135] To Gotō, accommodation of the island's traditions meant discovering customs that could be used to strengthen the Japanese hold and encouraging these while discouraging less congenial habits.

He enlisted first-rate scholars to undertake an extensive investigation of Taiwanese law and custom and found their studies very helpful. Among other things the research of these scholars revealed laws which colonial courts promptly adopted for disputes among Taiwanese, and research also familiarized the Japanese with the *pao-chia,* the old Ch'ing collective security organizations. The administration promptly revived them in the form of the *hokō* (*pao-chia*) system, which, as an auxiliary to the police, was a key instrument of social control throughout almost all the colonial period.[136] In education as in agriculture, industry, transportation, and sanitation, Gotō recommended policies according to the needs of the situation; always he stressed the importance of research and experimentation.[137]

Gotō's experimentation and his utilization of indigenous institutions received the wholehearted support of his superior.[138] He needed it. There were many in the home government and in the colonial government, too, who believed Taiwan should be governed by the laws and procedures that ruled Japan, and only Kodama Gentarō's powerful backing enabled Gotō successfully to resist pressures from those clamoring to outlaw native practice and introduce Japanese law wholesale.[139] In education as in other areas, Gotō was sure that any attempt to enforce a sudden radical change in Taiwanese lives would fail completely; the flounder's transmutation to sea bream (if it were possible at all, and he admitted he had some doubts) would be a long and gradual process.

He elaborated upon this theme in a speech to a consultative conference on education affairs on November 10, 1903.[140] Stressing the difficulties of changing the hearts, minds, and customs of a foreign people, he reminded Japanese educators that Taiwanese had been Chinese for three hundred years. He himself did not think their spiritual and material lives could be drastically transformed in two or even three generations. He believed that until at least twenty-five years had passed the Japanese could make no definitive policy decision regarding education. What were Japanese teachers to do in the meantime? Their task was to spread the use of the Japanese language, but he cautioned them against opening too many schools too quickly and against looking too soon for favorable results. Japanese teachers were to content themselves with setting high standards of personal conduct; even if they could not speak the language of Taiwanese adults, their devotion to the children could build a bridge of trust. Gotō told his educators that although Taiwan was a test case for assimilation, successful assimilation was by no means assured. Warning that colonial assimilation policies had been known to bear unwanted fruit, he cited the educational efforts of the United States to assimilate the Filipinos as a dismal failure.[141]

This emphasis on the limitations of education for the Taiwanese underlined the Kodama-Gotō policy of transferring more and more of the costs of common schooling to the well-to-do Taiwanese at whom it was aimed. Until 1897 all Taiwan public educational expenses were paid by the Japanese government, much to the satisfaction of Izawa Shūji. [142] But from the beginning the wisdom of such educational expenditures had been challenged; [143] and after the establishment of common schools, school expenses were charged to local taxpayers, that is, the wealthier Taiwanese in the school districts. (See Table 2.) By 1903 educational costs paid from regional and town and village funds equaled those paid by the central administration. By 1906 the combined payments of the regions and the municipalities were three times greater than those of the central administration. Henceforth, new schools could only be opened when the local people were willing and able to pay for them.

The administration's heavy investment went into public works. Railroad lines were extended, the harbor at Keelung was improved, spacious government offices and lodgings were constructed. Expenditures on land and census surveys ate up government-general funds as did the subsequent purchase of absentee landholding rights in the island's complicated landholding sys-

TABLE 2. Sources of educational expenditures, 1896-1906 (in yen)

Year	Government expenditures	Regional taxes	Town and village fees	Total
1896	141,441	0	0	141,441
1897	211,661	0	0	211,661
1898	190,233a	0	22,782	213,016
1899	173,307	140,683	47,723	361,713
1900	223,153	157,047	52,537	432,737
1901	219,981	174,718	82,239	476,938
1902	183,612	194,518	79,483	457,613
1903	189,299	215,995	93,091	498,385
1904	127,467	294,041	80,381	501,889
1905	102,035	328,241	171,375	601,651
1906	162,985	357,686	272,732	793,403

Source: Yoshino, p. 237.

aThis figure includes those educational expenses which were paid by the regional taxes.

tem. Simplified landholding and accurate population information raised land tax revenues; and government monopolies of salt, camphor, tobacco, and opium netted profits. However, costly public works, which formed the infrastructure for the Japanese capital Kodama and Gotō were beginning to lure to the island, kept the colonial government dependent upon subsidies from Tokyo until 1905. In that year the administration's highly successful deficit financing through public bonds achieved economic self-sufficiency for the colony. But government-general spending continued to be largely upon public works. The bulk of the expenditures for education, definitely a low priority budgetary item, went to such expensive institutions as the medical school and the Japanese Language School and to educate colonial Japanese. Very little money was left in the administration's coffers for common schools.[144]

Izawa's only real interest in the education of Japanese within the colony was in the training of Japanese for the schools he dreamed would one day bring Japanese language and culture to every native islander. For Kodama and Gotō, schooling for their compatriots was also an afterthought. Nevertheless Kodama and Gotō took care to establish high standards for primary school and other Japanese school facilities and teachers. This was not only to remind Taiwanese and aborigines of the superiority of their rulers.[145] Gotō also considered it absolutely necessary that life for the Japanese community in Taiwan be made attractive enough to give those who had crossed the sea a vested interest in the colony and to persuade first-class men to join the colonial service. High salaries and inviting living conditions were the weapons he used against the *dekasegi* mentality.[146] (*Dekasegi* is leaving one's home for residence elsewhere only because of employment opportunities; the intention is always to return home when possible.)

The educational tracks were more sharply separated and more unequal than Izawa had intended. Izawa's mind was capable of imagining young Taiwanese rising to the top of the Japanese educational pyramid and making their way into the ranks of the elite that governed the empire. In the memorandum he handed Kabayama, Izawa's language courses in Japanese for Taiwanese and in native languages for Japanese were proposed on an equal footing, similar in length and curricula. In another formal note to his governor-general he had urged that the (racial) discrimination that was characteristic of colonial education be kept out of Taiwan.[147]

To his teacher trainee recruits he always insisted that it was just as important for Japanese to learn the languages of the natives as it was for the natives to master Japanese. The higher educational opportunities for Taiwanese were also more severely limited than Izawa had originally planned. The Japanese Language School's language course for Taiwanese, in Izawa's view, was to qualify graduates for higher training as well as for immediate employment.[148] Normal schools for natives had been an important part of his proposal too, and he had hoped to see these expanded, not curtailed.

Izawa agreed with Kodama and Gotō about the importance of accommodating local institutions and respecting Chinese culture. When he encountered Japanese troops in Taiwan using Confucius' temple as a field hospital, he immediately petitioned to have the hospital moved and the temple restored and protected, and he heartily endorsed most of the principles of the Chinese classics that the *shobō* masters taught, even if he disapproved of the attention they devoted to archaic literary styles.[149]

But on the question of assimilation of Taiwan's Chinese population Izawa Shūji was an opponent of Gotō Shimpei and his chief because in Izawa's mind there was no doubt that assimilation could and should take place. He admitted that when assimilation had been attempted by the Western colonial powers the results had been less than impressive, yet he insisted that Japan would be able to succeed where they had failed. This would happen, thought Izawa, because Japanese and Taiwanese already shared so much — they were of the same race, revered the same Confucian teachings, and wrote with the same script.[150] The task would be arduous. But as long as the government general's commitment was large enough, Japanese educators would be able to accomplish it. Izawa was never a gradualist who believed education facilities should be available only to those who could pay for them or be deliberately limited to avoid producing overeducated natives. It was because he refused to accept any but the highest priority for education that he finally quarreled with his superiors and was forced to leave Taiwan.

3/ Expansion: Suitable Education for a Colony

The administrations of Governors-General Sakuma Samata (April 1906-May 1915) and Andō Sadayoshi (May 1915-June 1918) built upon the foundations laid by Kodama and Gotō. A separate school system for Japanese children catered to the growing needs of Japanese residents. As the Japanese community grew, new primary schools were opened, a second middle school for Japanese boys was founded in Tainan in 1914, and three years later a second higher girls' school for Japanese girls was opened there too. Meanwhile the quality and quantity of common schooling for Taiwanese children was steadily improving, while efforts to Japanize Chinese private schools and to reduce their numbers were made. Higher schooling for natives was developed slowly, sparingly, and with extreme reluctance.

The government general continued to place great importance upon getting young children of native elites into Japanese schools. Officials felt that if new attitudes and values could be inculcated in the leadership classes, they would be passed along to the more humble folk. Administrators who hoped to create a demand for common schooling assumed that if gentry and other prominent figures sent their youngsters to the new schools, others would eventually follow their betters' example. Even if they did not do so, the association of native elites with Japanese education could only solidify the government general's prestige and legitimacy. Thus all leadership classes, even aborigine chieftains, were wooed.[1] Although serious attempts to educate aborigine children were minimal during this period, Japanese policemen stationed in aborigine villages were ordered to make sure the lads who would some day be chieftains were given a rudimentary Japanese education.[2]

Overtures to upper-class Taiwanese met with some success. In 1907 there were 34,382 Taiwanese children in common school;

eleven years later 107,659 names were on the common school rolls. In these eleven years the number of common schools had jumped from 190 to 394.[3] The Japanese calculated that while the 1907 common schools took in only 4.5 percent of the native elementary school aged population, in 1918 the common schools accommodated 15.7 percent of this population.[4] The overwhelming majority of these pupils came from homes of the well-to-do.

This was at least partly because only the salaries of teachers were paid from taxes collected by the regional administrators. All other expenses, including capital expenditures, had to be borne by the Taiwanese living in the city, town, or village in which a school was located.[5] Wherever the people were unable or unwilling to maintain a common school, no such school was opened. To establish and to maintain a common school usually meant that wealthy Taiwanese in the district would have to make generous personal donations.[6] Still, financial demands made of Taiwanese communities were not as heavy as what had been required of local taxpayers in Meiji Japan, upon whose backs the country's modern primary school system had been built.[7]

When Japanese administrators considered what was happening in the overseas possessions of the Western powers, they were all the more convinced that a slow, controlled expansion of predominantly elementary school facilities was a wise policy. Education in British India was the great negative example: the thought of India's "educated unemployed" worried Japan's colonial policy makers.[8] Some suggested that American rule in the Philippines also demonstrated the dangers inherent in educating a subject people. Takekoshi Yosaburō (1865-1950), scholarly politician of the Seiyūkai, for instance, remarked that as the natives in the Philippines had learned to read they had become increasingly unhappy with American rule. He warned:

> Generally when one country annexes another, the annexing country, from its own point of view, has considerable reason for doing so, but from the view point of ordinary humanity (*ippan jinrui*) it is a great tragedy. Therefore, unless the annexer gains the gratitude of the annexed people by providing several years of good government and law, the stain of this tragedy cannot be wiped out. If the annexer teaches the natives to read and opens schools before good government and law are impressed upon the hearts of the people, this will only make the annexed people

remember their tragedy all the more vividly and will only cause their hateful resentment to grow all the stronger.[9]

Officials on the spot in Taiwan were particularly keen students of comparative colonialism, although what they observed in other colonies were often points to be avoided rather than emulated. In 1907 Mochiji Rokusaburō, head of the education bureau in the government general, made an extensive tour of the American Philippines, Dutch Java, and British India. His report on his findings stressed aspects of education in each of these colonies that he felt Taiwan could do without.

The Americans in the Philippines, he claimed, spent one sixth of their colonial budget on education, while they neglected the building of railroads and the encouragement of industry which would contribute to the population's well-being. This policy spelled disaster, he argued, because too much education and too little economic development would not enable the Filipinos to maintain their independence even if the Americans gave it to them. He doubted that the Americans would in fact grant independence. Mochiji noted that almost a decade had passed since the American President William McKinley had promised the Philippine people self-rule when they were ready for it. In the interval, Japan's rise as an imperialist power in the Pacific and heavy American investment in the Philippines had turned opinion in the United States away from support of this promise.

In the East Indies he found the Dutch putting little effort and few funds into native education, although they provided excellent schooling for Dutch children there. In India he observed a confused and complicated education system, which he concluded was a result of lack of planning and policy on the part of the British. Many, he claimed, blamed the troubles in India solely on British education with its emphasis on freedom and rights. While Mochiji acknowledged that a firm connection between the English education of Indian intellectuals and their anti-British political activities existed, he felt that there were more fundamental causes of rebellion in India. He pointed to the long years of British economic exploitation in the area and the victory of Japan in the Russo-Japanese War, which had awakened an Asian racial consciousness in peoples under the white man's rule.

Compared to what he had seen in Java, India, and the Philippines, schooling in Taiwan looked very good indeed, Mochiji told colonial educators in 1908.[10] Not that the Japanese in Taiwan could not learn something from the colonies visited — the energy and enthusiasm of American teachers in the Philippines, for example, was inspiring. But on the whole, Mochiji concluded, education in these regions reached far too few natives, lacked coherent planning, or cost too much.[11]

In 1911 another Taiwan administrator, Tōgō Minoru (1881-1959), expressed his doubts regarding Western colonial education policies more bluntly in an article in *Taiwan jihō* (Taiwan Times) entitled "In Opposition to Assimilation."[12] Tōgō pointed to France as the "great advocate of assimilation," which saw "a colony as an extension of the mother country," and noted Algeria and Indochina as examples. He claimed, however, that the dismantling of Algerian society had generated native hostility toward the French, and the raising of political hopes that would not be fulfilled in Indochina had also produced Frenchmen opposed to assimilation.[13]

English experience, although different, was unhappy too. Tōgō was convinced that the "almost unlimited freedom of publication" permitted in the British domains would turn natives against the British. Although Lord Macaulay's education proposal to give Western philosophy and literature to an Indian elite was meant to provide India with culture and law, instead it merely destroyed native Indian morality and made Indians want to become officials in the administration. With the administration able to absorb but a limited number of natives, discontent would grow and the people rebel against their British rulers. Efforts to assimilate Germany's eastern Slavs by means of the German education system and suppression of their native languages had also turned these people against the German state, according to Tōgō.[14]

Tōgō felt that these attempts to liquidate customs and cultures one thousand years old invited failure. These countries failed abysmally, he announced, as had all colonial powers in recorded history that adopted assimilation policies. To import systems, especially education systems, from the mother country spelled disaster. To disseminate knowledge which encouraged an individualistic mentality was to poison the social order. After all, colonial rule existed not for the individual but for the social order. He claimed that when Indians received a Western-type education they destroyed English order, as, thinking only of their own individual goals, they subverted the social system.[15]

Common Schools and Their Competitors

With the terrible example of India in mind, government-general officials worried that a common school education might come to be regarded by the native population as a stepping-stone for Taiwanese who hoped to better themselves through collaboration with their rulers. These administrators were aware that their continued quest for pupils among the children of the well-to-do had unwittingly encouraged this impression. The steady increase in the number of native children attending school was most satisfactory, but in the eyes of the government general, numbers were not the only criterion of educational success. They considered it of utmost importance that common school graduates accept the economic and social positions of their parents, and that the common schools give young islanders new skills and goals which would make them more efficient practitioners of their customary professions and trades.

Uchida Kakichi (1864-1933), Director of Civil Administration from August 1910 to November 1915, expressed this resolve straightforwardly at a conference of local officials in May 1915. Uchida first remarked that the keen desire of common school graduates for higher education had resulted in an enthusiastic and successful campaign for a middle school for Taiwanese. Then he continued:

> Education, that is, education in a colony, is not purely for the purpose of advancing education. A colonial education system must correspond to social conditions and the people's cultural level. It is absolutely inadvisable to offer advanced courses. Teaching such courses has often done irreparable damage. Thus it is imperative that careful attention be devoted to deliberation concerning the establishment of such facilities. Virtually all colonial powers pursue a policy of promoting vocational education to provide students with practical skills. The people of Taiwan should be taught practical skills too so they may earn a living and enjoy happiness.[16]

The message was clear. The government general would resist Taiwanese pressures for advancement through education.

Attention devoted to the common school curriculum during the first two decades of the twentieth century reflected official concerns. Much energy went into devising a curriculum as responsive as possible to what the government perceived to be Taiwanese needs. Twice during this period, in 1907 and in 1912, the common school curriculum underwent a major revision.

The revised Common School Regulations of 1907 introduced flexibility into the length and content of the common school course. Four-year and eight-year variations of the standard six-year courses were authorized to accommodate local conditions, and the timing of school terms was to be in harmony with agricultural seasons where planting, harvesting, and other tasks kept children from attending school all year around. Chinese language, music, and sewing could be omitted if local conditions so advised. On the other hand, the optional subjects—agriculture, commerce, and manual arts—became compulsory in schools which offered them. The teaching of these subjects was designed to fight the deep-rooted repugnance literate Taiwanese felt toward manual labor. The government general urged its teachers to conquer this prejudice by making sure that Taiwanese children learned the satisfaction of honest manual work.[17]

The 1907 revision turned out to be a preview of the more thorough-going amendment of the Common School Regulations which occurred in 1912. The 1912 move was intended to make common schooling more practical, more vocational, more directly applicable to the daily lives of the pupils. Arithmetic classes were to teach everyday uses of numbers, not to impart theoretical knowledge. Science, hitherto taught only in the seventh and eighth grades (that is, only in the expanded eight-year course), was now to begin in the fifth grade. Science lessons were to give the children a feeling for nature. Lesson material was to be relevant to the youngsters' daily lives and directly related to what they were learning about homemaking, health, agriculture, and commerce. Teachers were told to use science to destroy popular superstitions. Plant fibers, bamboo, wood, metal, and other familiar substances were designated as suitable materials for manual arts, the object of which was to acquaint children with physical labor (kinrō) and to inculcate in them respect and appreciation for it. Agriculture, taught in rural schools, was also intended to cultivate respect for manual labor and to teach work habits, as well as to give practical information about soil cultivation (saibai), livestock, sericulture, and tree and fish farming. The commerce curriculum, directed at children living in the towns, put high values upon keeping accounts, and upon calculating and computing skills. Lessons in sewing and household management for girls were supposed to encourage thrift, diligence, order, and circumspection (*shūmitsu*), as well as to transmit practical skills.[18]

These new regulations were accompanied by a confidential memorandum to teachers and other local officials, which contained harsh words about the Taiwanese. They were described as frivolous, fond of idle show and foppishness, interested only in the hollow phrases of Chinese learning. The [upper class] Taiwanese, claimed the memorandum, despised manual labor and had nothing but contempt for honest and useful occupations which required physical skill or exertion. In order to carry out "the great hundred-year plan" [outlined by Gotō Shimpei] of transforming the Taiwanese into Japanese, educators were urged to trade the seventh and eighth grades of eight-year common schools for vocational departments. Because in the majority of schools seventh and eighth grades did not exist, and because of a shortage of facilities and teachers, vocational departments could not be set up everywhere immediately; but until such departments could be opened in all common schools, all teachers were entreated to teach vocational subjects in extracurricular time. Even if the elders remained hopeless, such action on the part of teachers might make the next generation of native leaders less prejudiced against agricultural, commercial, and manual occupations.[19]

Although Japanese teachers dominated the schools — principals and senior teachers were Japanese — by this time many Taiwanese normal school graduates had joined the Japanese staff in common schools. It would be interesting to know if they too received this memorandum on the assumption that they were Japanized enough to agree with it, or whether the memorandum was intended for Japanese eyes alone.

In support of the goals of the 1907 and 1912 regulations, government-general officials wrote, compiled, and edited sets of common school textbooks, teachers' manuals, and other classroom materials. In 1912 the colonial government published thirteen such curriculum aids, and the following year thirteen additional books were published. In addition to the lessons found in a pupil's version of a text, teachers' versions of the same book contained extensive instructional commentary.

Many of the publications were materials for studying Japanese and ethics, which were the two subjects which administrators believed held the key to cultivating morality and loyalty to Japan.

There were in addition a series on calligraphy, another for teaching arithmetic, some general manuals of instruction for teachers, and a book with the intriguing title of *Japanese Language Agricultural Reader* (*Kokugo nōgyō tokuhon*). During the following five years this core of teaching materials was joined by a variety of publications. These included books for arithmetic, agriculture, manual arts, commerce, physical education, singing, Chinese-character texts for Japanese language readers, and composition (*tsuzurikata*) books. As well, more Japanese language readers, ethics textbooks, and general instruction manuals were issued. Production of textbooks for aborigine schoolchildren began in 1916 with the appearance of the first three volumes of *Aborigine Reader* (*Banjin tokuhon*).[20]

At first glance, it might seem that this thrust toward practical instruction was because educational policy in Japan had taken a turn in this direction. Official commentary upon the revisions suggest as much: the administration-based Taiwan Education Society's *The Development of Taiwan Education* (*Taiwan kyōiku enkaku shi*) states that, since vocational courses in agriculture, industrial arts, and commerce had recently become more important in the elementary and secondary schools in Japan, it was fitting that such studies should be expanded in the colony also.[21]

In Japan during the 1890s vocational schooling came into its own. Japan's industrial preparation for the Sino-Japanese War heightened awareness of the primary school's role in the training of a modern labor force, especially in the minds of Inoue Kowashi (education minister from May 1893 to July 1894) and his "brain trust" of young education ministry officials. Associating elementary education and a disciplined labor force with an industrial economy and a strong rich country, Inoue and his subordinates led a drive to improve attendance at primary school. Although Inoue's resolution to help poorer children gain an elementary education was tempered by his acceptance of the higher priority of other demands made upon the national treasury, he pushed for a system of at least limited subsidies from national funds to support needy primary schools. The Imperial Diet rejected his proposal in 1893 but three years later approved it when it was put forward by his successor. A system of restricted subsidies finally got underway in 1900.[22]

However, it was at the secondary and tertiary school levels that Inoue developed the vocational and technical facilities for which he is famous. He persuaded the government to provide funds for setting up apprentice schools, commercial schools, agricultural schools, industrial and commercial continuation schools—at the postprimary level. The primary school curriculum was not remodeled to emphasize vocational training at this time or during the years that followed. Rather, primary schooling, which imparted basic literacy and arithmetic, appropriate work habits and discipline as well as selected spiritual or ideological values, was viewed as an essential experience for the Japanese masses because it provided them with the general "readiness" which would enable them to master more specialized skills later.[23]

About fifteen years afterwards, when officials in Taiwan perceived an increased need for vocational studies, their concern was also in response to changing economic conditions. The government general's railroad, road, and bridge construction projects had vastly improved communications; the island's two main harbors, Keelung in the north and Takao in the south, were now joined by rail and carried on an expanding shipping business. Japanese capital, encouraged by handsome subsidies from the colonial government, had enlarged and modernized the operations of Taiwan's sugar industry, the most important industry on the island.[24] Government experimental farms, irrigation, and flood control projects stimulated the movement of Japanese capital into other important industries as well: tea, camphor, rice, pineapple, and banana production, for example.[25]

The colonial government had no intention of sponsoring technical schools and colleges to produce the manpower that the island's modernizing agricultural sector and the newer trade, transportation, communication, and administrative facilities required. As Tables 3 and 4 illustrate, Taiwanese had begun to be needed in the lower echelons of new occupations, but as Yanaihara Tadao observed late in the 1920s, unlike some other colonial powers, the Japanese in Taiwan felt they "could always obtain technicians from the home country."[26] Japanese migrants to Taiwan had been providing and were continuing to provide technicians, administrators, managers, professionals, and skilled workers to develop the economy. In 1905, 59,618 Japanese resided in the colony; in 1915 there were 137,229 Japanese residents of Taiwan.[27] Of these the overwhelming majority were government administrators or professionals in managerial or other skilled professions.[28]

TABLE 3. Employment of Taiwanese, mainland Chinese, and Japanese in Taiwan by job category as of October 1905, 1915, 1920, respectively (in units of one hundred people)

Job category	Taiwanese						Mainland Chinese						Japanese					
	Male			Female			Male			Female			Male			Female		
	1905	1915	1920	1905	1915	1920	1905	1915	1920	1905	1915	1920	1905	1915	1920	1905	1915	1920
Total	10,537	10,973	11,002	3,083	4,671	4,444	124	132	168	–	5	7	280	539	638	42	102	109
Agriculture and forestry	7,311	7,724	7,579	2,618	3,880	3,746	–	3	3	–	–	1	3	34	28	–	11	12
Fishing	318	296	270	17	28	16	–	–	3	–	–	–	2	7	14	–	–	–
Mining	80	122	156	2	4	10	3	–	4	–	–	–	16	15	15	–	1	–
Manufacturing	535	651	846	179	443	352	28	51	72	–	3	4	55	160	174	5	13	12
Fabricated metals	64	59	44	2	2	2	2	5	5	–	–	–	2	5	5	–	–	–
Machinery	17	22	27	–	–	–	–	–	2	–	–	–	2	3	5	–	–	–
Chemicals	79	114	106	8	32	37	–	–	–	–	–	–	3	13	11	–	3	2
Cotton	2	4	18	6	7	61	–	1	2	–	–	1	–	–	4	–	–	1
Weaving, knitting, dyeing	20	13		8	8		–	–		–	–		–	1				
Paper and pulp products	31	32	33	26	39	34	–	–	–	–	–	–	–	2	1	–	–	–
Leather products	2	–	–	–	–	–	–	–	1	–	–	–	–	–	–	–	–	–
Wood and bamboo	84	113	136	21	41	36	6	11	13	–	–	–	5	9	16	–	–	1

Seafood processing	–	–	–	–	–	–	–	–	–	–	–	–	–	–	–
Sugar, foods, beverages	133	157	220	60	75	92	15	14	15	1	5	49	64	1	3
Clothing and laundry	20	25	27	48	237	78	2	11	17	1	4	9	7	3	7
Construction	67	88	114	–	–	2	2	5	9	–	28	58	39	–	–
Printing and photography	4	8	10	–	–	1	–	–	–	–	2	4	2	–	–
Others	12	16	111[a]	–	2	9[a]	1	2	8[a]	1	4	7	20[a]	1	–
Commercial activities	770	798	836	70	123	122	22	38	45	1	46	95	96	20	37

Source: TWT, pp. 132-137.

[a]This marked increase was due to the fact that by 1920 a number of new industries hitherto negligible became too large to be ignored. For example, cement and glass products, pottery, and ceramics were separated from the old classification of mining.

[b]By 1920, the category "transportation" included the newer "communication." The breakdown of this category for 1920 is as follows:

	Taiwanese		Chinese		Japanese	
Job category	Male	Female	Male	Female	Male	Female
Transportation	35,428	1,378	2,727	3	7,466	413
Communications	1,582	111	2	–	939	279
Transportation	33,846	1,267	2,725	3	6,527	134

[c]The category "professionals" includes ministers of various religions, teachers, lawyers, doctors, writers, journalists, and artists.

Table 3 (continued)

TABLE 3. (continued)

Job category	Taiwanese						Mainland Chinese						Japanese					
	Male			Female			Male			Female			Male			Female		
	1905	1915	1920	1905	1915	1920	1905	1915	1920	1905	1915	1920	1905	1915	1920	1905	1915	1920
Retailers	648	689	687	62	106	94	13	24	28	–	1	1	25	60	55	6	11	11
Wholesalers, brokers	50	41	53	1	1	2	3	3	4	–	–	–	–	2	4	–	–	–
Banking, insurance	3	6	18	–	–	–	–	–	–	–	–	–	4	9	14	–	1	2
Restaurants, entertainments	65	62	76	6	14	26	5	11	13	–	–	–	12	21	23	14	25	48
Others	4	–	2	1	2	–	1	–	–	–	–	–	5	–	–	–	–	–
Transportation and communication	231	295	354b	1	6	14b	21	31	27b	–	–	–	39	62	75b	–	3	4b
Army and Navy	–	–	–	–	–	–	–	–	–	–	–	–	9	5	6	–	–	–

56

Government and municipal employees	83	68	95	—	5	—	—	—	91	114	131	—	2	
Professionals^c	74	89	135	2	12	—	—	1	14	30	38	3	11	15
Others	1,135	930	731	194	167	50	9	14	1	5	17	61	14	26	3

Source: TWT, pp. 132-137.

a This marked increase was due to the fact that by 1920 a number of new industries hitherto negligible became too large to be ignored. For example, cement and glass products, pottery, and ceramics were separated from the old classification of mining.

b By 1920, the category "transportation" included the newer "communication." The breakdown of this category for 1920 is as follows:

Job category	Taiwanese		Chinese		Japanese	
	Male	Female	Male	Female	Male	Female
Transportation	35,428	1,378	2,727	3	7,466	413
Communications	1,582	111	2	—	939	279
Transportation	33,846	1,267	2,725	3	6,527	134

c The category "professionals" includes ministers of various religions, teachers, lawyers, doctors, writers, journalists, and artists.

57

TABLE 4. Clerks and factory technicians employed in manufacturing industries in Taiwan during 1911 and 1916[a]

	Office clerks			Factory technicians		
Year	Taiwanese	Japanese	Total	Taiwanese	Japanese	Total
1911	839	577	1,416	182	236	418
	(59.2%)	(40.8%)		(43.5%)	(56.5%)	
1916	2,402	760	3,162	558	570	1,128
	(75.9%)	(24.1%)		(49.4%)	(50.6%)	
1911/1916	2.86	1.31	2.23	3.06	2.41	2.69

Sources: *Taiwan sōtokufu dai jūhachi* [1913] *tōkeisho*, pp. 400-407; *Taiwan sōtokufu dai nijūsan* [1918] *tōkeisho*, pp. 425-433.

[a]Figures in parentheses indicate the percentage ratio of ethnic group to total persons in job category. Clerks and factory technicians generally had completed elementary school.

However, vocational training was to be given to common school pupils. Like leaders of Meiji Japan, colonial officials in Taiwan during the 1910s understood that education could help prepare members of a traditional society to become productive workers in a modern economy. Thus they hoped to expand the common school system until it eventually took in all of the island's native children. But they were not satisfied that the basic arithmetic, literacy, general knowledge, and ethics taught to Japanese children were entirely suitable for young Taiwanese. The "readiness" officials demanded of Taiwanese masses was not so much readiness to learn skilled trades or professions as it was readiness to pursue old occupations more efficiently and to provide reliable unskilled and semiskilled labor for new industries.

Meiji schools did encourage respect for authority and the status quo—in 1881, for instance, "Instructions to Primary School Personnel" ("Shōgakkō kyōin no kokoroe") stated that "the teacher should avoid arousing too much ambition in his pupils."[29] But on the whole, Japanese schools during the Meiji period, like the military service, were a great equalizing force. They were "classless" in the sense that they went a long way toward providing equality of opportunity; a bright boy of humble origins could, with health and luck, go on to middle school, higher school, Tokyo Imperial University, and eventually a coveted career in government service.

In spite of the 1881 instructions and similar injunctions, children were encouraged to be ambitious as well as obedient.[30]

The common school curriculum, on the other hand, was designed to discourage any hopes of such a meteoric rise. It aimed to disseminate knowledge which would streamline traditional occupations, to upgrade health standards, and to spread Japanese ideas and customs. It was classless in the sense that it fostered attitudes, discipline, and habits deemed proper for all Taiwanese.[31]

In addition to their focus on vocational subjects, the common school regulations of 1912 singled out ethics and Japanese language as special vehicles for transforming the Chinese of Taiwan into Japanese. To hasten the children's mastery of Japanese, language lessons were increased from nine to twelve hours a week in the first grade. In later grades, hours spent on Japanese were reduced slightly on the assumption that pupils would become fluent in the language through its use in the teaching of all subjects, for the regulations designated Japanese as the sole medium of instruction and communication for all grades above the first.[32]

Problems of implementation apart, even in theory this Japanization was not as thoroughgoing as officials would have liked. Written Chinese, which remained the main means of communication between Japanese and literate Taiwanese adults, was still taught; five hours in grades one through four and four hours in grades five to six were spent on Chinese.[33] This was necessary to enable the new schools to compete successfully with Chinese private schools. In 1912 the government general recognized 541 *shobō* with a total of 16,302 pupils. Although this represented a significant decline from 1905 (1,080 *shobō* with 21,661 pupils), it was almost equal to a third of the Taiwanese attending the 248 common schools of 1912. It was only in 1918, when *shobō* students had been whittled down to 12,725 and common school attenders increased to 107,659, that administrators dared reduce weekly class time spent upon Chinese from five or four hours, depending upon the grade, to only two hours in each grade.[34] The government general really wanted to banish Chinese completely from the common school but even at this date felt it unwise to do so.[35]

When Chinese was demoted in 1918, Japanese language lessons were increased by two hours in the first four grades, and schools began to give ethics lessons twice a week instead of once. Geography was added to the curriculum "to show the Taiwanese the

honors and benefits accruing to subjects of the empire and because of the necessity of familiarizing them with conditions in our
country."[36] The object of all these changes was "to thoroughly
cultivate the Japanese spirit (kokumin seishin)."[37]

Physical education and music, which had no place in shobō,
were popular with common school pupils. The youngsters considered exercises upon the school playgrounds, sometimes equipped
with tennis courts and other sports apparatus, to be among the
chief attractions of a Japanese education.[38] Julean H. Arnold, the
American Consul in Taiwan and an interested observer of common schools in session, reported in 1908 that

> One of the most hopeful features in the education of the Chi-
> nese native lies in the interest he manifests in athletic games. The
> public school-yard, during the fifteen minutes recess at the end of
> each hour, presents as animated a scene as does that of any west-
> ern school. The Chinese child loves play and takes a keen delight
> in all games. Already interclass and interschool athletic meets
> have been held, and not only do the pupils delight in them, but
> the parents exhibit a surprising amount of pleasure at seeing their
> children participate in these sports.[39]

Singing was also greeted with enthusiasm. Arnold also noted
that "one has only to visit a class of native pupils engaged in their
singing exercises to appreciate the usefulness of the subject as
part of the daily program. The Chinese child is fond of singing
and has a better ear for music than the Japanese lad. He enters
into his singing with a spirit of enjoyment far in excess of that
which he exhibits in any of his other work and for this reason
much good language instruction may be imparted through this
medium."[40]

With physical education and music thus attracting pupils to
common schools, the government general tightened control of
the shobō. In 1909 a Chinese language reader was distributed to
native academies. It was compiled by education officials and was
intended to provide children with practical information about
daily living, as well as to give them clear and easy-to-read compositions to study. At this time its use was not made compulsory and
very few shobō teachers referred to it. It was probably most frequently consulted by common school pupils who, after common
school classes were over, went to a Chinese schoolmaster for extra
study.[41]

Two years later a directive demanding more thorough supervision of Chinese school texts and teaching materials was sent to all regional administrations. The directive noted that although regulations required permission from the head of the regional administration before a textbook could be used in a *shobō,* regional officials were not systematically checking to see if unauthorized texts were in fact employed; it also claimed that negligent officials had approved textbooks on the basis of their titles alone, without actually reading all the contents of the works carefully. Specific categories of books published in China were singled out for prohibition. These included introductory works in ethics, geography, Chinese language, and Chinese history. Local authorities were ordered to encourage the use of Chinese language textbooks written and published by Japanese, to see that the Japanese language and arithmetic were taught in all *shobō* and to persuade old-style schoolmasters to take the teacher training courses run by the government.[42]

This directive was little more than an order to enforce regulations on the books since 1898. Now that the *shobō* were decreasing numerically and in some areas common schools had established themselves as successful competitors to *shobō,* the colonial government felt able to take stricter measures against these native institutions. The potential for subversion harbored by these strongholds of Chinese learning and cultural values did not escape the Japanese; at the very least the *shobō* were a visible link with the past, reminding islanders of their Chinese identity.

The 1907 attempt to accommodate academic years to local agricultural calendars supported teachers' campaigns to exact daily attendance from all their pupils. There were, however, many reasons besides work in the fields to keep children home from school. As children—especially girls—became older they became more useful at home in a variety of capacities. Illness was a frequent excuse for absence; in spite of the salutary results of the administration's often harshly imposed sanitation measures, Taiwan was still a disease-ridden island.[43] And, as Arnold observed in 1908, "Chinese festivals and feast days are numerous, and, moreover, the Chinese boy who really desires to find an excuse for absence from school has a long list of relatives among whom marriage and funeral ceremonies . . . are bound to occur."[44]

The Japanese still complained that Taiwanese fathers had no

serious taste for education and often saw common school merely as a place for learning a little Japanese language.[45] However, persuasion and patience were the recommended policies toward recalcitrant parents; Japanese principals and teachers constantly visited parents and earnestly talked to them about the importance of sending their offspring to school regularly. Children were lectured in class about the same subject; the model child presented in ethics lessons was one who never missed a day of school and always arrived on time.[46] Competitions were staged with awards of individual prizes — which could "be transferred into cash for personal use" — and class banners for good attendance.[47]

Such efforts seem to have reaped some success because, as Table 5 illustrates, the difficulties of getting pupils to attend school regularly lessened markedly during the 1910s. By 1916 over 92 percent of the children on the common school rolls were apparently present on an average school day.

But much less progress had been made in persuading even wealthy Taiwanese to send their daughters to common school. As late as 1920 less than 10 percent of the female Taiwanese elemen-

TABLE 5. Daily attendance at common schools, 1907-18[a]

Year	Average daily attendance as percentage of students enrolled
1907	69.96
1908	75.96
1909	78.99
1910	83.55
1911	84.80
1912	87.35
1913	89.36
1914	90.90
1915	90.90
1916	92.67
1917	92.67
1918	92.00

Source: Yoshino, pp. 315-316.

[a]High attendance rates seem almost too good to be true. Perhaps anyone frequently absent was considered to have dropped out. These high attendance rates may be a reflection of the family backgrounds of the pupils.

tary school-aged population was attending classes, as compared to 39 percent for males.[48] This failure distressed administrators. If Japanese customs were ever going to be accepted and absorbed, the female half of the population would have to go to school too. But from the Taiwanese point of view there was little to be gained from sending girls to common school.[49] Parents may have feared that school would give their daughters unsuitable ideas or encourage unfortunate connections. Disappointed but not discouraged, Japanese officials knew that the same kinds of barriers had once kept girls out of primary school in Japan; they found the slowly but steadily increasing number of common school girls comforting, even if these girls were outnumbered by boys four to one.

Common School Leavers

Not all pupils finished the common school course. Table 6 demonstrates that between 1906 and 1918 many students left before completing the full course. Girls especially tended to drop out before graduation.[50]

TABLE 6. Percentages of common school pupils who left school before completion of the common school course by sex, 1906-18

Year	Boys	Girls
1906	35.0	42.5
1907	31.0	51.0
1908	27.4	47.9
1909	28.7	41.9
1910	23.7	38.5
1911	24.4	48.4
1912	20.3	26.6
1913	17.9	25.7
1914	15.1	21.8
1915	13.9	20.6
1916	11.9	17.5
1917	10.9	16.7
1918	11.8	18.4

Source: TWT, pp. 1232-1233.

[a]Unfortunately no data were available regarding the numbers of pupils dropping out of the individual grades of common school.

The regime encouraged both dropouts and most graduates to follow their parents' professions. Exceptionally able common school graduates were urged, as earlier, to take up teaching or medicine. Those who were not suited for these two professions and who rejected the traditional Taiwanese occupations were directed toward semiskilled work in the new industries developed by the Japanese.

On the whole, the government's objectives seem to have been fairly well fulfilled. Those who did enter new professions almost inevitably became teachers or doctors. Nevertheless, the number of Taiwanese passing through the common school department of the Japanese Language School in the 1910s was not large. In 1910 sixty-six Taiwanese teacher trainees were graduated; in 1915 ninety-eight; in 1918, 134.[51] The medical school took in even fewer common school graduates, graduating twenty-nine in 1910, thirty-two in 1915, and forty-four in 1918.[52] As Tables 3 and 4 suggest, growing numbers of Taiwanese did find employment in new and modernizing industries. And large numbers must have been absorbed in agricultural and commercial occupations.

A higher proportion of education and medical students completed their studies, although the drop-out rate was still significant. An article in the Chinese language section of the May 1909 issue of the periodical *Taiwan jihō* observed that the 1909 medical graduating class of twenty-four had originally numbered thirty-seven when beginning the medical preparatory course five years before. In the same year the Japanese Language School was graduating twenty-five Taiwanese teachers out of a class of eighty who had entered the department four years earlier.[53] Although some education and medical students left for reasons of illness or family necessity, perhaps the heavy Japanization that was very much a part of their programs was more than some could bear. All education and medical students were expected to live in Japanese-style dormitories, speak Japanese at all times, and live strictly according to the customs of the ruling country.

In 1907 the medical school took responsibility for offering training to traditional native doctors. From the beginning of the Japanese period, these *isei*, as they were called, had been permitted to practice traditional Chinese medicine, although the government kept track of them and hoped eventually to replace them with physicians trained in modern methods. By 1916, largely thanks to the medical school, there were 583 doctors and 927 accredited *isei* in the colony.[54]

From its inception, the medical school concentrated upon problems of medicine relevant to the island. It maintained a serious research interest in tropical medicine; for example, in 1918 a special one-year graduate course in tropical medicine was instituted. In the same year the medical college established a course for Japanese students. Its prerequisites were the same as those of medical colleges in Japan. Again the distinction between Japanese and Taiwanese was maintained. Taiwanese doctors had six years of common school, one of medical preparatory classes, and four of the regular medical course, and were licensed to practice in the colony only. They were not considered to be as qualified as those who would graduate from the medical course for Japanese. However, the facilities and the faculty of Taiwan's medical school were excellent enough by 1918 to offer Japanese a medical education on a par with that given in Japan.

Japanese policy was one thing; Taiwanese desires quite another. Well-to-do Taiwanese who sent their offspring to common school were not happy with the limited opportunities for study and employment available to common school graduates. Medicine was a lucrative profession; the more successful physicians made much more than Japanese teachers and other lower-ranking bureaucrats.[55] Teachers' salaries were far less inviting. A Taiwanese teacher got one third or less of the salary of a Japanese teacher, who was also provided with living quarters.[56] However, ambitious young islanders with slender means could get scholarships to see them through teacher training. Consequently, there were always many more applicants for medical school and teacher training than openings available. Competition to enter the medical school was particularly fierce, but even the Japanese Language School's teacher training course had three times as many applicants as it could accept.[57]

Frustrations of common school graduates increased, and more and more of the families who were able to do so sent sons to Japan. According to government-general records, there were but thirty-three Taiwanese studying in Japan in 1907, while four years later there were 320 Taiwanese at school in the ruling country.[58]

Japan had rapidly become a popular destination for ambitious young islanders because there Taiwanese, who in the colony would have been restricted to the facilities provided for their race, freely entered schools of their choice provided they could pass the required entrance examinations. Finding the barriers to Japan's higher schools to be scholastic not ethnic, wealthy Taiwanese began to send youngsters to primary school in Japan. Older students, competing equally with Japanese and studying side-by-side with them in an environment with less racial bias and ruling class consciousness than the colony's, often found their years of study abroad to be an exhilarating experience. Much of their excitement was communicated to their peers and juniors when they returned home. But many more young scholars wanted to go to Japan than were able to do so. Study in the ruling country was usually only possible for those whose families were wealthy enough to support such luxury or for those lucky enough to find a rich patron.[59]

At the same time, agitation for middle school facilities for Taiwanese boys grew. The government general was worried about the exodus of young natives to the "dangerous" intellectual atmosphere of Tokyo; in 1915 it reluctantly bowed to the pressure, and the first middle school for Taiwanese boys was opened. The struggle for this seemingly modest achievement was intense, and is worth examining in some detail.

A Campaign for a Taiwanese Middle School

In 1914 Itagaki Taisuke (1837-1919), a prominent liberal politician in Japan, paid two visits to Taiwan. During and after his first visit, in the spring, he publicized the idea of a Taiwan Assimilation Society (Taiwan dōkakai), the goal of which was to be equality for Taiwanese and Japanese citizens of the island. The original initiative for such a society came both from a few Taiwanese intellectuals and from two Japanese in the Taiwan administration, "who appear to have been both idealistic and politically ambitious, as well as frustrated with their minor posts in the Taiwan Customs Office."[60] However, as the Taiwanese and the Japanese initiators both knew, such a controversial proposal needed a sponsor of Itagaki's stature to make it even remotely realistic.

Itagaki had two political goals in mind. First was the strengthening of Japan's position in East Asia, which he felt assimilation of the Taiwanese would further. He expected that this concern for Japan's international stature would appeal to a wide range of Japanese opinion. Second, and equally important, was the elimination of Japanese discrimination against Taiwanese in the colony. As an old warrior in the fight for "people's rights" in Japan he was confident that this goal too would attract widespread Japanese support.[61] Itagaki's enthusiasm for equal treatment of Japanese and Taiwanese drew Taiwanese intellectuals; but neither Japanese colonists nor the government general shared their enthusiasm.

While Itagaki was in Taiwan, the administration kept a guarded though respectful watch on his movements and speech-making. After his departure in the spring, they reacted with growing concern to accounts of his publicity drive for the Taiwan Assimilation Society in Japan. Itagaki was proclaiming the necessity for equality between Japanese and Taiwanese, and was critizing the narrow educational opportunities available to the latter. He argued that if Taiwanese had full access to educational opportunities — as full, for instance, as the Japanese had enjoyed during the Meiji period — their leaders would not be driven to rebel and seek independence.[62] Itagaki's energetic campaign to win support for these views in high governmental circles in Tokyo made him even less welcome, in the eyes of the colonial government, when he returned to Taiwan in late November of 1914.

However, even in retirement Itagaki remained a senior politician of national renown, and the government general could do nothing but arrange the formal welcome due to such a statesman. Ironically, Gotō Shimpei, who happened to be in the colony at the time, also greeeted Itagaki.[63] (Earlier, when Itagaki had circulated his proposal for the Taiwanese Assimilation Society among government officials and politicians in Tokyo, Gotō had replied politely and diplomatically, but of course without granting his approval.)[64] Although Gotō must have been far from pleased with the object of Itagaki's visit to Taiwan, he remained as always the astute politician and welcomed him courteously.

Taiwanese intellectuals received Itagaki warmly, and on December 13 the Assimilation Society was given official authorization by the government general. On the twentieth the opening ceremony was held in Taihoku; headquarters were shortly established and two main branches set up.[65] A month later the society had attracted 3,178 members — including 44 Japanese — and its assets, composed of donations and membership fees, totaled 4,660 yen.[66] Conversely, most Japanese residents in Taiwan were hostile to the new organization, as was the administration. Itagaki's prestige meant that no action could be taken against the society while he remained in Taiwan, but immediately upon his departure on December 26 the campaign began.

Attacks appeared in the colony's newspapers; complaints about the activities of Itagaki and his followers were printed; Taiwanese leaders were vehemently denounced. The Chinese edition of the newspaper *Taiwan nichi nichi shimpō* curtly warned Taiwanese not to expect Itagaki to achieve civil rights and equality for them. Then on January 26, 1915, Governor-General Sakuma ordered the Taiwan Assimilation Society dissolved.[67] The Japanese in Taiwan also made their views known in Tokyo: "Following the departure of Itagaki, officials about the island, as well as representatives of various Japanese professional groups there, besieged key figures in Tokyo with letters and telegrams. Gotō Shimpei, who had not held office in Taiwan for almost eight years, received a number of messages denouncing Itagaki."[68]

Although the initiative had come from a handful of bold Taiwanese and disgruntled Japanese, who chose as their leader a figure completely outside Taiwanese society, the 1914 movement immediately struck a responsive chord among upper-class Taiwanese, especially among the young. It was not difficult for colonial authorities to break up the Assimilation Society after its figurehead had returned to Tokyo, but they did not possess the same powers of political suppression in the ruling country. Crushing of the movement in the colony encouraged young Taiwanese to go to Japan. Officially they went to continue their education but actually in the hope that they might persuade other Japanese, individuals like Itagaki, to understand their desires and ambitions.[69] In 1913, the year preceding Itagaki's visits, the government general recognized 268 Taiwanese studying in Japan; during 1915 this figure jumped to 337, and this was just the beginning.[70]

The administration's anxiety regarding this desire to become a student in Japan was exploited by Taiwanese leaders who had been trying in vain to persuade the Japanese to improve educational opportunities for common school graduates. Lin Hsient'ang (1881-1956), a rich and famous landholder in the Taichū region and a key actor in Itagaki's Assimilation Society, had been campaigning for some time for a public middle school for Taiwanese boys and had met with nothing but obstruction from the government general. Official opinion, as the speech of Uchida Kakichi quoted earlier illustrates, opposed higher schooling for natives on the grounds that it was intellectually dangerous and likely only to breed discontent. But Lin and his colleague Kan Te-chung (1883-19?) used Itagaki's 1914 movement to wring from a reluctant administration authorization for the first middle school for Taiwanese.[71] Much as officials deplored establishment of such a school, they reluctantly concluded that it was a lesser evil than a steady exodus of young Taiwanese headed for Tokyo to pick up ideas that could disturb the colony's peace when they returned home.

As the regime had not encouraged the founding of the Taichū middle school, it is not surprising that it was begun with heavy support from Taiwanese; the costly grounds and buildings for example, were paid for by Taiwanese donations. In fact, it is probably more accurate to say that the Taiwanese built the school, gaining the necessary authority from an unenthusiastic administration. In April 1915 entrance examinations held in Taihoku, Tainan, Taichū, and Kagi (Chia-i) selected one hundred students out of 306 applicants for classes which began in May.[72]

Like medical or educational students, all students at the Kōritsu Taichū Middle School were required to reside in a dormitory. Here they spoke Japanese, ate Japanese food, wore Japanese clothing, took hot baths and became accustomed to other Japanese habits. This type of dormitory existence seems to have been imposed on all islanders receiving postprimary education for two reasons. Many Japanese objected to advanced education for Taiwanese on the grounds that native tastes and customs made them unworthy of higher schooling; and, conversely, many thought it dangerous for natives to acquire specialized skills unless they were Japanized as intensively as possible at the same time. Whatever the other results of such dormitory programs, they are known to have produced frequent and acute cases of homesickness.[73]

In spite of Taiwanese aspirations, the Kōritsu Taichū Middle School did not equal the standards of Japanese middle schools; officials who insisted that "the education needs of the Taiwanese are not the same as those of the Japanese" made sure of this.[74] The Taichū school accepted boys who had completed four years of common school, its course was one year shorter than a Japanese middle school course, and vocational subjects (agriculture or commerce) were compulsory in all grades. (See Table 7.) Neither was the school's course a prerequisite to any higher training program in the colony. As a result, well-to-do Taiwanese still looked

TABLE 7. Curricula of the Taichū Middle School and of a Japanese middle school

Curriculum of the Koritsu Taichū Middle School (for Taiwanese) in weekly hours

Year	Ethics	Japanese and written Chinese	History and geography	Mathematics	Science	Vocational subject	Law and economics	Handicrafts and drawing	Singing	Physical education	English	Total
First	1	12	2	4	3	2	0	3	1	2	0	30
Second	1	12	2	4	3	3	0	3	1	2	0	31
Third	1	12	2	4	3	5	0	1	1	2	2[a]	31 or 32
Fourth	1	10	1	4	3	5	2	1	1	2	2[a]	31 or 32

Curriculum of a Contemporary Japanese Middle School in weekly hours

Year	Ethics	Japanese and written Chinese	Foreign language	History and geography	Mathematics	Natural history	Physics and chemistry	Law and economics	Drawing	Singing	Physical education	Total
First	1	7	7	3	3	2	0	0	1	1	3	28
Second	1	7	7	3	3	2	0	0	1	1	3	28
Third	1	7	7	3	5	2	0	0	1	1	3	30
Fourth	1	6	7	3	5	0	4	0	1	0	3	30
Fifth	1	6	6	3	4	0	4	3	0	0	3	30

Sources: TKES, pp. 749-750; Mombusho, Gakusei hyakunen shi, I, 356.
[a]Optional subject.

to Japan as a place to send sons who wished to get ahead. By 1918 nearly five hundred Taiwanese scholars in Japan were acknowledged by the colonial government.[75] Some of them were becoming more and more interested in means by which they might loosen the government general's grip upon their island.

Postprimary Education for Girls

During the first years of Japanese rule colonial educators had established an advanced course of handicrafts in the first elementary school opened for native girls. In 1906 the pupils in the elementary division were transferred to a common school. The upper section of the school which remained became the colony's first higher girls' school for Taiwanese. It was renamed the Japanese Language School's Second Attached School, and its advanced course of handicrafts became a three-year course of ethics, Japanese language, mathematics, science, sewing, calligraphy, singing, physical education, and, for those who chose them, flower arrangement and embroidery. The object of this course was to prepare young Taiwanese women to teach domestic science and handicrafts in the common schools.[76]

Besides its accent on subjects to be taught to girls, the training for women teachers differed in two important respects from that which men received. First, women were accepted after completion of four years of a common school course, while men could only enter the Japanese Language School's education course for Taiwanese after finishing six years of common school. Second, the handicrafts course was a year shorter than that required for Taiwanese male teachers. Taiwanese women teachers thus received three years less schooling than males. Also, native female teachers in common schools were paid much less than native men. All this corresponded to patterns familiar in the education world in Japan.[77]

Small though the Second Attached School was, it deserves attention. Although most Taiwanese families had little reason to provide their daughters with a postprimary education, this school managed to attract steadily increasing numbers. By 1918 enrollment exceeded two hundred.[78] (See Table 8.) Many or perhaps most of the girls who passed through this school were preparing for teaching careers in the common schools as the regime encouraged, and some were attracted by the prestige the school had gained as a colonial finishing school.[79]

TABLE 8. Handicraft course of the Japanese Language School's Second Attached School (for Taiwanese girls): entrants, graduates, total students enrolled, 1907-18

Year	Entrants	Graduates	Students Enrolled
1907	46	10	53
1908	39	8	66
1909	25	22	81
1910	39	25	86
1911	42	21	93
1912	47	29	106
1913	47	28	113
1914	47	26	116
1915	45	40	130
1916	48	36	126
1917	92	37	165
1918	92	37	208

Sources: TKES, pp. 723-725; Yoshino, pp. 331-332.

For a very few ambitious and fortunate young women from wealthy Taiwanese familes that permitted or encouraged girls to seek higher schooling and careers, study in Japan was a goal from at least the late 1910s. It was unusual but not unheard of for a Taiwanese family to enroll a daughter in a primary school or higher girls' school in Japan so that later she might enter a women's normal school or a women's medical college there.[80] Christian missionaries, like the Presbyterians from Britain and Canada, whose advocacy of schooling for girls and women predated Japanese occupation of the island, encouraged young Taiwanese Christians to go to Japan to complete their studies.[81]

Of course the majority of upper-class Taiwanese families neither wished to have their daughters trained as common school teachers nor did they see graduation from the government general's higher school for Taiwanese girls as a necessary prerequisite for marriage and the duties that marriage involved. The Japanese deplored this, but it must have come as no surprise to them, especially since in Japan many educational professionals were beginning to feel that postprimary school for girls was something less than desirable. In the autumn of 1918 a special education conference (*rinji kyōiku kaigi*) convened by the Ministry of Education discussed problems related to higher education for women. Almost all the participants agreed that higher education of women in Japan had produced women with "dangerous thoughts" who were less dutiful as wives, daughters-in-law, and child bearers than were their less educated sisters. It was pointed out that higher girls' school graduates bore fewer children than any other group of Japanese women.[82]

Japanese Schooling

Gotō Shimpei's desire to lure to the colony men who would have pursued successful careers in Japan had resulted in splendid housing and recreation facilities for the Japanese in Taiwan.[83] Indeed, the grandeur of the government-general buildings in Taihoku struck some visitors from the ruling country as unnecessarily extravagant.[84] The large hospital in Taihoku offered medical services which could match those available in the best of Japanese hospitals, and Gotō proudly called it "the Vatican of Formosa."[85]

Schooling for Japanese children was also liberally funded. Pains were taken to bring outstanding teachers to the colony and to see that the primary schools for young colonials boasted facilities equal to the best endowed primary schools in Japan. Primary school teachers were paid higher salaries than they would have received in Japan.[86] By 1918 there were ten primary schools with twenty branches to serve Japanese children in Taiwan, 95.2 percent of whom were now attending school.[87] Since most Japanese now resided in the major cities and towns, all of which were well equipped with excellent primary schools, very few Japanese children were without easy access to elementary instruction. Now only four traveling primary teachers were needed to serve the Japanese children in isolated areas.[88] Throughout the 1910s, dormitory accommodations, financial grants, and railway passes had brought country children to primary schools in urban centers.[89]

The colony's middle school population grew dramatically during the 1910s; from 314 students in 1908 it reached 1,063 in 1918.[90] The student body of the Taihoku higher girls' school for Japanese expanded too. In 1908 there were 228 girls enrolled at this school; ten years later—two years after a higher girls' school was opened in Tainan—there were 791 higher girls' school students in the colony.[91] In spite of Izawa Shūji's early hopes that young Japanese would seriously study the languages and cultures of Taiwan's native peoples, curricula of colonial middle and higher girls' schools were almost identical to those of their counterparts in Japan.

The Boarding School Experiment

Yet during the 1910s, at least for boys, an alternative to standard Japanese middle schooling did exist. Not surprisingly, this was part of Gotō Shimpei's plan to have the best of everything for the colonial Japanese of Taiwan. Gotō's aim was to establish in the colony an independent, character-building school for Japanese boys, frankly modeled upon the British public school.

A canny student of comparative colonialism, Gotō admired the way the British governed their far-flung empire.[92] One of the first things he did when he took up his post in Taiwan was to have Sir Charles Prestwood Lucas' many-volumed *Historical Geography of the British Colonies* translated into Japanese. His subordinates were then encouraged to read about the topography, peoples, products, industry, wars, religions, education, administrations, finances, and other aspects of the regions of the world under British rule.[93] Gotō applauded the British rulers' manipulation of local institutions to tighten their grip on the peoples they controlled, and he seems to have been equally impressed with the elitist mentality of British overseas administrators.[94] To Gotō it was clear that it was the public school which prepared the upper-class English boy for membership in a ruling class which directed the destinies of millions of Englishmen and dominated "lesser breeds" all over the globe.[95] In contrast to British statesmen, he found Japanese leaders of the early twentieth century sadly lacking in the confident self-reliance needed for directing affairs of state.[96]

Gotō was highly critical of Japan's education system which he claimed produced nothing but "machine-like carbon copies."[97] While he headed the civil bureau in Taiwan he often went out of his way to recruit subordinates who had not emerged from the education ministry's conventional assembly line.[98] His boarding school was to be an alternative to regular middle school and would prepare a small number of young men to govern Taiwan, to rule the Japanese nation, and—if the Japanese were ever to go beyond Japan—to lead the world.[99]

The boarding school was to have its own botanical garden, orchards, and vegetable patches tended by the students; there were to be meadows, pastures, and yards for horses, sheep, and pigs; team games like football and baseball would be played on the school's own playing fields; and there was to be a large swimming pool. Classrooms, study areas, and libraries were to be equipped with the latest and best in instructional resources, and laboratories would be stocked with first-class scientific apparatus.[100]

The regime of studies was divided into three parts. The first, "intellectual activities," included classes in Japanese, English, history, science, and mathematics. The second, "discipline for the body and the hands," was composed of indoor labor, handicrafts, outdoor labor, gymnastics, military exercises, swordmanship, jujitsu, team sports, swimming, and boating. The third division, "esthetic education," covered singing, concerts, and social entertainments. Indoor and outdoor labor aimed to give the boys first-hand experience of problems involved in making a living and to teach them to be independent. They were to keep the school stocked with food from their gardens and their animals.[101]

Milk and bread were to be served at breakfast; luncheon was to be a Western-style meal of meat, vegetables, and pudding. Fruit and sweets came at tea time and dinner meant vegetables and fish. After dinner the students were to do all their own laundry; lower classmen were to be taught by their seniors how to take care of the school uniforms and costumes for work and games they had been allotted. Western-style showers as well as Japanese baths were installed, and character-building cold showers were expected to be frequent.[102]

With the cooperation of men in the colonial government who once had been his loyal subordinates as well as the support of Governor-General Sakuma, Gotō was able to open his boarding school in 1908. Maximum admissions were set at thirty-five, and thirty-three boys were chosen for the first class. The school accepted boys who had completed only five years of primary school, whereas entrants to the regular middle school had to have completed all six years. However, the school kept students for a year longer than did the middle schools, so all graduates were of the same age.

All students were required to reside in the school's dormitory, where they lived a strictly regulated life under a monitor system; this was based upon the prefect structure of the British public school. This method of internal self-government, with considerable freedom for older boys and demands of obedience on younger ones, was aimed at "instilling independence in the pupils."[103] A Canadian teacher, a Miss Septon, was engaged by Gotō as dormitory mistress to encourage individual character development and to demonstrate appropriate etiquette for social intercourse. The table manners she taught were mandatory at all meals.[104]

The fate of Gotō's cherished school poignantly illustrates what happened to Japanese educational institutions—in the colony as well as at home—which attempted to remain independent of the education ministry's prescriptions. Or, as Gotō read it, its demise demonstrated what happened to ventures in initiative or imagination which strayed from the ministry's conventional paths. The boarding school had powerful backers. Governor-General Sakuma as well as Gotō personally made substantial gifts to it.[105] Yet from the beginning it was in trouble with the Ministry of Education. When it and the regular middle school applied to the ministry for official recognition in 1908, the latter received accreditation almost immediately; but the boarding school was refused on the grounds that its regime was too far removed from that of an ordinary middle school. Accreditation was essential, for without it the school's students could not transfer to middle schools in Japan when they left the colony, nor could its graduates apply to higher institutions of learning. Negotiations with the ministry continued, but recognition was not granted until 1911, after the school agreed to increase the hours of certain subjects as demanded by the ministry.

During the following few years, the ministry used accreditation as both a stick and a carrot, little by little whittling away at the school's distinctive character. In 1914 the prefect system was replaced by a dormitory life style which required weekly approval of all activities by the principal. In the same year the competitive sports program in swimming, boating, baseball, football, lawn tennis, and Japanese self-defense skills came to an end, and the education ministry's physical education course for middle schools was instituted. With the school's two central pillars gone, it rapidly became indistinguishable from an ordinary Japanese middle school.[106] In 1917 complete defeat was acknowledged; the school stopped taking in new students. Even Gotō Shimpei could not hold out against the Ministry of Education.[107]

Yet the school did provide, during its short history, an elite education for a number of Japanese colonials. The kind of education it offered was welcomed by at least some of the Japanese in Taiwan. It drew applicants throughout its existence, in spite of education ministry harassment and accreditation difficulties.

Conclusion

From 1906 to 1918 education policy makers in Taiwan expanded and upgraded the common school system. At the same time they did their best to ward off the creation of a demand among Taiwanese for higher education, superior social status, and better employment opportunities. As the years passed, the common school curriculum became more like that of Japanese primary schools and less like that of a Chinese *shobō*; it reached more and more islanders and kept a greater number of them occupied for longer periods of time. While common school leavers were expected to return to agriculture or commerce or to become unskilled laborers in the new industries, teaching and medicine were the two main safety valves by means of which a small number of Taiwanese might legitimately seek upward mobility.

Given the role education played in Taiwan before 1895 and its traditional function throughout most of China's history, it is probably not surprising that Taiwanese quickly perceived Japanese higher education as a means of bettering their situations in life. Certainly physicians made a great deal of money, and a few lucky islanders who managed to gain specialized trades apparently did well too. Thus competition for access to such skills was intense.[108]

Yet Japanese education appears to have acquired a certain amount of prestige for its own sake. Recognition of the higher school for Taiwanese girls as a respectable finishing school has been mentioned. It is interesting that Lin Hsien-t'ang and his associates lobbied for a public middle school offering the academic subjects studied by Japanese teenaged boys rather than for a second medical school or another specialized vocational institute.

The warm response of Japanese-educated Taiwanese to Itagaki's Assimilation Society suggests that a yearning for equal treatment of Taiwanese and Japanese had definitely been nurtured by their Japanese education, in spite of the administration's careful policy. After the speedy suppression of Itagaki's movement, Taiwanese intellectuals and professionals watched with envy or approval as some of their number and younger students went off to Japan to seek Japanese who, like Itagaki and unlike the Japanese in the colony, would understand their problems and accept them as equals. Those who went abroad were filled with optimism. Those who stayed behind in their dormitories to take hot baths, wear *yukata,* breakfast on *miso* soup, and master their Japanese textbooks were less so. They knew that no matter how well they learned the new ways they were not going to be held in high regard by those young men in another dormitory, who, after a cold shower and a brief struggle with their Western-style uniforms, were now politely consuming bread and milk at Miss Septon's table.

4 / Systematization and Integration

From mid-1918 to mid-1923, the tone of government-general policy statements underwent a drastic change. Praise of "the great hundred year plan" for the gradual evolution of Taiwanese society via liberal accommodation of indigenous institutions and specially designed schools for native children gave way to a new watchword, assimilation (*dōka*). By 1922 officials were claiming that, in the field of education at least, assimilation had been translated into full equality of opportunity between Taiwanese and Japanese.

After twenty years of Gotō's gradualism, the switch to assimilation appeared abrupt and dramatic, even though it took five years to get the new policy into full gear. While many Taiwanese applauded the new promises to abolish separatism in education and other areas of colonial rule, old colonial hands among the Japanese were shocked. Yet the new policy was, to a large extent, simply a reflection of rapid changes taking place outside the sleepy colony.

The most dramatic alterations came with World War I, but even before the war the world was changing. In Western Europe old ways and old worlds were crumbling. In Russia rebellion became revolution, which demonstrated new models of statescraft and raised the hopes of champions of the oppressed everywhere. During the first world war the Allied Powers' slogan Self-Determination of Peoples caught the imagination of peoples far beyond the borders of the European communities to which Wilson meant it to apply.[1] This slogan was picked up by Chinese struggling against treaty port domination, by Japanese trying to insert a racial equality clause in the Covenant of the League of Nations, and by spokesmen for populations under alien administrations in all the corners of the earth.[2] When the war ended so did an era for established governments everywhere.

The government of Japan was no exception. From the beginning of the century Japanese political parties had steadily advanced their claim to share power with the elites which governed
the country.[3] Although the parties represented but a small "privileged group of landlords, businessmen and other taxpayers"[4] —
until the 1919 electoral reform only 1.5 million had the vote out
of a population of fifty-three million, and male universal suffrage
did not come until 1925[5] — they gained an enormous boost from
the spread of democratic ideas associated with the winning powers of World War I.

By the time of the war most of the autocratic statesmen of the
Meiji period were dead. The aging survivors, having mellowed
somewhat, had begun at least to tolerate leaders from the political party ranks who cultivated them respectfully while simultaneously strengthening relationships with prominent men in the
bureaucracy and the armed forces. In September 1918 Hara Kei
(1856-1921), leader of the Seiyūkai, one of the largest parties, at
long last became the premier of Japan's first party cabinet; under
Hara all ministers except the heads of the military service minis-
tries were Seiyūkai members.[6]

Not only did political party cabinets instantly alter domestic
government structures; they soon changed the face of the colonial
administrations as well. The criteria for appointment of governors-general of Taiwan and Korea were modified. Although after
1919 they "donned civilian clothes," military officers continued
to head the Korean government general.[7] But in Taiwan civilian
instead of military officials served as chief executives from 1919
until 1936, when Japan's international position brought about a
return to the old system of military governors.

The decision to appoint civilian governors-general and the new
assimilation policy are generally seen as closely associated: it is
true that Hara's choice of Den Kenjirō (1855-1930) for the first
civilian governor-general of Taiwan intentionally made Den a
key agent in the introduction of the new policy to Taiwan. Nevertheless, the last of the early military governors-general of the island, Akashi Motojirō (1864-1919), was every bit as instrumental
in making "assimilation" the policy of the Taiwan administration. These two men both labored to overturn the long-standing
policy of gradualism and to prepare Taiwan for closer integration
with the ruling country. They worked in different ways, but each
saw educational reform as a major factor in the achievement of
his goals.

Akashi Motojirō's Systematization

Although Akashi Motojirō served in Taiwan before the Tokyo government changed its colonial policy to one of assimilation and integration, he was an avowed assimilationist. But assimilation meant many things to many men and was espoused for a variety of motives. We have seen how Itagaki supported assimilation both because he saw Taiwan as an important support of Japan's expanding influence in East Asia and believed in equality between Japanese and Taiwanese.[8] We have also seen that Itagaki's aim to grant Taiwanese the same rights and status that Japanese enjoyed was regarded by most Japanese residents in Taiwan as unthinkable. In their minds, Gotō's gradualism was, in 1919 as in 1914, by far the most sensible policy. This policy did not, of course, rule out assimilation sometime in the remote future, but such a phenomenon was always a possibility only, and was always a long way off.

Although in all likelihood Gotō was heavily influenced by the social Darwinist influences of his youth, he had modestly claimed that as a medical man trained in science he was simply practicing what he called biology politics.[9] That is: he claimed that his philosophy of colonial administration was based on the biological principles of evolution as discovered and clarified by Darwin and other great nineteenth-century scientists. According to Gotō, human communities, like nature, evolved only slowly over long spans of time: hence any attempts to initiate sudden changes into Taiwanese life and society would be folly—such action would run contrary to the workings of both nature and civilization.[10] His protégés and successors had reiterated this theme enthusiastically. Tōgō Minoru's "In Opposition to Assimilation" of 1911, for instance, faithfully echoed Gotō's claim that nineteenth-century science was the basis of the colonial policy of Taiwan.[11]

Outside the colony perhaps the most articulate exponent of Gotō's gradualism had been Takekoshi Yosaburō, newspaperman, traveler, critic, author, bureaucrat, historian, party politician elected five time to the Diet's House of Representatives.[12] Takekoshi's interest in colonialism took him to "nearly all the Dutch, French and English colonies, making a special study of the customs and sentiments of the native populations, their relations to the mother countries, and their administrative and legislative methods" as well as to Japan's own overseas territories.[13] In addition to freely advising his fellow countrymen on appropriate colonial policies for Japan, Takekoshi took it upon himself to explain Japanese policies to the West.[14] For an American audience he published the following in 1912:

> There are countries such as France and the United States, which endeavor to transplant in their colonies the laws and civilization of the mother country, and to assimilate the natives in the quickest way possible. This method is not pursued by the Japanese. They understand that in the matter of national policy they must make the colony work in line with the mother country, but that at the same time they must respect the manners and customs of the natives, even in cases where there may be some objectionable phases as viewed from a higher standard of civilization. An exception to this general principle of leniency toward native institutions is, of course, however, made of those customs which are absolutely unpardonable from the standpoint of civilization, such as slavery. Otherwise the natives are allowed their own customs . . . The success of our colonial policy in Formosa made us extend the principle to Korea, newly annexed to Japan . . . The Koreans can be slowly and gradually led in the direction of progress, but it is against all the laws of sociology and biology to make them enter a new life at once . . . The history of different colonial enterprises will, I am sure, dissipate most of the criticism aimed at the general colonial policy pursued by the Japanese—a policy that has been founded upon the conclusions of sociology, biology, and history.[15]

Words like these were welcomed by the Japanese residents of Taiwan. If the Taiwanese were to be rapidly assimilated, the privileged position of the colonial Japanese would soon be threatened. The Japanese in Taiwan were well aware that they enjoyed a ruling class status at the expense of the people they ruled. Japanese monopolies reaped profits; Taiwanese were paid half the wages Japanese received for performing the same tasks; through the *hokō* collective security organizations Taiwanese were forced to maintain roads and provide a host of other services; Taiwanese taxpayers supported well-endowed schools for Japanese while their own children studied in inferior facilities.[16] Accommodation of native customs also meant compulsory confinement of natives at the bottom of colonial society.

If Akashi Motojirō's references to assimilation had pertained only to the dim future, the Japanese community would have been less uneasy. But he had an annoying habit of talking about assimilation here and now. Yet surely this army veteran, who possessed an awesome reputation for firm handling of the subject populace in Korea, was no wild-eyed idealist like Itagaki. The question was what kind of an assimilationist the new governor-general was.

Lieutenant General Akashi Motojirō arrived in Taiwan in June 1918 with definite ideas about how a colony should be ruled. As a military attaché in St. Petersburg between 1902 and 1904, he had been a diligent student of the colonial policies of Russia, and from 1907 to 1914 he served in the colonial administration of Korea.[17] In Korea, he served first as head of the gendarmerie of the regency general and then as Governor-General Terauchi Masatake's (1852-1919) powerful director of police affairs. In the later post he dealt mercilessly with Korean insurgents and suspected rebels alike, killing and torturing with little regard for legal process.[18] To the core a soldier, Akashi believed that the police and the army were the most important instruments of colonial rule.[19]

The armed forces, he felt, must be constantly prepared in order to guarantee Japanese control of Taiwan. Control for Akashi included thought control as well as political control. Therefore, rooting out "dangerous ideologies" which might lead the colony's natives to question the validity of the established order was an important responsibility of the police.[20] During his administration in Taiwan he grudged his police neither funds nor manpower. Viewing money spent on the police and the army as investments in insurance premiums to guarantee law and order, he drew up ambitious plans to improve conditions of patrolmen in the colonial police force and of noncommissioned officers in the armed forces.[21]

Yet just as Akashi unquestioningly accepted maintenance of Japanese rule of Taiwan by force and terror if necessary, so he also believed in ultimate assimilation of the island's natives. For his predecessors assimilation had been at best a distant policy goal,[22] but in the mind of Governor-General Akashi there was no doubt that it could and must become reality. Discussion among his subordinates as to whether or not the Taiwanese *could* be assimilated irritated him no end. He insisted that assimilation *must* take place in order to ensure Japan's permanent hold upon the island, and he forbade all debate on the matter.[23]

Alert to the appeal of Wilsonian self-determination and aware of the changing world, Akashi feared that Taiwan might become the center of an international diplomatic incident and Japan would then risk losing the island altogether. This might well happen, he reasoned, if the inhabitants of Taiwan were not encouraged to become unmistakably Japanese, if instead an unwise policy of creating an outcast (*eta*) type of separatism was pursued. This was to be prevented at all costs, because the island was essential both to the defense of the home islands and to future economic and military expansion into south China and the South Seas.

Akashi flatly stated that the Taiwanese must be educated to be Japanese in order to cement Japan's hold upon Taiwan. It would be no easy task to break down barriers of language, custom, and tradition, but he urged his officials to do this even if it appeared to them to be an impossible assignment. Akashi bade those who believed assimilation to be impossible to remember that in ancient times separate Izumo and Yamato tribes became one harmonious Japanese people. With education his chosen vehicle of assimilation, he indicated that he would soon be making the colonial school system a major area of policy change.

Many of Akashi's subordinates had strong doubts about his policy. After Akashi silenced those who protested that assimilation was impossible, these men began to argue that from an economic point of view benefits to be gained from assimilation were minimal. After all many of them had been in the administration for years carrying out gradualist policies in the name of changing governors-general. They must have thought that they rather than a new governor-general from Tokyo knew best what was possible and practical. Lieutenant General Akashi was an impressive figure but his colonial experience had been with the police and the military in Korea: he was not familiar with more peaceful Taiwan where civilian rule had prevailed in fact if not in format from the time of Kodama and Gotō.[24]

Even among his senior staff, who were presumably closest to him, Akashi had trouble gaining support for assimilation plans, which featured a broad expansion of public school facilities for Taiwanese. When he presented his proposal for educational revision to his bureau and department heads on December 18, 1918, it met with strong opposition—which Akashi characteristically overruled.[25] Subsequently the lieutenant general seems to have successfully commanded the cooperation of even those who did not agree with him. Undoubtedly he was aided in this by growing

Taiwanese pressure for more and better higher education. Government-general officials, regardless of their stand on assimilation, knew that these demands had to be met in some way. Akashi's decision was also supported by the manpower demands of the island's economy, which had changed a great deal since the first years of Japanese rule. His proposal became the education rescript of January 1919 which for the first time welded all the colony's public schools for Taiwanese into a single, coordinated system.

This system is outlined in Figure 2. At its base were the com-

Figure 2. Akashi's systematization: school system for Taiwanese as outlined by the 1919 Rescript

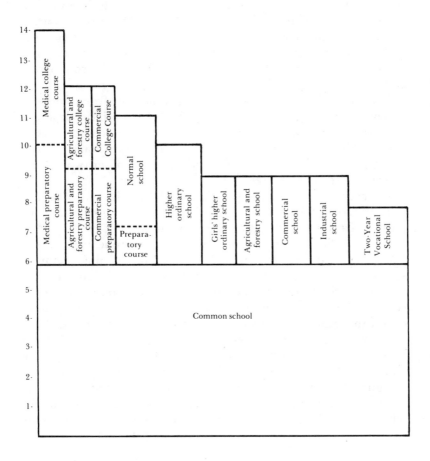

mon schools. Between them and the secondary level were two-year vocational schools, essentially a continuation of common school vocational studies.

Above these, secondary schooling was made up of (1) a higher ordinary school (the middle school for Taiwanese boys) with a course one year shorter than that of a Japanese middle school and containing more Japanese language, classical Chinese, and vocational training and less physics and chemistry than did that of a Japanese middle school; (2) a girl's higher ordinary school, roughly equivalent to a three-year vocational higher girls' school (*jitsuka kōtō jogakkō*) in Japan but involving more Japanese language, sewing, and handicrafts and less mathematics than did such Japanese institutions; (3) two normal schools with a one-year preparatory course and a four-year regular course; (4) three technical schools: a commercial school, a school of agriculture and forestry, and an industrial school, all with three-year courses. Above the secondary level were three specialized colleges (*senmon gakkō*). These were the upgraded medical school and two new institutions, an agriculture and forestry college and a commercial college. Each college program required a college preparatory course which students took after graduation from common school. The preparatory courses of the commercial college and the agriculture and forestry college were both three years in length. The medical preparatory course was a year longer. Medical college training was four years long and the other two colleges offered three-year courses.[26]

In addition to fashioning an orderly hierarchy out of a haphazard array of institutions, Akashi's reform improved and increased Taiwanese educational opportunities. All existing post-primary facilities were upgraded and several new ones were added. The old vocational continuation programs of some common schools became independent two-year vocational schools; in 1919 six such agricultural schools had a total of 341 pupils and eight commercial institutes had 512 pupils.[27] An industrial training center in Taihoku was transformed into an industrial school and two new vocational institutes were opened, a commercial school in Taichu and an agriculture and forestry school in Kagi. The admission requirements of both the higher ordinary school and the girls' higher ordinary school rose from completion of four years of common school to graduation from the six-year common school course. The two normal schools (the former Japanese Lan-

guage School and its branch school in Tainan) were also upgraded because a one-year preparatory course was added to their
four-year regular course. Medical training was lengthened three
years and a college of commerce and a college of agriculture and
forestry were created.

While the 1919 rescript recognized existing private schools it
banned the creation of any more private equivalents of common
schools, higher ordinary schools, and girls' higher ordinary
schools. Henceforth, new private education ventures had to be
vocational institutions or special schools for the handicapped or
otherwise unfortunate.[28] Although this proscription was due in
part to the emphasis upon vocational education, it was also probably a result of Akashi's experience in Korea. Korean private
schools and colleges had frequently been associated with anti-
Japanese sentiment and leadership, so Akashi was sensitive to the
potential of private education — especially if directed by the colonized people themselves — for development of nationalistic or
other "dangerous" thought. Indeed, government initiative in
founding Taiwan's first colleges was intended to "forestall establishment of any unsuitable schools" at this level.[29]

Colonial facilities for Japanese nationals were completely outside the system. After middle school, Japanese boys who hoped to
continue their formal education in the colony had a choice of the
medical course for Japanese or a higher commercial school established in 1919; and academically ambitious Japanese girls had
nowhere to go after higher girls' school but to Japan. Elementary
and secondary schools for colonial Japanese, which of course did
not accept any Taiwanese pupils, were governed by the rescripts
of the ruling country's Ministry of Education. Whenever Japanese
shared premises with islanders — for instance, at the medical
school and at the normal schools where programs to produce
common school teachers and teachers for Japanese primary
schools were specially set up for Japanese young people — strict
segregation of the two ethnic groups was maintained. Pains were
taken to give Taiwanese institutions titles distinctly different from
the common appellations for Japanese schools.

Akashi's main concern was postprimary vocational training.
Even the secondary academic schools for Taiwanese resembled
Japan's technical schools more than the standard middle schools
and higher girls' schools. So that no one should miss the point the
rescript clearly announced that these institutions were not to pre-

pare students for college or university. Teacher training courses of one year's duration were to be instituted in these two types of school and in the secondary technical schools too; in the latter case the intention was to recruit teachers for the two-year vocational schools.[30]

Overall, the reform aimed to integrate Taiwanese into the colonial economy's rapidly growing industrial and commercial sectors. By giving the Taiwanese a greater stake in the economic development of the colony, Akashi hoped to bind their interests more tightly to those of their rulers. At the same time the new plan would help meet the increased demands for skilled and semiskilled labor. Although it was intended that Japanese should continue to fill the managerial and higher engineering positions needed by industry and commerce, Akashi's new educational policy signaled a resolve to depart from the officially encouraged practice of recruiting workers with technical skills almost solely from Japan. Whereas previously islanders had been purposely denied postprimary vocational schooling, the government general now set up a number of courses for new skilled trades as well as modern training programs for old occupations.

As Tables 3 and 4 indicate, by the end of the second decade of the twentieth century manufacturing and other industries were already employing fairly large numbers of natives with some technical or commercial skills. Economic arguments against secondary vocational schools—claims by earlier administrations that such schools would drain the government-general treasury only to produce graduates who would be unable to find employment— must have lost much of their punch.[31] Although vigorously resisted by education authorities and other government-general officials, Akashi's education policy seems to have met with no opposition from Japanese employers and managers in private and public industry.[32] Since a Taiwanese employee was usually paid roughly one half of what a Japanese worker with the same skills commanded, this is not surprising.

The new education system's accent upon secondary vocational schooling and its continuance of strict racial segregation illuminate Governor-General Akashi's concept of assimilation. Akashi was by no means encouraging or even permitting assimilation on all levels of the colony's economic, social, and political life. Mingling between the two ethnic groups would, at least in the foreseeable future, occur fairly far down the ladder in paraprofessional, skilled, and semiskilled occupations. And for many years to come this mingling would probably not be numerically significant; the highest ranking of the new institutions for Taiwanese, the commercial college and the college of agriculture and forestry, only admitted a total of eighty-eight students during their first year of operation.[33]

Akashi encouraged his regional administrators to persuade the Taiwanese to stay in agricultural occupations—they should be opening up those still vacant lands in the eastern part of the island, he insisted—and to keep them from studying politics and law, subjects which would make them fit only to become lawyers or government clerks. "These days Taiwanese are inclined to be snobbish and this certainly is not in accord with our plan," he complained to subordinates.[34] He believed that colonial education should uphold the hierarchical social order. In a speech to his regional administration chiefs on June 9, 1919, he severely chastised teachers for not paying enough attention to proprieties.

> Education must be suitable to time and place. If what you teach is unrelated to time and place you are just making a pretense and calling it education . . . This does harm to Japan . . . It is poison to the true spirit of governing. When I was on a tour of inspection in the east [the most undeveloped and remote part of the island, much of which was aborigine territory] I examined the schoolchildren's footwear. Some of their clogs were homemade; some had been bought in town. Some bore expensive floral patterns—and such "rich man's clogs" as these could not have been homemade. Is such a thing, is the wearing of floral-pattern clogs in aborigine territory in the east, an example of the application of so-called educational methods to time and place? Should not [the children] be taught not to wear [such clogs] with their everyday clothes?[35]

Probably these children were not wearing their everyday clothes but were in fact all spruced up in their best in honor of Akashi himself. In all likelihood their teachers would never have allowed them to come to school in such fancy footgear on any occasion less than a governor-general's visit, and a visit from the colony's chief executive would have been the highest honor any school could ever receive. As these were poor children in an out-of-the-way district, Akashi perhaps mistook their very best costumes for their everyday garments but immediately spotted the festive Japanese-style footwear that children who could afford them proudly put on to receive him. Akashi's anger at the incident is revealing; consciously or unconsciously he was probably appalled that any of these humble, native children actually owned store-bought clogs.

To Akashi then assimilation did not mean equality with the Japanese. He would have thought Itagaki's approach insane, despite the fact that the two men shared one important motive for assimilation—the desire to preserve and expand Japanese influence in East Asia and the Pacific.[36] Although warnings to his subordinates suggest that Akashi believed that someday the Taiwanese and Japanese must become one, he undertook to assimilate Taiwanese at the bottom and at the lower-middle portions of the social pyramid where he thought they belonged.

Nevertheless, his 1919 education rescript did genuinely extend educational opportunities for Taiwanese youth. Moreover, as officials were quick to point out when the rescript was superseded by another three years later, Akashi's reform provided for its own amendment.[37] Article three of the rescript, which declared that "education must be applicable to the state of progress of the people and to the times," could be interpreted as encouraging change.[38]

While ambitious Taiwanese who did not possess the means to study in Japan welcomed the new schools and improved courses, the 1919 rescript did not entirely satisfy longstanding Taiwanese demands for higher education. Upper-class Taiwanese wanted first-rate secondary and college academic programs, not vocational training. And while Akashi's education system faithfully mirrored elementary schools and lower-level technical institutes in Japan, it lacked the middle schools, higher schools, and universities for young Japanese men headed for their country's political and economic elites. Denied access to colonial primary and middle schools, wealthy Taiwanese continued to send their children to primary school, middle school, higher girls' school, college, or university in Japan.

The goals of such study were not always purely academic or career oriented: when the colonial government snuffed out Itagaki's Assimilation Society, young Taiwanese embarked upon a serious search for sympathizers among the Japanese of the home islands. Yet an education in Japan continued to be a sound investment. It was easier to enter one of Japan's several medical colleges or faculties than it was to get accepted in the colony's only medical college, and Taiwanese who qualified in Japan as medical doctors could almost always be sure of a lucrative practice when they returned home.[39] Anxiety regarding the "dangerous ideologies" in Tokyo notwithstanding, government-general efforts to dissuade Taiwanese from circumventing the segregated, lower-standard schooling of the colony by sending their sons and occasionally their daughters to Japan were no more successful after January 1919 than they had been before that date.[40]

Den Kenjirō and His Integration Rescript

Whatever long-range influence the edict might have exerted remains shrouded in might-have-beens because Akashi, failing in health, died in October 1919, and the next governor-general amended the education system even more drastically than Akashi had done. This man was none other than Den Kenjirō, the first civilian governor-general of Taiwan. Den's appointment was testimony to the Hara government's determination to convert Taiwan into an extension of Japan proper, ruled in the same fashion as the home islands.

Hara Kei and Den Kenjirō had served side-by-side in the Taiwan Affairs Bureau (Taiwan jimu kyoku) of Prime Minister Itō Hirobumi (1841-1909), which had been established when Taiwan was acquired in 1895. When the bureau staff debated over choosing a military or a civilian governor-general to head the new territory, Hara and Den both came down squarely on the side of civilian rule. Hara's proposals for ruling Taiwan as an extension of Japan, as Alsace-Lorraine was ruled as an extension of Germany, or Algeria of France, were rejected by the bureau, but they clearly reveal him as an early proponent of integration and Japanization for Taiwan.[41] More than two decades later as prime minister, Hara was still a supporter of integration for overseas territories.

After a massive rebellion against Japanese rule erupted in Korea in March 1919, Hara was even more convinced that Japan's colonial policy, in Korea especially, must rapidly undergo a fundamental overhaul. If Japan was to avoid alienating the native peoples of its overseas holdings a serious integration and assimilation policy must be formulated immediately. In Korea Hara wanted to begin by replacing military governors-general with civilians, substituting civil for military police, initiating equal education for Koreans and Japanese, increasing opportunities for Koreans to participate in local government, sending Korean representatives to the Japanese Diet, and appointing Koreans as government officials.[42] Static from powerful military figures prevented Hara from pushing changes in Korea as quickly or as fundamentally as he would have liked. But since Taiwan was not considered to be strategically important, there was less opposition to his desire to appoint a civilian as chief executive of the island.[43]

Akashi Motojirō unwittingly aided Hara in this latter objective. Although certainly not an advocate of civilian rule or of governing Taiwan as part of Japan, Akashi insisted that Taiwan's natives must be assimilated and took the first step by remodeling the education system to substantially improve Taiwanese chances to obtain better livelihoods. Since Akashi used the same word for assimilation (*dōka*) as Hara did, Akashi's support for assimilation facilitated Hara's campaign.[44] Moreover Akashi's sudden death gave Hara an early opportunity to appoint an integration-minded civilian as governor-general.

For this honor Den seemed an ideal choice. Not only had Den proven himself as an ally of integration in their Taiwan Affairs Bureau days, but Den was also an influential member of Yamagata Aritomo's (1838-1925) following; Hara knew that support from Yamagata was crucial to allaying military prejudice against civil governors-general.[45] In addition, Den was not a member of Hara's Seiyūkai; so for once Hara Kei could not be accused of pursuing partisan interests.[46]

Den Kenjirō also prized his lack of party label: he saw his nonpartisan stance as freeing him from central governmental interference and saw this freedom as an essential prerequisite for the sucessful initiation of a new policy in Taiwan. He feared that a civilian governor-general might become dependent upon the party currently in power and therefore asked that the governor-general of Taiwan be made independent of both cabinet changes and the partisan political appointments that were so much a feature of Hara's Seiyūkai politics. Hara agreed.[47] Den also made a point of continuing to solicit Yamagata's good will. Before accepting the Taiwan post Den visited the old man ostensibly to ask his advice, actually to gain his approval. As governor-general, Den always visited Yamagata to tell him about developments in the colony whenever he came to Tokyo.[48] He was also on good terms with high ranking bureaucrats and party politicians both inside and outside the Seiyūkai.[49]

Upon taking up his duties in Taiwan, Den Kenjirō proclaimed that Japanization of Taiwan and assimilation of the Taiwanese were the goals of his administration.[50] An important part of his assimilation policy, as he had explained to Hara before accepting the governor-generalship, was educating the Taiwanese to be pure Japanese.[51]

In his first major policy speech, delivered in November of 1919, he declared that acculturation (*kyōka*) of the island's native population must be extended far beyond the boundaries of formal schooling (*gakkō kyōiku*).[52] This kind of education must take place in politics and in social life as well as in the classroom, he told his officials; for instance if a man was qualified for a high post within the government general, he must not be barred from it just because he was Taiwanese. The law which did not recognize marriages between Taiwanese and Japanese should be revised; for marriages between Japanese and foreigners who were not subjects of the Japanese emperor as were the Taiwanese received legal sanction. Compulsory education was to be brought in as soon as possible. Many more common schools were to be opened, in spite of complaints that attendance at existing common schools was not always as faithful as it might be. School attendance would be allowed to improve gradually; meanwhile more elementary schools must be provided for Taiwanese, especially in rural districts where schools and other facilities common in the urban areas were scarce. Den urged his administrators to begin preparation for one integrated school system embracing both Japanese and Taiwanese. He admitted that language differences would make integration at the elementary school level difficult, but insisted that at the postprimary level it could be quickly brought into effect.[53]

Soon after this speech, Governor-General Den handed his chief subordinate (*chōkan*)[54] a seven-point plan with which to begin working out the policies he had outlined in his address. Among his seven points were a feasibility study of integrated education of Japanese and Taiwanese in all schools and a proposal to establish a university with faculties of medicine, agriculture, and literature. The other five points were preparation for abolition of flogging (a punishment only meted out to Taiwanese); a scheme to increase the number of railway cars in Taiwan; a survey of the house registration system and the system of registering naturalized Taiwanese as a preliminary toward facilitating recognition of marriage between Taiwanese and Japanese; preparation for new legal government structures; and establishment of a commercial conference center. However, revision of the island's education system was clearly one of Den's top priorities.[55]

On December 27, 1919, secret instructions went out to district government heads and school principals. These ordered that "Taiwanese applicants who could meet the necessary academic standards be admitted without hindrance to schools educating Japanese" and that Japanese children who lived far from primary schools be allowed to attend nearby common schools.[56] Explaining that admission of Taiwanese to primary schools was to be on a trial basis, the instructions hinted that not all Taiwanese children who applied should be granted admission. Admission was to depend upon the level of the boy's or girl's education, the child's Japanese language ability, his or her family's position in the town or village, the extent of the family's education, and the family's wealth. Taiwanese children currently enrolled in common school who wished to transfer to a primary school were to take entrance examinations.[57]

These instructions suggest that trial admission of Taiwanese to primary schools was meant to be extremely selective. Educators could turn down applications for admission for several reasons other than academic or language qualifications, and applicants from literate and wealthy families were to be favored. The details of the instructions—probably prepared by unenthusiastic subordinates—allowed considerable room for any primary school principal who viewed the integration policy with skepticism or alarm to violate the spirit of Den's order.

Before the new school year began in April 1920, procedures for Taiwanese entering primary schools and Japanese entering common schools were formalized. Taiwanese starting the first grade of primary school were required to be between their sixth and seventh birthdays; transfers from common schools could be no more than one year older than the Japanese pupils of the grade they were joining; Japanese in common schools were to be exempted from classical Chinese lessons and, in the case of girls, from learning how to sew Taiwanese-style clothing. The following March these rules were altered slightly. Taiwanese coming into primary schools were allowed to be as much as two years older than their Japanese classmates; a Taiwanese child transferring from a primary school in Japan to one in the colony was required to have spent at least one full year at the school in Japan;

and as much as one third of a primary school class could now be made up of Taiwanese pupils.[58]

During the 1920-21 academic year sixty-seven Taiwanese children received permission to enter Japanese schools; during the following school year 216 Taiwanese children were given this permission.[59] Since in 1922 the primary school population was 21,801 and common school enrollment stood at 195,783, the experiment was indeed a limited one.[60]

The Japanese observed this experiment closely. Some authorities praised it as a way to keep Taiwanese from sending their children to primary school in Japan and, noting primary school officials' reluctance to admit native children, intimated that the requirements for Taiwanese were perhaps a bit too stiff.[61] Japanese educators carefully ticked off the advantages and disadvantages they saw in integrated elementary schooling. On the credit side they listed: removal of discrimination, a step toward racial harmony; increased understanding between the two ethnic groups, also a contribution toward greater harmony; possibilities for reducing tensions between the two ethnic groups in a given district, one of which was all for expanding and improving the common schools while the other was interested only in schools for Japanese children; savings to be gained from combining school facilities. On the other hand they feared that with Taiwanese children outnumbering Japanese, the Japanese might acquire the characteristics of their Taiwanese classmates; that teachers would be unable to use the same methods to teach Japanese and Taiwanese children; that the inferior Japanese language ability of native islanders would lower academic standards; that antagonism toward integrated education on the part of Japanese parents would undermine Japanese commitment to Taiwan as a place of permanent domicile.[62]

Although some officials welcomed integration, echoing Akashi's and Den's declarations that the Taiwanese and the Japanese were not as different from each other as ruled and rulers in the colonies of Western nations,[63] the majority concluded that the losses exceeded the gains. Of all the obstacles to integration they found the language barrier the most serious. They claimed that Taiwanese children were simply not fluent enough in Japanese to receive a Japanese primary school education from the first grade. And if integration were to begin in a higher grade, the time Taiwanese primary schoolers would have to spend on Japanese language would keep them well below standards achieved by Japanese children in other subjects as well. In the final analysis, education authorities rejected integration mainly on the grounds that it would impose lower elementary school standards upon Japanese nationals.[64]

Given this conclusion, the results of a comparative study of Taiwanese and Japanese schoolchildren, conducted by education experts for Den's administration, are most interesting. These researchers tested and compared the academic levels of a sample of 4,000 common school pupils and 8,000 primary school pupils.[65] The study included many comparisons: between boys and girls; between children in the same grade with several months' difference in their ages; and between Japanese children born in Japan and Japanese children born in Taiwan. Of most significance is the survey's evaluation of the overall performance and the subject-by-subject performance of Taiwanese common school children, as compared to those of Japanese primary school pupils.

In arithmetic, common school students did much better than primary schoolers in the same grades.[66] Moreover, their overall academic performance in all subjects was also rated higher than that of primary school pupils in the same grades.[67] The superior output of the Taiwanese children in the sample was explained by those who conducted the study as follows. Common school children tended to begin school a year older than their Japanese counterparts and therefore had the advantage of an extra year to develop. Taiwanese school-goers were a select group because they generally came from a particular type of family, but nearly all Japanese children in the colony went to primary school and their backgrounds varied.[68]

These reasons may indeed help explain the superior performances of Taiwanese children. Today there are teachers who would argue that in many if not most young children at least eight years of physical and emotional growth must take place before the basics of reading, writing, and arithmetic can be grasped easily.[69] In 1923 when the results of this study were published 28.6 percent of the Taiwanese elementary school aged population was in common school as compared to 97.3 percent of the Japanese elementary school aged population of the colony in primary schools.[70] On the other hand, primary schools enjoyed superior buildings, grounds, and equipment; their teacher-pupil ratios were much more favorable; and they employed more highly qualified professionals.[71] Surely of even greater importance, Taiwanese children were tested in their second language while Japanese youngsters were examined in their mother tongue. When this last fact is considered, the superior performance of Taiwanese children, especially in subjects other than arithmetic, is indeed impressive if not astonishing—even if these children represented a school population which was slightly less than one third of the number of school aged children in the general population.[72]

Certainly the study's results raise doubts about the validity and the sincerity of the claims that, with integrated schooling, the language handicaps of Taiwanese pupils would bring down academic standards. These standards might indeed have been endangered by integrated education, but only because integration would have forced Japanese children in primary schools to share their superior facilities and highly qualified teachers with larger numbers of Taiwanese youngsters and to give up their favorable teacher-pupil ratios. For unless education expenditures were to be vastly increased—and budgetary preference given to industry and commerce ruled this out—integration would inevitably threaten the privileged position of the primary schools. Yet to admit publicly that Japanese children could not be asked to make sacrifices for their Taiwanese counterparts would be embarrassing, since the governor-general had just proclaimed a policy of assimilation and equal treatment. Hence "Japanese language backwardness" provided a convenient rationale for restricting Taiwanese admission to the better-equipped schools. Needless to say, when the findings of the comparative study were published in 1923, public sale of the volume was prohibited and its circulation was restricted to administrative personnel.[73]

The decision to limit integration at the elementary school level probably came as a relief to most education officials, not to mention the personnel charged with balancing the government general's budget or the average Japanese parents of elementary school aged children. Assimilation had only been a respectable concept since 1918, enthusiastically advocated by the chief executive but often against the judgment of his subordinates. Without the prestige of his predecessor's military rank, Governor-General Den had to rely more upon persuasion and less upon orders than had Akashi. The decision was probably as much a concession toward deeply entrenched opposition to integrated education as it was acknowledgment of financial priorities and practicalities.[74]

Since ethnic segregation had always been maintained in government-general schools, Japanese resistance to total or even partial integration at the elementary school level is not surprising. Several administrations earlier, a single Taiwanese child had somehow managed to enter a Taihoku primary school in 1903 and it had caused a great scandal when officials discovered him there in the fourth grade in 1906.[75] He was removed at once and the following reminder was sent out to teachers, principals, and regional officials throughout the colony:

> As Article One of the Taiwan Primary School Regulations clearly states, a primary school is a place for the education of Japanese children. As Article One of the Common School Regulations clearly states, a common school is a place for the education of native children. In each of the two [types of school] the aim of education is different; mixing of the two is not permitted. This . . . is basic policy in this island. In spite of this, cases of Taiwanese entering primary schools and Japanese entering common schools have not been completely unheard of. Such incidents demonstrate supervisory negligence and reveal educators failing in their important responsibilities. Such infringements of established laws and regulations are contrary to education policy. They will not only prevent the attainment of desirable results from the education system but they will also be a permanent hindrance to [general] administration of the island. Therefore all officials are to abide by the provisions of the education code in order to realize the [desired] results from education.[76]

Authorities had even been reluctant to allow the offspring of Japanese fathers and native mothers to attend primary school. (A child born to a Japanese woman and a Taiwanese man was considered Taiwanese.) Lengthy deliberations took place in the government general before a request on behalf of such a child whose father was Japanese and mother Taiwanese was granted in 1910. Officials noted that, although in such colonies as British India or the Dutch East Indies children of "mixed blood" were admitted to schools provided for nationals of the ruling country, no such principle had been established in Taiwan. They stressed that authorization to admit this particular child must in no way be taken as a precedent for establishment of such a principle. Each time the parents of a cosmopolitan child wished to enter him or her in primary school, application would have to be made to the proper authorities, who would decide each case on the basis of its individual merits.[77]

So the new education rescript, which on February 4, 1922, replaced Akashi's, completely integrated schools only from the secondary level up. The new rescript declared all schools equally accessible to Taiwanese and Japanese. It named the common schools as institutions for non-Japanese-speaking children and the primary schools for Japanese-speaking children regardless of race. Japanese were now free to enter common schools, and Taiwanese who could meet the Japanese language criteria of a primary school were to be admitted. On the higher levels of the education system all schools (except normal schools) were to be governed henceforth by the same education ministry rescripts which regulated their counterparts in Japan.[78] Shortly after the rescript's promulgation, Akashi's ban on new private schools in any category other than vocational institution or special school was lifted.[79]

Publicly at least officials agreed that the brand new integration rescript, as they called it, "abolished discrimination in education."[80] "Originally . . . common school graduates were clearly of a somewhat lower standard than were primary school graduates . . . But have not common school graduates now become the equal of primary school graduates? There has been much debate over recognition of this. There has been a gradual increase in the use of Japanese language in [Taiwanese] homes . . . and in addition there are superior common school graduates and inferior primary school ones, with the former comparing favorably to the latter . . . Indeed, the aim of the education rescript is to banish discrimination between the two."[81] So noted the head of the internal affairs bureau (*naimu kyoku*) when the rescript went into effect. And the chief of the education bureau added: "The primary point of the revised education rescript is not just to abolish discrimination in the education of Japanese and Taiwanese. It [the rescript] does not recognize racial appellations like 'Japanese' and 'Taiwanese' at all. Its distinctions are based upon the use of the Japanese language, and even this distinction stops after elementary education."[82]

The common school curriculum was brought closer to that of the primary school. Japanese history was added, vocational subjects were shifted to the periphery, and classical Chinese, which was not taught to primary schoolers, became an elective. Many schools used this reorganization of subjects as an excuse to drop Chinese altogether, although the Taiwanese parents of their pupils — especially in the southern half of the island — objected strenuously.[83] The six-year common school course now consisted of ethics, Japanese language, arithmetic, Japanese history, geography, science, drawing, singing, physical education, vocational training, sewing, and home management, with Chinese sometimes offered as an option. Abbreviated four-year and three-year common school courses were authorized "where local conditions warranted such" but three-year schools never materialized and four-year ones were never popular.[84]

The declared objectives of teaching Japanese history were to provide a general introduction to the "national polity" (*kokutai*) and to cultivate the "national spirit" (*kokumin seishin*). The history of Japan was to be taught from ancient to present times and was to include lessons about the founding of the state, the unbroken line of Japan's ruling house, the chronological records of emperors, loyal and virtuous deeds of subjects, origins of the culture, and the rudiments of Japan's relations with foreign countries. In geography classes, knowledge of both nature and man was to be disseminated, in order to familiarize the children with the features of the home islands and to cultivate patriotism. The topography, climate, divisions, cities, products, and transportation system of Japan were to be the main areas of study. But the geography of south China, the South Seas area, and perhaps even other countries was to be covered in a general fashion, and the globe's composition and movements were to be explained. Literary Chinese was to be taught as before, although for the first time regulations did not instruct teachers to be sure that the Chinese words children learned to write included Taiwanese proper names and place names.[85]

Common schools were now authorized to offer the two-year advanced courses (*kōtō ka*) and the supplementary courses (*hoshū ka*) found in some primary schools.[86] Titles classifying the different common school teacher ranks became identical to designations for primary school instructors, but Taiwanese were still lower-ranking teachers with less training.[87]

In his policy speech Den had promised that compulsory elementary education would be brought in as soon as possible. When and how to introduce it was one of the problems he laid before his new consultative council (*hyōgikai*) in 1921. Up until that year the Consultative Council of the Taiwan Government General — its duty was to advise the chief executive on policy matters when asked to do so — "had been no more than a meeting of the governor-general's subordinates."[88] But Den altered the body's composition. It now consisted of nine senior government-general officials (including Den himself as president) and eighteen distinguished residents of Taiwan. Half of the eighteen nonofficial appointments he made were Taiwanese.[89] Den's inclusion of Taiwanese was undoubtedly window-dressing to give the appearance of native participation in the colony's political processes, for the consultative council mandate was only to offer opinions to the governor-general when he asked for them. Nevertheless the opinions of the Taiwanese members of the council on compulsory education and the administration's response to these opinions are interesting.

During the three sessions Den's consultative council held between June 1921 and June 1922, compulsory education was on the agenda twice. Several Taiwanese councilors were the keenest advocates of making elementary schooling mandatory for all Taiwanese children as soon as possible. Japanese on the council were far less enthusiastic and would not lend their support to a proposal from Taiwanese councilors to initiate compulsory education by 1928.[90] As a result Taiwanese hopes for a concrete program to introduce mandatory schooling were disappointed. The council's final report to Den on this issue, dated June 22, 1922, merely recommended that, because of the difficulties the local governments would have in financing a compulsory education system, four years of compulsory school should be instituted when the local administrations could bear the financial burdens involved.[91]

Such a recommendation might just as readily have come from a body composed entirely of administrative officials. It is interesting that in spite of Den's designation of compulsory education as soon as possible as one of his policy priorities, no alternative financial arrangements ever seem to have been seriously considered, not even subsidies from the central government-general treasury. Expense was a key factor in limiting Taiwanese admissions to primary schools; it was also an unchallengeable obstacle to elementary schooling for all Taiwanese children.

On the other hand a concerted effort to increase the number of common schools was made during Den's regime. The number of common schools increased from 438 in 1919 to 715 in 1923 and the numbers of common pupils rose from 125,135 to 209,946 during the same period.[92]

Beyond elementary school, the government general boasted of completely integrated, nondiscriminatory facilities. The integration rescript raised the standards of the formerly all-Taiwanese facilities, and thus held out better academic opportunities to the natives who would utilize them in the future. However, the rescript actually gave the colonial Japanese far more new opportunities than the Taiwanese, since, unlike Akashi's rescript, Den's did not set up new institutions nor expand existing ones.[93] Native students became eligible for the first time to admission to the previously all-Japanese middle schools, the higher girls' schools, and the commercial college. They were still excluded—not in theory but in fact absolutely—from the primary school teacher training course. Japanese students, however, gained new access to a wide range of institutions: at the secondary level, middle schools, higher girls' schools, the agriculture and forestry school, the commercial school, the industrial school; and at the specialized college level, the agriculture and forestry college and the commercial college.

Instead of enlarging Taiwanese educational opportunities, Den's reform actually reduced the number of Taiwanese who received higher training in the colony. Taiwanese scholars were subjected to stiff competition from Japanese. The year before the integration rescript was promulgated colonial authorities reported 224 Japanese and 640 Taiwanese enrolled in college level courses.[94] During 1923, the last year of Den's administration, specialized college enrollments totaled 330 Japanese and 314 Taiwanese.[95]

A closer look at the formerly all-Taiwanese agriculture and forestry college reveals what happened. In 1921 this all-Taiwanese school had 113 students; in 1922 it took in a total of 111 students, of whom seventeen were Japanese; the following year thirty-five Japanese and ninety-two Taiwanese were admitted.[96] In the other colleges the story was the same. The numbers of students admitted annually from 1922 did not expand to accommodate rising numbers of Japanese; instead, Japanese students took places previously occupied by Taiwanese. Even medicine, long established as a Taiwanese stronghold, did not escape the invasion. In 1921 the medical school had 343 Taiwanese students plus 93 Japanese in the special course; in 1923 Taiwanese places had fallen to 262 while Japanese had risen to 122.[97] The secondary vocational schools followed much the same pattern, although only a few Taiwanese boys were admitted to the formerly all-Japanese higher commercial school and middle schools.[98] For Taiwanese girls to get into a previously all-Japanese higher girls' school was also very difficult, despite the fact that this type of school, in less demand in both ethnic groups, was clearly out of the mainstream of career-oriented education.[99]

Japanese administrators claimed that aspirants from both ethnic groups were judged equitably in open competition and that the coveted places went to the most proficient. They explained the less successful performances of Taiwanese applicants in terms of language handicaps and lower academic achievements. In specific cases this may have been true, but it was an open secret that the Japanese who controlled admissions did not discard their longstanding practice of protecting the interests of the rapidly growing Japanese community.[100] For all the new policy's boasts of equal opportunity and equal treatment, Taiwanese youths still found it much easier to get into advanced schools in Japan than to gain admittance to comparable institutions in the colony.[101]

Yet surely Den was as sincere as Akashi had been in his plan to improve the education lot of native islanders. Why then, in at least one sense, did his rescript have a reverse result? As in the case of compulsory education, Den's hopes for the coeducation policy came up against the realities of colonial life. Government-general funds were still heavily earmarked for other areas than education; agriculture, industry, and commerce continued to come first. And the well-being of a growing number of Japanese colonists had to be secured. Much as Den wanted to improve the position of the Taiwanese, there is no evidence that he was willing to do this at the expense of his fellow countrymen. Akashi had autocratically overruled the objections of his staff and opened costly new schools in spite of protests. Den instructed his subordinates to seek ways to achieve his objectives, but when the conclusions of their investigations modified his policy he did not counter them. Perhaps he could not have done otherwise. Not only did Den lack the prestige of a lieutenant general, but he would never have been prepared as a last resort to call in the army to carry out policy, as Akashi might have been.

The governor-general of Taiwan had to spend a great deal of time in Japan every year, gaining support for his budgets and policies and answering questions about his administration in the Imperial Diet. Den performed these tasks conscientiously and adroitly, solidifying the support he had gained before accepting the overseas post and meeting new challenges skillfully.[102] But although he was successful in warding off outside interference, his duties kept him in Tokyo for such lengthy periods of time that the actual running of the colony was often left in the hands of the officials in Taiwan. The attitudes and loyalties of these men were shaped by their service in the colonial administration during the tenures of successive governors-general. To most of them protection of Japanese interests was undoubtedly their first duty. And their colonial background often led them to believe that they, rather than a more temporary chief executive, were the best qualified interpreters of Japanese interests. The Japanese official, like other Japanese in Taiwan, took his preferred status for granted. Like colonialists the world over, the Japanese residents of Taiwan were not prepared to consider natives their equals in education or in any other sphere. As a part of the larger ruling class community a large number of Japanese teachers must have shared this feeling. It is not surprising that educators and others in the administration used the integration rescript to answer Japanese demands for education.

There is also the question of the nature and length of Den's term as governor-general. Backed by Prime Minister Hara Kei, Hara's successor as prime minister, and other strong civil and military politicians, Den Kenjirō was the most powerful of Taiwan's civilian governors-general. Decidedly he was one of the most important of all the figures who headed the colony's administration throughout its fifty-one-year history; and his regime has been declared by an authoritative source to be second in importance only to Kodama Gentarō's.[103] Like Kodama he skillfully kept Tokyo politicians at bay and enlisted support at home for his overseas policies.

But Den inherited highly developed administrative machinery operating in favor of continuance of the status quo whereas Kodama started almost from scratch against a background of flux and chaos. Within the colony Den could count upon neither the authority which Kodama's military rank commanded nor a brilliant chief subordinate like Gotō Shimpei who was completely in tune with his policy aims and objectives. Gotō himself understood well the difficulties that would confront a civilian governor-general years before Den took office. While governor-general, Kodama once suggested that he resign his post and have Gotō appointed in his stead. Gotō refused, emphatically asserting that the authority of high military rank was essential for any governor-general of Taiwan.[104] Den's four-year stint was the longest term of all the civilian governors-general except the last one, who served four years and three months. Yet compared to Kodama's eight years or Sakuma's ten, the length of his regime is less impressive. And barely one and a half years after his education rescript was promulgated Den returned to Tokyo to become Minister of Agriculture and Commerce in a newly formed cabinet.

Like so many of Den's policies, like his police, local government, and marriage law reforms, the new educational system was more impressive on paper than in action.[105]

> On my assumption of the Governorship-General, I recognized the fact that the time was ripe for giving to the natives the same education as was given to the Japanese and introduced the system of co-education for a section of Japanese and Formosan children by way of experiment. As the result was excellent, the Educational Law was so revised, in February, 1922, that all discriminatory treatment in educational matters was done away with. Children who habitually use the Japanese language are taught in *sho gakko* (primary school), and all other children are sent to *ko gakko* (public schools). The system for co-educating Japanese and Formosans is adopted as a principle in respect to the middle school education. The distinction still existing in elementary education, I have no doubt, will sooner or later be abolished with the progress of civilization and further spread of education. The revised Educational Law has been enforced since April, 1922, and it is fully expected that it will produce far-reaching moral effect on the Formosans.[106]

So Den optimistically and confidently reported to readers of the English language periodical *The Trans-Pacific* in 1923.[107] Readers of *The Trans-Pacific* may have been impressed. But to Taiwanese who witnessed but a select few of their children entering primary school and who saw Japanese students cutting down the number of natives in advanced training programs, the claim to have abolished "all discriminatory treatment in educational matters" had a sour ring.

Perhaps Den did not consider the de facto discrimination against Taiwanese, which everyone in the colony knew about, as important as the fact that at last Taiwan's public schools had actually become integrated, unquestionably so from the secondary level up. After all he and his staff lived in an era which long preceded such a concept as affirmative action or indeed any concept of obligatory compensation for the discrimination experienced by disadvantaged groupings within society. To Japanese administrators, equality in education did not mean absolute equality of opportunity for every Japanese and Taiwanese. Even in the wake of Wilsonianism and Taishō democracy, the Japan of the early 1920s was a clearly demarcated hierarchy and in the colony ethnic differences divided rulers and ruled even more sharply. After the integration rescript some Taiwanese attained the same academic degrees as Japanese, and once admitted to advanced courses individual Taiwanese were officially recognized as equal to their Japanese classmates. This, to paternalistic Japanese eyes, was equal treatment bestowed upon a subject people by their benign rulers. To Den Kenjirō it was definitely a large step toward making Taiwan an extension of the home islands and making the colony's native inhabitants one with the people of Japan.

5/ After the Integration Rescript

The school system produced by the integration edict of 1922 remained essentially unaltered until Japan lost Taiwan in 1945, although the rhetoric changed as did the titles of some schools. Throughout the last two decades of Japanese rule the tension that had surfaced with the educational reforms of Akashi and Den remained strong. This tension—between the ideals of assimilation and the compulsion to maintain Japanese primacy—was present during the administrations of all the civilian governors-general who followed Den, in spite of the different personalities and outlooks of these men. The conflicts were still evident even after the pace of assimilation quickened, and under military governors-general again the policy became one of militant Japanization or imperialization (*kōminka*).

Den's civilian successors pursued his integrated education policy with varying degrees of enthusiasm. Uchida Kakichi took up the governor-generalship (September 1923-September 1924) when Den left. As Governor-General Sakuma's senior civil officer, Uchida had been opposed to higher education for Taiwanese, and it is unlikely that his views had changed much by 1923.

The next governor-general, Izawa Takio (1869-1949), who served from September 1924 to July 1926, "was greatly influenced by the assimilation ideal of his deceased elder brother, Izawa Shūji . . . Before departing for Taiwan Izawa Takio gave news reporters an impromptu interview, saying among other things that the object of his mission to the island was the three million Taiwanese rather than the smaller number of Japanese in Taiwan."[1] Needless to say, Izawa's views did not endear him to Taiwan's Japanese residents. They did not make many of his subordinates happy either. Izawa tried to retire a large number of the hostile old-timers in his administration by offering them lucrative lands at an advantageous price as a condition of retirement.

These lands had been reclaimed by Taiwanese peasants who lived on them, worked them, and considered them their own. Thus, ironically, one of Izawa's major efforts to organize a loyal staff in order "to look after the interests of the Taiwanese" made him the enemy of large segments of the Taiwanese farming population and of other islanders who sympathized with the dispossessed farmers. But Izawa felt that without personally loyal subordinates he would not be able to achieve any of his goals, one of which was to end discriminatory treatment of Taiwanese. This was an important goal to him because he believed that, with Taiwan as a bridge between China and Japan, together these two nations might halt European and American expansion in East Asia.[2]

The fourth civilian to hold the post (July 1926-June 1928), Kamiyama Mitsunoshin (1869-1938), went even further than Izawa Takio when he described what he wanted to see happen in Taiwan. Kamiyama used a phrase meaning fusion of races or fusion of peoples (*minzoku yūwa*, a fusion of supposedly equal elements).[3] Taking up the familiar theme of education as a bridge between the two ethnic groups, Kamiyama pointed out that a command of both Taiwanese and Japanese languages would contribute to the fusion he desired.[4] But the sixth civilian governor-general (July 1929-January 1931) was another old Taiwan hand; Ishizuka Eizō had gained his experience in colonial government during the anti-integration regime of Kodama Gentarō.

Whatever the personal hopes or ideals of successive civilian governors-general, after Den Kenjirō all the civilians except the last to hold the post served short terms. Moreover, unlike Den, they were heavily dependent upon changing party cabinets in Japan. Those who were veterans of earlier Taiwan administrations had local ties and experience to aid them, but these could also curb enthusiasm for newer policy objectives. Thus the patterns which appeared in education during Den's last year and a half continued unaltered throughout the 1920s and the early 1930s. It is interesting, for example, that despite Governor-General Kamiyama's championship of the languages of both Taiwanese and Japanese, Chinese language was not given a more prominent place in the common school curriculum, nor was it introduced to primary schools during his administration. The latter might have been somewhat difficult to achieve because the education ministry in Japan controlled what was taught in primary schools. However, the ministry's primary school curriculum did permit some electives in accord with local conditions. Taiwanese language already had a place in the advanced course of Taiwan's primary schools, which used science, drawing, and agriculture textbooks published by the government general.[5] Common school courses, on the other hand, were completely within the jurisdiction of the government general.

By the early 1930s, assimilation in Taiwan was receiving heavy support from Japan's changing foreign and domestic policies. In an increasingly expansionist Japan, civil and military politicians' thoughts turned toward south China and Southeast Asia as well as toward Manchuria and north China where Japanese interests were already extensive. Taiwan was now clearly viewed by many as a launching pad for southward advancement and thus gained new status in Tokyo circles.[6] As aggressive patriotism became popular, voices urging thorough cultivation of the "national spirit" grew louder and louder, and among other results, large doses of ultra-nationalism and militarism were injected into the curriculum of Japan's elementary schools.[7]

Taiwan did not escape the influence of these developments. By 1936, when military rule came again, the island was a naval base with a swelling garrison, and assimilation or Japanization of the native population had been a central concern of the government general from at least the beginning of the decade. In the words of Governor-General Kawamura Takeji (1871-1955), who served as chief executive from June 1928 to July 1929, the Taiwanese were to become imperial subjects who "dress, eat, and live as Japanese do, speak the Japanese tongue as their own and guard our national spirit in the same way as do Japanese born in Japan."[8] This was far from a new aim, but much more serious efforts were now being made to achieve it.

Some of these efforts were carried out within the schools, which, like Japan's, began to reflect the militarism and ultranationalism now evident in Japanese life and society. The imperial ordinance of 1925 which required that an army officer on active duty be appointed to each of Japan's schools above the elementary level applied to Taiwan's postprimary schools too.[9] Military instructors taught theoretical studies as well as military drill to male students and were responsible to superiors in the army as well as to the education ministry hierarchy. Thus the army gained substantive authority through them over what went on in the schools.[10] Chauvinistic content appeared in common school textbooks as it did in the books used in homeland and colonial primary schools. But as we shall see in Chapter 6, this material was not conspicuous in common school texts until very near the end of Taiwan's Japanese period, and even then it was not as dominant as might have been expected.

The Japanization policy of the 1930s and later did influence the schools significantly, but innovative implementation of the Japanization policy took place largely outside the formal education system from about 1930, when for the first time a serious endeavor was made to transform all Taiwanese rapidly into imperial subjects identical to "Japanese born in Japan." The special object of much of this effort was the Taiwanese who never attended elementary school and thus did not come into contact with the Japanization being carried on there. New measures to reach such people included social and economic betterment schemes as well as campaigns to spread Japanese language and culture and to increase common school attendance. The measures were particularly directed at the countryside, where, as the colonial government ruefully acknowledged, Japanese influence was especially light. These social education projects, as they were called, will be discussed in Chapter 7. Here it is important to remember that during the last decade and a half of Japanese rule, while the education system exhibited strong continuities with the public schools of the 1920s, a heavy Japanization program was being carried on simultaneously outside the schools.[11]

Elementary Schools

The integration rescript permitted Japanese to enroll in common schools, but few Japanese ever did. This provision was convenient for a few Japanese families stationed in remote areas, but most Japanese lived in the cities or larger towns.[12] The peak year for Japanese enrollment in common schools was 1940 when there were 396 Japanese out of a common school population of 621,450.[13]

It is doubtful if the entry of a few Japanese into mainly rural common schools had much impact upon the common schools as a whole; more important to these schools from 1922 on was their annual loss to the primary schools of from several hundred to several thousand of their most able Taiwanese pupils.[14]

However, while this flow invigorated primary school classes many bright children remained in the common schools — at least partly because of the limits put upon Taiwanese enrollment in primary schools. Although fluency in the Japanese language was the only legal requirement for entrance to the first grade of a primary school, an unofficial quota system made sure that Taiwanese made up no more than 10 percent of the primary school population.[15] It was not uncommon for some children in a Taiwanese family to attend one type of elementary school while their siblings went to the other type, depending upon the unofficial quota and the Taiwanese competition for entry into their local primary school each year.[16]

During the late 1920s and the early 1930s the common school's curriculum experienced little change. In 1927 the Ministry of Education's arithmetic textbooks for primary schools began to be used in common schools, but all other common school textbooks continued to be the products of the government general's textbook editing office.[17] By 1933 the colonial government seems to have concluded that too many common schools had become too much like academically oriented primary schools, because administrators moved to put some of the earlier vocational emphasis back into these schools, which they meant to serve mainly children whose education ended when they were graduated from common school. In that year, they made vocational studies in the regular six-year common school compulsory for girls as well as boys, and in the handful of four-year common schools that still existed optional vocational courses were made mandatory.[18]

In 1937 classical Chinese, so important during the first two decades of Japanese education in Taiwan, was banished from the common schools. This step was an integral part of the accelerated assimilation policy. Nevertheless it was by no means a radical departure from earlier education policy. Classroom time devoted to Chinese had been systematically reduced since the late 1910s, and in 1922 this subject had been made an elective. When a 1936 survey revealed that out of 625 common schools only fifty-five were still teaching classical Chinese, administrators, noting that now there were only sixty-two *shobō* with less than 2,500 pupils, felt that at last they might abolish this subject.[19]

Their stated reasons for doing so were practical as well as ideological. This subject had originally been introduced into native elementary schools, they pointed out, when written Chinese had been the main vehicle of communication between literate Taiwanese and their Japanese rulers. In those days Chinese had also been an essential language for islanders who carried on trade with the Chinese mainland. But now literate Taiwanese conversed and wrote in Japanese and the China trade had dwindled. Administrators also argued that it was desirable to take Chinese out of the common schools in order to make them as much like primary schools as possible — although their attempt four years earlier to keep common schools more vocationally oriented than primary schools surely raises doubts about this claim. Perhaps most important of all, they feared that even as an elective, the teaching of Chinese might awaken a latent Chinese mentality and thus impede mastery of the Japanese language and formation of a Japanese consciousness (*kokumin seishin*).[20]

Common school pupils were taught by both Japanese and Taiwanese teachers during the period 1923-45. The vast majority of teachers from both ethnic groups were male. Yet as Table 9 illustrates, there were always several hundred Japanese women and several hundred Taiwanese women teaching common school during these years.

In the wartime climate of 1942 the colony's 850 common schools and 150 primary schools were renamed national schools (*kokumin gakkō*) as were the primary schools of Japan. However, they remained essentially two separate types of elementary school

TABLE 9. Japanese and Taiwanese teachers in common schools, 1923-41

Year	Japanese		Taiwanese	
	Male	Female	Male	Female
1923	1,341	277	2,986	460
1925	1,446	259	2,833	457
1927	1,601	290	2,807	415
1929	1,708	348	2,876	356
1931	1,899	395	2,821	342
1933	2,165	464	2,817	317
1935	2,510	603	2,811	315
1937	3,226	856	2,779	381
1939	4,104	1,304	2,788	528
1941	4,407	1,904	3,357	1,347

Sources: Taiwan sōtokufu tōkeisho: 1926, p. 103; 1928, p. 109; 1929, p. 111; 1935, p. 137; 1937, p. 99; 1939, p. 93; 1941, p. 391.

—one for Japanese and a few Taiwanese, and the other for the bulk of the elementary-school-going native population. Ranks clearly identified their differences: primary schools became national schools of the first rank; six-year common schools became national schools of the second rank; and the much rarer four-year common schools were classified as national schools of the third rank.[21]

Of much more consequence than this simple name change was the decision to inaugurate compulsory elementary education. In the autumn of 1939 a government-general committee that had been investigating ways to initiate mandatory schooling recommended that compulsory education be enforced from the school year of 1943 and that it be made equally binding on Japanese, Taiwanese, and aborigine children. All children were to be required to attend school either between the ages of six and fourteen or until they had completed either the ordinary six-year common school or primary school course.[22] The recommendation was accepted and preparations for the 1943 academic year began immediately.

By 1943 when compulsory education made its debut, school authorities had managed to raise the Taiwanese elementary-school-going percentage to 65.7 (76.6 percent of the boys and 54.1 percent of the girls).[23] One year later 71.1 percent of Taiwanese school-aged children (80.7 percent of the boys and 60.7 percent of the girls) were attending school.[24] So even under the tight wartime controls of the early 1940s almost 20 percent of the boys and 40 percent of the girls in the colony's native population remained outside the schools. There were apparently limits to what the Taiwanese could be persuaded to accept, even under martial rule. Even more important probably, the costs of immediately providing additional facilities and staff to accommodate all the island's children were too much for a government general that, because of the war, had even more budgetary problems than usual.

There is no doubt that government-general campaigns to get girls into the common schools from the earliest days of Japanese rule were responsible for some impressive statistics in 1943—those which recorded over 60 percent of Taiwanese elementary-school-aged females in school. Before 1895 very few girls had ever been admitted to the Chinese academies and schools; it was only after the Japanese began pressing for female education that the number of girls in *shobō* rose, although females always remained a small proportion of the student bodies of these institutions.[25] When Taiwanese girls began to go to school in conspicuous numbers, it was to common school that they went.

This decision to institute compulsory education was accompanied by another long-awaited step, banning of the *shobō*. This was also a less drastic move than might at first seem, because during the last year of their existence in 1939 there were only seventeen or eighteen of these Chinese private schools left.[26]

Vocational Schools

The tendency toward Japanese domination of higher educational facilities which began during Den's regime continued right up to 1945. The only postprimary institution to escape this trend was the two- and three-year lower level vocational school, which, originating as the seventh and eighth grades of common school, fell somewhere between the elementary and the secondary schools in the colony's education pyramid. Most of these schools were agricultural but there were a few commercial, commercial and engineering, and fishery schools; from 1933 they included a women's technical school; and by 1940 there existed at least twenty schools of home economics for women.[27]

All other postprimary vocational facilities were soon dominated by Japanese enrollments. In the late 1920s, when a commercial school and two agricultural institutes were opened, these new secondary schools were largely occupied by colonial Japanese. On the highest vocational tier of the school system, the Taichū Agriculture and Forestry College catered to Japanese rather than Taiwanese applicants.

Normal Schools

Taiwan's normal schools, unlike other higher schools, remained outside the jurisdiction of the Tokyo Ministry of Education after 1922. Thus, although they followed the teacher training trends of Japan, they also retained some of their own peculiarities, the most prominent of which was the continued separation of primary school and common school teacher courses. In practice if not in theory, only Japanese were ever admitted into the primary school course.[28] Both Taiwanese and Japanese entered the common school program, which was called upon to recruit more and more teachers for the common school network.[29]

To help meet this need, a third normal school had been opened in Taichū in 1923. Four years later the Taihoku normal school split into two separate institutions, one to train primary school teachers and the other to produce staff for common schools.[30] The following year, 1928, one of the Taihoku normal schools took over the instruction of female common school teachers, who up until this time had been trained in higher girls' schools. From the late 1920s students of both sexes came to colonial normal schools to spend either six or seven years or one or two years before qualifying as teachers. From time to time the normal schools emphasized short-term and accelerated programs in response to particularly acute teacher shortages.[31]

Like Japanese postprimary institutions everywhere, each normal school in Taiwan was required to add a military instructor to its regular teaching staff in 1925. However when military drill was instituted the following year it was only given to male students from their fifth year up.[32]

In the same year, perhaps as a result of the same influence that brought military training into the schools, Japanese martial arts such as *kendo* and judo were added to the skills taught to male common school teacher trainees in physical education classes. Other curriculum amendments made at this time in the common school training program include reducing fourth- and fifth-year English to elective status, bringing arithmetic instruction up to the standard of what was offered in Japan's normal schools and permitting the one-year graduate course (*kenkyū ka*) to feature academic subjects as well as purely pedagogical studies. Although a mainstay of the normal school curriculum in Japan, English was made an elective because an island-wide survey had shown that after graduation from normal school only somewhere between one third and one half of the colony's teachers used their English. Thus normal school authorities thought that time usually spent upon English might be more productively devoted to vocational subjects or handicrafts.[33]

The normal school curriculum was amended again in 1933. Following the example of Japan's normal schools, the five-year main course was reorganized as a compulsory core of subjects for all students, who were allowed during their following final two years to develop areas of concentration in accord with their interests and aptitudes. Changes in subject content also followed the example of Japanese normal schools. The class in law and economics was abolished in favor of a less specialized social studies syllabus entitled civics (*kōmin ka*); physics, chemistry, and natural history were replaced by the more general subject heading of science; industry (*kōgyō*) was added to the roster of vocational subjects. Compulsory for men, industry was also offered to women as an elective. This time the emphasis reflected the climate of opinion in Japan as much as government-general policy, but once again the stress was upon education for practical everyday living and education for loyal, patriotic citizenship.[34]

When Japan's normal schools became equivalents of three-year specialized colleges in 1943 the format of Taiwan's schools followed suit, but the change meant more on paper than in fact for many students. Now middle school or higher girls' school graduates had to complete a three-year regular normal school course and thus their training was extended a year. But others entered this three-year course after completing first the two-year higher *kokumin gakkō* course (a two-year extension of the regular six-year elementary school) and then a two-year normal school preparatory course. As before, these students spent a total of thirteen years in school before qualifying as teachers.[35]

Middle Schools and Higher Girls' Schools

While heavy Japanese admissions to vocational and normal schools curtailed the number of places in these institutions available to Taiwanese after 1922, secondary academic schooling was even more obviously a Japanese domain. In Japan the race to enter secondary schools was a highly competitive one and many applicants to middle schools, higher girls' schools, and the like, failed to gain admittance.[36] In Taiwan virtually all Japanese applying to middle school or higher girls' school were accepted in some secondary institution. Japanese who did not do well enough in entrance examinations to gain admission to schools that had formerly been all-Japanese institutions were often accepted into what had formerly been a Taiwanese middle school or higher girls' school — even though their academic performances fell short of Taiwanese classmates in the same institution.

This of course was the norm for an overseas territory. H. A. Wyndham, the British author of a comparative study of colonial education in Asia, noted in 1933:

> Here [in Taiwan's middle schools and higher girls' schools] again the disproportionate number of Japanese pupils is natural.

No English child is uneducated in Ceylon, nor Dutch child in Java, nor French child in Indochina. All colonial powers make the education of the children of their colonial nationals a first consideration and afterwards do all that the colony's finances will permit for the education of natives. To allow the descendants of the former to degenerate through lack of education would be a retrograde step and a negation of the trusteeship which is the justification of empire building.[37]

The privileged position of the Japanese in Taiwan was not unlike that enjoyed by the nationals of Western colonial powers in their overseas holdings.

But the Japanese in Taiwan claimed that they were not like other empire builders because in 1922 they had stopped making "the education of the children of their colonial nationals a first consideration." The education rescript of 1922, they proclaimed, had abolished discrimination in education. Government-general officials continually asserted this throughout the twenty-three years of Japanese rule that followed 1922.[38] Thus it is against their own often repeated claim as well as in comparison with the records of Western colonial contemporaries that they ask to be judged.

In spite of the fact that the 1922 rescript ruled out race as a factor in admission selections, only a small percentage of Taiwanese applicants was accepted into middle school and almost none into a formerly all-Japanese school. The same holds true for higher girls' schools. It was common knowledge that, for those seeking a secondary academic education, Japanese birth was a greater asset than either intellectual ability or demonstrated excellence in school entrance examinations.

Taiwanese youths quickly learned that it mattered not how able or well-prepared they were; even for the most brilliant of them it was generally folly to apply to any of the formerly all-Japanese middle schools—especially the oldest and most prestigious of them—because each year only a token half-dozen or so native islanders were admitted to each of these institutions. Therefore they and higher girls' school aspirants usually sat only for the entrance examinations of the "Taiwanese" schools.[39] For despite government-general statements to the contrary, some middle and higher girls' schools were mainly for Taiwanese while others served a Japanese clientele. The proportions of the two ethnic groups in each school's student body clearly revealed which schools were for which. And the comparative disadvantage of the Taiwanese, as Tables 10 and 11 show, continued right up through the last years of the colonial government. As far as Taiwanese elementary school graduates were concerned, the middle schools were accommodating far too few of them, but the authorities appraised the situation differently. As the number of middle school graduates in the colony steadily rose year by year, administrators were once again haunted by their old fear of creating an educated native elite with poor employment prospects. Another government-general worry was that Taiwanese in middle schools seemed to be acquiring a taste for further academic and professional training, which would be open to very few of them. The Taiwanese lad who survived the fierce entrance competition had proven his ability and shown his determination by the time he began his middle school course. With five years to develop his scholarly interests and raise his aspirations, graduation was likely to be severely anticlimactic unless he was among the handful who managed to get into colleges or the higher school (from 1925) or unless his family could afford to send him to Japan.

Thus critics within the government general began to castigate the middle schools for their solidly academic programs. These

TABLE 10. Percentages of applicants accepted in major "Japanese" and "Taiwanese" middle schools, 1941-43[a]

Year	Japanese				Taiwanese			
	Taihoku 1	Taihoku 3	Taichū 2	Tainan 1	Taihoku 2	Taichū 1	Tainan 2	Tamsui Private
1941	53.6	35.1	64.8	70.5	15.2	16.0	16.7	27.2
1942	80.1	40.8	77.8	71.2	29.2	16.3	21.9	22.6
1943	69.6	70.6	74.7	80.8	21.9	26.5	24.3	26.7

Sources: Taiwan tsūshin sha, Taiwan nenkan 1942 (Taihoku, 1942), p. 238: Taiwan nenkan 1944, p. 505.
[a]It was customary for Japanese applicants who failed to do well in the entrance examinations of "Japanese" middle schools to be assigned places in "Taiwanese" middle schools. It is not clear if, in such cases, the Japanese applicants had also written the examinations of the "Taiwanese" middle school when they were regularly given. At any rate, this practice made it even more difficult for Taiwanese aspirants to get into a middle school than the above table suggests.

TABLE 11. Percentages of applicants accepted in major "Japanese" and "Taiwanese" higher girls' schools, 1941-43

	Japanese				Taiwanese			
Year	Taihoku 1	Taihoku 2	Taichū 1	Tainan 1	Taihoku 3	Taichū 2	Tainan 2	Tamsui Private
1941	55.9	35.0	49.3	81.5	23.8	18.9	27.7	48.8
1942	61.7	30.3	81.3	68.8	21.3	24.7	25.7	44.7
1943	68.9	56.2	79.7	71.9	19.7	33.0	22.7	38.9

Sources: Taiwan tsūshin sha, *Taiwan nenkan 1942*, pp. 234-240; *Taiwan nenkan 1944*, pp. 506-507.

schools, government authorities noted, were preparing their students solely for a higher education that most of them would never receive. This type of preparation was highly unsuitable for "the greater number of middle school students who, upon graduation, would have to go out into society to work."[40] It was the Taiwanese rather than the Japanese middle school students who were referred to here, because they were the graduates who usually had "to go out into society to work."

Uneasiness and dissatisfaction mounted until 1933 when the government general, perhaps encouraged by similar expressions of concern in education circles in Japan, finally took action. In that year revisions in the middle school curriculum attempted to strengthen general subjects and the now unfashionable vocational interests that had been so prominent in colonial schools in earlier times. Some of the changes paralleled those taking place in schools in the home country: for instance, Japanese martial arts were to be emphasized in order to underline the national identity. But there was also to be a new emphasis on the vocational subjects already taught as electives. A job training course to teach gardening, building, and other skills was added with the intention of inculcating "useful, everyday knowledge and a love of labor."[41]

In addition, to get away from the memorization and cramming that preparation for higher schools often implied, students were to be encouraged to embark upon their own freely chosen research projects — the only stipulations were that such a project be given any necessary guidance and that it be in harmony with a student's capacities, environment, and interests. Students could spend up to two hours a week on this research, which would take place outside of the classroom.[42]

The impact of these changes upon the academic orientation of the middle schools appears to have been marginal. Japanese middle schools had always provided preparation for college and university. Teachers in colonial middle schools knew they were responsible for their Japanese as well as their Taiwanese pupils, and the parents of the former expected them to get their sons ready for college or university. It is unlikely that gardening or building instruction slackened many Taiwanese ambitions. The chances of a Taiwanese middle school graduate remaining in school were not very good, but his prospects for immediate employment must have seemed even dimmer. The best jobs still went automatically to Japanese, and migrants from Japan poured into Taiwan during the last two decades of government-general rule.[43]

Senmon Gakkō and Other Postsecondary Options

Taiwanese hoping to advance to specialized colleges or to the higher school's university preparatory course (after it was founded in 1925) faced the greatest barriers of all. Government-general records clearly reveal what everyone in the colony must have known—that in both absolute and proportionate numbers fewer Taiwanese succeeded in entering the island's higher institutions of learning during each year that followed the 1922 rescript than received some college-level training in each year immediately preceding its promulgation.[44] Even in areas like agriculture and medicine where the regime had always encouraged Taiwanese interest, Japanese tended to take places away from Taiwanese college students after 1922. And Taiwanese entries to the higher school's university preparatory course were always kept well below the number of Japanese admitted.

Senmon gakkō and university preparation were for men. Although in Japan a small but significant number of specialized colleges had been established for women, no private or public equivalents existed in the colony. There is no evidence, however, that the limited educational opportunities available in the colony to higher girls' school graduates worried many in either Japanese or Taiwanese communities. In both ethnic groups parents who encouraged a son to climb high up the educational ladder were usually less concerned about formal schooling for a daughter who was expected to marry and join her husband's household.

In spite of this, certain factors did encourage—at least to a limited extent—higher education of females. In the first place, both Chinese and Japanese cultures harbored an ancient respect for learning for its own sake and in neither tradition had scholarship and literary accomplishment been confined entirely to men. Since all Japanese girls and a good many Taiwanese girls learned the same elementary school lessons as their brothers did, it is not surprising that girls as well as boys developed a taste for further study. For well-brought-up Japanese females an appropriate higher education could be a marriage asset; a higher girls' school graduate with an excellent school record, for instance, could be expected to raise intelligent sons and to be able to assist them with at least their early education. Under Japanese rule some Taiwanese families began to see similar values in higher schooling for their daughters. And, although it was true that educated women generally earned much less than educated men, schooling allowed women to gain respectable employment that could augment family incomes or make them self-supporting if the need arose.

During the last half of Taiwan's Japanese period, the influence of all these factors stimulated in both ethnic groups not only keen competition for higher girls' school places and the growth of a female vocational student population but also a real if small demand among women for postsecondary education.

This demand was large enough for the Taiwan Education Society to found the Taihoku Girls' Higher Academy (Taihoku joshi kōtō gakuin) in 1931. This institution, about which government-general records and the Taiwan Education Society's own *Taiwan kyōiku enkakushi* are strangely silent, offered a two-year regular course and a one-year graduate course to higher girls' school graduates. The academy's role in the colonial education system is, however, unclear, because little is known regarding its curriculum or the interests of its students. In 1940 there were seventy-three students at the academy which employed six full-time teachers and nineteen part-time faculty members who regularly taught at the university, a normal school, or a higher girls' school.[45]

Some Japanese and a few Taiwanese higher girls' school graduates completed the advanced course for common school teacher trainees offered by the Taihoku First Normal School from the late 1920s. However, hundreds of Taiwanese and perhaps thousands of Japanese who were graduated from higher girls' school probably finished an accelerated teachers' training course or received some sort of pedagogical instruction. This must have been the case because, as Table 9 illustrates, there were always many more female common school teachers of both races than there were women who finished the one-year normal school course for higher girls' school graduates.[46]

Some Taiwanese higher girls' school graduates trained as midwives in the training program available in the island's larger hospitals, but unfortunately it is not known how many did so.[47] It is known that medicine drew Taiwanese women as well as men. Tokyo Women's Medical College (Tokyo joshi igaku senmon gakkō) was a popular goal among ambitious Taiwanese girls in higher girls' school; and according to one Taiwanese writer, in Taiwanese "dreams of their children's future their boys became physicians and their girls became the brides of physicians."[48]

Taihoku Imperial University

A university of Taiwan had been one of Governor-General Den Kenjirō's ambitions. A higher school and a university had been an important part of his seven-point proposal of 1919, and article four of the 1922 rescript provided for university as well as *senmon gakkō* education.[49] However, Japanese imperial universities were never established easily, and in spite of Den's memoranda and the eagerness of the Japanese in Taiwan for a university, hopes for this highest educational institution only began to materialize in 1925 when the colony's three-year-old higher school gained a higher or university preparatory course. There was a clear understanding between the government general and the Tokyo Ministry of Education that when the preparatory course's first class was ready to graduate three years later Taihoku Imperial University would be ready to receive them. In 1928 Taihoku Imperial University opened the doors of both its faculties—literature and political science and agriculture—right on schedule.

The Japanese in Taiwan would have been happy to see the university open even earlier. Yet they had been spared the long wait, arduous campaigns, and financial strain that generally preceded a decision by the Japanese government to establish a new imperial university. Compared to the struggles which the people and politicians of Tōhoku or Hokkaidō were forced to wage before either region gained a public university, the agitation of the privileged nationals in Taiwan was short and soon rewarded.[50]

Nevertheless, by 1928 regular classes of the law and literature faculty and the medical faculty had been meeting for two years in Keijō Imperial University, which had been organized as a two-faculty university for Korea in 1926. The Japanese in Taiwan knew that there were important reasons why Korea had acquired a university before Taiwan—although relentlessly crushed, the Korean uprising of 1919 had precipitated a good deal of educational reform. Keijō's establishment had been hastened to undercut Korean nationalists who were agitating, organizing, and collecting funds for a private people's university to consist of a medical school, an engineering school, and a liberal arts college.[51] Still, it rankled old Taiwan hands that Korea, the younger colony, should be put first while Taiwan, because it was peaceful and orderly, was made to wait.

When Taihoku Imperial University's two faculties were ready in 1928, Taiwan government-general officials announced that all aspects of the policy of integrated education had now been implemented. Henceforth, even the highest education facilities enjoyed in the home islands would be available in the colony to Japanese and Taiwanese alike. At the same time it was clear that Taihoku was to have another function, even more important to colonial policy makers than its role as a teaching institution.

The founding of Taihoku was due as much to Japan's heightened interest in south China and the South Pacific as it was to the demands of colonists or the example of Keijō. From its beginning Taihoku was defined as a center for research focusing on the subtropical regions of south China and the South Seas with the understanding that future Japanese expansion might be in these directions.[52] Organized primarily for research, the new university stood in harmony with some very old concerns of the colonial government. The government general had always sponsored scholarly and scientific study to improve agriculture, to aid industrial development, to better sanitation, and to facilitate social and political control, as well as to learn more about the south China and the South Pacific regions.[53] Even purely historical and cultural studies of the island's pre-Japanese past had received government-general sponsorship.[54] The high ratio of faculty to students in Taihoku Imperial University testified to its function as a research institution.

Nevertheless, Taihoku did train students also. For the most

part these were not Taiwanese: very few natives ever managed to squeeze into either the literature and politics faculty or agriculture and science, and in spite of Taiwanese strengths in medical education a faculty of medicine was not opened until 1936. In that year, part of the old medical school became Taihoku's third faculty and the rest remained as a specialized medical college, now attached to the university (*daigaku igaku senmon bu*). Of the forty medical students admitted to the university in 1936 only sixteen were Taiwanese; out of the 265 students who remained in the medical college 136 were native islanders.[55] Predictably, the Taiwanese position in other fields was much weaker.

The problem for Taiwanese applicants to Taihoku was that Japanese were favored—not officially of course—in entrance selections, and since the number of places was small to begin with, only a few could ever hope to get in. For the Taiwanese who had no means of getting to Japan, where he knew he could enter a university much more easily, familiar frustrations mounted.[56] This situation remained essentially unchanged until the end of Japanese rule; once the Japanese in Taiwan had gained their university they hung on to it tightly. Yanaihara Tadao's description of Taihoku in 1929 was still true in 1945: "That Taihoku Imperial University is mainly a university for Japanese is clear and self-evident. Thus the highest of Taiwan's institutions of learning is occupied by Japanese from the island [Taiwan] and Japanese from the homeland. Taiwanese who have entered [Taihoku Imperial University] are, compared to the Japanese who have done so, very, very few."[57]

Private Education

From 1923 to 1945 private schools played a peripheral role in Taiwan's education system. By 1923 *shobō* were on the wane and the government general easily enforced its requirement that Japanese language, ethics, mathematics, and other common school subjects be taught in these native schools. Budget-conscious administrations had always encouraged private philanthropy, and training for the handicapped was considered a worthy private endeavor. The colony's two schools for the blind and the deaf began as private schools; one was started by the missionary, William Campbell, at the turn of the century and the other founded by a Japanese physician in 1917. But such facilities were costly to maintain, and the government general eventually took over both schools.[58] Authorities tolerated two religious institutes with missionary connections and permitted a few private vocational schools to operate. By far the most important private schools, however, provided a secondary academic education.

The outstanding contribution of a handful of middle schools and higher girls' schools was in the education of native islanders. A significant number of Taiwanese young people, by choice or necessity, attended these schools rather than the ones run by the government general. In cases of choice, it was sometimes because families of the youngsters were Christians. Prominent among the private schools were two secondary schools for boys and two for girls founded by the Protestant missionaries at Tainan and Tamsui and a distinguished higher girls' school operated by Catholic fathers.[59] On the other hand, many Taiwanese came to these schools because it was so difficult to enter public ones.[60]

Thus, these private schools did respond to the intense demand of Taiwanese elementary school graduates for secondary education, but their nongovernmental status created problems for their Taiwanese students too. Until 1938 no private middle school or higher girls' school received official recognition from the colonial government, and therefore before that date none of their graduates was entitled to sit for examinations to higher institutions. The two Tamsui mission schools were the first private middle school and higher girls' school to be granted official accreditation; by 1941 the Tainan Protestant schools were among the four private middle schools and two private higher girls' schools recognized by the government.[61] Yet even after a private secondary school was accredited, very few of its graduates were likely to be accepted in the colony's university preparatory course or colleges. One authority estimates that during the 1940s only four or five private middle school graduates went on to higher schools each year.[62]

Possibilities for private middle school graduates were not encouraging, but they were probably not quite as bleak as the above description suggests. The Christian schools had ties with Japanese believers and foreign missionaries in Japan and were often able to send their brighter and more affluent students to the schools, colleges, and universities associated with members of their faith in the ruling country.[63] Although Yanaihara Tadao complained in 1929 that in the colony Japanese Christians and native Christians had little to do with each other, there had been connections between Taiwan's mission schools and Christian schools in Japan since the beginning of Japanese rule.[64]

Although some young women sought postsecondary training, the education provided by a higher girls' school—public or private—was usually expected to be terminal. As a result, private schools for girls were better able to satisfy Taiwanese demands than could private middle schools. Held in high repute, the girls' schools were always inundated with student applications.[65]

Taiwanese Students in Japan

To acquire a higher education in the colony a young Taiwanese first had to get past education officials who favored students of their own race and worried about overeducating natives. By contrast Japan seemed to be a land of hope which offered true equality of opportunity. With a wider variety of schools and no racial quotas in Japan it was always easier for a Taiwanese to get into a university, specialized college, middle school, or higher girls' school there than it was to win one of the few places available in Taiwan. So many bright lads in Taihoku had their education cut off after middle school, but the Taiwanese boys who got to middle school in the ruling country nearly always went on to university or other training programs.[66]

Although medical college remained a popular destination, among the flow of Taiwanese scholars to Japan that continued unabated through the 1920s and the 1930s were students of law, politics, literature, economics, commerce, agriculture, science, and engineering.[67] In lesser numbers girls followed their brothers, often heading also for medical college.[68] However they too branched out and could be found studying dentistry or even economics.[69]

In vain the government general tried to discourage this trek. Attempts were always made to guide and direct the activities of those who did leave the island; the colonial government appointed supervisors (shidō kantoku) to oversee the students, and from 1912 on there was a dormitory for Taiwanese in Tokyo to make supervision more effective.[70] But as the years passed, just keeping track of the students became difficult. The government general's efficient police force did its best to keep a close watch on all Taiwanese in Japan as part of its responsibility to guard the colony against political, social, or cultural subversion. By the 1920s, however, there were so many Taiwanese in Japan that police surveillance was largely confined to politically active students, those displaying an interest in "dangerous ideologies" and those who appeared to be friendly with nationalistically inclined Chinese or Korean students. Although official records of the colonial government claimed that fewer than seven hundred Taiwanese were studying in Japan during 1922, confidential police estimates put the 1922 Taiwanese student population in the ruling country at at least 2,400.[71]

By the last decade of Japanese rule it must have been impossible for the government general to gain an accurate picture of how many Taiwanese were in the home islands. Rigorously enforced sanitary improvements and long years of peace had helped to produce striking increases in the colony's native population, which grew from 3,414,388 in 1915 to 5,682,223 in 1940.[72] With scientific exploitation of the island's agricultural, forest, and mineral resources and the beginnings of new industries had come prosperity. Even though Japanese took the lion's share of the new riches and wealthy Taiwanese remained but a small fraction of the whole Taiwanese population, the size and wealth of the Taiwanese upper class had obviously grown immensely. During these last ten years many more thousands were able to afford study in Japan than could have done so two or perhaps even one decade earlier. Transportation between the colony and ports in Japan was freely available and Taiwanese needed no visas or passports to make the journey.[73] Taiwanese in Japan who had completed their schooling and found gainful employment there were sometimes in a position to help younger relatives when they arrived. The colonial government's last counts of Taiwanese students in schools in Japan are given in Table 12; there must have been many more—perhaps thousands more—in the ruling country who were never included in the government-general statistics.

Mobilization for War

The war years were grim. As the fighting steadily ate up the colony's resources, administrators sought new ways to involve the Taiwanese more deeply in the tasks of self-sacrifice and patriotism required of Japanese subjects. Japanization reached new heights after 1940 with campaigns which forced Taiwanese to take Japanese surnames and penalized natives who spoke anything but the Japanese language. These heavy-handed efforts were often resented, but they were sometimes difficult to resist—

TABLE 12. Official estimates of the number of Taiwanese enrolled in schools in Japan, 1936-42

Year	Middle school and higher girls' schools		Vocational schools		Higher school and university preparatory		College		Universities		Miscellaneous schools[a]	
	Male	Female	Male	Female	Male	Female	Male	Female	Male	Female	Male	Female
1936	733	43	188	0	149	0	566	181	202	3	277	15
1937	829	76	217	0	154	0	651	229	209	2	422	23
1938	1,197	101	328	24	145	0	959	291	312	1	650	115
1939	1,635	148	462	16	177	0	1,211	343	337	0	914	164
1940	1,541	158	524	20	201	0	1,438	360	309	1	1,275	161
1941	1,556	267	603	31	249	0	1,640	352	303	0	1,493	182
1942	1,523	270	681	13	258	0	1,635	304	329	1	1,917	160

Sources: For 1936-39, Taiwan sōtokufu bunkyōkyoku, *Taiwan no gakkō kyōiku*, p. 121; for 1936-41, Taiwan sōtokufu bunkyōkyoku hen, *Taiwan no gakkō kyōiku shōwa jūroku nenban* (Taihoku, 1942), p. 124; for 1938-42, Taiwan tsushinsha, *Taiwan nenkan 1944*, p. 505.
aThe category "miscellaneous schools" probably included many private nonaccredited schools and colleges.

the children of families who refused to take Japanese names, for instance, were denied entrance to middle school and higher girls' school.[74] About the same time, a large-scale organization called the Imperial Subjects' Service Society (Kōmin hōkō kai) was set up with the governor-general as president and branches all over the island. The goal of this new society, according to its constitution, was to lead native islanders in "the way of the subject." That is, it was to see that the island's population was thoroughly imbued with a keenly patriotic outlook.[75]

School curricula were carefully checked to see that they conveyed as much patriotic content as possible, and teachers were constantly admonished to develop the national spirit of their pupils, while military instructors played a larger and larger role in school life. But greater disruptions to educational processes came from the voluntary military service system and the obligatory work brigades for young people and children into which Taiwanese were channeled during the 1940s.

In June 1941 the government of Japan decided that the Taiwanese, who as colonial subjects were not drafted into the regular armed forces, would henceforth be eligible for voluntary military service. This was enforced the following year and Taiwanese males were obliged to join one of the four so-called volunteer corps that provided coolies, translators, agricultural workers, and seamen for the Japanese armed forces in Taiwan, the home islands, and the South Pacific.[76] In the same year military deferments for higher school and university students were canceled and, while their Japanese classmates were drafted into the army, Taiwanese students who would otherwise have remained in school in the colony or the ruling country joined a volunteer corps. To refuse to volunteer was unusual and could be risky; a Taiwanese who was a student in Tokyo Imperial University in 1942 remembers: "My name remained posted as the only one who had not yet volunteered, and I began to fear arrest. I moved my lodging from time to time and went to the campus less and less often."[77]

Meanwhile, the young people who remained in school, in the colonies as well as in the home islands, were organized into labor teams. In Taiwan a government-general order in January 1942 created the public service brigades that were made mandatory for all students and staff in university, college, higher school, normal school, middle school, higher girls' school, and vocational school. The students and their teachers were ordered to assist in the production of foodstuffs and to do manual labor in factories and other places as needed.[78] During the same year elementary school children were all made members of children's brigades. These groups trained children in military drill, but as with the public service brigades of their elders the main purpose of these groups was labor.[79]

With young children and their teachers out working on the roads, in factory assembly lines, or down at the docks, and their seniors doing voluntary military services or conscripted into the army, there was not much time or many resources left for formal schooling. Taiwanese knew that in Japan the school system suffered equally, and they saw the disruptions impeding the education of young Japanese as well as that of their own children. At the same time, they did not see equal treatment being meted out. Applications to postprimary schools continued throughout the last years of the war, and so did the favoritism shown Japanese applicants. Taiwanese work corps were sent to the lines in the South Pacific but never to China, and Taiwanese were not drafted into the regular armed forces. Thus, concluded thoughtful Taiwanese, their rulers harbored doubts about their loyalty.[80] Life was harsh for everyone in wartime Taiwan, but ration coupons allotted to Japanese entitled their bearers to a superior quality of provision than that procured with ration tickets distributed to the emperor's Taiwanese subjects.[81]

The Education System Essentially Unchanged

Den Kenjirō saw his education rescript as the beginning of a fully integrated education system. As he had abolished separate education in postprimary facilities, so others would do the same for the lower schools. "This distinction still existing in elementary education, I have no doubt, will sooner or later be abolished with the progress of civilization and further spread of education," he confidently announced in 1923. This never happened. On the contrary, there continued to be two types of elementary school, one for natives and another for Japanese and a few natives. Den had also expected that compulsory education for all the colony's children, although regrettably unfeasible during his tenure, would come sooner or later, but it was only introduced two years before the Japanese left the island. Postprimary education remained Den's too. The coeducation of the two ethnic groups that his rescript produced remained essentially unaltered, although new schools, colleges, and a university were added.

That none of Den's civilian successors should alter the equilibrium achieved during his administration is not surprising. Although their outlooks differed, short tenures enhanced their dependency upon the career officials who ran their administrations and their need for the cooperation and support of all Japanese in Taiwan. Yet they could not command from subordinates nor the larger Japanese community the respect that a military governorgeneral could usually count on. And most of the Japanese of Taiwan — inside or outside the government general — continued to see equality of education and other such implications of the assimilation program as a threat to Japanese interests.

What is perhaps more startling is that the school system was left more or less intact by the military administrations that began in 1936. It is amazing that common school textbooks, for instance, did not undergo greater modification during the 1930s. One also wonders why a greater effort was not made to respond to Taiwanese demands for a fairer deal in the postprimary schools. Well aware of Taiwanese criticism of *de facto* discrimination in the schools, the government general also knew that Akashi Motojirō's educational move in 1919 to win Taiwanese support had been popular with the native population.

However, administrations headed by military governors-general during the last decade of Japanese rule had many problems besides Taiwanese education. Defense and the war effort became larger and larger priorities, to which finally everything else had to be sacrificed. The island's wartime economy allotted so little money and manpower to maintenance of existing educational institutions that educational planners felt forced to banish all thought of innovation. By the late 1930s compulsory elementary schooling was considered to be a long-overdue essential of the Japanization program. Yet when it was finally instituted it was not enforced with the vigor characteristic of earlier educational measures; the colonial government's energies and funds were obviously engaged elsewhere.

Between 1935 and 1942 the Japanese population of Taiwan increased by more than 102,000 to reach a total of 348,847.[82] As this population grew so did its demands for employment and high quality schooling for its children. Until the end of its days, the government general of Taiwan was under heavy pressure to provide for that very old interest, the well-being of the Japanese colonists in the island.

As the war on the Chinese mainland raged on, the Japanization policy displayed a growing ambivalence toward the Taiwanese. On the one hand, the colonial administration and the Tokyo government officially viewed Taiwanese as loyal Japanese subjects. At the same time, the Taiwanese were not considered reliable enough to be drafted into the regular armed forces or to be sent to the front in China even as nonfighting personnel. Japanization declared war on Taiwanese memories of their Chinese past, but in the minds of those who implemented Japanization this Chinese ancestry caused doubts and suspicions to linger. Ambivalent attitudes about Taiwanese worthiness may have made it easier for those who ruled Taiwan to emphasize duties and to neglect rights when they constantly reminded the Taiwanese that they were Japanese subjects. Hence from officials there was little talk of securing for the Taiwanese the equal access to education that was widely enjoyed in Japan, but there was continual exhortation to make sacrifices for the war effort as the people of Japan were doing.

In the last analysis, Japanization did not mean important changes in the education system because the schools were considered to be doing a good job. Admittedly, Japanization was most thorough in postprimary institutions, but ordinarily the small percentage of Taiwanese young people who applied to these had already absorbed a great deal of Japanese language and culture. It was in the more numerous elementary schools that the basic work was being done. For decades the common schools had been spreading Japanese values and customs among ever larger proportions of the island's children. Officials recognized this achievement and lauded it. What was needed, they felt, was not so much alterations in the process as reinforcement of it by action taken outside the school system.

In order to make the indoctrination carried on in the schools more effective, Japanization campaigns concentrated upon adults and upon children who did not go to school. Such campaigns aimed to make the atmosphere of Taiwanese society — into which the common school pupil stepped after graduation — more like the climate of opinion cultivated at school. A major goal was to increase the number of elementary school attenders in the island; this too underscored the government general's satisfaction with the school system. The Japanization policy attempted to make the outside world as Japanese as that of the playing fields and the classrooms and to give a greater number of islanders experience in both worlds.

6/ Japanization in the Common Schools

Japanese educators aimed at nothing less than a total transformation of each Taiwanese child that passed through the gates of the common schools. Many hours of Japanese language instruction supported by weekly ethics lessons were intended to accomplish this aim.[1] "It is not enough to give them the ability to speak Japanese. The goal is much more: it is to inculcate the Japanese way of thinking and of experiencing emotion and to cultivate the Japanese spirit," reminded a 1941 Japanese teachers' manual.[2] Twenty-eight years earlier, instructions to teachers of first-grade ethics had warned: "As the Japanese spirit rests in the Japanese language . . . as soon as possible you must put all effort into using as much Japanese as possible."[3] In Japan the object of language and ethics lessons was also to make loyal Japanese out of elementary school pupils. But education authorities in Taiwan felt that the task was much more difficult with Taiwanese children and their very different heritage.[4]

Teachers in common schools were enjoined to be patient and diligent. They were to encourage and praise their pupils, but they were also strictly to enforce the use of Japanese in and out of the classroom at all possible times.[5] To aid and inspire them, teachers were supplied with Japanese language readers, ethics textbooks, and curriculum manuals for both language and ethics classes. Specially compiled and edited by colonial education officers for use in common schools, these were similar to the volumes published by the Ministry of Education for use in Japanese primary schools, but they were by no means the same.

Language Readers and Ethics Textbooks in Japanese Primary Schools

In pre-World War II Japan, the publication of government elementary school language and ethics textbooks occurred during five distinct periods. The education ministry approved a set of

133

textbooks for both subjects in 1904.[6] These were used in primary schools until revised sets for both Japanese language and ethics were published in 1910. Subsequent revisions and republications took place in 1918, 1933, and 1941.

Karasawa Tomitarō has analyzed the content of the Japanese language and ethics textbooks used in each of the five periods.[7] According to his analysis, the books used between 1904 and 1910 expressed a youthful Japanese nationalism. The primary school child was urged to work hard to make his country great by achieving greatness and success in his own personal endeavors. In the Japanese readers this concept was conveyed by many lessons emphasizing scientific knowledge, that is, lessons dealing with geography, nature, agricultural production, industry, and so on. Such lessons insisted that scientific knowledge was to be used to achieve civilization and enlightenment for Japanese individuals and for their country. As an example of this, Karasawa singled out a lesson from a Japanese reader of this period entitled "The Earth." Teachers were instructed to use this lesson to impress upon the children that although the earth is large and Japan is small, any country, small or large, will rise or fall according to the efforts of that country's people.[8]

In the ethics textbooks there was heavy emphasis on individual and social morals as routes to national greatness. Pupils were urged to be industrious and to cooperate in order to benefit society as well as themselves; they were taught not to block the freedom of others. Examples of exemplary conduct were drawn from the lives of such figures as Socrates, Isaac Newton, Benjamin Franklin, Henri-François d'Agresseau, and Florence Nightingale, as well as from the exploits of famous people in Japanese history.[9]

In the Japanese language readers used during the second period, from 1910 to 1918, Karasawa found more emphasis on military power and state controls as prerogatives of the state. He also found an abundance of material directly related to daily life. In the ethics textbooks the emphasis on loyalty, patriotism, the family-state, and the family system became heavier. Children were still encouraged to rise in the world. But at the same time, dutiful servants faithfully serving their betters received praise. Children were taught that there was a close connection between the service of humble individuals and the industriousness and the progress of a state.[10]

From 1918 to 1933 both readers and ethics books reflected the trends of Taishō democracy. Internationalism was expressed in the language readers with almost twice as many Western personalities appearing in their pages as the preceding period. The industrialist was also a respectable figure in these readers. Nationalism continued to be an important element, however, as expressed in such lessons as "The Order of the Golden Kite" and "The Divine Wind." Ethics textbooks carried lessons on "The Public Benefit," "The Duties of a Citizen," "Hygiene," "Labor," "The Spirit of Progressiveness," "The Manual Worker," and "Cooperation," as well as on "Our Country," "The Meiji Emperor," "Yasukuni Shrine," and "Loyalty."[11]

Karasawa characterized the fourth period, from 1933 to 1941, as one in which "fascism raised its head."[12] The Japanese language was described as the property of the Japanese race and was named as the repository of the Japanese people's spirit. The language readers began to stress racial consciousness in stories of the founding gods and warriors of old. Stories of contemporary Japanese military life were also included. Heavy doses of science remained in such lessons as "The Automobile," "The Water's Journey," and "The Invention of the Telephone," and material related to everyday life continued to appear. Ethics textbooks strengthened their emphasis on "the way of the subject." The ideal Japanese subject was portrayed as obedient, loyal to the emperor and the state, and true to the "national essence" (*kokutai*).[13]

During the fifth period Karasawa saw in the textbooks the culmination of the nationalistic and militaristic trends of the 1930s. He described the years from 1941 to 1945 as a period of ultranationalism and saw militarism as the dominant characteristic of the language and ethics books. In the readers, Japan was portrayed as the sacred country of the gods. From his analysis of Japanese language teaching manuals of primary school teachers, he concluded that 76.4 percent of the Japanese language lesson content in primary schools was aimed at inculcating ultranationalistic sentiment, and during the last two grades of primary school he found this content to reach 95 percent.[14] He also found that ethics textbooks reflected this trend, teaching the unique nature of the Japanese nation and people with appropriate examples from Japanese historical tales.

Karasawa's exhaustive examination of Japanese textbooks — not just ethics and language textbooks and not just primary school textbooks—is impressive. I agree with most of his characterization of the ethics texts for all these periods and with his assessment of the earlier language texts.[15] However, I think he has exaggerated the militaristic and ultranationalistic content of primary school Japanese language textbooks during the last two periods. For the last period especially, I think he has over-emphasized the militaristic content of the language readers. The content is certainly there in larger quantities than before, but it is not as all-pervasive as he suggests.

He bases his conclusion regarding the very high percentage of ultranationalism and militarism in primary school language lessons on the aims and goals for Japanese language teaching outlined in teachers' manuals during the fourth period. In these he found teachers advised to stress militarism and patriotism in the teaching of a very high proportion of the readers' lessons—from 50 percent in the first grade to about 95 percent in the fourth and fifth grades.[16] An examination of the readers does not reveal such a high percentage.

For example, in the second reader of the series *Yomikata,* a reader used in the first grade, there were five lessons out of a total of twenty-six which might be called nationalistic or militaristic. These ranged from a long lesson about children playing war games to a lesson on "radio language," which mentioned that radio broadcasts were in standard Japanese, the national language.[17] Similarly, the two *Yomikata* readers used in grade two contain seven out of twenty-six and ten out of twenty-five ultranationalistic lessons respectively. These second grade readers contain more nationalistic lessons than do the first grade ones, but still the percentage is nowhere near Karasawa's 76.4 percent.[18] The range in ultranationalistic lessons is also considerable. In *Yomikata 4* such lessons included one featuring big brother's send-off as he goes to take up military service and one in which the only nationalistic content is the red sun painted on the kite in the illustrations.[19] Significantly, Karasawa's "representative examples" from the readers of this period in his *Kyōkasho no rekishi* (A history of textbooks) are generally the most chauvinistic of the lessons.

Such examples are certainly typical of one strong trend, but they are not representative of the series' entire contents. A great deal of continuity can be found in the language lessons dealing with children's games, nature, riddles, letter writing, and folk tales—especially stories featuring animals—which appeared repeatedly during all five periods. A good deal of this material remains in the 1941 readers. Many of the morals and principles embodied in earlier readers also show up in later reader lessons.[20] In his otherwise excellent treatment of the history of Japanese language textbooks, Karasawa underestimates the extent of such content in both the 1933 readers and the 1941 readers, but especially in the later ones.

On the other hand, the great increase in ultranationalism and militarism in ethics textbooks during the last two periods, particularly during the last period, was quite extraordinary.[21] A similar development occurred in primary school history textbooks.[22] However it must be remembered that ethics lessons and history lessons took up only a few hours a week, while a large part of the primary school curriculum was devoted to Japanese language.

Japanese Language and Ethics Textbooks in Taiwan

Taiwan government-general education officers had been writing and compiling textbooks since the beginning of the colony's history, but with one exception, arithmetic texts for teachers, it was not until after the 1912 common school regulation revision that completed sets of common school textbooks resembling the Ministry of Education's editions for primary schools began to be published.[23] The first such set, a twelve-volume series of Japanese language readers for grades one through six, was completed in 1913. During the next few years a similar set of ethics textbooks for common school grades one through six was also completed. The education bureau also prepared teachers' manuals to accompany these. Both the Japanese language and the ethics series were used in common schools until the promulgation of the 1922 education rescript. From 1922 a new set of Japanese readers and a new set of ethics books were issued. These were used at least until the middle of the 1930s and in most cases probably until 1941.[24]

Common school language and ethics textbooks before 1922. From the second decade of the twentieth century on, a substantial number of Taiwanese children learned to read and write Japanese in the island's common schools. The Taiwanese child spent most of his or her first four weeks in school doing oral language drill and therefore began using a Japanese language primer later than did the first grader of a Japanese primary school. During this first month or so the first grade teacher, by means of about twelve formal lesson-hours of Japanese language a week and presumably by using Japanese in all other possible situations as well, attempted to banish the child's own tongue from the classroom. The description of this procedure in the teachers' manuals coincides with the complaint of Ts'ai P'ei-huo (1889-   ), a Taiwanese advocate of political and educational reform. "As soon as our children enter the gates of the school they revert to babyhood and have to rid themselves of all the language and thought that they have learned during their [first] six years at home . . . mimicking like babies."[25] Ts'ai related what was apparently a familiar story when he told of the Japanese teacher pointing to his chest and repeating "teacher," whereupon the Taiwanese pupils took the Japanese word for teacher to mean heart.[26] After the four weeks of spoken language drill, the teacher began to teach written Japanese and to use the first reader. By the end of the school year the children were supposed to have completed two readers. Two readers were to be completed in every common school grade, just as in primary schools.

Much of the content of common school readers resembled the books used in primary schools, and indeed some of the lessons were almost identical. This was especially true of lessons made up of folk tales, children's stories, or poems. However, most of the common school readers' material dealt with matters close to Taiwanese schoolchildren. There were many lessons about nature, scenery, school, good pupils, home, shopping, the post office, and adults at work. The settings of such lessons were all Taiwanese. Taiwanese children and adults were featured in the stories and the illustrations displayed Taiwanese scenery, houses, furniture, and clothing.[27]

Common school ethics textbooks also exhibited a strong Taiwanese flavor. The illustrations and stories in the children's books and the instructions in the teachers' manuals all stressed material intended to show young Taiwanese living as their Japanese rulers would have them live. The first lesson in the first grade ethics textbook was entitled "School." It was illustrated by a picture of a common school classroom full of Taiwanese pupils listening attentively to a teacher and by another which showed a teacher playing with children in a schoolyard. Teachers were instructed by the teachers' manual to introduce the lesson with the following little talk:

School is to make you a good person. But as you heard at the school entrance ceremony, you cannot become a good person automatically just by coming to school. There are several things you must do. Even if it is hot and windy, even if the roads are bad, even if you are not feeling well, still you must come to school. You must heed what your parents say and what your teacher teaches. And (introducing the two pictures illustrating the first lesson) you must be like the children in these pictures: you must study hard and you must play hard.[28]

The second lesson was about a Taiwanese boy who, during his four years at common school, had never been late. This was followed by other lessons featuring Taiwanese children in stories illustrating tidiness, cleanliness, appropriate deportment, obedience to parents, friendliness among siblings, the importance of improving one's Japanese language, owning up to one's errors, protecting helpless animals, understanding the difference between one's own belongings and those of others, and avoiding annoying others. Another lesson taught truthfulness, using the story of the boy who cried "Wolf! Wolf!" — only in this verson the boy cried "Tiger! Tiger!" There was another lesson without a story which urged the children to remember always the great debt they owed their parents, and still another in which the children were taught about the Japanese emperor and his concern for his Taiwanese subjects. Common school teachers were reminded by the manual, as were primary school teachers, always to use solemn deferential language and demeanor when speaking of the emperor. The last lesson in the first grade ethics book was entitled "The Good Child." It described the attributes of a model first-grader and was intended to be a review of all the morals taught in previous lessons.[29]

Common school language and ethics textbooks, 1922-1941. Although the Japanese language readers used in common schools during the 1920s and 1930s continued to have a strong Taiwanese flavor, they resembled contemporary and earlier primary school language readers in many ways. Taiwanese children first approached their readers as relative strangers to the Japanese language. Nevertheless, as they progressed beyond the first grade there appeared less and less evidence of efforts to simplify the Japanese they were taught. By the time the Taiwanese child had reached the fourth common school reader in the second half of the second grade, he was doing language work equivalent to that of the Japanese primary school second-grader. From this level onward, there is little difference between the number of words and syllables per page, the number of Chinese characters introduced per volume, the number of pages per reader, and the complexity of the grammar and sentence structure in the readers used in equivalent grades in common schools and primary schools. By the time both common school and primary school pupils had completed the entire twelve readers in their respective sets they had been exposed to about equal standards of written Japanese. The one exception to this was that the Japanese readers contained more literary language (*bungo*) than did the textbooks for Taiwanese, the majority of the lessons of which were presented in more colloquial Japanese.[30]

The pace of teaching Japanese to common schoolers may also have been slower, for although the number of pages in both sets of readers was usually about the same, the Japanese readers in all periods usually contained more lessons than did the common school readers published during the 1920s.[31]

The topics introduced and the morals stressed in the Taiwanese readers of this period and in the two contemporary periods of Japanese readers (1918-33 and 1933-41) shared many themes. Both sets contained material about occupations, nature, geography, and elementary science. Both sets were liberally sprinkled with folk tales and animal fables, particularly in the early volumes. Lessons about everyday behavior — stories about children helping out at home, for instance — were to be found in both Japanese and Taiwanese readers. There were practical lessons about buying and selling and about the post office in both sets. In both were children's riddles, letters, and diaries. Rhythmic poems — sometimes identical poems — appeared in both about such subjects as a kite, a plane, or a sports meet.[32]

Although stories from Japanese history and mythology appeared in both, in the Japanese readers such stories appeared earlier and more frequently.[33] In the readers compiled by colonial education officers, historical tales and the morals they illustrated were more likely to be drawn from Chinese history or Chinese and Japanese history combined.[34] In lessons dealing with Japan and foreign countries, anything revealing the power and prestige of Japan vis-a-vis other countries tended to be emphasized in the Taiwan textbooks, and anything which deemphasized this tended to be omitted. For instance the twelfth readers of the Ministry of Education 1918-33 set and the Taiwan 1922-41 set both contained similar lessons about the Meiji emperor. There was one notable difference in each version, however. The Taiwan reader's lesson lacked the fifth article of the Meiji emperor's charter oath which called for Japan to seek knowledge from all the nations of the world. This part of the Japanese lesson was replaced in the Taiwanese reader by mention of the Meiji emperor's concern for Taiwan.[35] In the eleventh Taiwanese reader, a lesson dealing with the Russo-Japanese War made much of Japan's power compared to that of other countries.[36]

The Taiwanese readers also tended to contain more lessons about boys and girls the same age as the children who studied them. Such lessons usually portrayed Taiwanese children in virtuous actions. Public-spirited conduct was particularly conspicuous. Lesson Nine of the fifth reader, taught to children in the first half of the third grade of common school, is a typical example. In this lesson a child went to a railroad station to buy a train ticket. He joined the end of a long queue of ticket buyers and patiently waited his turn—unlike the person who tried to break into the middle of the line and was prevented from doing so by a watchful policeman. On the crowded platform the youngster helped an old woman who was struggling with a large bundle.[37]

Lesson Thirteen in the same reader illustrated honesty with a story of a child who found that his neighbor's hen had laid an egg in his yard. He decided to take the egg to the rightful owner, the neighbor, but not before he had been tempted to take it into his own house for himself and his mother to eat.[38] The fourth reader contained a similar story in which two boys turned over a wallet to the local police authorities—again not before one of the two had been tempted to pocket its contents.[39] The Taiwanese child was consistently shown in these readers going straight home from school, doing homework carefully, being kind and helpful to those in distress, keeping promises, heeding the words of the teacher, and helping parents in their work.[40]

Primary school readers also portrayed children's conduct, but the lessons did not always preach as overtly as those in the common school readers. For instance, the lesson "Harvesting" in the sixth Japanese reader of the period 1910-18 dealt with the same topic as "Rice Reaping" in the sixth Taiwanese reader published during the 1920s. The Japanese lesson was a step-by-step explanation of how the harvesting was carried out. The common school lesson appeared to take such knowledge for granted. It described a farmer's son bringing lunch to workers in the field. The Japanese text imparted information; the Taiwanese text had strong overtones of good conduct.[41]

Not all the stories in common school readers featuring Taiwanese children were heavily moralistic. There were also lessons about boys and girls playing doctor, visiting their grandmothers, discovering an echo, describing home life, all very like lessons in Japanese readers.

The Taiwanese language textbooks also taught more about health and hygiene than did their primary school counterparts. The instruction was often particularly relevant to Taiwan. For instance, in Lesson Three in the sixth reader of the 1922-41 period, a father carefully explained to his son the connection between mosquitoes and malaria.[42] A similar lesson in the fifth reader began with a schoolboy's report that one of his classmates was in the hospital with typhoid fever. The boy asked his mother how one caught typhoid fever. Her answer explained to him that flies spread the disease. The lesson ended with the mother showing her son a leaflet from the local government office calling for a campaign against flies.[43]

The ethics textbooks used in common schools after the 1922 rescript were essentially the same as those used previously. A few lessons were amended but usually only very slightly.[44] These books were also very like those used in Japanese primary schools from 1910 to 1918 and from 1918 to 1933. The differences between the Ministry of Education's second grade primary school ethics textbook, published in 1919, and the one put out by the Taiwan authorities in 1931 were mainly in the illustrations. In the pictures in the Taiwanese book children and adults appeared in Chinese-style clothing living in Chinese-style homes filled with Chinese-style furniture. The background scenery was semitropical, like Taiwan's.[45]

The ethics textbooks used in the higher grades of common schools and primary schools resembled each other more than the language readers. In these grades, Taiwanese as well as Japanese ethics textbooks concentrated more heavily on instances of exemplary conduct drawn from Japanese history. Far more Japanese historical personages appear in common school ethics textbooks than in the common school Japanese language readers published during the 1920s.

The fourth grade common school ethics textbook contained lessons entitled "Be on Time" and "Take Care of Your Health." It included the tale of a Chinese official in pre-1895 Taiwan who, at the price of his own head, made an aborigine village give up headhunting. But it also featured stories of such familiar figures from premodern Japanese history as Ninomiya Sontoku (the hero of four lessons), Ogyū Sorai, Itō Jinsai, and Aoki Konyō. This volume ended with a lesson entitled "The Good Japanese" as did the contemporary primary school fourth grade ethics textbook.[46]

Common school language and ethics textbooks, 1941-1945. In 1941 common schools as well as primary schools were provided with new textbooks to serve a nation at war.[47] Much of the Taiwanese setting of common school Japanese language readers disappeared. Children with Taiwanese names and dress were replaced by characters named Hanako and Taro who wore Japanese clothing. Adults with Japanese names also appeared. An increased amount of the content was devoted to nationalistic and military topics. The teacher's manual for first grade Japanese language instructed teachers to present the lesson entitled "The Soldier" with special care and attention. "This lesson is to instill in the children respect for and gratitude toward the soldiers. It is also to plant in them the desire to carry out the splendid duty of becoming soldiers when they grow up. It is important that you talk to them so they come to understand that our imperial forces are the strongest, the most disciplined, and the kindest to children [of all the forces] in the world."[48]

Although this kind of content was increased in the common school readers, the amount was apparently far less than that in the education ministry Japanese language readers of 1941. Out of forty-six lessons prepared for first graders in elementary schools for Taiwanese children in 1941, only four could be classed as ultranationalistic or militaristic, if one does not consider the mere use of a Japanese instead of a Taiwanese name to indicate ultranationalism or militarism.[49] This content is far less chauvinistic than that found in even the grade one volumes of the 1941 Japanese reader series, *Yomikata.* Taiwanese first graders still read many old animal folk tales and everyday accounts of the lives of boys and girls their own ages.[50]

Taiwanese 1941 ethics textbooks also seem to have fallen short of Japanese elementary school textbooks in ultranationalistic content. For instance, an examination of the Taiwanese 1941 second grade ethics textbook and the Japanese 1941 second grade ethics textbook suggests this quite clearly. The Japanese book contained twenty lessons; the Taiwanese, twenty-seven. Both books began with a lesson entitled "Second Grader" and ended with a lesson called "The Good Child." In between, the Japanese volume contained eight lessons with nationalistic content: "Profound Obeisance," "The Festival of May," "Uncle and Aunt," "To the Soldier," "Meiji Festival," "The Emperor," "Empire Day," and "The Country of Japan." The common school textbook had four such lessons: "The Emperor," "Loyalty," "Do not Forget the Debt You Owe" (*on o wasureruna*), and "Empire Day." Each of the two books contained one lesson about a local festival or local gods, which need not be considered nationalistic.[51]

Conclusion

Japanese language and ethics taught in common school were indeed used to Japanize the Taiwanese child. Language lessons, occupying so many of the pupil's weekly school hours, played a particularly large role in this. As in Japanese primary schools, ethics classes were designed to reinforce much of what the child learned as he mastered reading and writing. The principles, rules of conduct, attitudes, and personal and public habits stressed by common school teachers were essentially the same as those being pressed upon Japanese schoolchildren in the colony or in Japan.

Yet an examination of textbooks published for Taiwanese common schoolers reveals that the colonial authorities were less concerned to make the Taiwanese child feel that he was Japanese than they were to have him learn to behave in his Taiwanese home, school, and community in ways they deemed appropriate. He was to think like a Japanese, but he was not necessarily to think that he was a Japanese. He was to learn to act like an obedient, hard-working Japanese subject, but he was not taught much about the privileges or opportunities that a Japanese might be tempted to claim. The Japanese reader often included stories of individual achievement, of men and women rising in society by their own efforts. Taiwanese language textbooks put more accent on harmony within the family and the local community and on sons taking up the same occupations as their fathers.

An ethics textbook, for children who continued in common school after finishing the regular six grades, had an interesting lesson entitled "Occupations." Its message was that a person's first duty was to earn a living, although one also had an obligation to use one's knowledge and skills for the sake of society. It advised children to follow the same occupations as their fathers and grandfathers had. Anything else was to be considered second best.[52] Many lessons in common school language readers portrayed fathers and sons working together at the same occupation or children assisting their parents in their work. The striving, ambitious individual was definitely overshadowed by the cooperative, hardworking, public-spirited one. The eighth reader of the series published after 1922 contained a lesson about the Meiji statesman, Itō Hirobumi. The lesson did not mention Itō's humble origins as primary school textbooks usually did. Instead it stressed the honesty he displayed even as a child at play.[53] Similarly, the same reader had a story about the Tokugawa pioneer of textile weaving, Inoue Den. The story did not emphasize personal striving or achievement on the part of Inoue; rather, it dwelt on the fact that the superior loom he invented made his native Kurume in Kyūshū a great industrial center.[54]

Near the end of the Japanese colonial period in Taiwan, details were changed in these textbooks, making their settings and heroes less Taiwanese and more Japanese. The proportion of their content dealing with the Japanese empire and nation was also increased. Still, Taiwanese common schoolers appear to have been exposed to less nationalistic material in their textbooks than were Japanese or the relatively few Taiwanese who attended Japanese primary schools.

Common school Japanese language and ethics textbooks suggest that the common school was definitely meant to assimilate Taiwanese but only at the bottom of the Japanese social order. As individuals or as a group they were not encouraged by the schools to rise to positions of power or decision making. Their textbooks aimed to make of them faithful Japanese followers, not able Japanese leaders. Given this, it is interesting that the curricula of these schools were not generally of a lower academic level than what was taught in primary schools. Common school textbooks were not watered-down versions of primary school books; only the ideological content was significantly modified.

7/ Japanese Education and Taiwanese Life

What sort of changes did the schools bring about in the lives of Taiwanese who attended them? Equally important, how did these institutions affect Taiwanese who never attended them? What kind of educational work was carried on outside the formal school system? In the final analysis, what influence did Japanese education have upon Taiwanese life and society?

Governor-General Den Kenjirō had carefully distinguished between *kyōiku* (education) and *kyōka* (acculturation) when he outlined the essential ingredients of the assimilation policy. *Kyōiku* was primarily a function of the schools, but *kyōka* meant education in a much broader sense—enlightening, civilizing, evangelizing the Taiwanese were all part of *kyōka*. Although Den and some of his immediate successors did their best, acculturation did not begin in earnest until 1930, partly because not until then did policy priorities demand accelerated assimilation or intensified Japanization. Also, projects aimed at Japanizing the general Taiwanese population had at last begun to show signs of becoming moderately successful.

Social Education, Japanese Language, and Literacy in the Countryside

In the countryside Japanese influence was lightest in the most basic sense: rural stretches of the island enjoyed few of the roads, water works, and hospitals in which the colonial government took such pride. Elementary schools were also much scarcer and not as well equipped as those in the cities and towns.[1] In a poor district, a common school serving only a few of the richest families generally failed to become a focus of community activity or concern.[2] To improve the effectiveness of such schools, the government general decided that new bridges would have to be built between local schools and the village people, ways would have to be found

146

to help pupils retain their Japanese language after they left school, and school attendance would have to include more children from all segments of the rural population.

Common school attendance was highest in the cities, but between different rural districts and even within single districts it varied widely.[3] (See Table 13.) In 1930, for example, more than 83 percent of school-aged boys in one village in Taichū province were attending school, while in another Taichū village only 19 percent attended.[4] The latter village also held the record in 1930 for low female enrollment in elementary school — less than 1 percent.[5] Girls' enrollments always lagged behind boys', but how far behind depended upon the area.[6] Although absenteeism and dropout rates also varied greatly, they were higher in the country and among girls.[7] As the percentage of Taiwanese children going to school rose year by year, regional differences and disparities between the sexes sometimes lessened, but they did not disappear.

Apart from the regional and sexual variations, children who did attend common school in rural areas tended to be the sons or more rarely the daughters of landlords or fairly prosperous owner-farmers. Children of poor owner-farmers, tenant-farmers, fishermen, day laborers, or families engaged in other humble occupations were far less likely to be sent to school.[8] Plans to spread Japanese language and culture among these classes by social education projects as well as by drives to increase common school attendance were at the heart of the accelerated Japanization policy.

Such projects were not unknown before 1930. From the earliest years officials had talked about the need for adult education to reinforce the work of the common schools, and from about 1914 the Japanese language began to be taught here and there to groups of Taiwanese adults, usually in evening sessions run by teachers or policemen. These instructors were not always skillful; they usually translated directly from Taiwanese dialects, often failing to keep the interest of their audiences. Consequently most results of such classes were not encouraging. In some places, common school graduates were brought together to listen to lectures given by local representatives of the colonial government or distinguished Japanese-speaking guests. Wherever common school graduates showed any sign of interest in this practice, the lectures became year-long courses. Rare at first, the local lecture series became fairly common by the 1920s. In many places police officers induced household heads and groups of housewives to attend

TABLE 13. Percentage of Taiwanese school-aged children enrolled in elementary school, 1907-44

Year	Boys	Girls	Total
1907	–	–	4.50
1908	–	–	4.93
1909	–	–	5.54
1910	–	–	5.76
1911	–	–	6.06
1912	–	–	6.63
1913	–	–	8.32
1914	–	–	9.09
1915	–	–	9.63
1916	–	–	11.06
1917	–	–	13.14
1918	–	–	15.71
1919	–	–	20.69
1920	39.11	9.36	25.11
1921	–	–	27.22
1922[a]	43.47	11.80	28.82
1923	–	–	28.60
1924	–	–	28.69
1925	44.26	13.25	29.51
1926	43.00	12.45	28.42
1927	43.96	13.13	29.18
1928	44.68	13.78	29.79
1929[a]	45.96	15.34	31.11
1930[a]	48.86	16.57	33.11
1931[a]	49.55	17.95	34.20
1932[a]	51.00	19.70	35.87
1933[a]	52.83	21.17	37.44
1934[a]	54.71	23.04	39.33
1935[a]	56.83	25.13	41.47
1936[a]	59.14	27.37	43.79
1937[a]	62.04	30.28	46.69
1938[a]	64.49	34.12	49.82
1939[a]	67.17	38.10	53.15
1940[a]	70.56	43.64	57.56
1941[a]	73.59	48.70	61.60
1942[a]	73.55	48.66	61.56
1943[a]	76.56	54.25	65.82
1944[a]	80.86	60.94	71.31

Sources: For 1907-19: *TKES*, pp. 408-410, Yoshino, pp. 315-316; for 1920: Taiwan sōtokufu, *Taiwan jijō* 1923, p. 137; for 1921: *TKES*, p. 410; for 1922, 1929-38, Taiwan sōtokufu, *Taiwan no gakkō kyōiku*, p. 119; for 1939, Taiwan sōtokufu, *Taiwan jijō 1940*, p. 183; for 1940-44, Taiwan sōtokufu, *Taiwan tōchi gaiyō*, p. 52.

talks given by school principals, policemen, or other regional officials who spoke about hygiene, road repairs, tax obligations, and the necessity of education. However, translation usually made such presentations unwieldy and the villagers were often bored.[9]

By 1928 the government general had decided to back its encouragement of Japanese language and social education projects with monetary support.[10] Communities all over the island were urged to set up Japanese language courses and institutes for their non-school-going members, and in 1931 such enterprises became eligible for government subsidies to aid their operations.[11]

Along with the subsidies came a new determination to involve local Taiwanese leadership in this work. The absence of such involvement in the past was seen as a mistake. Administrators now realized that no matter how intensely they preached or applied pressure, Taiwanese village life would never be substantially altered until at least some inhabitants in each village took the initiative themselves.[12] As one authority on rural social education wrote in the 1930s: "Formerly social education was carried out by officials—from government offices, from schools, from police stations. While this remained the case the goals of social education could not possibly be achieved."[13]

Indeed, during the 1930s local initiative did appear in numerous villages and the smaller units of settlement, the hamlets (*buraku*).[14] Villages and hamlets which demonstrated outstanding social educational efforts were showered with praise by local officials and their superiors in the central administration. The most outstanding of them were awarded prizes and given citations by provincial and central governments. Information about them was published by the government general's education department, and their activities were publicized in local and island-

---

aPercentages for these years include aborigine children attending elementary school (mainly the aborigine education centers). A larger percentage of aborigine than Taiwanese children was reported to be attending school. However, since Taiwan's aborigine population was extremely small, the resulting increases in the percentages for these years are insignificant. In 1942, for example, 61.52 percent of Taiwanese school-aged children were enrolled in school. When aborigine enrollees are added, this percentage rises to 61.56. In 1943 the percentage of Taiwanese children in school was 65.76 and the percentage of Taiwanese and aborigine school-attenders combined was 65.82. The percentage of the Taiwanese school-aged population enrolled in school in 1944 was 71.17; that of the Taiwanese plus aborigine school-aged population was 71.31. See Taiwan sōtokufu, *Taiwan tōchi gaiyō,* pp. 51-52, for such comparisons.

wide newspapers, all of which, with one exception, were published and managed by Japanese.[15] But one wonders just how numerous these model rural communities actually were. Perhaps it was their relative scarcity that brought them fame.[16]

The litany of achievements of one such model hamlet, San-shih-chang-li, a part of the village of T'ien Wei in Taichū province, was impressive. This hamlet's campaigns to better itself included improving hygiene and comfort in hamlet homes and their surroundings, planting victory forests, fruit orchards, and vegetable gardens (cabbages raised in the gardens were sent to Japanese troops), building tennis courts, and organizing a drive against "harmful customs."[17]

San-shih-chang-li was also active in attempting to improve its residents' Japanese language skills. With a population of 1,882 as of December 1939, it boasted no fewer than six different kinds of Japanese language institutions, as well as a day-care center for small children during busy agricultural seasons, where presumably Japanese was spoken to even the youngest members of the community. These six institutions accommodated a total of 1,059 students in a variety of Japanese language courses. There were full-year courses, one-month courses held every year in March and September, and other one-month and two-month courses. These were all for adults, but there were also two facilities for the hamlet children who did not attend common school.[18]

In addition, this hamlet carried out an ambitious "Japanese Word a Day" campaign with a special calendar which featured a new Japanese word or phrase for every day from June through March. Youngsters, divided into three groups according to their educational backgrounds, led the elders in their families in the use of new Japanese vocabulary. This cumulative language program began with "thank you" on the first day of June, progressed to "on top of the mountain" by November, and ended with "Your efforts have really been appreciated" on the last day of March.[19]

The smallest of this hamlet's language programs was the one for women. It served only sixty-one students.[20] Although increased schooling for girls and women remained a major goal of the government general, the campaigns to spread Japanese language and to reinforce common schooling in the villages appear to have been aimed mainly at the male members of the rural population. This may well have reflected, at least partially, Taiwanese leadership in the social education movement. Of San-shih-chang-li's many projects, few concerned women specifically. The leaders in this hamlet's social education movement were nearly all men.[21]

A priority among San-shih-chang-li's efforts was support for the local common school. In 1939, 235 hamlet children went to common school, but another 160 did not. By that year the hamlet could claim ninety-eight common school graduates and another 160 residents who had attended school but left before graduation.[22] For the graduates especially, who risked losing their reading and writing skills if they did not use them, the hamlet ran a small library of Japanese books. In 1940 the library's two hundred volumes included works of literature, history, biography, science, and young people's drama. It also subscribed to three newspapers: *Taiwan shimbun,* a periodical of the Taichū region, *Taiwan nichi nichi shimpō,* published in Taihoku, and the popular Taiwanese-owned and -managed *Taiwan shinminpō,* which contained both Japanese and Chinese language columns until the Chinese ones were banned in 1937.[23]

San-shih-chang-li was not the only model hamlet. And even in the many villages and hamlets which were far from model in the eyes of the authorities, some of the programs which made such places as San-shih-chang-li relatively famous were begun. Construction of a village or hamlet meetinghouse was a particularly popular project, because such a structure could be used for many other purposes than Japanese language classes or lectures by local officials. It could serve as a day nursery for young children during busy agricultural seasons and could also house wedding receptions, parties, festival celebrations, and a host of other functions.[24]

Japanese language courses for adults and children who did not go to school were also organized throughout the island. The frequency with which individuals taking such courses met varied, but typically they would come together about seven o'clock on designated evenings. The session would open with group singing in Japanese led by a teacher. Informal talks or free conversation would follow, with a teacher guiding the participants' Japanese conversation about their experiences of that day. After this, the assembly would divide into smaller classes for about two hours of instruction in Japanese language, arithmetic, singing, gymnastics, and perhaps sewing for women if any were present. Afterwards the larger group would reassemble for another song before dispersing.[25]

Youth groups for both teenaged boys and girls were set up in all the colony's provinces and districts. Overall participation of girls in such groups fell behind that of male adolescents, but here again there were many regional differences. In the sparsely settled eastern part of the island in the districts of Taitō (Taitung) and Karenkō (Hualien-kang), male and female membership in youth groups was almost equal.[26] The groups were organized primarily for young people whose formal schooling ended after elementary school; their adult leaders were generally elementary school principals or teachers, with policemen and other local officials acting as advisers. By 1936 entertainments, musical activities and sports, as well as group companionship, had attracted 23,355 boys and 9,951 girls to these organizations.[27] The primary purpose of the groups was not, however, to entertain and organize pleasant leisure time activities. Formal statements declared that their goals were to cultivate citizenship and morality, to teach the spirit of self-government, to provide vocational training opportunities, and to encourage physical education.[28] The groups put a particularly important emphasis upon maintenance of common school skills and encouraged reading Japanese newspapers, writing letters in Japanese, and using the abacus.[29]

Although the girls' groups shared the same objectives, they tended to concentrate on such domestic concerns as household management, sewing, and the health of small children. Girls studied such Japanese accomplishments as the tea ceremony, flower arrangement, and traditional singing and dancing, but their leaders also tried hard to encourage them to take an active part in community affairs officially deemed suitable for women — usually government-sponsored women's groups. In addition, girls' leaders sought to stimulate young women to seek employment outside their homes, pointing out that women working in industrial enterprises made a significant contribution to Taiwan's economy. The girls were reminded, for example, that the broad-brimmed hats woven by island women were an important export.[30]

Was common schooling, reinforced during the last fifteen years of Japanese rule by various social education schemes, able to give the rural Taiwanese a modicum of literacy and fluency in Japanese? The question is hard to answer, just as literacy and fluency are hard to measure precisely from Japanese statistics on "Japanese speaking" percentages of the Taiwanese population.[31]

Literacy, even functional literacy, is nearly always difficult to define and gauge, as Gunnar Myrdal has pointed out:

> A person may have a little ability to read and write but not enough to enable him to put his skills to practical use. In the literature, therefore, we meet with the term "functional literacy." It is extremely difficult to give definite meaning to that concept. The definition of functional literacy as the ability to read, write and reckon intelligently for one's own practical needs accords with common sense but is not specific enough to be very useful. "Arithmetical literacy" is a vital aspect of functional literacy; from the standpoint of economic development it is at least as important as "verbal literacy." Obviously, the ability not only to read and write figures with understanding but also to add, subtract, multiply and divide is of importance in all industrial work, in rationally managed agriculture, in commercial and credit transactions, and of course, in such specific development efforts as planning on the local level and building up a network of cooperatives.[32]

The prominence of arithmetic in the common school curriculum and the high quality of common school arithmetic textbooks suggests that, for many common school graduates at least, there were opportunities to gain arithmetical literacy.[33] But what about those who did not finish common school? And how great were the language and arithmetic skills of those who attended only short evening courses? Contemporary descriptions and recollections of the short courses held for adults tell one little about how well these actually taught people to read or do sums.[34] What was the general level of literacy and Japanese language skill in the countryside during the last decade of Japanese rule in Taiwan?

Opinions differed.[35] Ts'ai P'ei-huo, writing in the Japanese periodical *Kyōiku* (Education) in 1936, claimed that only about 5 percent of the island's native population spoke Japanese and that nearly all of these lived in the larger cities. In order to wipe out illiteracy among the rural masses, he made a plea for propagation of the simple Taiwanese vernacular script first transcribed by British missionaries seventy years earlier and now banned by the Japanese.[36] "When children leave common school they have few opportunities to keep up the practice of their Japanese language," he declared.[37] Another contributor to *Kyōiku* was more optimistic. Two years later in the same journal Hasuda Zenmei asserted that, at that time, 50 percent of the Taiwanese population understood the Japanese language. This he considered to be an excellent record, as little more than forty years had passed since Japan had annexed Taiwan. The goal, which he was optimistic about reaching, was to wipe out Taiwanese dialects completely, not just to add Japanese as a second language.[38]

Neither Ts'ai nor Hasuda was a completely disinterested observer. The former was a leader in the Taiwanese movement against Japan's tight hold on the island; the latter was a Japanese assimilationist who looked forward to the day when the Taiwanese would become wholly Japanese. Yet both could claim to be fairly well-informed observers. Their vastly different assessments probably exaggerated certain tendencies but they underline the great range of opinion on this subject.

With wide disagreement among contemporaries, later researchers must exercise considerable caution in attempting to ascertain the depth of literacy and the extent of the practical skills provided by the schools, adult education classes, and social betterment schemes in the countryside. Undoubtedly, as one writer complained in the early 1930s, those who needed literacy and new knowledge the most—the poorest and least efficient rural workers and their families—often had little access to them.[39] Nevertheless, in some areas some of the poorest children went to school, and in some places an atmosphere favoring retention of literacy and other skills was consciously created. Twenty-four years after the Japanese had left the island individuals could be found everywhere in the central, eastern, and southern countryside who, although claiming no more than a common school education, could still speak and sometimes even read Japanese with surprising fluency.[40]

There is no doubt, however, that the values regarding sanitation, orderliness, and cooperation taught to common school pupils and to adults and children through social education programs, penetrated rural life to a considerable degree. The Japanization of customs and habits perhaps never did reach the core of "traditional Chinese culture brought over from southeastern China" in the eighteenth and nineteenth centuries, but it did make many far from superficial changes in the lives of the people who inhabited rural Taiwan.[41]

Such changes have been recognized by Taiwanese who have had experience both under Japanese rule and under the Nationalist Chinese regime.[42] Concerning sanitation, where attitudinal change was particularly important, a rural elementary school teacher interviewed in 1969 remarked:

> Japanese colonialism was very bad. It kept the Taiwanese people down, giving nearly all the good job opportunities to the Japanese in Taiwan. It kept clever Taiwanese out of the higher schools. But one good thing it did do. It made great differences in people's health because the Japanese made people pay a great deal of attention to cleanliness. We learned this in school from the first grade. Why in the early days [of the Japanese period] there were people here who wouldn't dream of taking a bath every day. Now, not to bathe would be unthinkable.[43]

The Japanese gained and to a great extent maintained social control by working through indigenous institutions, but they often modified such institutions and employed them to initiate change. The *hokō* system became an especially important vehicle of rural change. While many of its functions had to do with maintenance of law and order, "the *hokō* system should also be given considerable credit for enabling the Japanese authorities to rid the Taiwanese of their age-old undesirable customs such as opium-smoking, foot-binding, queue-wearing, gambling and the habit of burying gold and silver coins underground as a method of saving."[44]

A great many rural islanders came into contact with the Japanese policeman, the lowest-ranking representative of governmental authority. Among other things, the police supervised the compulsory housecleanings that all Taiwanese households had to carry out. Sometimes police methods were extremely crude, but nonetheless effective. For instance, during Governor-General Sakuma's administration the police undertook several successful drives to exterminate rodents. For each Taiwanese household they set, according to the size of the house, a monthly quota of rats. Households that failed to catch and deliver their quotas were fined.[45] Force was not as obviously an ingredient in social education projects or common schools because, while policemen commanded, teachers only preached. But the message was the same in both cases and the one reinforced the other.

There is much in the attitudes of Taiwanese in the postcolonial period which suggests that even in the countryside Japanese rule left its mark. Of course in Taiwan today the results of Japanese rule are judged differently by different individuals. In 1969 a

Taiwanese man in his sixties, when asked if he thought any greater differences existed between Taiwanese and mainland Chinese than among Chinese from different parts of mainland China, replied: "We Taiwanese are Chinese all right. We are the same as other Chinese—except for one difference. Under fifty years of not-so-pleasant Japanese rule we learned to respect law and order. But that dust [the Nationalist Chinese] which blew over from the mainland after the war has no respect for one law that applies equally to everybody. They just take all they can get for themselves and their families."[46] At the other extreme was a remark made about the same time by a mainlander resident of Taiwan in his fifties: "Those stupid Taiwanese. All they learned under the Japanese was to line up in queues."[47]

Japanese Influence in the Cities and Towns

Taiwanese in the urban areas were more likely to come into contact with Japanese residents in the places in which they lived, worked, and went to school. It was in the larger towns and the cities that more of the teachers tended to be Japanese; it was there that most of the Taiwanese children who attended Japanese primary schools lived; it was there that secondary and higher schools were usually located. It was also in urban areas that one found the greatest abundance of Japanese books, periodicals, and other reading matter.

The urban common schooler was more likely to receive a thoroughly Japanese education from the first grade. His or her teacher was most likely to be either a Japanese or a Taiwanese who was very much at home in the Japanese language. Taiwanese informants who had attended city common schools frequently recalled that their Taiwanese teachers were stricter than the Japanese in requiring the use of Japanese language.[48] These individuals also reported that use of the Japanese language among Taiwanese children in city schools was fostered by the fact that many of the children originally came from different parts of the island and spoke different dialects at home. "Japanese became our language of play and friendship as well as of school," remembered one woman.[49]

Other graduates of urban common schools recollected, with some bitterness, that teachers often overtly favored those Taiwanese youngsters who were most fluent in Japanese. All reported that much stress was put upon mastering the Japanese language from the first day of the first grade. A man who had attended common school in a small town thought that Japanese language training had been efficient in his school, because Japanese teachers there had been assigned to the junior grades while their Taiwanese colleagues taught the older children, who had a firmer hold on the Japanese language.[50]

The smaller number of urban Taiwanese who attended primary schools after 1922 were exposed to even greater Japanization. Taught by Japanese teachers and outnumbered by their Japanese classmates, it is no wonder that many of them felt themselves to have been truly assimilated. Some were from the few families which had been singled out by authorities as "Japanese-speaking families" entitled to some ruling-class privileges — the better class of wartime ration tickets during the 1940s, for instance.[51]

Still, some friction did develop between children from such families and their Japanese classmates. A man from such a background recalled a fist fight he once had with a classmate: "I remember one really bad fight I had with a Japanese boy at primary school. Did I fight him! He called me a *changoro* [a derogatory Japanese term for a Chinese] and I pounded him. I was so mad. I was not mad because *changoro* was an insulting name for a Taiwanese or a Chinese to be called. I was mad because I was no *changoro*. I was every bit as Japanese as he was! Or so I thought at the time."[52] Recollections of fights between "assimilated" Taiwanese schoolboys and "unassimilated" Taiwanese youngsters were even more common. Informants in the unassimilated category asserted that they had felt little respect for "those so-called assimilated Taiwanese."[53]

Urban Taiwanese, who after common school or primary school went on to higher institutions, sometimes remembered their elementary school days as being relatively free of racial tensions. It was often when they entered middle school or another secondary institution that they first became aware of differential treatment of the two ethnic groups on the part of education authorities, or of anti-Taiwanese prejudice among their Japanese classmates. One primary school graduate remembered that during his last few months in primary school his father had surprised him with the remark that he would soon be attending Taihoku Second Middle School if he successfully passed the entrance examinations. He had inquired why he should not be sent to Taihoku First

Middle School. After all, he knew he was a top student and every-one knew that Taihoku First was the best. His father's blunt reply that Taiwanese boys went to the Second Middle School and not to the First gave him a rude shock. This was the first time in his life, he said, that he realized that he was Taiwanese and not Japa-nese.[54]

A resident of Taipei, in his middle fifties in 1969, revealed how he learned of differential treatment when he entered Taihoku Second Middle School:

> There were no Japanese pupils in my common school and the teachers treated us all alike. Japanese and Taiwanese all took the same middle school entrance examination, so naturally I thought it was fair. When I was assigned to the Second Middle School, that seemed right too. But in our middle school, although we were mostly Taiwanese, we had a small number of Japanese students. And were they stupid! I realized that they could not possibly have passed the entrance examination that brighter Taiwanese boys had failed. They had just been put in our school, the Taiwanese school, because they were not bright enough to get into the First Middle School, the Japanese school. If they had been Taiwanese I am sure they would never have been admitted.[55]

Higher up the ladder, differential treatment appeared more obvious. Informants who had been among the small number of Taiwanese who studied at Taihoku Imperial University during the 1930s reported harsh treatment from Japanese professors and sometimes from Japanese classmates too. Repeatedly they con-trasted their difficult experiences with those of fellow islanders who had been treated much better at school or university in Ja-pan.[56]

Taiwanese middle school graduates who possessed no means for study in Japan, yet failed to gain admittance to the colony's highest schools, were particularly frustrated and bitter. They deeply resented the favoritism education authorities showed toward Japanese applicants to Taiwan's highest educational insti-tutions. As one thoughtful informant remembered: "The discon-tent was not so great among industrial school and commercial school graduates who began work at about thirty-five yen a month. It was very strong among middle school graduates who, although they had high aspirations, could not go to school in Japan because their families were not rich enough to send them. They had to be satisfied with positions which paid thirty yen a month."[57]

Taiwanese living in the towns and cities were also more likely to come into frequent contact with discrimination in employment. They could see Taiwanese and Japanese performing the same tasks for different remuneration. They watched Japanese monopolizing the better paying positions even when others were as well or better qualified to fill them.[58]

On the other hand, it seems that urban Taiwanese also best appreciated some features of Japanese colonial life. Taiwanese who grew up in the towns sometimes mentioned that they had been favorably impressed by the cleanliness and orderliness of their rulers. City dwellers, Taiwanese as well as Japanese, benefited from the sewers, hospitals, and other sanitary amenities instituted by the colonial government. One Taiwanese remarked that Taipei in the late 1960s could do with some of the cooperation and public-spiritedness that had existed before the Japanese left.[59] Others noted that in those days no one needed to build high fences around their homes as protection against robbers.[60] Even the ubiquitous Japanese police, who had meddled in so many aspects of Taiwanese life,[61] were accorded some words of respect: "I saw a Japanese policeman arrest a drunken Japanese for urinating in public. With my own eyes I saw it. I was very impressed. It was not just the Taiwanese who had to pay when they broke the law. Japanese law-breakers had to pay fines too."[62]

Taiwanese Responses to Japanese Education in Perspective

The record of Japanese education in Japan's other major colony, Korea, offers a comparative focus for an assessment of Taiwanese receptivity to this aspect of colonial rule. The political and organizational approaches taken by Japan to the two colonies were in many ways similar.

Administrative structures in Taiwan and Korea were the same. Korea was also ruled by a government general headed by an executive who possessed great discretionary power, and who until 1919 was required to be a senior naval or army officer on active duty. Divisions of authority within the Korean government general were organized in much the same way as the units that made up Taiwan's central and regional administrations. Koreans were subject to laws and regulations like those imposed upon the Tai-wanese; in Korea too there existed a bandit punishment law with a death penalty and a *hokō* system.

In two ways Korea was considered to be special, but neither had much influence upon the manner in which the colony was governed. First of all, unlike Taiwan, Korea was not a prize of war but had been annexed by Japan, supposedly with the consent of the royal Korean government but actually by force. The Japa-nese tried to make it look as if Koreans had agreed to the annexa-tion and were participating in the government of the colony. As a result, more natives could be found within the ranks of govern-ment-general officials in Korea — especially during the early years — than were ever employed in Taiwan's administration, but this was purely window-dressing. Second, because the Korean penin-sula was located between Japan and her adversary, Russia, the colony was considered to be of special strategic importance. Thus Korea did not receive a civilian governor-general as soon as Tai-wan did. Yet the administrative reforms actually instituted after 1919 were at least as extensive in Korea as they were in Taiwan.[63]

Educational policies in the two colonies were almost indistin-guishable. Within both administrations "educational affairs" had a similar status and was staffed by officers assigned similar du-ties.[64] Even before Korea's annexation in 1910, Japanese "ad-visers" to the shaky Korean government were looking to Taiwan for educational models; they called in Gotō Shimpei as an educa-tional consultant as early as 1903.[65] Accommodation of native Chinese schools and overtures toward Confucian scholars oc-curred during the early days of Japanese rule in Korea, much as they had in the older colony. In Korea, as in Taiwan, Japanese educators gradually fashioned a bottom-heavy pyramid of public education which emerged as an inferior, "colonial" version of public schooling in the home islands. In both colonies schools and curricula were alike; in both a new education edict was promul-gated in 1922 to implement the post-1919 assimilation policy. In the two countries the goals of Japanese education were identical: the natives were to be transformed into loyal Japanese subjects and taught how to live in modern society.[66] Colonial school sys-tems in Korea and Taiwan had much more in common than either had with Japanese education in Manchuria, where the policy was entirely different. In Manchuria, Japanese authorities not only made no serious attempt to use the schools to assimilate or Japanize the native population, but they actually supported schooling in the Chinese language.[67]

And yet, despite the close similarity of government and educational policies in Korea and Taiwan, the results of Japanese rule and schooling in the two colonies were in many ways quite different. In both Taiwan and Korea, administrators tolerated traditional Chinese schools until their own elementary schools were well established but afterwards did their best to discourage these institutions. In Taiwan this was not a difficult policy to carry out because, as Japanese schools multiplied, Taiwanese demands for a *shobō* education decreased. Koreans, on the other hand, clung to their Chinese schools tenaciously; as late as 1940 over 4,000 of them still existed. Similarly, while in Taiwan "modern" private schools never gave government schools any serious competition, in Korea they continued to be the first choice of thousands of families who were well aware of the economic penalties attached to such a choice. In Taiwan the sports and games which were introduced along with Japanese education became extremely popular and created substantial Taiwanese good will toward their rulers. Koreans also became fond of sports but never of the Japanese as a result of them; on at least one prominent occasion Korean participation in Japanese-sponsored games provided an outlet for the strong anti-Japanese feelings of the Korean populace.

In Taiwan public education did much to reconcile the islanders to their government and the institutions it introduced. Generally, the more Japanese education a Taiwanese received, the more assimilated she or he tended to be. At the same time, it was among Japanese-trained intellectuals that an anticolonial movement against Japanese rule originated. But a large segment of this movement was extremely moderate, with leaders who worked completely within Japan's legal and governmental structures. In sharp contrast, the Japanese schools of Korea turned out class after class of anti-Japanese militants. Many of them joined graduates of native-run private schools in a long, uncompromising fight to drive the Japanese out of Korea.

The Korean Background

By the beginning of the twentieth century, three distinct branches of the education system were firmly rooted in Korea. Oldest among them were the traditional Chinese schools, long encouraged by dynastic governments and supported by the *yangban,* the Korean aristocratic class. From the mid-1880s on, these were joined by educational enterprises of Western Christian missionaries. Last on the scene was a host of "modern" secular schools, started by the Korean government and by private Korean groups and individuals in the decade after 1894.

In Yi dynasty Korea (1392-1910), Chinese schools were generally of two kinds. In each county the royal government sponsored a *hyanggyo,* a provincial school supervised by the local county administration. Much more numerous were the *sŏdang,* the private schools which could be found everywhere in the country. These were patronized by the *yangban,* and by others who desired the Chinese classical education customarily acquired by upper-class Koreans. Like the Chinese schools of Taiwan, the *sŏdang* taught written Chinese and calligraphy and introduced Korean children to ancient Chinese books and the Confucian ethics they embodied. Also, like the *shu-fang* of pre-Japanese Taiwan, individual *sŏdang* varied greatly in the standards they maintained and the resources they commanded. The Japanese classified *sŏdang (shōdo)* into the following four categories: "(1) those founded by individual *yangban* and powerful families who engaged teachers to educate their own children and those of their relatives; (2) those set up by groups of families who combined forces to provide school buildings and to secure teachers for their children; (3) those established by individual teachers who instructed children in their own homes; (4) those with no permanent school buildings that were taught by traveling teachers who held classes at various places."[68]

Although the Korean government signed a treaty of "friendship and commerce" with Japan in 1876, it was 1882 before similar pacts were made with Western powers. In that year the United States was the first Western nation to successfully negotiate such a treaty with Korea but agreements with Great Britain, Germany, Austria, Russia, Italy, and France soon followed. Under the protection of these treaties, Western missionaries, among whom Protestant Americans were most numerous, freely entered Korea. Until the end of the century the missionaries' primary emphasis was evangelical rather than educational; for instance, they did not encourage nonbelievers to attend their secondary and higher educational institutions.[69] However, the missionaries soon found that in order to convert they had to teach.[70] They also found that it was extremely difficult and perhaps not wholly desirable to limit mission education to Christian Koreans only.[71]

Like their counterparts in Taiwan, they opened numerous elementary schools offering the basics of literacy (in simple Korean) and religious training to the children of their followers.[72] Rapidly they began founding postsecondary institutions as well. In 1886 Mrs. M. F. Scranton of the American Methodists opened in Seoul the country's first secondary school for girls, with one pupil. The following year a Presbyterian missionary founded another girls' secondary school in Seoul. During 1898, 1903, and 1907 other secondary mission schools for girls were opened. From 1886 to 1908 missionaries were also busy opening secondary schools for boys.[73] These schools often taught secular as well as religious subjects. At the earliest mission secondary school for boys, established in Seoul in 1886, "Students were given lessons in Chinese characters, English, astronomy, geography, biology, mathematics, handicrafts and Bible, and they learned Western sports such as baseball, soccer, and tennis. Students were strongly admonished to keep and respect the laws of the country and to abstain from using alcoholic beverages and obscene language."[74] In 1903 the U.S. northern Presbyterian mission founded a medical college with a seven-year course in medicine and a three-year course in pharmacy. Three years later Union Christian College was organized, along the lines of a small denominational college in the United States. In 1910 Mrs. M. F. Scranton, with Methodist support, founded Ewha College for Women.[75]

As part of a series of reform measures that began in 1894 the Yi government created a new education system which embraced a number of elementary schools, middle schools, foreign language schools, vocational schools, a normal school, and a medical school.[76] Western influence in the curricula of these government schools was heavy.[77] About the same time Korean leaders began to found private schools which also taught Western-style subjects and employed the Korean *ŏnmun.* This alphabet of phonetic symbols had reportedly been invented by King Sejong in 1443 but was long held in contempt by the *yangban,* who "had not been trained in reading materials in the Korean script, the use of which had been left to women and persons of the lower classes."[78] The rapidly growing use of the *ŏnmun* did a great deal to boost literacy among the nonaristocratic classes. The *ŏnmun's* appearance in newspapers during the 1890s, especially in the influential *Tŏngnip shinmun (The independent)* of the patriotic reformer Philip Jaisohn (Sŏ Chae-p'il, 187?-1951), did much to popularize it.[79] By about 1905 a country-wide movement of "education for the nation" had sprung up. As a result of this, a large number of night schools, laborers' schools, laborers' night schools, and "short training" centers (*kōshusho*) were opened. Changes began to occur in the curricula of some *sŏdang,* and periodicals and other publications focusing on education found eager readers.[80]

Even before Korea became a protectorate of Japan in 1905, the Japanese in Korea tried to stem the tide of "education for the nation," which they believed to be against the interests of Japan. For instance, Shidehara Hiroshi (1870-1953) was sent to Seoul in 1904 as an educational councilor (*gakubu san'yo-kan*) to the Yi government, in an attempt to exert greater influence upon Korean educational developments. After the protectorate was proclaimed, Japanese supervision of Korean education tightened. The Residency General took over the most promising of the Yi government's new schools and refused authorization to any private school suspected of harboring anti-Japanese sentiment. This last was a powerful move, because now private schools had to obtain permission of the Residency General in order to continue to exist. By the end of June 1909 only 820 out of 1,995 requests from private schools for permission to operate had been granted — 778 to schools with religious connections and 42 to others.[81]

After Japan annexed Korea in 1910, the government general of the new colony showed no signs of relaxing its harsh attitude toward "education for the nation." The first governor-general of Korea, Terauchi Masatake, almost immediately made a policy speech in which he articulated Japanese fears that private education in Korea nurtured a national consciousness, which encouraged Koreans to strive for independence from Japan.

> Among the private schools, there are schools that teach songs and use other materials which encourage independence and incite rebellion against the Japanese empire. This is forbidden, and utmost care must be exercised to ensure that the prohibition of these [activities] is enforced. Koreans themselves should deeply reflect upon the consequences of fostering this kind of thought. For instance, the cry for independence will eventually lead Koreans to rebel against Japan. Will this promote the happiness of Koreans? Japan will just suppress such rebellion with force. This will not hurt Japan; only Koreans will suffer.[82]

Koreans in all walks of life deeply resented the Japanese takeover, and Korean-run private schools returned the government general's hostility in kind. The authorities found "the number of private schools with 'Independence to Great Korea' and 'Restoration of the State' printed upon posters or written on their school walls to be countless" and "all these schools to be teaching nationalistic philosophy, language, and economics."[83] The colonial government hastened to close the doors of such institutions and to initiate instead a system of Japanese schools, particularly elementary schools, which emphasized Japanese language and ethics and preparation for vocational and technical training.

Christian schools, some of the most important of which were directly operated by foreign missionaries, were generally treated with more leniency.[84] At first this was partly because at the time of the annexation missionaries were still protected by remnants of the unequal treaties which Korea and Japan had signed with Western nations. The Japanese did not wish to offend powerful Western governments.[85] Nevertheless there was also genuine respect for some of the content that the Christian schools taught. Japanese authorities freely acknowledged that Western missionaries had been the pioneers of modern, scientific education in Korea.[86] They also praised the missionaries for their pedagogical efforts on behalf of girls and women, who in traditional Korea had neither been sent to school nor encouraged to become scholars.[87]

On the other hand, Christian educators were by no means considered above suspicion. Terauchi complained that missionaries, who had been given a free hand in the past, were inclined to mix religion and politics.[88] After the private school regulations were promulgated in 1908, government-general officials were irritated when a large number of mission schools continued operations without receiving the required authorization.[89] Mission schools were soon subjected to the same stringent controls and strict surveillance that other private schools experienced. They too had to meet Japanese standards which demanded that teachers who had completed Japanese teacher training courses be employed and that Japanese subjects—especially the Japanese language—be taught. And, in the face of energetic protests from the missionaries, five years after annexation came an ordinance forbidding (after a ten-year period of grace) the use of school buildings or classroom hours for religious instruction. Rigorously applying the private school regulations, the government general during the first four years of its existence reduced the number of schools run by missionaries from 746 to 473.[90] Missionaries urged their native followers to obey the laws and the government that ruled them, but clearly the cause of the Christians was not the cause of the Japanese state.[91] The colonial government was especially suspicious of Korean Christians.[92]

By contrast, early government-general policy toward the *sŏdang* was friendly. Although half-hearted attempts were made to persuade those who ran them to add the Japanese language to the subjects taught, regulations governing these schools were not issued until 1918 and serious controls were not put on them before 1929.[93] In part this tolerance was a function of an official policy of reconciliation and respect toward Confucian learning and scholars, but there was a very practical reason for it too. As Izawa Shūji had hoped to do with the Chinese traditional schools of Taiwan, the Korean government general employed the *sŏdang* as makeshift substitutes for the public schools that could not be opened everywhere at once. In regions where government schooling did not yet exist or was inadequate the authorities actually encouraged *sŏdang* education.[94] Certainly these institutions thrived. Korean government-general records report that *sŏdang* numbers rose from 16,540 in 1911 to 23,441 in 1915 and only began to decline after 1920.[95]

As in Taiwan, the Korean government general energetically established public education facilities, although there were some important differences between government schools in the two colonies. The colonial government in Korea developed a network of elementary schools which emphasized the Japanese language, Japanese morality, Japanese customs, and practical, vocational studies. At the postprimary level the government encouraged vocational training rather than academic education. However, until 1922 the elementary schools in Korea offered a four-year course instead of a six-year one as in Taiwan. (In 1922 the Korean elementary school course was lengthened by two years.) And although Taiwan's public schools for Taiwanese taught no vernacular native languages, Korean language as well as written Chinese was taught from the first grade of these elementary schools.[96] Even under the educational revisions of 1938 on behalf of the heavy-handed Japanization of the time, Korean language study, although changed from a compulsory to an elective subject, could—at least in theory—still be offered in some government schools.[97]

In spite of the fact that the Korean language was taught in public schools and that the colonial government took a repressive stance in regard to private education, Koreans appear to have been much more reluctant to send their children to Japanese schools than were Taiwanese. In the early days the authorities had to resort to extreme measures in order to get any Koreans to send their youngsters to school. It was commonplace enough for public schools to entice Korean pupils by providing them with textbooks, school supplies, and lunches free of charge, or to send the *myŏn* (district) chief and the police to "persuade" families to send their children to school. But sometimes officials went so far as to hold parents in detention and release them only on the condition that their children attend school.[98]

As the years passed, some of this hostility toward Japanese schools faded, yet throughout the colonial period Koreans consistently showed a marked preference for private schools run by their compatriots (or in some cases operated by foreign missionaries) and for the traditional *sŏdang*. As the Korean demand for education increased it was in large part a demand for private schooling. Thus, private schools that survived the first few years after annexation flourished, and new ones were opened later. In striking contrast to Taiwan, a rapid expansion of private secondary education occurred late in the period.[99] Private *senmon gakkō*, not all of which had their origins in preannexation Korea, also played an important role.[100] In 1942 there were 3,118 Korean students enrolled in private *senmon gakkō* compared to 580 Korean students in governmental *senmon gakkō*.[101] In Taiwan, of course, there were no private *senmon gakkō*.

Life was not always easy for individuals who operated, taught in, or attended Korean private schools, but the demand for what these schools offered was always strong. Missionaries claimed that government pressures jeopardized continuance of Christian schools because the latter lacked funds to meet government standards for buildings and equipment. They complained that they could not meet the demands of their students for the fashionable athletic uniforms or school excursions enjoyed by the students in public schools. They pointed out that the graduates of their schools were systematically excluded from higher educational institutions and were permitted few opportunities for attractive employment. They found the government's curriculum requirements —that Japanese language, history, and ethics be taught and religious instruction not be given—particularly onerous.[102] Non-Christian private schools experienced similar difficulties but in spite of being forced to adapt to government requirements they too continued to draw students.[103] (The situation improved somewhat for private educators after the anti-Japanese rebellion of March 1919 when Governor-General Saito Makoto relaxed the prohibition against religious instruction, among other educational reforms.)[104]

Sŏdang also held their own. Although after the first decade of Japanese rule the authorities no longer felt it necessary to encourage *sŏdang* education and tightened control of them, they continued to educate large numbers. In 1930, although they had been in a decline for almost a decade, there remained more than 10,000 of these traditional Chinese schools in Korea. Ten years later, the year Taiwan's last seventeen or eighteen Chinese schools were closed, the Korean government-general statistical yearbook reported that as of the end of March 1940, there were 158,320 *sŏdang* students in Korea.[105]

When public elementary schools became firmly established in Taiwan, the *shobō* were forced to teach Japanese, ethics, and arithmetic in the same manner as the common schools did. But they did not adopt the common school's popular music exercises nor the much-appreciated physical education. Thus, although they were forced to become much like the common schools, they did not possess the latter's most alluring programs. Probably this was an important reason for the sharp decline in their popularity once the Japanese schools were numerous. A man in eastern Taiwan who had been a student in a *shobō* during the late 1910s recalled his experience there with repugnance. "Those places were most unhealthy. The teacher had long, long fingernails and the children got no exercise at all. My parents eventually took me out of there, thank goodness. We had no exercise, no sports at all. It was no fun."[106]

By the late 1910s sports and games, which had been introduced along with Japanese education, had won fairly wide acceptance among Taiwanese who at first had been suspicious of these alien rituals. When the parents of the first Taiwanese students to attend the Japanese Language School at the beginning of the period saw their children performing gymnastic exercises they were horrified. They were sure their offspring were being trained to serve as soldiers.[107] Public school sports soon altered this perception. At first mainly the medical school and other higher institutions but eventually common schools too held sports meets, participated in competitive league games, put on physical culture displays, and in various other ways did a great deal to familiarize the Taiwanese public with athletics.[108]

Girls and boys played on school teams, soon acquainting their parents and older relatives with a wide range of athletic activities. Students of both sexes enthusiastically took part in track and field exercises and swimming meets and played lawn tennis, basketball, and volleyball. Boys alone played rugby, soccer, hockey, and baseball.[109]

The genuine pleasure that school children took in both playing and watching games was soon communicated to the larger Taiwanese community. Beginning in 1912 Taiwanese adults began to organize local athletic meets.[110] In the countryside eventually whole hamlets would turn out for radio calisthenics. Baseball became especially popular. It was played all over the island. A variety of adult leagues were organized as well as those for young boys and their teenaged brothers. Visits to Taiwan by first-rate Japanese teams — islanders saw the Waseda University team play in 1916 — were enthusiastically welcomed by Taiwanese and helped boost the game's already extraordinary popularity.[111]

In Korea the response to Japanese initiative in the realm of sport was much cooler. Games were popular in Korea, but, perhaps because mission schools had sponsored them before the country became a colony of Japan, in the minds of Koreans athletics do not seem to have been closely linked with Japanese schools. Missionaries felt that the public connected them with mission schools. "Baseball, tennis, football, hockey, skating, and various forms of track athletics were, for the most part, introduced by missionaries and are associated with mission schools, although at present they are engaged in by all schools and by town and village clubs. Match games, and tournaments where mission schools participate, draw the attention of the general public to the activities of mission schools, and extend the influence of these schools further among the people."[112] Koreans rejoiced in the summer of 1936 when two of their compatriots won first and third places in the marathon of the eleventh Olympic Games. Yet although the two heroes were members of the Japanese Olympic team, the jubilant celebration of their victory by the Korean public and newspapers had strong anti-Japanese overtones.

The *shobō* of Taiwan were not the only traditional Chinese schools that discovered that athletics could be subversive. As a student of the education revolution in early twentieth-century China has pointed out, in China physical education helped Western studies usurp the position once held by classical scholarship and its values: "As expressed in the motto: 'The body, hair, and skin are received from parents, none should dare to injure or ruin them,' such filial piety is being violated by participation in sports and games."[113] Yet in spite of the popularity of school athletics as well as the requirement that *sŏdang* teach the Japanese language and Japanese ethics, significant numbers of Koreans clung to these schools.

Despite this loyalty on the part of Koreans and their preference for modern-style private schools run by fellow natives, Japanese schooling dominated the colony's educational world, as it did in Taiwan. Government-general schools set standards and provided (compulsory) models; often they were the best outfitted. After the early difficult years many Koreans accepted them as necessary paths to occupational opportunities and material rewards. After the collapse of the 1919 independence uprising there was a phenomenal increase in the Korean desire to attend them and of government efforts to provide them. "Between 1919 and 1925, the student enrollment in common schools [elementary schools for Koreans] was more than quadrupled and the rate of school attendance in the age group of 7-14 was more than doubled."[114]

Acceptance of the schools, however, did not necessarily mean acceptance of Japanese culture or values. On the contrary, some of the most knowledgeable scholarship on the Japanese period in Korea has clearly shown that the public schools, which aimed to assimilate the native population, in actuality played a crucial role in the formation of modern Korean nationalism with its heavy anti-Japanese content.[115]

Male and female students from public schools as well as private schools played a conspicuous part in the 1919 uprising.[116]

> In the early stages of the movement, only the students of middle-school level and higher were involved, but pupils in elementary schools participated later. Japanese government statistics indicate that out of 1,251 schools in Korea, including elementary schools, 203 schools took part in the movement; out of a student population of 133,557 there were 11,113 who took part, mostly from the middle schools and above. Immediately after the movement began, most schools closed for several weeks. Those in Seoul were

not reopened until June. [The movement began on March first.] The school closings, caused either by student or teacher strikes, contributed to what might be called, from the Japanese viewpoint, a subversive atmosphere.[117]

The students' anti-Japanese activity did not end when the 1919 rebellion was crushed. During their summer vacation students traveled throughout rural Korea giving lectures—often highly nationalistic ones—and courses aimed at reducing illiteracy.[118] Student strikes also occurred from time to time in public schools. Such strikes reached a peak in late 1929 and early 1930 when an incident between Korean and Japanese students in Kwangju set off a rash of strikes all over Korea.

> On Nov. 3, 1929, the birthday of former Japanese emperor Meiji, fisticuffs were exchanged between Korean and Japanese students in Kwangju. In a show of apparent favoritism for the Japanese students, the police punished the Korean students alone. All Korean students in the city rose up in a mass demonstration and the police arrested the representatives of the demonstrators. This police action touched off waves of student demonstrations across the country. Angry students left their books, paraded through the streets and scattered leaflets denouncing the inhuman nature of Japanese imperialism.[119]

About 54,000 students from 194 schools (including private and public institutions) eventually took part in these strikes, and the main thrust of their protest was against the attitude of superiority shown by Japanese students and teachers.[120]

The colonial government recognized that it was extremely difficult for educators to separate Koreans from their traditional culture and learning, and that Korean ethnic pride was continually being wounded by Japanese actions. Thus they reluctantly allowed Korean language classes to remain a substantive part of elementary school studies until 1938. And as part of the reforms which took place after the 1919 revolt, Korean history and geography were added to the curriculum of public elementary schools. According to the *Japan Year Book 1943-1944* this was done "out of respect for Chosenese [Korean] sentiment," but of course these subjects were taught from a Japanese imperialist point of view.[121] Such attempts to make concessions to Korean sentiment appear to have been in vain. In *The Politics of Korean Nationalism*

Chong-sik Lee came to the conclusion that by 1919 "the strenuous effort to Japanize Korea through education had brought about its countereffect."[122] By the end of the colonial period, the Japanese-educated Taiwanese of the island's native middle and upper classes had absorbed a whole spectrum of Japanese tastes and attitudes. In Korea these same classes were seething with militant nationalism; 1919 had taught them costly lessons about the futility of open rebellion but defiance was far from dead. The psychological gap between ruler and ruled was enormous.

The Contrast between Korean and Taiwanese Responses

Why did Japanese education evoke such different results in Taiwan and Korea? Like all questions that deal overtly or subtly with "national character," this cannot be answered easily. Certainly factors other than the educational also helped elicit the intense anti-Japanese response of the Koreans.

In 1895 Japan acquired an outpost of the Ch'ing empire, populated largely by Chinese who were there because they, their parents, grandparents, or other immediate ancestors had found it difficult to scratch out a living on the mainland. When Taiwan was ceded in Japan or shortly afterwards, Ch'ing officials and most of the higher gentry, classes one would expect to be most deeply committed politically and culturally to China, left the island and returned to China.[123] Since the Japanese government provided a two-year period of grace during which the Chinese of Taiwan were to decide to become Japanese subjects or to leave for China, members of the gentry who stayed behind more or less chose to do so.

In annexing Korea, Japan acquired an entire country with its own proud imperial traditions and ancient civilization. The capital which governed Yi dynasty Korea was Seoul, located in the heart of the country which the Japanese so conspicuously occupied, and not some faraway city like Peking. Koreans who objected to their new rulers could not leave for a life under the old regime somewhere else. The upper classes with their political and cultural attachments as well as the lower classes were forced to stay. The Korean royal family also remained in the country. Although it was now a captive of the Japanese it kept alive memories of the days when Koreans ruled Koreans, and provided a rallying point for countrywide challenges to the government general.

In neither traditional Chinese society nor frontier Taiwan was heredity the single most important determinant of a family's status and power. And throughout Chinese history foreign invaders had conquered China and established themselves as a ruling class apart from the Chinese; indeed, Ch'ing rule had begun this way. Thus, the shifts in influence and wealth within the Taiwanese community that occurred after the Japanese arrived probably came as a great shock to few members of that community. Legally and socially treating all Taiwanese as one class and all Japanese as another was not a totally unfamiliar concept either. In addition, many well-to-do Taiwanese were merchants who could appreciate the Japanese interest in commerce and trade. But Yi dynasty Korea was a highly stratified world in which each individual's status was largely decided by birth. The privileged position of the *yangban,* whose only profession was government employment, was a function of traditional class distinctions. Thus, when the Japanese espoused equality among all Koreans they made enemies of the entire aristocratic class.[124]

Before Japanese rule in Korea, the kernels of a modern nationalist movement already existed, thanks to Western-educated reformers like Philip Jaisohn. From the 1890s on many new schools established by Koreans and missionaries showed Koreans that Japanese education was not the only possible road to modernization. The presence of a large number of Christian missionaries prevented the Japanese from being the only visible foreign contingent in the country. Koreans were able to make comparisons between the behavior of the two.

Geography was also against the Japanese in Korea. The country was six times as large as Taiwan and communications were primitive. Throughout the peninsula there were many isolated communities. To secure Japanese authority and establish schools in all parts of Korea was a much more difficult and time-consuming task than in Taiwan.

Policies which in the abstract were identical turned out to be anything but similar in the two settings. For instance, in Taiwan Japanese overtures toward Chinese scholarship and esthetics displayed a great deal of respect for the high culture of so many of the islanders' ancestors. After the victories of the Sino-Japanese War, Japanese awe of Chinese civilization diminished somewhat, but in Japan China continued to be recognized culturally as the cradle of East Asian civilizations, including Japan's own.[125] In Korea, protection and patronage offered to Confucian scholars and Chinese schools were recognized as gestures toward a respected but certainly not indigenous culture. The Japanese looked down upon Korean culture; the Koreans knew and resented it.

The Japanese command that the subject people give their allegiance to the Japanese emperor was probably easier for Taiwanese to bear than Koreans. The notion of a mandate of heaven which throughout China's history had been passed from one ruling dynasty to another—even to invading foreigners—was not an unfamiliar concept to the Chinese of Taiwan.[126] In any case, the Ch'ing emperor still ruled over continental China, and it was not impossible for Taiwanese to take up residence within his domains. In Korea the continued presence of the dethroned royal house served to remind natives of their older loyalty. To Korean eyes, Japanese treatment of Korea's royal family was at once contemptuous and treacherous.

Because of differences in size, climate, natural resources, and proximity to Japan, economic development in the two colonies was not the same. In both countries the bulk of the population was farmers. In Taiwan, land policies and agricultural technology brought a good deal of prosperity to the rural elite and some material benefits to the rest of the agrarian community. In any case, Japanese rule did not worsen the lot of any conspicuous segment of the rural population.[127] Almost the entire Korean farming population—and most Koreans were farmers—suffered enormously from the land registration policies and the switch, which came after annexation, from a barter-based to a monetary-based economy. To make matters worse, as Koreans lost land held for centuries, Japanese immigrants to Korea—more numerous than to Taiwan—acquired more and more land.[128] "Although a small number of Koreans did become rich landowners, the rise of Japanese landlords was more obvious. It was natural for the generally poverty-stricken Korean farmers to blame much of their misery upon the newcomers, practically all of whom were prosperous, or seemed to be so."[129]

By many other indices, agricultural and industrial policies brought more benefit to Taiwanese than to Koreans. Korean rice was in greater demand in Japan than was Taiwanese; hence, even after 1929, when rice consumption was steadily decreasing in both colonies, Taiwanese ate twice as much as Koreans.[130] Many more Taiwanese homes were furnished with electricity. In 1937, 36.3 percent of Taiwanese families enjoyed electric lighting compared to 11.9 percent of Korean families; yet in this same year Korean production of hydroelectricity almost tripled Taiwanese production.[131] Wage differentials between Japanese and natives performing the same jobs differed in the two colonies too: they were much greater in Korea than in Taiwan.[132] Workers in Taiwan, regardless of their ethnic group, tended to receive higher wages than their counterparts in Korea.[133] And in Taiwan the percentage of people employed was more than twice as high as it was in Korea.[134] Furthermore, in Korea Japanese workers represented a larger percentage of the employed than they did in Taiwan.[135]

Perhaps because the option of return to China existed at the beginning of the colonial period, Japanese government of Taiwan was never seriously opposed by patriotic attachments to the old regime. And although the Taiwanese remained a subject people at the base of the island's society, Japanese rule brought them peace and stability, and made some of them wealthier and most of them healthier than they had ever been before. As Taiwanese awareness of their disadvantageous position and self-confidence in relation to their rulers matured over the years, articulate Taiwanese voices demanded a larger slice of the unevenly divided colonial pie, rather than destruction of the pie itself. Japanese education was one obvious way to obtain a larger slice. Indeed, medical training repeatedly had meant a rags-to-riches story for some lucky islanders. Although resentment against educational discrimination and obstacles to advanced training was strong, Japanese education, especially higher education, tended to draw its Taiwanese recipients closer to the nation that ruled them.

Perhaps in Korea national consciousness was more advanced at the beginning of the colonial period. At any rate, many factors militated against the development of good will toward the colonial government: Japanese alienation of the *yangban* class as well as of the agrarian masses; what Koreans perceived to be shabby treatment of the royal family by the Japanese; Japanese lack of respect for Korean culture; and the presence of other foreigners who represented an alternative model for modern development. Koreans eventually sent their children to Japanese public schools in order to reap employment opportunities, but the material rewards of collaboration appear to have been less generous and less widely available than in Taiwan. Koreans in Japanese schools had less to look forward to materially, while at the same time they had before them the example of more "patriotic" peers who attended schools managed by Koreans or missionaries. It is no wonder that the Japanization message of the colonial schools "brought about its countereffect" upon students in such an ambivalent situation.

Similar colonial education policies, then, do not necessarily produce similar results. Whatever else may be stated about Taiwanese responses to Japanese education, they were certainly more positive than those of the Koreans.

8/ Japanese Education, Taiwanese Intellectuals, and Political Activism

By the 1920s Taiwanese upper- and middle-class demands for higher education were highly visible. These demands were too large to be satisfied by the colony's advanced educational institutions, which after Den's rescript tended to be monopolized by the Japanese population. In spite of their reluctance to permit the creation of a highly educated native elite, government-general officials knew these demands had to be at least partially met if widespread alienation among the most affluent and articulate native classes was to be avoided. As a safety valve, from 1920 on administrators slackened their customary efforts to restrict the number of Taiwanese going to Japan to study.

As a result, higher schools, colleges, and universities in Japan joined the colony's facilities in producing hundreds and then thousands of Japanese-trained Taiwanese intellectuals. These men and women were fluent in the Japanese language, familiar with Japanese culture, at home in Japanese social settings, and well versed in the laws and institutions that governed the ruling country as well as those under which Taiwan was ruled.[1] It was here at the top of the educational pyramid that the assimilation policy seems to have been most successful. Taiwanese physicians, lawyers, clerks, journalists, and urban school teachers appeared much closer to their Japanese rulers in lifestyle and attitude than they did to the poor Taiwanese peasants of rural villages.

Indeed, the evidence suggests that assimilation of the Japanese-educated Taiwanese was far from superficial. Ō Ikutoku, a scholar of Taiwanese history, not likely to overlook distinctive Taiwanese characteristics,[2] has concluded that thousands of Taiwanese who received postsecondary training in Taiwan or in the home islands "entered the ranks of Japanese [intellectuals], becoming almost indistinguishable from them."[3] Ō has also pointed out that during the Pacific War, people in China, Manchuria,

177

and the South Seas could not distinguish Taiwanese from Japanese.[4]

However, assimilation was not the only hallmark of the Japanese-trained intellectual. Like colonial rulers elsewhere, authorities on the island found that native intellectuals educated in their rulers' mold became organizers of anticolonial movements against the Japanese. By the 1920s this tendency had become quite apparent. How much, then, did Japanese education help Taiwanese intellectuals realize their differences from the Japanese? Did their educational experiences help them rediscover their Chinese origins? How much of the Japanese educational package did Taiwanese political activists ultimately accept? Certainly they rejected the disadvantaged position of colonials within the Japanese imperial framework. But how much of the framework itself did they reject? Even tentative, exploratory answers may help elucidate the ways in which Japanese education influenced islanders who actively opposed the colonial government and also the larger number of Taiwanese intellectuals who emerged during the last half of the colony's history.

Taiwanese Students in Japan Turn toward Politics

By 1920 steadily increasing numbers of young colonials were finding Tokyo and other major Japanese cities alive with social, cultural, and political ideas. Democracy, liberalism, and socialism — home-grown or imported — were gaining ground in Japan. Woodrow Wilson's concept of self-determination for nations and peoples was very much in the air. At Tokyo Imperial University the distinguished legal scholar, Minobe Tatsukichi (1873-1948), was expounding his "organ theory" of the Japanese constitution; Yoshino Sakuzō (1878-1933), another professor of law at Tokyo Imperial, was campaigning in favor of *minponshugi,* a brand of democracy he and others claimed was particularly fitting for Japan's institutions.[5] The problem of the poor and the working classes had also caught the interest of intellectuals. In 1916 *Bimbō monogatari* (Tales of the poor) caused a stir when it appeared in serialized form in the *Ōsaka asahi shimbun.* Its author, Kawakami Hajime (1879-1946), one of the most original figures in the history of Japanese Marxism, was drawing students to his economics lectures at Kyoto Imperial University.[6] Since late 1917, when the first student-worker society (the Rogakkai) had been founded, university students in Kyoto and Tokyo had been entering the Japanese labor movement.

Taiwanese students in Japan imbibed the exciting new atmosphere not only through the books and articles they read, their contact with Japanese students, and the lectures they heard. Many of them "also came into close contact with scholars and thinkers of the liberal school."[7] Meanwhile, other young Taiwanese were getting to know Japanese leftists. Some absorbed socialist ideas at meetings organized by such groups as Tokyo University's Shinjinkai (New Man's Society), a student activist group formed in 1918.[8] Others became involved with off-campus radicals.[9]

Taiwanese in Japan also met patriotic Chinese and Korean students and began learning about the dramatic events that had recently taken place in these countries. The struggles of Chinese nationalists, particularly the student-led May Fourth Movement of 1919, had aroused sympathies in Japan's liberal and leftist academic circles.[10] Another tumultuous upheaval during 1919, the March First Independence Movement in Korea and its brutal suppression, had also moved Japanese liberals and social reformers.

The Taiwanese students were as moved by the Korean independence movement as they were by developments in China.[11] They were

inspired by the heroic demonstration of the Koreans and were prompted to compare and contrast their native land with Korea . . . In terms of financial capacity, according to these Taiwanese, Taiwan had been independent of Japan's treasury since 1904 while Korea was still dependent on Japan's financial subsidies for its governmental expenditures, and the scale of enterprises in Taiwan and the wealth of its residents excelled those of Korea. The Taiwanese intellectuals of the time also believed that the Taiwanese educational level was superior to the Koreans because primary education was much more widespread in Taiwan than in Korea . . . Taiwanese intellectuals had little difficulty pointing out, among other things, that the Taiwan governor-general, when served by a military man, could also command the Japanese garrison on the island while his counterpart in Korea was not allowed to have the same authority over the Japanese forces in Korea; that the Japanese colonial authorities employed a greater percentage of Koreans in the administration of Korea than of Taiwanese in the governing of Taiwan; that, unlike Korea, which had several daily newspapers in Korean, Taiwan had no newspaper in the Taiwanese languages.[12]

The largest concentration of Taiwanese in Japan was in Tokyo with its many schools, colleges, and universities. And it was the Taiwanese students in the Tokyo area who came in closest contact with new political and intellectual influences. Like other students from other colonies in other capitals, it was in the metropolitan center that young Taiwanese became conscious of problems at home. The Taiwanese student dormitory in Tokyo had been built because the government general thought that such a facility would aid supervision and control of the young colonials. Ironically, it became a place where Taiwanese from different parts of the island came together to share increasingly critical ideas.[13]

By 1920 Taiwanese studying in the capital region had been meeting regularly for some years. Originally the meetings had been for social purposes, but gradually, for the more politically conscious at least, discussions of the wrongs of Taiwan had become more frequent. Out of these discussions emerged two distinct streams of political activism, which—at least in relation to each other—can be described as being conservative and radical.[14]

The Conservative Activists: Political Action

In 1920 leaders of what was to become the conservative stream organized the beginnings of a persistent opposition to the colonial authorities. This did not end until 1936, when legal antigovernmental agitation became impossible. The key figure in the 1920 move was Lin Hsien-t'ang, the wealthy Taichū businessman who for many years had been searching for ways to initiate political reform in Taiwan.[15] With support from Lin, the Taiwanese in Tokyo who had been meeting for political discussions formed early in 1920 the first Taiwanese political organization, the New People's Society (Shinminkai).[16] "It is not clear how many Taiwanese joined the society. A Japanese police record, however, estimated that the New People's Society had more than one hundred members and gave the names of fifty-seven of the more prominent ones. All of the fifty-seven individuals listed, with the exception of probably three or four (including Lin Hsien-t'ang), were students or graduates of colleges and universities in Tokyo. They accounted for about 10% of the total number of Taiwanese students and graduates of colleges and universities in the Japanese capital at the time."[17] There was a fairly wide range of opinion among the society's members, but they all agreed that the situation in Taiwan demanded reform.[18]

The New People's Society was soon organizing against renewal of controversial Law No. 63, which was due in 1920 to be either repealed or extended by the Diet. Since its enactment in 1896, Law No. 63 had given the governor-general of Taiwan broad lawmaking powers within the colony. However, the law's duration was limited; first it was in effect for three years, and later this was extended to five. Consequently, governors-general were forced to go before the Diet periodically to defend their claims that their extraordinary discretionary power—which critics declared to be a violation of the constitution—was still necessary.[19] The New People's Society was anxious to see the law repealed.

There were several reasons why the Society favored such a position. First, it was assumed that the abolition of the law would terminate numerous harsh and discriminatory regulations which the governor-general had long relied upon to intimidate the Formosans. Most of all they feared and despised such regulations as the Bandit Punishment Ordinance, which made the death penalty mandatory for any two persons who acted as a group to commit violence, and the *Hō Kō* (or *Pao Chia* in Chinese) Ordinance, which held the entire community responsible for a crime committed by any one of its members. This ordinance, it was clearly stipulated, was not applicable to Japanese residents. Second, the repeal of the law would mean the extension of Japanese laws to the island, with the result that the governor-general would be made more accountable to the Imperial Diet vis-à-vis the Japanese public which was far more responsive to Formosan complaints than the Japanese residents of the island. Lastly, some members of the Society cherished the notion that the abolition of the controversial law would eventually open the way toward electing Formosan representatives to the Diet.[20]

In essence, what society members opposed when they campaigned against Law No. 63 was a legal and governmental system which denied Taiwanese equal treatment with Japanese. By implication, their demand was that they be treated as Japanese. This position surfaced early among the conservatives. It closely resembled the stand Itagaki Taisuke's assimilation movement had taken in 1914, and it was an argument with which Taiwanese intellectuals were familiar. Lin Hsien-t'ang's active role in the 1914 movement was fresh in their minds.

Not surprisingly, this argument found a great deal of sympathy among some Japanese in the home islands. Many felt it was but a call for simple justice. The Taiwanese activists were quick to see possibilities in the responsive chord they had struck, first in the campaign against Law No. 63 and later on behalf of other endeavors. They aimed eloquent and logical arguments at the Japanese politicians and intellectuals they sensed might be won to their cause.

Soon after 1920 the dominant conservative-activist position shifted to advocacy of home rule and the special needs of the Taiwanese people. However, the complaint that Taiwanese were not being treated as full-fledged Japanese continued to be aimed at Japanese audiences long after "equal treatment" and "genuine assimilation" had ceased to satisfy all but the meekest of Taiwanese activists.

An excellent example of use of the earlier demand for extending Japanese law to Taiwan to argue the case of the later stand, home rule, can be seen in a 1928 book written by Lin Hsient'ang's protégé, Ts'ai P'ei-huo. As suggested by the title, *To the Homeland Japanese* (*Nihon honkokumin ni atō*), Ts'ai had already given up on the Japanese in the colony, but still held some hope that the Japanese in Japan would listen to his plea.[21] By 1928 Ts'ai, whose credentials as a would-be politician reformer dated back to the 1914 movement, had publicly become a champion of home rule and Taiwanese society's unique requirements. *To the Homeland Japanese* argues passionately on behalf of both. Yet throughout the book are constant reminders that Taiwanese in the colony are never accorded the rights of Japanese. Readers are repeatedly told that in spite of the assimilation policy Japanese and Taiwanese are not treated as "subjects equal in the eyes of the emperor."

Ts'ai naturally felt a need to educate Japanese about conditions in Taiwan, concerning which — as Yanaihara Tadao pointed out in the preface — they were abysmally ignorant.[22] Ts'ai may also have felt that a thorough exposure of the failure of the assimilation policy strengthened the case for home rule; if assimilation could not bring justice to the Taiwanese, surely home rule could. But so frequently and so stoutly did Ts'ai denounce the treatment of the native islanders that a reader might reasonably conclude that what Ts'ai really wanted for his compatriots was equal rights and equal justice, and that home rule was only sought out of a despair born of the failure to achieve an integrated solution. The author did insist that a local legislature and encouragement of native languages and culture were necessary. But the ringing rhetoric of the passages which denounced Japanese discrimination against the Taiwanese were as stirring as the ones that argued for separate development under the imperial umbrella.[23]

In Ts'ai's view, the mentality embodied in Gotō Shimpei's theory of gradual assimilation was just an excuse to continue to deny equal treatment of the Taiwanese.[24] "The majority of the 180,000 Japanese in Taiwan treat us Taiwanese as incompetents, as second-class citizens," was the complaint in *To the Homeland Japanese*.[25] "Is assimilation just another name for exploitation? If the authorities really believed in assimilation would they have been so keen to prevent us from sending our children to be educated in Japan? . . . [If the authorities really believed in assimilation] would they not have instituted compulsory education? . . . Clearly all the higher educational facilities—like Taihoku Medical College and Tainan Commercial College—are for the children of the Japanese."[26]

The book challenged the notion that the Japanese were a unique people into whom assimilation could not be easily accomplished. Ts'ai mocked a popular Japanese claim that their "3,000 year history"[27] entitled them to preferential treatment. Japanese assertions that they had displayed loyalty to an unbroken line of emperors for 3,000 years while the Taiwanese had known a much shorter time to cultivate this loyalty were sheer nonsense, wrote Ts'ai. He pointed out that the "unique" loyalty of the Japanese people to their emperor was a phenomenon which appeared only after the opening of Japan to foreign intercourse in the middle of the nineteenth century. Far from having any unique national character to be so proud of, the Japanese were a very ordinary people, and there was no reason why the Taiwanese should not be granted immediate equality with them.[28] After all, *To the Homeland Japanese* maintained, "We [Taiwanese] have shown every bit as much loyalty as Japanese have. Every year we contribute more than 1,000,000 yen to the central government treasury. What is all this about [our needing] to cultivate citizenship?"[29]

How much was this exposure of the hollow assimilation policy intended to politicize Taiwanese and to catch the consciences of sympathetic Japanese? How much did it stem from a pragmatism which reasoned that, while local self-government was most desirable, imperfect reforms that made good the promises of assimilation were better than no reforms at all? At any rate, through the 1920s and even later, conservative activists like Ts'ai P'ei-huo continued to call upon the government general and the people of Japan to fulfill the promises of the assimilation policy.

They demanded that de facto as well as de jure restrictions upon Taiwanese participation in political, social, and economic life be removed. They sought many reforms: abolition of the *hokō* system of mutual responsibility and forced labor; access to higher positions in the colonial administration; relaxation of Japanese control of the island's economic enterprises; abolition of Japanese control of the mass media; institution of compulsory education; and an end to Japanese monopolization of higher school facilities. All these they declared were rights due the Taiwanese as loyal subjects of the Japanese emperor.[30]

Activists accused government-general officials of not listening to Taiwanese opinion. They pointed out that, although new leaders had emerged among the Taiwanese middle and upper classes, the authorities continued to consult only those few prominent Taiwanese families who had collaborated with the Japanese in the first days of Japanese rule. Governors-general changed, administrators came and went, but Taiwanese advisers remained the same. When such advisers aged or died their sons or younger brothers replaced them. Consequently, the rulers of Taiwan were quite out of touch with Taiwanese public opinion.[31]

Grievances concerning the education system were legion. Government-general officials rejected Taiwanese demands for compulsory education on the grounds that this would cost too much. But were not Taiwanese paying for Japanese educational privileges while their own children were being neglected? Did not the money spent upon primary schools and denied to common schools come from Taiwanese pockets? Was it not the Japanese who benefited from so-called integrated education? Did not the government general's own records clearly demonstrate that fewer Taiwanese gained access to higher schools in the colony after the educational reform of 1922 than before?[32]

Even those few Taiwanese who did struggle to the top of the education pyramid were denied the just rewards of their outstanding achievements. Ts'ai P'ei-huo pointed out that in 1928 there were only five Taiwanese senior officials in the administration. Among junior ranking appointees in the administration, in 1928 only thirty were Taiwanese out of a total that exceeded

1,500. With the exception of these few, all other native employees of the government general were clerks, junior technicians, teachers, or assistant patrolmen. Improvements in the position of Taiwanese civil servants were always gestures without substance. For instance, in Governor-General Den's time the colonial police force dropped the designation of assistant patrolman, and classified patrolmen as class A and class B. Nevertheless, Taiwanese policemen remained at the bottom of the heap. The only difference was that their titles were changed from assistant patrolmen to patrolmen class B.[33]

Of course the tendency to write and speak as if denial of complete Japanese citizenship was the major source of the critics' discontent was tactical. In the colony, efficient police machinery prevented public expression of any view that urged substantial alterations in the colonial status quo. Yet there is a ring of sincerity in at least some of the Taiwanese demands for their due as the Japanese emperor's subjects.

However, distaste for this type of mentality was expressed almost as soon as the conservative activists began to organize. A minority of the New People's Society members immediately opposed the campaign to repeal Law No. 63, on the grounds that it supported a concept of integration akin to that espoused by Itagaki in 1914. Lin Ch'eng-lu (1887-?), a spokesman for this dissident group, heavily criticized the society's failure to recognize the culture and traditions of the Taiwanese as distinctly different from those of their rulers. Justice would not be rendered, he argued, by a simple extension to Taiwanese of the laws of Japan. Lin's alternative solution was a local legislature for Taiwan.[34]

Lin was a graduate of Meiji University who had taught political science at Hunan University in China; his experiences were broader than those of some of the other Taiwanese in Japan. Back in Tokyo in 1920 he was in touch with Yanaihara Tadao, who espoused home rule for Korea and Taiwan.[35] But Lin's position was a minority one. It was not his argument but action by the Imperial Diet which brought around the majority of the New People's Society members to support home rule for Taiwan. In November 1920 the Diet extended Law No. 63 indefinitely. Some revisions were made in it, but these were very minor. The revised version enjoined the governor-general of Taiwan to implement as much of Japanese law as he found feasible, but it continued to give him legislative power wherever he deemed Japanese law to be unsuitable. With all hope for abolition of Law No. 63 now gone, the New People's Society concluded that Lin's proposal was the only practical alternative.[36]

The shift to home rule brought the society a step further toward a position of self-determination or Taiwanese nationalism. Yet its members maintained their willingness to stay within the Japanese empire. This attitude contrasts sharply with that of their Korean contemporaries. Korean students in Japan always tended to be more outspoken regarding the need for political reform in their country than their Taiwanese counterparts.[37] After suppression of the 1919 independence movement, for instance, the Greater Japan Society for Peace (Dai Nihon heiwa kyōkai), a private organization, invited Korean and Taiwanese students in Japan to a conference of round table discussions. The Japanese participants in these declared that Japan must quickly grant both Korea and Taiwan home rule. While the Taiwanese students greeted this proposal enthusiastically, the Koreans left the conference in protest. To them anything less than independence was unthinkable.[38]

Beginning early in 1921, in Taiwan as well as in Japan, New People Society members circulated copies of a petition which they urged Taiwanese to sign. Within a month signatures of 178 supporters—mostly Taiwanese in Tokyo—had been collected and the petition was handed over to sympathetic Japanese Diet members for presentation to both houses of the Diet.[39] The petition and parts of its preface are translated below.

> *Preface*
>
> We humbly submit that the Great Empire of Japan is a constitutional monarchy and that Taiwan is an integral part of the Empire. Therefore . . . it should go without saying that the administration of Taiwan should also be based upon the principles of constitutional government.
>
> . . . At this important juncture in time, the Empire, which is charged with maintaining peace in the Orient, must pursue friendship with foreign nations and cultivate within the country a cooperation which will solidify the national foundations. Therefore in regard to administration of the new territory, Taiwan, it is imperative that the aspirations of the people, part of a worldwide trend of emerging thought, be recognized and that the races be treated equally in accord with normal standards of constitutional

government. A parliament of Taiwan made up of members publicly elected by the residents of Taiwan should be established. Through it the people of Taiwan would be permitted to enjoy the Emperor's sacred pronouncement regarding equal treatment and to benefit from the blessing of constitutional government. It is most urgent that, through the measure described above, the Taiwanese be allowed to perform their special geographical and historical mission as loyal subjects.

If their desire is not fulfilled and the present system continues, or if civil rights are suppressed and the civil will suffocated, there is no guarantee that these new subjects will not come to question the rule of Imperial Japan. For the sake of our nation we the undersigned petitioners are gravely concerned. It will be fortunate if the wishes of the undersigned petitioners are adopted and a parliament of Taiwan is established with powers to participate in the formulation of special laws for Taiwan and in enactment of the budget for Taiwan . . . This will not only bring happiness to the people of Taiwan; it will also be a singularly great achievement in Imperial Japan's history of governing new territories. This is why we are submitting this petition. We humbly request that the petition be given serious attention.

Petition

As stated above, we beg to request that a parliament of Taiwan made up of members publicly elected by the residents of Taiwan be established, and that a law be enacted to give this parliament powers to participate in the enactment of special laws and a budget for Taiwan.

The above petition is submitted by the undersigned through the good offices of Ebara Soroku, Member of the House of Peers, and Tagawa Daikichirō, Member of the House of Representatives.

January 1921[40]

As their statement reveals, the petitioners' terms of reference were those of Japanese constitutionalism. They felt sure that a legislature in Taiwan composed of members "publicly elected by the residents of Taiwan" would not in any way violate the constitution of Japan. Although they assailed the official assimilation policy, they never questioned the Japanese government's right to formulate such a policy.

Their declaration of constitutional intentions and profession of loyalty did not go unchallenged. Appearing before the petition committee of the House of Peers on February 28, 1921, Governor-General Den Kenjirō denounced the petition as an attempt to acquire for Taiwan a self-government which would be equivalent to the independence that Britain's Australia or Canada enjoyed. This, declared Den emphatically, was directly opposite to the policy objectives of Japanese rule in Taiwan. Japan's Taiwan policy was to raise the island's cultural level gradually until it paralleled that of the home country. Once this had been accomplished, Den promised, then Taiwan might be included within the territory directly ruled by the government of Japan.[41]

When the petition committee in both houses rejected the petition, the petitioners began a full-scale campaign to muster support and signatures for future petitions. From 1922 to 1934 fourteen petitions were presented to the Diet. Although the wording sometimes varied, all were essentially the same as the 1921 document. All fourteen were rejected. None of them got past the petition committees and consequently none was ever debated upon the floor of either house. In spite of repeated failures, the Taiwanese conservative activists campaigned tirelessly until 1934. With experience, the sophistication of their methods increased.[42] But they never stepped outside the boundaries they had set for themselves with their claims of complete loyalty to Japan.

In the first place, right up until the end of the petition movement, these Taiwanese activists continued to place their ultimate hopes in the government of Japan. All the petition campaigns sought single-mindedly to move the Japanese government to take legislative action. And if — as actually happened — Japanese legislators should prove to be unresponsive? The answer seemed to be to patiently stage another campaign and to try harder to persuade Diet members and other influential figures on the national scene.[43]

During the 1920s liberal and democratic currents flourished in Japan. In 1925 the various coalitions that had been agitating for a drastic enlargement of the electoral franchise happily witnessed the passage of a universal manhood suffrage law. A great deal of attention was focused upon the national legislature, and the prestige of the political parties was at its peak. This atmosphere abetted the petitioners' efforts to win Japanese backing. Liberal and social democratic politicians, university professors, and even a few prominent newspapers willingly gave them support.[44]

Some of the democratic climate even spilled over to the colony. This aided the home rule petitioners because their leaders felt that, in addition to Japanese support, what their petitions needed most was Taiwanese signatures—particularly those of prestigious and educated Taiwanese.[45] Canvassing for these in Japan was not too difficult. Most of the Taiwanese residents of Japan who signed were students or graduates of Tokyo schools, although circulation of the petitions was by no means limited to the capital region.[46] Collecting names in Taiwan was a more formidable undertaking. However, it might have been quite impossible if democratic trends in Japan had not exercised some influence upon the colonial government.

The colonial government was totally against the home rule movement. The governor-general possessed the power and the means to stop public discussion of home rule and signature collecting within the colony. Yet, given contemporary opinion in the home islands, it was awkward for him to prohibit orderly activity that was so obviously within the law. After all, the government general was publicly committed to extending Japanese constitutionalism to the island. When Governor-General Den's police chief asked how the petitioners were to be dealt with, Den pointed out that they were only exercising their constitutional rights and advised trying to restrain them by means of "friendly persuasion."[47]

Friendly persuasion easily slid into harassment, which often included threatened or actual economic sanctions. In 1922 friendly persuasion made Lin Hsien-t'ang withdraw from leadership of the home rule movement. Lin had borrowed a huge sum from the governmental Bank of Taiwan. If the government general had demanded immediate repayment of this loan, Lin might have been ruined.[48] He was also vulnerable because a relative of his was a suspect in a case involving defacement of the memorial stone of the member of the imperial family who perished during the taking of Taiwan.[49] Others involved in the movement were treated less gently. Teachers and other government employees who signed the 1922 petition were forced to resign their positions, while signatories "who enjoyed the privilege of distributing or selling government monopoly commodities had their licenses suspended."[50] The colonial government also urged private corporations to take similar action. Since most private companies were either Japanese-owned or dependent upon the government, they usually complied.[51] "Those petitioners who were self-employed but dependent on loans from government banks had their loan applications rejected or were compelled to repay their debts immediately."[52]

In spite of, or perhaps because of, such pressure, the petition leaders, who had been working largely through their personal memberships in the Taiwan Youth Association (Taiwan seinen-kai) in Tokyo and the Taiwan Cultural Association (Taiwan bunka kyōkai) in the colony, decided they needed an organization devoted solely to home rule. Early in 1922 they applied to the Taihoku police for permission to found the League for Establishment of a Taiwan Parliament (Taiwan gikai kisei dōmeikai). When their application was turned down, they moved on to Tokyo, where police authorities granted the necessary permission. This irritated the colonial officials. From October 1923 when the league's organizers began to return to Taiwan, government-general administrators were watching closely. The island was now the responsibility of Governor-General Uchida Kakichi, the old colonial hand who took over from Den in September. Uchida was even less disposed than Den to rely upon persuasion.[53]

In mid-December, as the newly returned leaders and their associates on the island were preparing for the next bout of signature collecting, Uchida's police rounded up everyone connected with the league that they could find. Since the arrests were made during a total news blackout, it is not clear exactly how many people were detained. However, a later report in the *Ōsaka asahi shimbun* claimed that eighty-five were served with summonses, fifty-six had their homes searched, and forty-four were taken into custody.[54] According to recollections of some of those arrested, forty-nine were arrested and another fifty received summonses or had their houses searched.[55] Of those arrested, twenty-nine were charged with contravening the Peace Preservation Police Law (Chian keisatsuhō) by creating in Tokyo the League for Establishment of a Taiwan Parliament which had been banned in the colony.[56] Charges were dropped against eleven of the twenty-nine, but the remaining eighteen were held over for trial.[57]

Widespread publicity surrounding the arrests, trial, and two appeals helped bring new Taiwanese recruits to the cause. During court sessions, spectator benches were packed with islanders whose noisy support of the defendants periodically interrupted the proceedings.[58] Taiwanese students in Peking, Shanghai, and

Amoy held meetings to declare their support of the defendants.[59] The affair dramatically escalated the political consciousness of Taiwanese in Japan. They quickly came together to pledge solidarity with the individuals on trial and determination to carry on the league's work. They saw that the petition, signed by seventy-one Taiwanese students and residents in Japan, got to the Diet on schedule early in 1924.[60]

Skillfully the conservative activists mobilized their Japanese contacts. Sympathetic legislators asked questions in the Diet. Legal experts went to Taiwan to help prepare the accused for their trial. Three famous Japanese criminal lawyers — Watanabe Noboru, Kiyose Ichirō, and Hanai Takuzo — defended the eighteen, first in Taihoku district court, then in the higher court, and finally before the appeals department of the higher court.[61] After the first judgment, Tagawa Daikichirō, who had been a friend in the Diet for years, and Kanda Masao, a newly elected member of the House of Representatives, visited Taiwan to meet and speak with supporters of the home rule movement.[62]

At the trial and the subsequent appeals, defense lawyers argued that Taiwanese associated with the League for Establishment of a Taiwan Parliament had in no way violated any law. On the contrary, defense attorneys insisted, their clients had been quite properly using their constitutional right to petition. Elsewhere, other Japanese supporters were vehemently proclaiming that the Taiwanese activists had followed all appropriate legal procedures for registering the league and publicizing their cause. Kanda Masao later intimated that the government general was well aware that the home rule movement was not an independence movement. Government-general opposition, he hinted, was really on behalf of the Japanese living in Taiwan, who would naturally be unhappy with the loss of privilege that meaningful Taiwanese participation in the island's government would bring.[63]

Not so, insisted the government general and its agents. In Taihoku district court, the prosecutor hammered away at what he claimed was the motive of the defendants rather than at their actions. The real desire of the founders of the League for Establishment of a Taiwan Parliament, he alleged in a lengthy discourse, was Taiwan's self-government and separation from Japan.[64]

On August 18, 1924, all eighteen were acquitted. However, the government general immediately appealed the decision, and within two months the higher court had overturned the verdict for all but five of the defendants. Although defense lawyers lodged an appeal against this, the judgment was upheld. Seven of the defendants were given prison terms of either three or four months, and six were fined one hundred yen each.[65]

But the sentences were not heavy enough to discourage the defendants, who had become famous through all the publicity. They had shown that they could effectively exercise their rights as Japanese subjects—even against the powerful colonial government.[66] They discovered that the government had reluctantly learned the limitations of its heavy-handed methods. They found that Japanese policemen, who bullied ordinary Taiwanese readily enough, were beginning to treat them with some respect. This was not only because the home rule activists were generally upper-class Taiwanese, who had been educated in the prestigious institutions few police officers had ever had a chance to attend. It was also because their confident and intricate knowledge of the laws and their applications either equaled or bettered that of the average patrolman.[67] The Taiwanese people also felt encouraged because many more of them signed subsequent petitions. Signatures on petitions increased to 782 in 1925, 1,990 in 1926, and 2,470 in 1927.[68]

This legalistic, reformist approach dominated the conservative activists' other political activities too. In 1921 they founded the Taiwan Cultural Association in Taihoku. Ostensibly dedicated to improving the cultural level of the Taiwanese people, the cultural association actually functioned as an island-based front for petition campaigns. From the beginning some of the cultural association's members felt the association should get involved in other areas of political protest, but the conservative leaders demurred. In 1927, when radical activists captured decision making in the association, the conservatives left to found the Taiwan Popular Party (Taiwan minshūtō), the only legal Taiwanese political party ever to exist in Taiwan under Japanese rule.[69]

For Taiwanese support, the Taiwan Popular Party competed with the radicalized Taiwan Cultural Association, now heavily involved in organizing laborers and supporting a growing agrarian protest movement. Stimulated at least partly by the example of their opponents in the Cultural Association, a number of Popular Party members were becoming convinced that more fundamental alterations in Taiwan's social, economic, and political structures than those espoused by the conservatives were necessary. By 1929 the Taiwan Popular Party was rent with ideological struggle. Among the critics of the party's strictly reformist policies were such conservative stalwarts as Chiang Wei-shui (1890-1931), a key figure in the founding of the original Taiwan Cultural Association in 1921, and Hsieh Ch'un-mu (1902-?). The latter was a sparkling propagandist who wrote many articles on China as well as on conditions in Taiwan for the journal the conservative activists put out in Tokyo until 1927, when it finally received permission for daily publication in the colony. However, the bulk of the conservatives stood firm.

Finding themselves outnumbered, they left the Taiwan Popular Party to Chiang, Hsieh, and others and launched their final venture in opposition politics, the League for the Attainment of Local Autonomy (Taiwan chihōjichi renmei). This organization, which eagerly sought members among Japanese as well as Taiwanese residents of the colony, was the most moderate of all the conservative enterprises. The league's goal was nothing higher than extension of the home island's system of local government to Taiwan.[70]

The league, which lasted until 1936, signed up 4,000 members, nearly all of whom were Taiwanese.[71] The public meetings which it held to gain supporters proved overwhelmingly successful. During the first six months of the league's existence alone these meetings brought out more than 18,000 islanders.[72] The league presented proposals for local autonomy to the government general and had petitions for local autonomy introduced into the Imperial Diet. Its demands were moderate, but it must be remembered that they were put forward during the early 1930s when almost any kind of political agitation by nongovernmental or nonmilitary groups was becoming difficult.

Why did the conservative activists remain willing to pour energy into such limited politics? They told themselves that "improvements in the local government system would provide an ideal opportunity for training the Taiwanese people in the fundamentals of democratic systems and would also be beneficial to future political movements."[73] They also saw their work in the local autonomy league as encouragement for those Japanese officials within the government general who favored reform.[74]

It has been persuasively argued that the acquiescence to the authorities and reliance upon Japanese channels were always for the conservative activists but a means to an end, just a necessary tactic in their dogged struggle to achieve independence.[75] This tactical approach was required, so the argument continues, because any overt resistance to Japanese rule would have been quickly suppressed. The certainty of this had been vividly demonstrated by the bloody reprisals against the Korean March First Movement, which began as a peaceful demonstration against the government general of Korea.

This kind of analysis does not deal with the question of why other anticolonial leaders elsewhere, facing equally repressive power structures, refused to limit themselves to the political opposition allowed by law. The contrast with Korean activists is a striking one. In colonial schools and in educational institutions in Japan, young Koreans were subject to the same kind of influences as Taiwanese students. Yet no fragments of the Korean anticolonial movement found issues like home rule and local governmental autonomy worth fighting for.[76] Korean independence leaders often chose exile because they found they could not work for their goals under Japanese rule.

In colonial Vietnam, the French Sûreté suppressed anti-French "subversives" as efficiently as did the police in Taiwan and Japan. Yet anticolonial Vietnamese of the conservative scholar-gentry class seriously strove to force the French to leave Indochina. In the face of the Sûreté's ubiquitous network, they attempted to train themselves and their followers for armed upheaval and tried also to secure promises of military aid from other Asians. They too organized native students who were studying abroad and drew activists from their ranks. But they did not encourage young Vietnamese to go to Paris to study, and the French capital never became an important base for their operations.[77]

Like Korean militants, such Vietnamese leaders found reform within existing colonial arrangements irrelevant. They rejected proposals for gradual progress toward nationalistic goals which accepted the colonizer "for the time being."[78] They clearly recognized the either/or juxtaposition of assimilation and independence that the great Filipino nationalist, José Rizal (1861-96) had articulated so vividly in his famous novel, El Filibusterismo (The Subversive).[79]

Analysts who regard the reformist approach of the conservatives as completely tactical also tend to overlook the anticolonial contribution of other Taiwanese activists who rejected this approach.[80] Nevertheless, such analysts probably accurately portray the real feelings of the conservative leaders.[81]

Government-general officials were then undoubtedly correct in concluding that the ultimate end of the home rule movement was Taiwan's independence from Japan.[82] Yet the methods pursued on behalf of this goal are revealing. Always the movement leaders worked within Japan's legal and governmental frameworks. They lobbied and publicized exhaustively through Japanese media as well as attempting to rally Taiwanese support. In a totally Japanese fashion, they cemented personal relationships with politicians and opinion makers in Japan. Most of all they sought out those with power and influence. But they were willing to approach any respectable individual or group of almost any political color or bent — from the prime minister down to a labor union alliance.[83] They appeared astonishingly willing to wait patiently until Japanese institutions and actors implemented the changes they were trying to bring about.

Even more significant is the nature of the Taiwan they intended to govern once they had succeeded in gaining independence. Although individuals like Chiang Wei-shui leaned toward union with China, most of the conservative activists seem to have accepted the economic and political structures the Japanese had planted in Taiwan.[84] During the first decade of the twentieth century Lin Hsien-t'ang had sought help for Taiwanese from prominent Chinese nationalists, but, like the Vietnamese anticolonialists who about the same time asked the Chinese for aid against the French, Lin received no encouragement from this quarter.[85] By the 1920s Lin retained no thought of assistance from China. Among the conservative anticolonialists of Taiwan there existed interest in Chinese political developments and admiration for the trail-blazing intellectuals of China's new cultural movement, but the political confusion and infamous warlord system on the continent were not attractive.[86] Given the business and other connections of many of the conservatives, they probably had no intention of cutting trade or other relations with Japan. Men like Lin Ch'eng-lu said that Taiwan's separate cultural development was essential, but they were educating even their younger children as if they intended them to enter first-class higher educational institutions in Japan.[87]

What then did independence mean to these individuals? Den's accusation that the home rule group wanted to establish a self-

governing entity, related to the home islands as Canada and
Australia were related to Britain, was meant to expose the activists' hopes for withdrawal from the Japanese empire. But this
comparison to the British dominions also illustrated the very
moderation of the home rule leaders' "most extreme intentions."
A nationalism comparable to that of contemporary Canadians or
Australians (who thought of themselves as British) pales beside
the nationalism of other anticolonial leaders in Asia, many of
whom shared the upper-class background and conservative outlook of the home rule leaders. The only other Asian anticolonialists who exhibited a comparable willingness to accept and lobby
through the governing processes of the ruling country were the
leaders of the Philippine independence movement. And the Filipinos at least had promises — albeit ambiguous ones — of eventual
independence from their colonial caretakers. They also had been
allowed to participate more in the governing of their country
than the Taiwanese were permitted to do in theirs.[88]

It is true that the Taiwanese leaders, unlike nationalists in
India or Indonesia, had at their disposal no religious force that
could be used to arouse their compatriots.[89] In Taiwan they
labored under a press censorship that was more thorough than
that exercised in the British and Dutch colonies.[90] But in many
respects the Taiwanese situation was akin to that of the Korean
nationalist leaders, whose opposition to Japanese consumer goods
took their cues from anti-British economic campaigns in India.[91]
The Koreans' avoidance of government schools and their attempt
to found a national university correspond to anticolonial national
school movements in such different settings as India, Burma,
Malaysia, Vietnam, and Indonesia.[92] Taiwanese conservative-
activists, on the other hand, put little energy into noncooperation
or passive resistance.[93]

The Conservative Activists: Cultural Identity

The question of the conservatives' cultural nationalism is a
knotty one. Under the assimilation policy, Taiwanese were not
permitted to openly encourage any non-Japanese ethnic consciousness. Thus the depth of the conservative activists' cultural
awareness cannot be gauged from actions alone. In addition,
there is a further complication. It is not always clear how much of
the anti-Japanese cultural identification to the Taiwanese intellectual of the 1920s represented an affirmation of a Chinese identity and how much of it expressed something else.

The New People's Society conservatives founded the Taiwan Cultural Association and dominated it until 1927. Since they regarded cultural separatism as a step toward independence from Japan, public lectures, plays, and other functions held under the association's auspices often deliberately fostered anti-Japanese feelings.[94] But the conservatives urged their fellow-Taiwanese to express these anti-Japanese feelings by signing home rule petitions. And the most outspoken of the anti-Japanese speakers at association rallies were generally not from the conservative leadership's ranks. They were instead younger Taiwanese intellectuals who were critical of the petitioning approach.[95]

Not only is the depth of the conservatives' cultural nationalism unclear, but the content of this cultural movement is ambiguous too. The association's championship of the Taiwanese as culturally distinct from the Japanese was unequivocal from the beginning. But was this culture Chinese or Taiwanese? Chiang Wei-shui, who with Ts'ai P'ei-huo and Lin Hsien-t'ang was one of the association's principal organizers, declared in an inaugural statement:

> The Taiwanese people are charged with a mission. They are to serve as an intermediary for Chinese and Japanese friendship. Sino-Japanese friendship is a prerequisite for confederation of the peoples of Asia. Union of the peoples of Asia is a prerequisite for world peace and in world peace lies humanity's greatest happiness and aspirations . . . In plain words, the Taiwanese hold the key to one door to future world peace. Is not this mission a heavy responsibility? This association has been formed to enlist individuals with the talent to accomplish this mission. But the Taiwanese are ill. If we do not heal that illness we shall not be able to produce talented individuals. Thus this association's first task must be to treat the cause of this illness, which is, according to my diagnosis, a lack of intellectual nourishment. A cultural movement is the one and only treatment.[96]

There is a strong suggestion here that the mission charged to the Taiwanese could only be carried out by subjects of the Japanese emperor who were Chinese. Dr. Chiang—for he was a physician—was an ardent admirer of the Chinese nationalists. He personally thought the treatments applied by Sun Yat-sen and his Kuomintang to the ills of their country were good ones.[97] The Taiwan Cultural Association sponsored summer school and night school courses in Chinese literature, language, history, and geography. Speakers at the association's public meetings told about political events in China as well as about anticolonial movements around the globe. The conservatives' journal, *Taiwan seinen* (Taiwan youth), which served as the house organ of the home rule movement, carried many articles on China. It was read eagerly by members—particularly the young—of the Taiwan Cultural Association.[98]

On the other hand, some scholars attach little importance to Chiang's hint that the Taiwanese and the continental Chinese were one and the same.[99] The association's plays and operas were in Taiwanese dialects, as were the popular public lectures that drew upon the experiences of those who attended them. It was the dramas and lectures that reached large numbers of islanders, while academic courses and seminars touched the minds of very few. (More than 117,000 islanders attended 315 public lectures in 1925 and more than 112,000 attended another 315 lectures in 1926.)[100] And one of the Taiwan Cultural Association's most important campaigns was a crusade endorsing the banned romanized script of the major Taiwanese dialect.[101]

To what kind of cultural identification were the thousands of Taiwanese who joined the association responding? The association was more broadly based than the New People's Society or the League for Establishment of a Taiwan Parliament; its members numbered 1,032 when it was inaugurated in October 1921 and according to one observer they grew to a total of 13,014.[102] The membership came from the Japanese-educated middle and upper classes. Physicians, lawyers, businessmen, landlords, journalists, teachers, and other white-collar workers joined along with students. In 1921 a quarter of the association's members were students registered in secondary or postsecondary schools in Taiwan.[103]

Students who were hungry for information about the outside world, and receptive to the anti-Japanese tone of the association, flocked to join it. *Taiwan seinen* was published in Tokyo because the colonial authorities would not permit such a publication in the island. But in Taihoku, Taiwanese students in middle school, normal school, and medical school greedily devoured issue after issue, reading them in secret to evade the censorious eyes of the school authorities.[104] Students at these schools who joined the Cultural Association became involved in defiant acts and anti-Japanese incidents to such an extent that the government soon forbade students to hold memberships.[105]

Students were not the only Taiwanese who were stimulated by the anti-Japanese orientation of the association. Speakers whose "cultural lectures" freely ridiculed Taiwan's rulers delighted large audiences. Mockery of the Japanese policeman was especially popular with the Taiwanese from all walks of life who crowded the lecture halls.[106] But the cultural consciousness of the older rank-and-file members and sympathizers of the Taiwan Cultural Association was, if anything, even more indefinite than that of the students or the association's leadership.

The Radical Activists

The radical stream of Taiwanese political activism has left less prominent traces than that of the conservatives. For one thing, the radicals did not restrict themselves to the narrow range of legal activities permitted by the colonial government. In addition, besides campaigning in their own right they labored anonymously within enterprises directed by conservatives. Although they managed sometimes to publish in the conservatives' journal, they did not themselves control a periodical issued regularly over several years, like *Taiwan seinen* or its successors. And no survivors of Taiwanese radical activism of the 1920s and 1930s have yet published a work like the conservatives' *Taiwan min-tsu yün-tung shih* (A history of the Taiwanese Nationalist Movement).[107] Nevertheless, radical activists played an important part in the Taiwanese anticolonial movement. Not only did they offer young Taiwanese intellectuals and others an alternative to the conservatives' model of protest; they also influenced the direction that conservative activism took.

Like its conservative counterpart, radical activism surfaced in the Taiwanese student community in Tokyo around 1920. About that time, some leftist-leaning students emerged among the members of the Taiwan Youth Association, which for years had functioned as a social club.[108] They could also be found in the New People's Society. P'eng Hua-ying (1895- ?), a young Taiwanese who had become active in the Japanese student-worker movement, was one of the society's charter members.[109] In 1921 an article by P'eng entitled "An Introduction to Socialism" appeared in the society's organ, *Taiwan seinen*. This is considered to be the earliest work on socialism written by a Taiwanese.[110]

P'eng and Fan Pen-liang, a young Taiwanese disciple of the Japanese anarchist, Ōsugi Sakai, joined militant Korean students in public denunciations of Japanese colonial rule. For example, in

June of 1921 Fan and P'eng addressed a meeting held at the Kanda Y.M.C.A. in Tokyo.[111] From various standpoints they argued for the independence of Taiwan. As a result, police halted the meeting and even detained Fan. From then on the two found their movements in Japan hampered by constant police surveillance. Within a month P'eng left for Shanghai and in August Fan was off to Peking, to meet left-wing Taiwanese who would introduce them to a world inhabited by Chinese nationalists, Communists, anarchists and Soviet agents.[112]

One of the Taiwanese P'eng met on the continent was Hsü Nai-ch'ang, a sociology student at Shanghai University. In August 1924 Hsü went to Moscow to study, but by 1925 he was in Tokyo entering Nihon University.[113] Hsü, six other Taiwanese students in Tokyo universities, and a Taiwanese printer formed a Socialist study group attached to Tokyo Imperial University's New Man's Society. The study group soon moved into the Taiwan Youth Association, because its members hoped to increase left-wing influence within that organization.

They soon succeeded in doing so. By 1927 Hsü and his comrades felt strong enough to be able to urge the Taiwan Youth Association to recognize their study group as a full-status branch organization pledged to building relationships with Chinese and Korean revolutionaries. The program they proposed for the enlarged study group featured regular lectures by Tokyo Imperial University professors and a close liaison with the New Man's Society. The Taiwan Youth Association executive opposed them but was voted down by the membership at a general meeting. Two weeks after this vote was taken on October 30, 1927, an even larger showing of the general membership ousted incumbent members of the executive and elected Hsü and several of his friends in their place.[114]

While Taiwanese interest in socialism was obviously increasing in Tokyo, the Taiwanese studying in China tended to be even more radical. For young Taiwanese, study in China was still a relatively recent phenomenon. During the 1910s Taiwanese students in Japan had met Chinese who came seeking educational programs not available in their own country. But China's modern schools and universities were developing rapidly, and with the May Fourth Movement of 1919 Chinese students had dramatically shown themselves to be an important force in national life.[115] Taiwan government-general records listed only nine Taiwanese students in China during 1919, but two years later reported that this figure had jumped to 273.[116] Police observers noted that the attractions included the political atmosphere as well as schools with low fees and easy entrance procedures.[117]

From 1923 to 1927 the Kuomintang received aid and advice from the Soviet Union, while members of the Chinese Communist Party (founded in 1921) worked within the Kuomintang. Comintern agents and Soviet advisers were a part of the landscape and in intellectual circles anarchist, Communist, and nationalist influences abounded. Taiwanese students not only participated in Chinese organizations and movements; they also founded groups of their own and formed alliances with Koreans who were dedicated to overthrowing Japanese imperialism.

By 1924 Taiwanese students in China had become severe critics of the Taiwan parliament petition movement. Petitioning the Japanese capitalist imperialist authorities was hopeless, they argued. As a league of Taiwanese, Korean, and Chinese leftists in Shanghai put it: "No matter how many hundreds of heads bow low the result is the same . . . It is just like trying to scoop up [the reflection of] the moon from the water."[118] Taiwanese students in the Shanghai league called upon their compatriots to join with other conquered peoples in Asia — Indians, Koreans, and Filipinos — to seek their independence from the capitalist-imperialists who ruled them.[119] The Taiwanese radicals in China felt that even if the petition movement did eventually succeed, the achievement would only benefit the island's wealthy classes. They began to refuse to sign petitions.

By 1927 Taiwanese students in China had few incentives to linger on after their formal studies were finished. In that year Chiang Kai-shek's murderous attack on the Chinese Communists put a definitive end to the honeymoon between the Kuomintang and the Communist Party. The environment, hitherto conducive to radical politics, suddenly changed drastically. The Taiwanese students in Peking, Shanghai, Amoy, and other centers returned to Taiwan, and like some of those coming home from Japan they brought their discontent with the petition movement with them.

Returning radicals found that every move they made was of interest to the well-informed police.[120] In spite of painstaking precautions, the authorities were discovering that radical ideas were also growing in Taiwanese soil. Young islanders who had never left the island or who had only been abroad for very short periods were also beginning to join left-wing groups.

The Japanese population in the colony stood so firmly behind its government that it would have been difficult to draw the line between official and private Japanese attitudes in Taihoku. Across the ocean in the Dutch East Indies, administrators found they could not be too exacting about the ideological orientation of the Dutch who applied for employment in the Indies. The number of Hollanders willing to go to the colony was too small for them to be able to pick and choose. Hence individuals from the ruling country whose ethos clashed with the ideas of the Indies government easily secured employment in the colony.[121] The government general of Taiwan, however, carefully investigated all residents of Japan who applied for positions in Taiwan. No Japanese with known radical tendencies were permitted to enter the colony. But it was less easy for the government to keep out Japanese with "dangerous" ideas when these individuals had been born or raised in Taiwan.

Yamaguchi Koshizu was the daughter of a Japanese Shinto priest in Taiwan. After graduating from Taihoku First Higher Girls' School with a brilliant record, she attended Tokyo Women's Higher Normal School (Tokyo joshi kōtō shihan gakkō) for a while. But in 1921 she left that institution without finishing its course and returned to Taiwan, possibly because of illness, because two years later she died of tuberculosis. While at the Tokyo school she worked her way through groups concerned with liberal democracy, social reform, and Marxism. Becoming an enthusiastic participant in socialist circles, she established close relationships with Yamakawa Kikue (1890-) and her husband, Yamakawa Hitoshi (1880-1958), both influential figures in Japanese socialism. When Yamaguchi returned to Taihoku she was employed to teach composition in a private girls' school. Apparently she did not teach socialism during school hours, but she moved in company that was engrossed in socialist studies and labor problems. What she had imbibed from the Yamakawas she passed along to a Taiwanese friend called Lien Wên-ch'ing (1895- ?) who was active in the Taiwan Cultural Association.[122]

A petty clerk in a Taihoku office, Lien had only received a common school education, but with Yamaguchi's help he managed to go to Japan for an Esperanto conference in 1924. There he met the Yamakawas; he stayed at their home while he was in Tokyo and like Yamaguchi took the couple as his ideological mentors. Lien's connections with the Yamakawas remained close after he had returned to Taiwan. For Yamakawa Hitoshi he

gathered data dealing with Taiwan's economy, society, and politics. These materials (and perhaps Lien's additional assistance)
enabled Yamakawa Hitoshi to begin the following year on a pene-
trating critique of Japan's first colony entitled *Taiwan under
Colonial Policy* (Chokumin saku ka no Taiwan). Through Lien,
who became an important figure in the Taiwanese anticolonial
movement, the ideas of Yamakawa had a great influence upon
anticolonial struggles in Taiwan.[123]

Another young Japanese colonial who furnished a link between
the Japanese left and receptive Taiwanese was Ozawa Hajime,
who was born in Taichū province. Son of a Japanese patrolman,
Ozawa entered Taihoku First Middle School, but during the summer vacation of his fourth year he went to Tokyo and did not
return to school when the vacation was over. In Tokyo he attended art school and was employed as a lithographic worker. He
became friendly with anarchists and was soon seriously involved
in labor activities. In June of 1925 his affairs took him back to
Taihoku, where he immediately began to organize young Taiwanese in anarchist groups. After a three-month stay he returned
to Tokyo, leaving an organization called the League of Black
Youth (Kokushoku seinen renmei) behind him. In 1926 he again
had to go to Taiwan. This time he took the opportunity to
organize on behalf of anarchism both in Taihoku and in his home
town in Taichū province.[124]

These anarchist groups drew island youths who had received
some secondary schooling, as well as young urban blue-collar and
white-collar workers with less formal education. They provided a
focus for radicals returning from China and Japan. Through
these groups, ideas picked up abroad were passed along to people
who had never left the colony. The members of these groups, like
the students in China, were critical of the conservatives' petition
campaigns.

The young anarchists met in secret, but not without reason.
Whenever they tried to organize openly the police stifled every
action before it got out of the planning stage. Lien Wên-ch'ing
and four comrades—including Chiang Wei-shui for whom Kuo-
mintang-Communist Party cooperation in China had stimulated
interest in socialism—tried to organize a socialist study group in
Taihoku in 1923. But police in that city halted their proceedings
before they held their first meeting.[125] During the same year
Lien, Chiang, and twenty-eight others tried to form a youth

group under the auspices of the Taiwan Cultural Association. But the authorities found the ideas of the participants dangerous enough to stop this too. Other attempts by leftists to organize legally were quickly crushed.[126]

Although young leftists in Taihoku and other cities and towns were critical of the Taiwan Cultural Association leadership's preoccupation with home rule, there was really no place for them to go but into the Cultural Association.[127] The efficiency of the police made even clandestine operations difficult, and legal groups of their own were forbidden. Taiwanese returnees from China and Japan were joining the Cultural Association for the same reasons. Consequently, the Taiwan Cultural Association's active membership soon included a substantial left-wing contingent.

Young leftists threw themselves into the association's speechmaking activities. Especially eager to address audiences of peasants or urban workers, they took part in the association's islandwide "cultural lecture" circuit. As speakers they were daring in their condemnations of the Japanese in Taiwan. Traveling theater groups organized under Cultural Association sponsorship gave some of them another outlet for their oratorical talents. The government general found the performances of these troupes as hostile to the colony's ruling authorities as the "cultural lectures."[128] Leftists also led the association's youth clubs, wherever the government allowed these to exist.[129]

Leftists heartily approved of the association's involvement with peasant farmers, who from about 1923 had begun to organize in order to fight threats to their livelihoods from large agricultural corporations and the colonial government. The atmosphere created by Cultural Association lectures and meetings held in rural districts encouraged farmers to get together and defend their economic rights. In individual struggles the Taiwan Cultural Association usually proved willing to lend a hand. During 1924 and 1925, for instance, the association helped farmers in Taichū and Tainan provinces fight the sale of bamboo forests to the Mitsubishi corporation, which intended to use the trees for pulp. Supported by the association, protesting farmers, who had always used the bamboo to supplement their meager farm incomes, refused to fulfill their hokō obligations, to pay taxes, or to send their children to common school until their interests in the bamboo lands were recognized.[130] Inspiration for such tactics came from left-wing members of the Cultural Association.

Sometimes the association's participation in agricultural disputes did not officially involve the organization as a whole, but was nonetheless influential. Such was the case in the famous Erhlin incident of October 1925. Before the incident occurred, sugarcane farmers in the area had attended meetings to hear visiting Cultural Association speakers criticize the Lin Pen-yuan Sugar Corporation that dominated the farmers' lives.[131] Under the leadership of the local physician, who headed the Erh-lin branch of the Cultural Association, four hundred farmers formed Taiwan's first sugarcane farmers' union. The union refused to deliver cane to the corporation's mill on the company's monopoly terms and insisted that three demands of the farmers be met. (The three were freedom to buy fertilizers of their choice and to use methods of fertilization as they chose; the right to witness the weighing of the cane; and establishment of a price for the cane before it was cut.) When the company, which refused to negotiate on these demands, sent scab labor to harvest the crop, a bloody battle ensued and the police arrested ninety-three individuals. When some of these were tried in Taichu district court, prominent lawyers who were active in the Taiwan Cultural Association defended them.[132]

During other struggles, the Cultural Association directly or indirectly aided the farmers involved. Initiative which resulted in Taiwan's first permanent peasant farmers' union was taken by a tenant farmer in the Feng-shan region of Takao province, who had been influenced by the enlightenment movement (*keimō undō*) of the Taiwan Cultural Association.[133] Whatever the issues —eviction of tenant farmers, disputed ownership of land, sale of lands to retired government-general officials—the tenants' opponents were generally the colonial government, Japanese corporations, or large corporations owned by Taiwanese "government stooges" (*goyō shinshi*) but staffed with Japanese managers.[134]

The conservative leadership of the Cultural Association approved of the peasant movement because it enhanced the farmers' sense of their Taiwanese identity and taught them the value of solidarity. After all, the peasants' antagonists were the Japanese and their most visible collaborators. Association leftists, on the other hand, were more interested in the peasant movement's lessons in class struggle. Yet recognizing that class cleavages in Taiwan were complicated by the presence of the colonial ruling power, they supported an all-Taiwanese effort against large-scale

Japanese capitalism and its agent, the government general. Thus they shared some of the goals of conservatives who backed the agrarian movement. But the leftists felt that more of the association's resources should have been going into the peasants' struggles. They also wanted to see the association turn its attention to the colony's embryonic industrial sector and the problems of factory workers. They were highly critical of the priority given to the petition campaigns.

Within the association's central executive the left wing and the right wing were held together tenuously by the efforts of Lien Wên-ch'ing and Chiang Wei-shui. Since Chiang's model for political action was the Kuomintang's effort to build a national mass movement in China, he agreed with the leftists on the importance of organizing peasants and workers. Lien, the young radicals' champion, also accepted the primacy of nationalist struggle over class struggle because of the peculiar colonial context of Taiwan. Lien's position is clearly expressed in Yamakawa Hitoshi's *Taiwan under Colonial Policy,* which Lien may have helped write. This work, published in 1926, does not attack the conservatives. Indeed it points out that the oppressed agricultural workers of Taiwan organized to fight Japanese capital, not Taiwanese bourgeois landlords.[135] Lien called for alliance between Taiwanese radicals and conservatives to build a national movement. What he had no patience for was the parliamentary petition movement and its famous leaders. Lien felt that change would come to Taiwan because of the efforts of young Taiwanese "nobodies," not through campaigns led by prominent members of the island's native bourgeoisie.[136]

By 1926 the divergent forces that had been building up within the association were ready to explode. Young islanders back from China and a leftward-moving student community in Tokyo added their articulate voices to the leftists' call for working-class action. Conservative founders of the association were indignant at younger intellectuals, who urged them to give up strictly cultural activities and the petition movement. Those who did not want to commit the association to the proletariat, but who did value organization of mass movements, were caught in the middle. Ts'ai P'ei-huo's old-line leadership, although still prestigious, was out of step with much of the membership. Chiang Wei-shui's middle ground was not enough for many of Lien Wên-ch'ing's comrades. After a series of arguments and maneuvers by all the interested parties, Lien's faction emerged dominant early in 1927.[137]

The association's new leaders tried in vain to placate right-wing feelings by insisting that conservatives and radicals could cooperate in common causes even when their reasons for cooperation differed.[138] The association's new statement, "Taiwan of 1927," listed Taiwanese landlords and capitalists among the ranks of islanders oppressed and exploited by Japanese capitalism.[139] But Lien and the other new leaders—who included a few landlords and capitalists—could contain neither the conservatives nor rank-and-file leftists' resentment against them. Led by Lin Hsien-t'ang and Ts'ai P'ei-huo, the conservatives bolted the association to form a new political group of their own. Moderates like Chiang Wei-shui and Hsieh Ch'un-mu went with them.

The radicalized Cultural Association continued antigovernmental speech-making and public meetings, but its main focus became organization of the rural and urban masses. Even before the 1927 split, association leftists had developed close ties with peasants. Under left-wing leadership the association now worked closely with the island-wide Taiwanese Peasant Farmers' Union (Taiwan nomin kumiai), who also had connections with leftist bodies in Japan.[140] Organizing industrial workers, on the other hand, was a newer field of endeavor. The association sought to build unions and to lead strikes among machine workers, lacquer workers, laborers in cement and iron works, and other workers. It found itself competing with the organizational efforts of Chiang Wei-shui, who on behalf of the conservatives' new political group was encouraging urban workers to form less militant associations than those sponsored by the Cultural Association.[141]

While fighting Chiang's brand of unionism on the labor front, the Cultural Association had to contend with an upsurge of internal factionalism. A number of influences from the Chinese and Japanese left contributed to this, but it hardened into a fight between a group led by Lien Wên-ch'ing and one headed by another veteran of the earliest years of the association, Wang Min-ch'uan (1889- ?). Wang and Lien had worked together before the 1927 split in the association, but afterwards Wang came to spearhead an attack on Lien's "Yamakawaism," a position which recently had been rejected by the Japanese Communist Party. Just as Yamakawa Hitoshi lost out in Japan when he insisted it was more important to develop mass organizations than to concentrate on a Leninist vanguard party—the necessity of which he never denied—Lien, Yamakawa's disciple in Taiwan, eventually lost to others within the Cultural Association whose ideas were more in tune with Communist strategies in Japan, China, and elsewhere.[142]

The factionalism was intensified by attacks upon Lien and the Cultural Association by the Taiwan Communist Party, which by the end of the 1920s had superseded the association's influence in the peasant union. At the same time, the government was bearing down hard upon the radicalized association. In December 1932, when the colonial police arrested more than a dozen of the association's leaders, the embattled Taiwan Cultural Association collapsed.

In some ways the Taiwan Communist Party appears as a distinct segment of the island's radical anticolonial stream. Because the larger international movement to which it belonged played an important part in shaping its policies, it has been considered as a particularly foreign element in Taiwanese anticolonialism. It was founded in Shanghai in 1928 with the understanding that it would work closely with the Chinese and Japanese Communist parties. (There were some disagreements among its founders concerning which of these two parties it should consider itself a part of.) However, once they began work within Taiwan, the women and men of the Taiwan Communist Party tended to be cut off from direction from abroad. Their tasks were continually disrupted by the colonial police; unwillingly or willingly they were usually forced to depend upon their own judgments.

Members were few—never more than a few dozen at most—but they were active in all left-wing enterprises and exerted a surprising amount of influence. Before 1928 was finished they had taken over the direction of the peasant movement, and in 1929 they managed to get Lien expelled from the Cultural Association for his "Yamakawaism." On the other hand, they cooperated with non-Communist leftists on many issues. One of the most prominent of their slogans, "Independence for Taiwan," inspired many young Taiwanese anticolonialists.[143]

As among other Taiwanese leftists, key figures in the Taiwan Communist Party had studied abroad—nearly all the important party members had been students in China or Japan.[144] Like other Taiwanese leftist groups, the party also attracted islanders with only elementary schooling.[145] And also as in the case of non-

Communist radicals, a self-made intellectual with little formal education could become an important leader in the party.

Lien Wên-ch'ing had only finished common school, but Hsieh Hsüeh-hung, "the parent of the Taiwan Communist Party," was even farther removed from the ranks of Taiwan's highly educated native elite. Born to a poor family in the eastern part of Taichū province in 1900, Hsieh lost both her parents when she was thirteen and was sold as a concubine two years later. Afterwards she worked as a laborer for a sugar company for a while, and managed to get to Kobe in Japan in 1917. At Kobe seventeen-year-old Hsieh opened a hat shop and studied Japanese and Mandarin Chinese. Three years later she returned to Taiwan. There she joined the Taiwan Cultural Association when it was organized and was active in women's movement activities. The police, however, soon recognized her leadership qualities, and by 1925 she was fleeing to Shanghai. The next few years gave her experience in the Chinese student movement and took her to Moscow, where she became acquainted with Chinese and Japanese revolutionaries. She went back to Taiwan briefly, and then was off to Shanghai in 1928 to play a central role in the founding of the Taiwan Communist Party. Soon she was back in Taihoku, where she ran a bookstore as a front for party business. She was one of the most influential Communists in the Cultural Association, the peasant movement, and labor movement until her arrest in 1931, the year in which massive police round-ups put an end to Communist activities within the colony.[146]

Hsieh, incidentally, was by no means the only prominent figure in the Taiwan Communist Party who was female. Out of the eight or nine individuals who occupied the most important positions at the center of the party, at least two others were also women.[147] The conservatives' platforms always included support for women's rights, but it was from Communist Party ranks that women significantly emerged as power holders.

Seminal influences upon Taiwanese radical anticolonialism came from China as well as Japan. In both these countries Taiwanese students tended to learn their lessons in radicalism outside their classrooms rather than in them. Nevertheless, some young Taiwanese also studied the theory of revolution-making seriously while abroad, and many of their teachers were Japanese. Leftists inside the colony, opposed at every turn by an efficient and knowledgeable police force, could not easily maintain ties with Chinese colleagues unless they left the island periodically—as indeed a few did. Once students had returned to Taiwan, contacts with Japanese sources of inspiration were generally easier to keep up because Taiwan was a part of the Japanese empire. In spite of severe police repression, Taiwanese radicals drew upon the resources of the Japanese left, much as conservatives turned to Japanese liberals for support. Activists in the peasant movement, for example, were close to left-wing unions and political parties in Japan, and when arrested were repeatedly defended in colonial courts by Japanese lawyers sent by these groups.[148]

It has been argued by no less eminent a commentator than Yanaihara Tadao that the left-wing element in Taiwan's anticolonial movement was entirely imported from abroad. In sharp contrast to the radicals with their alien (Marxist) ideology, Yanaihara saw the conservatives as nationalists struggling against the foreign imperialists who ruled their country.[149]

Certainly the radicals shared ideals held by people in other parts of the world. The models for social change they chose came not only from their Japanese experiences but also from apprenticeships served with Chinese—and in a few cases even Russian—comrades. But when they organized and agitated in Taiwan they by no means applied wholesale what they had learned abroad. Radicals in the peasant unions were usually local leaders who were highly sensitive to local conditions and problems. Taiwanese leftists preached class struggle, but for all practical purposes they defined the oppressed class as the people of Taiwan and the oppressor-class as the ruling Japanese. Rather than leading agricultural and industrial workers against capitalists and landlords irrespective of their ethnic origins, they tended to concentrate on fights against Japanese corporations, the colonial government, and its most visible collaborators. While from 1927 they also wholeheartedly supported tenant farmers' struggles against Taiwanese landlords, they never stopped insisting that Japanese imperialism was the islanders' real enemy.[150] Left-wing anticolonialism in Taiwan was ridden with internal squabbles after 1927, but even the Taiwan Communist Party, the organization with the tightest foreign ties, supported a national revolution. Why was organization, solidarity, and resistance to the Japanese as preached by the leftists a less nationalistic message than that of the conservatives?

Close to the conservatives, Yanaihara Tadao perhaps naturally sympathized with them. His conclusion regarding the radicals' contribution to Taiwanese anticolonialism, however, does not tally with the record of leftist activism. It reveals more about Yanaihara's expectations regarding Marxists than it does about the role leftists actually played in Taiwan's anticolonial struggles.

Conservative or radical, Taiwanese anticolonialism was a product of Japanese education. Modern Japan no longer held mysteries for the Taiwanese. Their rulers, by schools, teachers, and the printed word, had thoroughly acquainted them with a society once alien but now understood only too well. If educated Taiwanese accepted the premises upon which this society stood, they soon discovered that they, who in competition had proved themselves capable of first-class performance, were treated as second-class citizens. This discovery turned many intellectuals into anticolonialists. Educated Taiwanese who questioned the values of this society saw that there were Japanese in Japan who were repelled by the same inequities that troubled them. From these Japanese opponents of their country's establishment, they drew much of their vision of a new kind of Taiwan.

Conservative or radical, Taiwanese anticolonialism was largely a movement of intellectuals. Although a few outstanding self-schooled individuals like Lien Wên-ch'ing and Hsieh Hsüeh-hung played important parts, both wings were led by highly educated Japanese-trained islanders. Even in the peasant unions, where anticolonialism probably came closest to large numbers of humble Taiwanese, the leaders were usually teachers, physicians, lawyers — individuals with some advanced education and often direct contacts with groups and colleagues in Japan. Indeed, among the farmers and industrial workers who were organized a surprising number were common school graduates. The thousands of Taiwanese who signed petitions and joined the conservatives' Cultural Association and later their League for the Attainment of Local Autonomy were nearly all Japanese-trained members of the island's middle and upper classes. If one considers colonial Taiwan as a developing country, where an intellectual may be anyone with some modern education, then not only the leadership but a great deal of the rank-and-file of the Taiwanese anticolonial movement can be called intellectuals also. And although some internationalist content and Chinese experience went into the making of Taiwan's anticolonial intellectuals, leaders and followers alike were overwhelmingly products of Japanese education.

9/ Conclusion

In 1895 the Japanese arrived in Taiwan with two-and-a-half decades of building a modern education system behind them. With this experience, they began to construct a colonial school system modeled upon the one that was rapidly maturing in the home islands. As in Meiji Japan, Taiwan's education was to consist of a large base of public elementary schools for the general populace topped by a small number of specialized institutions for a select few. In their first colony, the Japanese were determined to match the impressive record their nation-building efforts were creating at home.[1]

The basic approach was the same in Japan and Taiwan. Education was a servant of the state. Its largest task, that of universal elementary schooling, was twofold. It was to unite the entire population psychologically and instill loyalty to the state in each of its members, and at the same time to provide them with the discipline, skills, and attitudes Japan's version of modernization required of its people. With appropriate socialization and preparation to enter a labor force, Japanese and Taiwanese schoolchildren would both become effective instruments of Japan's national goals.

But Taiwan was a colony and its people, although of the same Asian stock and with a partially-shared cultural heritage, were not Japanese. The Taiwanese not only lacked any kind of emotional commitment to Japan; they were entirely unfamiliar with everything the Japanese state represented. While this was not completely unlike the mentality of many ordinary Japanese before the Meiji Restoration, even the least nationalistic of late Tokugawa commoners would probably have been easier material for modern Japanese educators to work with.[2] For one thing, despite important linguistic variations, people from different parts of the Japanese islands shared a common language.

Realizing that they faced challenges far greater than those of early Meiji, the Japanese in Taiwan wondered if the Japanese language could be used to unify and nationalize the Taiwanese too. Officials debated this question, but to Izawa Shūji there was really no choice. He had already decided upon Japanese language-education before he left Japan. When a British Presbyterian missionary, who had been teaching in Taiwan for twelve years and had found it necessary to teach in the native languages (although he had tried instruction in English at first), urged him to educate in the vernacular, Izawa only became more adamant.[3] Vernacular education might have imparted new skills and knowledge, but would it have encouraged identification with Japan? As a student of colonial education in British Malaya noted:

> Through the vernacular the child, to begin with, enters into the thought and feeling of those with whom he is most closely linked both in the home and in the village; through the vernacular he also enters into the minds of those who, in song and story, have given voice to their deepest and inmost thoughts; through the vernacular he becomes heir to the social customs and ceremonies of his people. Thus the child comes to value his mother tongue not only as a medium of self-expression, but also as the means whereby he can secure for himself all that is worthy of his loyalty and devotion to his cultured past . . . It is the vehicle he chooses for the expression of his highest thoughts and feelings and of the loftiest flights of his imagination. It is rare for great literary heights, particularly in poetry, to be reached by writers using a foreign tongue . . . It can be stated without hesitation that no system of the highest and most natural development of the individual can afford to exclude the vernacular at any stage of progress.[4]

However, the Japanese in Taiwan were less interested in "the highest and most natural development of the individual" than they were in the highest development in each individual of loyalty to Japan. They wanted to detach each Taiwanese from any past he or she might perceive. Vernacular education in Taiwan would have meant Chinese education. And the Chinese intellectual tradition might well have challenged some Japanese goals.

On the other hand, administrators like Gotō Shimpei and Mochiji Rokusaburō were aware of the dangers of replacing old traditions with new aspirations. The new education was not to encourage natives to rise above their stations in colonial life. The pupils were not to think that they were equal to their Japanese teachers—at least not for a long, long time. A critic of English education in India has described the kind of situation which Taiwan's colonial administrators worked hard to avoid: "The educated Indian became ashamed of the language his parents spoke, of their dress, their manners and traditions. He would not return to the village but sought a life in the society he had learned to admire."[5]

Repeatedly, measures were taken to keep the common school curriculum suitable for a predominantly rural clientele who would take up the same occupations as their parents. Loyalty, filial piety, obedience to legitimate authority—all found within the Chinese Confucian tradition—were emphasized with this end in view. At the same time, great efforts were made to instill a very non-Confucian idea in Taiwanese schoolchildren. This was that manual labor was a dignified and honorable pastime for a scholar as well as for anyone else. Again and again, educational authorities urged teachers to show that the man who worked with his head also worked with his hands. Children were taught to clean and tidy their schoolrooms and to work in their school vegetable patches. Japanese teachers were commanded to set good examples for the children to copy.

Japanese administrators reasoned that higher education, especially in law, literature, politics, and philosophy, would encourage unrest and even rebellion. Therefore it was to be avoided as much as possible. Apparently this was the lesson they drew from their studies of earlier and contemporary Western colonialism, but they could have learned as much from watching higher education in Japan.[6] Irresistible Taiwanese demands for higher education were to be channeled into professional studies which would produce the kind of trained natives the colony required. Thus, during the first decades of colonial rule, higher education for Taiwanese meant either normal school or medical school.

This attitude was not at all like that of British administrators in India in the middle of the nineteenth century, who thought that higher education in English would turn Indians opposed to British rule into enthusiastic supporters of it.

> The young men, brought up at our seminaries, turn with contempt from the barbarous despotisms under which their ancestors groaned, to the prospect of improving their national institutions

on the English model. Instead of regarding us with dislike, they court our society, and look upon us as their natural protectors and benefactors: the summit of their ambition is to resemble us . . . So far from the idea of driving the English into the sea uppermost in their minds, they have no notion but such as rivets their connection with the English, and makes them dependent on English protection and instruction.[7]

wrote Charles Trevelyan of the Bengal Civil Service in 1838.

Unlike the British, the Japanese did not particularly want to replace one high culture with another. They did not wish to substitute Japanese philosophy or science for Chinese classical learning. Their main concern was to give a rudimentary education to a much larger number of Taiwanese than had ever gone to school before.

What the Japanese Achieved

Implementation of the hopes for elementary education was, on the whole, fairly successful. Although the common schools probably convinced more Taiwanese of the importance of boiling drinking water and washing one's hands after using the toilet than of the majesty of the Japanese emperor, by the end of the period these schools were touching the lives of even rather humble islanders. There were failures. Considerable wastage occurred in the common school system. Many who entered the first grade did not finish, probably because, as in Burma, when children were old enough to be useful many parents kept them home.[8] And in poor areas common schools, patronized only by a handful of children of the local well-to-do, stood apart from the main stream of community life.[9] For many common school graduates there were difficulties in retaining language and other skills while living and working in an all-Taiwanese environment.[10] Despite superficial influence in some spheres of Taiwanese life, the overall record of Japanese elementary education, in terms of the number of people it reached and what it taught them, is impressive. By the end of the colonial period it had gained widespread acceptance. Indeed, the limitations of common schooling during the last part of the Japanese period stem at least as much from government-general reluctance to increase investment in common schools as from Taiwanese attitudes toward these schools.

The resolution to curb higher education was much harder to

carry out. As the years passed, Taiwanese pressure for advanced schooling became increasingly difficult to resist. Reluctantly administrators concluded in 1915 that it was probably less dangerous to tolerate a secondary academic school for natives within the colony than to drive ambitious young Taiwanese to Japan. And when the economy proved ready to absorb indigenous paraprofessionals and technicians, an autocratic governor-general managed to initiate and expand vocational studies at secondary school and college levels despite resistance from old Taiwan hands. Shortly afterwards, when the policy of assimilation was announced and the 1922 education rescript was promulgated, this too was partly in response to Taiwanese pressure for higher education.

Officials claimed that the 1922 edict abolished all ethnic discrimination in the schools, in accord with the accelerated assimilation policy. But Taiwanese knew better. Assimilation under Den, in spite of his hopes and reforms, still meant assimilation chiefly at the bottom of Japanese society, just as it had meant under Akashi. Elementary school lessons for Taiwanese were still rewritten to delete tales of humble Japanese who rose to dizzy heights. Taiwanese who could afford it still sent their offspring to Japan to study, because it was easier for Taiwanese to enter Japan's first-rate colleges and universities than to gain admission to the integrated institutions of the colony. Official insistence that discrimination had been abolished only increased the resentment of Taiwanese intellectuals, especially among those who could not afford to go to Japan to study.

In India, British education soon mocked Charles Trevelyan's optimism, as from its embrace emerged forces for a militant anti-British movement.[11] Ironically, in Taiwan, where authorities had tried hard to withhold the higher education Trevelyan recommended for natives, many highly educated islanders responded much as Trevelyan had expected the Indians to do. Of course, while British education in India usually meant liberal arts, most Taiwanese intellectuals were products of specialized professional training. In the British colony "the study of English history and political theory indoctrinated the native intelligentsia with ideals and aspirations incompatible with the existing political order in India."[12] Educated Taiwanese had usually been prepared for careers in medicine, pedagogy, applied science, or commerce. Even so, before the period was out hundreds, perhaps thousands, of Taiwanese had studied such subjects as law, literature, arts, political science, economics, philosophy, and pure science mainly in the colleges and universities of Japan. Among these people, too, alienation from their rulers seems to have been comparatively weak.

Consequences for the Taiwanese

What consequences did Japanese education have for the Taiwanese identity? They were perhaps not very significant for the majority of the population. In the villages Chinese patterns of family and community life continued. Intergroup warfare, common before 1895, no longer existed but old allegiances remained, as did ethnic subgroup separations that were reinforced by differences in dialect and custom. However, the Japanese presence often softened the edge of these divisions, especially in the cities where working-class Taiwanese from all quarters of the island lived together. Since most of the Japanese resided in the cities, differences between Taiwanese and Japanese lifestyles were most visible there. Thus urban experience may have aided formation of a "Taiwanese consciousness" among city Taiwanese of all classes. At the same time, most of the modern improvements associated with the Japanese were in the cities and the Japanese atmosphere was strongest there. The Taihoku teacher's explanation of his pupils' blessings as Japanese subjects must have seemed less remote than the same message when preached in village schools.

The relationship between Japanese education and the identity of the Taiwanese middle and upper classes is a much more complex problem. Certainly Taiwanese intellectuals educated during the colonial period absorbed at least an overlay of Japanization. But how deep did the overlay go and what was at the core?

Much of the Taiwanese experience would have been familiar to other nationals who acquired higher education under a colonial regime. In many ways the Taiwanese student in Tokyo was cousin to young Indochinese in Paris and Indians in London. Happy or not with their situation, these intellectuals had entered the dominating country's culture. Like colonized elites elsewhere, even Taiwanese intellectuals who opposed Japanese rule sometimes clung to Japanese institutions and values.

But the cleavage between the 1920s or 1930s student in Tokyo and most of his three and a half or four million compatriots at home probably was not as severe as the gap that separated Western-educated Indians, Indochinese, Indonesians, and Africans from the masses in their countries. Indeed, as Taiwan's administrators were so fond of pointing out, Taiwanese and Japanese were both Asian peoples and did share some common traditions. But perhaps by the 1920s or 1930s it was equally important that the Taiwanese university or college student in Japan had begun his or her education with the same or a similar curriculum as that with which a large number of Taiwanese of all classes as well as nearly all Japanese had become acquainted. Western colonial school systems, on the other hand, tended to be composed of different kinds of schools for different groups or classes of natives at each level of schooling. At the elementary level especially, these included a variety of vernacular schools, partly vernacular schools, and schools which taught in the language of the colonial ruler.[13] Many of them were vastly different in kind as well as in standard from European schools, but ambitious natives often were expected to move from such institutions into more Westernized schools at a postprimary level.[14] And the educational link was not the only factor that made the Taiwanese intellectual seem less an outsider in metropolis or colony. Under fifty years of Japanese colonialism life in Taiwan generally became much closer to life in Japan than was the case in any colony under Western rule.[15] Perhaps because of this, educated Taiwanese were spared some of the anguish of the assimilated intellectual caught between two worlds.[16]

Contact with Chinese students in Japan, experiences on the Chinese mainland where schools became fairly accessible to them after 1920, and China's epoch-making modern history itself brought many Taiwanese intellectuals closer to their Chinese heritage. Yet they continued to feel at home in other places, comfortably moving back and forth among Chinese, Japanese, and Taiwanese colleagues. Affinity with China was part of the anticolonial movement, despite government hostility toward identification with China, but the movement contained a local, Taiwanese content too. For Taiwanese intellectuals who rejected Japanese imperialism, Chinese influences were often germane. However, the identity of these men and women was by no means primarily a national one.

While the deeper question of cultural or national identity cannot be answered definitely, it is clear that Japanese education brought decisive change into the lives of all classes of Taiwanese.

Schools were effective innovators because they were an integral part of a parcel that contained other instruments of change — railroads, telegraphs, post offices, streamlined landholding arrangements, agriculture testing stations, hydroelectric works, agricultural cooperatives, factories, banks, law courts, hospitals and clinics, policemen, and the *hokō* system. Of course the educational impact was greater among some groups than among others.

The Taiwanese opposition to Japanese rule which emerged after 1920 was also a product of Japanese education. After a taste of a freer life in the ruling country, returning students understandably found the restrictions placed upon them in colonial society harder to bear. In addition, Taiwanese who never left the island reacted against discrepancies between schoolbook descriptions of the Japanese empire and the realities of colonial life. Yet, despite their restlessness and resentment, Japanese-educated islanders did not necessarily reject the world their conquerors had created; schools in Taiwan and Japan tended to turn out less aggressive rebels than did study in China. Police repression also helped keep the anticolonial movement in legal channels, but a large proportion of the discontented were genuinely more interested in acquiring bigger shares of existing economic, political, and social rewards than in fundamentally disturbing the status quo. The paucity of native content in school curricula irritated them, but generally they lashed out at the niggardly education provisions for their children, in comparison with what was offered to colonial Japanese, rather than at the education system itself.

The Changing Status of Women

One group for whom Japanese education meant particularly radical change was the female half of the Taiwanese population. Nothing in Chinese high or folk culture supported public education for females. Yet, as Table 13 in Chapter Seven illustrates, by 1935 one quarter of the Taiwanese female elementary school-aged population was in school, and nine years later this percentage had jumped to 60. They studied the same curriculum as their brothers, and although textbooks did deal with differences in boys' and girls' roles, a surprising amount of the books' didactic content was addressed to both sexes.[17] Pictures and stories in readers and ethics books portrayed both sexes doing similar things; little boys as well as little girls could be found doing domestic tasks, like caring for an ill mother or sweeping up rubbish. In elementary school and at higher girls' school Taiwanese girls became as enthusiastic participants as their brothers in gymnastics, track and field, swimming, tennis, basketball, and volleyball. During the latter half of the period the high Taiwanese demand for higher girls' school shows how acceptable female education had become, for although attendance at such a school could help one acquire credentials as a teacher, for many it was essentially a finishing school experience.

Increased schoolgoing for girls was closely related to other new directions for women. An end to footbinding and entrance into the colony's industrial work force were two important changes. For twenty years the government encouraged Taiwanese to give up the custom of binding women's feet to produce a "lily-foot" of approximately half the normal size, a practice common in China since at least the Sung dynasty (960-1126). But officials concentrated on supporting native efforts, aware that this reform would be most effective if initiated by islanders themselves.

In 1900 the administration backed a natural foot society organized by a traditional medical practitioner named Huang Yü-chieh. Governor-General Kodama himself honored the society by attending its first large meeting, and later by presenting members (who were men who had sworn not to allow their sons to marry girls with bound feet) with silk sashes upon which, in his own calligraphy, he "wrote the Confucian maxim that filial piety began with our not daring to injure our persons."[18] Huang's argument for giving up the custom was both traditional and revolutionary. He wanted women to be better able to serve their families and menfolk in familiar ways, but he also suggested that they play new roles. In the society's inaugural address he stated:

> Now Taiwan has become a part of the Japanese empire, and the government is carrying out reforms. The Taiwanese are also a people of reform . . . We must continue striving forward, hoping that women can keep their Heavenly endowments. Natural-footed women can pound the mortars, draw water from the wells, and sew garments diligently in the service of their in-laws. Going one step further, they can enter schools to study the Japanese language, embroidery or calligraphy, and perhaps specialize in arith-

metic, accounting, science or other fields. If successful, they will create a worthy livelihood and greatly help society by assisting men who are too busy to accomplish certain deeds.[19]

Huang and his followers made some gains but for at least a decade unbound feet continued to be a popular target of male ridicule. However, by 1914 feeling had grown fairly strong, and Lin Hsien-t'ang's influential family in Taichū organized another anti-foot-binding society which successfully persuaded hundreds of women to let out their bindings. The following year the authorities decided that such action could be made mandatory: "On the fifteenth of April, an official order of prohibition was issued. The decree was effective and by August more than 763,000 women had obeyed. Recalcitrants were forcibly dealt with, more and more Taiwanese complied, and the custom disappeared, owing to strict government prohibition and the development of public feeling against it."[20]

On unbound feet women moved into the factories and offices that were beginning to appear. In 1914 there were only 21,859 factory workers on the island but about 28 percent of these were female. While the factory work force expanded each year, the female proportion of it did not rise significantly until the late 1930s; in 1938, out of 95,641 factory workers 35,878 or roughly 37 percent were women, and three years later this percentage exceeded 40. More women were employed in some industries than in others. They outnumbered male laborers in the manufacture of woven goods—mainly the fiber hats which became a famous island export. In the largest manufacturing industry, foodstuffs, they amounted to about half the number of men employed by the middle of the 1930s and by 1941 amounted to 30,941 out of a work force of 67,020. But very few women were ever employed in machinery and tool production. Employers preferred factory workers, female as well as male, who had been to school. Educated men vastly outnumbered their female counterparts for decades: it was 1938 before there were even half as many girls in common school as boys. But as the gap narrowed during the last years of colonial rule the proportion of schooled factory workers jumped faster for women than for men.[21]

Schooling was even more important for women seeking jobs in offices and shops. By 1943, 93 percent of the females employed in offices and shops had been to school and almost all of these were at least common school graduates, while at the very least 38 percent were graduates of higher girls' school, or of equivalent or higher institutions.[22] More of these white collar women may have been Japanese than was the case for factory workers, but the bulk of them were native islanders.[23]

Only a few Taiwanese women began careers after completing specialized professional studies, but their importance far exceeded their numbers. As pioneers in prestigious new fields they provided for females role models that had never before existed. Their appearance was probably one of the most radical of all the changes that occurred during the Japanese period. Unfortunately, however, data available on these trail breakers are scanty and imprecise. In educational statistics those who studied in Japan are often hidden away in private schools or miscellaneous schools categories. While biographical dictionaries published during the colonial period reveal the educational backgrounds of hundreds of Taiwanese men, in only one entry in one dictionary is the subject a woman.[24] However, thanks to a Chinese *Who's Who* published in Taiwan during the postcolonial period, and to other sundry scattered sources, it is known that by the end of the period Taiwanese women had been trained both in the colony and in Japan for careers in medicine, midwifery, dentistry, pedagogy, commerce, home economics, esthetics, economics, and science.[25]

Most of the highest-ranking female professionals appear to have been trained in Japan, and this in itself was no mean feat. There were very few colleges or other facilities in the ruling country to accommodate the most ambitious of the hundreds of thousands of Japanese girls who were graduating from higher girls' schools by the late 1930s. In 1914 the first three women ever to enter a government university enrolled in Tōhoku Imperial. From then on the government universities regularly admitted small numbers of women students, and by the late 1930s at least three or four Taiwanese women had gained entrance.[26] Only two or three of the private universities recognized women and permitted coeducational attendance at lectures; and while in 1937 the Japanese government supported ninety-six universities and higher educational institutions for men, it provided on the highest level only two higher normal schools for women, plus a coeducational music school in Tokyo.[27] There were also fifty specialized colleges for women in 1937, out of which six were governmental.[28] Competition to enter most women's colleges was stiff, but several hundred Taiwanese women managed to get a college education, many of them in medicine.[29]

Employment opportunities were always less generous for professional Japanese women than for their male counterparts. After the Manchurian incident in 1931 which led to a full-scale Japanese occupation of Manchuria, the loud demand of the antimodernists that patriotic Japanese women should first and foremost be "good wives and mothers" made the situation even more difficult.[30] Thus after 1931 Taiwanese graduates of women's colleges had to face not only longstanding islander prejudices against professional women but also a Japanese climate of opinion which was becoming less and less tolerant of them. Given the circumstances, it is amazing that any of them entered professional life.[31]

Higher education sent Taiwanese women as well as men into politics, in spite of the authorities' disapproval. Individual women were active in both conservative and radical wings of the anticolonial movement. Although they achieved central leadership roles only in leftist circles, a women's rights movement was an integral part of the moderates' campaigns.

Given the direction the Japanese nation took after 1931, it is rather ironic that Japanese colonial policies pushed Taiwanese women into professional and public life. When the Japanese occupied the Philippines during the course of the Pacific War, they were not entirely happy to find thousands of Philippine women in professional life and hundreds of them elected to public office (they had gained the franchise in 1937). After surveying conditions in this former American colony, they were "forced to conclude that the position which women occupy in the Philippines as a political factor, direct and indirect, cannot be ignored."[32] But they saw no reason to allow this situation to continue. "The character of political activities of women should be changed," recommended Royama Masamichi in a report commissioned by the Japanese military administration. He continued:

> When the women of the Philippines again turn their attention to matters relating to family, education, nutrition, public health, morality of men, and so forth, they will find in those fields an important mission for them to discharge, apparently negative, but actually distinctly positive. In this sense, the women of the Philip-

pines will profit by the example of their sisters in Japan, who work quietly and unobtrusively in the family and for the neighborhood associations, enabling their husbands to work outside, completely freed from the cares of their families, thus drawing to themselves the unbounded gratitude and respect of their men.[33]

The Japanese in Comparison to Other Colonial Rulers

In comparison with the educational opportunities other colonial rulers offered the people they dominated, the Japanese in Taiwan were far from niggardly. With the exception of the Americans in the Philippines, no other colonial power in Asia or elsewhere approached native education with anything like the seriousness of purpose of Japanese educators in Taiwan. The care that went into formulating and executing educational plans was outstanding. The Philippines excepted, no colonial education system under a Western flag received such a generous input of funds and skilled personnel.

In Dutch and French colonies the advanced education that selected elites received was famous for its high standards. But the maze of vernacular and European (Chinese, vernacular, and European in Indochina) schools which formed the base of the educational pyramids in Dutch and French colonies made it impossible for all but a very few natives to get the preparation necessary for entrance to the fine schools at the top. And for the general populations, Dutch and French colonial governments provided very little education. When the Dutch left Indonesia after centuries of rule only about 10 percent of the population was literate — one of the lowest rates in the area.[34] The stinginess of elementary schooling in the Netherlands Indies was rivaled only by its counterpart in Indochina.[35] The story was the same in other parts of the globe: in 1939, after a great increase in elementary school facilities for natives, the French in Morocco were able to boast that about 2 percent of the Moroccan school-aged population was in school.[36]

As colonial educators, the British were more liberal, although the standards of their higher institutions were not considered as excellent as French or Dutch.[37] In Britain's overseas territories, governments and missionaries tended to concentrate upon the education of the middle and upper classes and to rely upon a principle of downward filtration to reach the masses.[38] Because public support for education in British colonies commonly took the form of grants-in-aid to recognized private schools, governments frequently were less directly involved educationally than was the case elsewhere and had greater difficulty ensuring that educational planning remained an integral part of general policy making.[39] All in all, there was a good deal of laissez-faire in British colonial education. Perhaps this was why British colonial schools frequently failed either to provide people with marketable skills or to foster hoped-for attitudinal change but did succeed in turning out individuals totally unfit for traditional occupations and lifestyles.[40]

Some of the success of Japanese education in Taiwan, as in the Philippines, was because the new rulers took over a people who already possessed a well-established tradition of learning and schooling not completely unlike the one being introduced. Even on the outskirts of the Ch'ing empire, Chinese schools and scholars were teaching the classics to young members of the gentry class. Japanese language, which employed Chinese characters in its script, was not as strange to literate Taiwanese as Western languages might have been. Similarly, in the Philippines, the Americans inherited a land that had acquired a strong taste for learning from the Spanish friars.[41] English, which replaced Spanish as the medium of instruction, was not as different from Spanish as, for instance, a non-European language would have been.[42]

However, as J. S. Furnivall has illustrated in his study of Burma under the British, a high educational base at the beginning of a colonial period does not guarantee still higher educational levels at the end of the period:

> The progress of education under all its forms in Burma during the period between 1923 and 1940 shows a notable contrast with that achieved in neighbouring countries . . . Sixty years ago Upper Burma, under native rule, had far more children at school than any country outside Burma in the tropical Far East; in 1900 Burma as a whole still held the lead, but by 1940 it had sunk to the fifth place, and in respect of institutions managed or helped by Government, was little ahead of Netherlands India, where general public instruction dates only from 1907 . . . It might be claimed sixty years ago that Burma was the best educated country in the tropical Far East, with the possible exception of the Philippines. It would be difficult to repel the charge that at the time of its separation from India it was the worst educated.[43]

One of Furnivall's shrewdest criticisms of colonial education in South and Southeast Asia was that it did not prepare individuals for "the business of life" but only for "the life of business" few of them would ever pursue.[44] Colonial educators in Taiwan and the Philippines were exceptional because the school systems they fashioned seriously attempted to prepare their students for "the business of life." American education was meant to prepare the Filipinos for independence; the Japanese was meant to assimilate the Taiwanese completely. In spite of such diametrically opposite goals, public education in the two countries shared a great deal. In no other colonies did rulers devote so much energy to indoctrinating the subject people in their own world view, while at the same time taking extraordinary pains to present this view in a way which would be in harmony with the local environment.[45]

The United States, which at least officially did not intend to rule the Philippines forever, steadily increased native participation in colonial political processes over the years and allowed Filipino critics of American rule to publish freely under a "policy of permitting full semantic outbursts short of acts of sedition."[46] Thus it does not seem surprising that — unlike nationalist movements under less permissive rulers — Filipino anticolonialism remained within constitutional and legal orbits. What is more astonishing is that in Taiwan, where the political climate was so different, the anticolonial movement should tread similar paths. In Taiwan improved standards of living for many retarded alienation from the regime. But in both countries acceptance of the rulers' education appears to have acted as an important force for moderation in the choice of methods for political protest.

American rulers of the Philippines spent much more of their colony's revenues upon education than did the Japanese in Taiwan. A survey of Philippine education in 1925, for instance, reported that "out of a general government expenditure of slightly more than ₱ 100,000,000 educational contributions from taxes amount to ₱ 23,000,000."[47] But the Japanese probably expended educational funds more effectively, at least at the lower levels of the school system. The 1925 Philippine survey also reported that 82 percent of Filipino schoolchildren did not get past the fourth grade of the six-year elementary school course, that many dropped out after the first or second grade, and that the average length of time taken to complete four grades was five years.[48] As late as 1946 Filipino educators reported that only 58 percent of the country's elementary schoolchildren continued in school after the second grade, and that large numbers of youngsters were re-peating grades or taking longer than one year to pass each grade.[49]

Generally, segregation in Western colonial education did not stop at a demarcation between ruled and ruler. With the exception of the American Philippines, most administrations tended to make different qualities of schooling available to different classes or groups of natives.[50] Dutch schools for natives in Java were organized strictly upon class lines: the offspring of Javanese aristocrats alone were permitted to enter first-class native schools, while a second-class grade of native school accommodated the sons of commoners.[51] Similarly, the British in Malaysia established special elite schools for selected Malays of good birth and much more primitive facilities for most of the rest of the population.[52] Japanese education in Taiwan was much more egalitarian. In the beginning the Japanese made overtures toward the better-educated natives, but a single school system was established for Taiwanese of all classes and no Taiwanese class or group was denied access to it. For some individual Taiwanese families, Japanese education functioned as a vehicle of soaring upward mobility.[53] In fact, by the end of the period education had clearly become an important determinant of membership in the island's native middle and upper classes.

But the Japanese claimed too much for this egalitarianism when they declared that after 1922 Taiwanese and Japanese in the colony were treated alike educationally. Abolition of educational discrimination in 1922, they argued, proved that, unlike the racially prejudiced Western nations in Asia, Japan did not discriminate against or exploit the people it ruled. This attitude of self-deception or hypocrisy — or perhaps a combination of the two — remained strong in Japanese government circles long after 1945. As late as 1964 the Japanese foreign ministry published a book which still complacently claimed that Japanese education in Taiwan was aimed at integrating the Taiwanese and raising their cultural level and that the Japanese were unique among colonial rulers because of the abundant educational opportunities they gave the people they ruled.[54] In actual fact, however, the Japanese in Taiwan were much like other colonizers in their attitudes toward the people they governed. And the Taiwanese, whether or not they were aware of this, knew that Japanese residents in Taiwan showed no signs of willingness to give up their privileged position even after the assimilation policy was in full force.[55]

Heritage for Postcolonial Taiwan

The Taiwanese paid dearly for Japanese education, but it did give them some positive assets with which to start postcolonial life.[56] Training of teachers and physicians, urgently needed in developing countries but generally neglected by colonial regimes,[57] was emphasized during Japanese rule in Taiwan. The traditional contempt for manual work, which Gunnar Myrdal found so pernicious and tenacious in South Asian countries, is relatively weak in postcolonial Taiwan.[58]

In *Asian Drama* Myrdal has described the type of educated young people he believes developing countries need today: "In their efforts to modernize their economies and adopt advanced technology, the South Asian countries need young people who . . . have functional literacy, mastery of basic mathematics, certain mechanical skills, especially in the use of tools and machinery, a basic knowledge of the sciences and of the world around them, and rational attitudes toward work. Thus prepared they will be adaptable and mobile, ready for advancement."[59] The schools of Taiwan contributed a great deal toward mastery of such skills and formation of such attitudes.

Appendixes
Notes
Bibliography
Glossary
Index

Appendix A
Aborigine Education

The aborigines of Taiwan were bullied and driven from their lands by Chinese settlers, taxed and converted by the Dutch, isolated by Ch'ing officials, and slaughtered by Japanese troops. As Mochiji Rokusaburō pointed out, during the first two decades of Japanese rule, an education system for aborigines, who made up about 2 percent of the island's population, existed only on paper. Taiwan's new rulers appeared to be waging a war of extermination, as fierce tribal resistance engaged Japanese forces in expeditions to annihilate or contain in mountainous areas the island's oldest inhabitants. At least as late as 1916-18, Japanese planes were dropping bombs on aborigine villages.[1] Only gradually did formal educational programs come to assume a role of any importance.

However, from the beginning such programs—referred to as "taming"—were acknowledged as one of two valid methods of aborigine management.[2] Taming supplemented the other important prong of the aborigine policy, which the government labeled suppression and employed with special vigor against the energetic head-hunters of the north.

> The northern tribe is a wild and ferocious people, and look upon head-hunting as the highest aim in their life. Moreover, they take advantage of the natural stronghold of their territory, which prevents an invasion of the outsider, and depending on themselves for their fighting force, have always committed the most barbarous crimes. Not infrequently, under the influence of wine, after they were treated hospitably by officers in the [police] station, they have killed some of their benefactors and carried back to their tribes the heads of such officers as trophies. Massacres have frequently been perpetrated by these savages in various places from time to time, and it was considered quite a failure to attempt to control them simply by the method of taming.[3]

Despite the attitude which the above quotation from a 1911 government-general report illustrates, in certain localities a few
schools were opened for aborigine children, and police officers
stationed in aborigine territories tried to teach Japanese and
arithmetic to at least the children of village chieftains. However,
tribal rebellions which closed schools and beheaded policemen-
teachers sometimes disrupted such efforts.[4]

From 1910 to 1912 an interesting experiment was attempted in
some aborigine villages. In April 1910 fourteen Buddhist priests
of the *shin* and zen sects were sent to fourteen different aborigine
areas throughout the island to study the languages of various
tribes. The following November, at a three-day conference held
to discuss their experiences, they decided they would like to edit a
reader for aborigines. Subsequently they and others were sent by
the aborigine affairs bureau of the police force to teach in tribal
villages. (All aborigine affairs were the responsibility of the police
from 1902 on.) Those who were sent first went through a week of
intensive preparation in Japanese language and teaching methodology. By 1912 there were twenty-two such missionary teachers
with a total of 147 pupils in mountain villages. But in 1913 aborigine affairs switched back to a heavy emphasis on search-and-
destroy missions against the tribes and the priests were brought
out of the mountains.[5] Henceforth, "although employees at
police stations occasionally happened to be Buddhists and engaged in 'ordinary education' work, they were not encouraged to
carry on missionary activities."[6]

Even on paper aborigine education programs were rather meager before the 1920s. In 1900 the educational affairs chief presented a plan for aborigine education. It called for community
centers that would concentrate as much on schooling for adults as
on instruction for children. Courses were not to be fixed; standards were to be low; the length of the school year was to be flex-
ible. Five years later the administration outlined a plan of studies
in the Japanese language, ethics, and arithmetic for aborigines
who were judged ready for instruction. The plan called for four
years of elementary education modeled on the common school
curricula but of a much lower standard. A great deal of leeway
was given to local administrators who were to determine school
terms, vacation periods, requirements for entrance to the program, and so on.[7] Aborigine common school regulations were
promulgated in 1914, but these could be applied as the heads of

regional administrations saw fit. They outlined an abbreviated (three or four years), lower-standard version of regular common school studies. However, in 1917 only four out of ten administrative regions had any aborigine common schools at all.[8] For a few years around 1920 there existed as many as thirty aborigine common schools with a total of approximately 4,600 pupils, but by 1935 only five aborigine common schools could be found in the entire colony.[9]

Most aborigine children who received any formal Japanese schooling at all got it in the humble education centers (*kyōiku sho*) which grew out of the early efforts of policemen to teach Japanese and arithmetic to the children of chieftains in "pacified" areas. Children would be collected together and given rudimentary instruction in exchange for the medicines police officers handed out to their parents. By 1910 there were about two dozen of these education centers with over two hundred pupils and the government had established regulations for them. By 1916 they existed in every administrative district which included aborigines; altogether there were sixty of them with 1,452 children enrolled. By 1920 there were 2,179 aborigine children enrolled in 103 education centers, and fifteen years later there were 183 centers with a total enrollment of 8,291.[10]

The local policeman, with perhaps his wife as teaching assistant, gave the education center pupils very simple lessons in Japanese language and a few other subjects. Sometimes conversational Japanese was almost all that was taught. As a rule teaching materials were edited by the police force's aborigine affairs bureau, but primary school ethics and language textbooks were recommended as references for instructors. By 1915 the government general's textbook editing office had published books for aborigine children, but education officials had no say in their use. The policemen teachers often had no or very little pedagogical training, but it was 1932 before the education bureau managed to get one of its school inspectors attached to the police department's aborigine affairs bureau. Teaching was only one of the policeman's duties. In the villages he was also required to supervise such enterprises as livestock raising, silkworm cultivation, simple industry (*kan'i kōgyō*), medical aid, trade, transportation, and general farming.[11]

Administrators early and late argued that aborigine education was to be based on aborigine needs. Yet although surveys of aborigine lands took place and data on the different groups' customs and life patterns were conscientiously collected, none of this ever seems to have been used to plan educational programs.[12] Western visitors to the colony who were otherwise impressed with its administration remarked on the lack of sympathy the Japanese felt toward the aborigines and "the generally severe treatment of these native peoples."[13] What educators and administrators seemed to mean was that aborigine education was to meet Japanese needs. It was hoped that schooling would make the tribesmen "good, obedient people and defense soldiers."[14] *Takasago zoku no kyōiku* (Education of the Taiwan aborigines) was published by the police department in 1941 as a review of the history and contemporary state of Japanese education among the island's tribal people. This work states that as of 1940 the curriculum of an aborigine education center under a policeman teacher ideally consisted of the Japanese language, ethics, arithmetic, drawing, music, gymnastics, and manual arts or vocational studies (usually agriculture).[15] It appears that in 1941 the education centers were where the common schools were in 1898.

The number of police-directed education centers increased rapidly during the later years of the colonial period. By 1940 the police department claimed that a high proportion of aborigine children were attending school in these centers. Indeed, they claimed that this proportion amounted to 80 percent of a school-aged population which included the children of all but one of the island's seven aborigine groups.[16]

Some aborigines who attended school at centers during the 1930s and the early 1940s remember their policemen teachers as terrifying disciplinarians, who rounded them up periodically and took them off to classes which they attended only under duress.[17] They rated the education they received as worthless because "it didn't even teach one to read and write."[18] An examination of the educational record of graduates of these centers lends considerable credence to their claims that what the education centers taught was of a very low standard. By 1940 the police department could point to a total of only eighteen aborigine secondary school graduates during forty-five years of Japanese rule. By this year two aborigines had been graduated from the medical school, six from normal school, one from middle school, six from agricultural and forestry school, two from girls' higher school, one from a commercial and industrial school.[19] And even this handful, in all likelihood, reached higher institutions only after attending primary or common school.[20]

Official accounts of Japanese education for aborigines reveal a picture not unlike that sketched by the thirty-four-year-old grandson of an aborigine chieftain in 1969 — although this man's account suggests more educational achievements during the latter part of the Japanese period than do the government general's own records.

> At first the Japanese policy was to control and to limit the number of mountain people [aborigines] in Taiwan. The Japanese were not interested in improving our health or education because they wanted to reduce our numbers. There were no common schools, only so-called education centers. There policemen made sure aborigines could use a few Japanese phrases. The Japanese concentrated on reaching the people through the chieftains. They tried to get control of the chieftains and control the people through them.
>
> Later the Japanese found out that the mountain people could also be made into good soldiers — better even than Japanese soldiers. They discovered that mountain people could be excellent students — some even went to Japan to study. The Japanese consequently changed their policy to include education for mountain people, although we did not have the same common school opportunities which ordinary people (*heichi min*) [Chinese-Taiwanese] had.[21]

Appendix B
Finance

Central administration outlays on education went mainly to the higher schools: notably the specialized colleges, some normal schools (*kanritsu shihan gakkō*), the higher school, and Taihoku Imperial University after its establishment in 1928. The central administration also paid the salaries of teachers in middle schools, higher girls' schools, vocational schools, and provincial normal schools (*shiritsu shihan gakkō*). This left elementary education to the coffers of the regional administrations and the municipalities. District governments paid the salaries of teachers in common schools and primary schools. All other common school and primary school expenses, including capital expenditures, had to be borne jointly by the districts, cities, towns, and villages in which the schools were established. The districts' and municipalities' ratios of education expenditure to total expenditure were much higher than was that of the central administration.

How were the funds spent on education apportioned? What shares of them did the island's Japanese, Taiwanese, and aborigine children receive? An examination of per capita expenditures on children attending primary schools, common schools, and aborigine education centers offers the best answer. There were never enough Japanese in common schools or even Taiwanese in primary schools to make these two institutions anything other than separate vehicles of elementary education for the two main racial groups. (And, it must be remembered, although government outlays to the higher schools benefited some Taiwanese they were enjoyed mainly by Japanese.)

A consistent pattern clearly emerges. On a per capita basis the authorities spent approximately twice as much money for the education of Japanese children as they did for that of Taiwanese children. The aborigine child received much less than was spent on the Taiwanese child. As the following tables illustrate, the two regional government levels combined expended fifty to sixty yen annually on each child in primary school and twenty-five to thirty yen annually on each child in common school. The central government level, responsible for outlays to aborigine education, expended from 6.5 to eighteen yen annually on each child in the education centers. Teacher-student ratios were more favorable in primary schools than in common schools, and common schools had a greater proportion of junior-ranking faculty. These facts also suggest that Japanese schoolchildren received the largest share of education funds.

TABLE B.1. Ratio of educational expenditure to total expenditure of the central, the district, and the municipal governments

Year	Central Government	District Government	City Government	Town and Village Government
1896	—	0	0	0
1897	—	0	0	0
1898	—	—	—	—
1899	0.97	—	—	—
1900	0.88	—	—	—
1901	1.12	—	—	—
1902[a]	0.85	—	—	—
1903	0.81	—	—	—
1904	0.86	—	—	—
1905	0.73	—	—	—
1906	0.66	—	—	—
1907	0.75	—	—	—
1908	0.72	—	—	—
1909	0.83	—	—	—
1910	0.76	—	—	—
1911	0.75	—	—	—
1912	0.79	—	—	—
1913	0.93	—	—	—
1914	0.96	—	—	—
1915	1.34	—	—	—
1916	1.23	—	—	—

Source: TWT, pp. 986-989, 1016-1020.

[a]In April 1902 the primary fiscal responsibilities of education were shifted to the district government. However, it was not until 1921 that the district government increased the educational expenditures.

[b]In October 1920 the central government revised the tax structure and the fiscal responsibilities of primary education were transferred to the district and additionally to the municipal governments. This tax reform went into effect fully from 1921.

(continued)

TABLE B.1. (continued)

Year	Central Government	District Government	City Government	Town and Village Government
1917	1.22	--	–	–
1918	1.26	–	–	–
1919	1.20	–	–	–
1920[b]	1.36	16.1	–	1.9
1921	1.97	42.0	35.6	36.0
1922	2.10	43.2	23.0	36.8
1923	2.58	49.0	19.3	30.8
1924	2.78	51.5	17.5	31.5
1925	3.03	51.0	18.3	29.5
1926	3.26	51.5	17.7	31.2
1927	3.20	50.0	13.2	28.6
1928	3.96	50.9	13.9	27.0
1929	3.89	48.0	13.3	25.6
1930	4.25	46.5	15.4	25.3
1931	4.57	45.5	14.9	27.8
1932	4.40	44.6	14.5	27.1
1933	4.34	42.0	17.1	27.5
1934	3.96	41.0	16.9	25.6
1935	3.71	32.4	14.6	23.5
1936	3.62	35.8	14.2	28.9
1937	3.34	36.6	17.1	31.8
1938	3.45	38.6	17.3	30.8
1939	3.34	39.8	15.8	31.2
1940	3.36	42.5	17.2	38.5
1941	4.06	41.5	15.2	38.9
1942	3.45	37.4	16.1	40.4
1943	3.45	40.1	17.0	36.8
1944	2.62	37.8	14.3	33.8

Source: TWT, pp. 986-989, 1016-1020.

[a]In April 1902 the primary fiscal responsibilities of education were shifted to the district government. However, it was not until 1921 that the district government increased the educational expenditures.

[b]In October 1920 the central government revised the tax structure and the fiscal responsibilities of primary education were transferred to the district and additionally to the municipal governments. This tax reform went into effect fully from 1921.

TABLE B.2. Per capita expenditures on primary school pupils[a]

Academic year (April-March)	(1) No. of pupils enrolled	(2) District government expenditure	(3) City, town and village expenditure	(4) Total educational expenditure (2) + (3)	(5) Per capita educational expenditure (4) ÷ (1)
1915[b]	12,912	− yen	− yen	− yen	− yen
1916	14,145	−	−	−	−
1917	15,300	−	−	−	−
1918	16,622	−	−	−	−
1919	18,048	−	−	−	−
1920	19,784	−	−	−	−
1921[c]	21,901	−	−	−	−
1922	23,034	−	−	−	−
1923	23,983	−	−	−	−
1924	24,211	−	−	−	−
1925	25,730	−	−	−	−
1926	26,236	−	−	−	−
1927	27,638	−	−	−	−
1928	29,772	−	−	−	−
1929	31,980	−	−	−	−
1930	34,184	−	−	1,716,181	50.2
1931	36,744	1,182,831	760,827	2,036,511[d]	55.2
1932	38,388	1,283,961	605,311	1,889,272	49.3
1933	40,246	−	−	−	−
1934	41,251	1,278,583	671,328	1,949,911	47.1
1935	42,156	1,278,756	806,373	2,085,129	49.3
1936	42,968	1,371,587	1,085,783	2,462,370[d]	57.5
1937	44,074	1,527,864	1,259,076	2,822,974[d]	63.5
1938	44,758	−	−	−	−
1939	46,877	1,459,370	815,027	2,310,531[d]	49.5
1940	48,087	1,499,344	868,771	2,405,802[d]	50.0
1941	−	−	−	−	−
1942	50,023	−	−	−	−
1943	51,865	−	−	−	−
1944	53,797	−	−	−	−

Sources: Taiwan jijō, 1920, 1923, 1924, 1926, 1927, 1928, 1930, 1931, 1932, 1934, 1935, 1936, 1937, 1939, 1940, 1942.

[a]Salaries and personal expenses of teachers were paid by the district government. Other school expenses (maintenance and materials, capital expenditure) were borne by city, town, and village governments and partly by the district government.

[b]The only data available from this year concerned the number of pupils enrolled.

[c]The year when the new tax structure went into effect fully. From this year on, the local governments bore primary fiscal responsibilities for education.

[d]Total expenditure is larger than district, city, town, and village government expenditures combined. The difference was made up by special subsidies from the central administration.

TABLE B.3. Per capita expenditures on common school pupils[a]

Academic year (April-March)	(1) No. of Pupils enrolled	(2) District government expenditure	(3) City, town and village expenditure	(4) Total educational expenditure (2) + (3)	(5) Per capita educational expenditure (4) ÷ (1)
1915[b]	66,078	− yen	− yen	− yen	− yen
1916	75,545	−	−	−	−
1917	88,099	−	−	−	−
1918	107,659	−	−	−	−
1919	125,135	−	−	−	−
1920	151,094	−	−	−	−
1921[c]	185,555	−	−	−	−
1922	218,211	−	−	−	−
1923	231,919	−	−	−	−
1924	240,543	−	−	−	−
1925	241,985	−	−	−	−
1926	232,821	−	−	−	−
1927	231,228	−	−	−	−
1928	235,164	−	−	−	−
1929	249,384	−	−	−	−
1930	257,028	−	−	7,629,335	29.6
1931	275,207	5,043,333	2,726,895	8,068,394[d]	29.4
1932	291,990	5,028,116	2,537,286	7,565,402	26.0
1933	316,094	−	−	−	−
1934	344,686	4,852,059	3,023,797	8,505,856[d]	24.7
1935	373,892	5,806,479	4,149,234	9,955,713	26.5
1936	407,614	6,197,046	4,554,583	10,751,629	26.4
1937	450,032	6,723,110	5,326,728	13,187,460[d]	29.2
1938	505,545	−	−	−	−
1939	557,135	8,179,229	2,356,054	13,322,267[d]	24.0
1940	624,986	9,257,787	7,217,045	16,706,139[d]	26.9
1941	−	−	−	−	−
1942	790,670	−	−	−	−
1943	745,638	−	−	−	−
1944	797,729	−	−	−	−

Sources: Taiwan jijō, 1920, 1923, 1924, 1926, 1927, 1928, 1930, 1931, 1932, 1934, 1935, 1936, 1937, 1939, 1940, 1942.

[a]Salaries and personal expenses of teachers were paid by the district government. Other school expenses (maintenance and materials, capital expenditure) were borne by city, town, and village governments and partly by the district government.

[b]The only data available from this year concerned the number of pupils enrolled.

[c]The year when the new tax structure went into effect fully. From this year on, the local governments bore primary fiscal responsibilities for education.

[d]Total expenditure is larger than district, city, town, and village government expenditures combined. The difference was made up by special subsidies from the central administration.

TABLE B.4. Per capita expenditures on aborigine education center pupils[a]

Academic year (April-March)	(1) Total educational expenditure	(2) Fund for postelementary schooling[b]	(3) Expenditure for education centers[c]	(4) Number of pupils registered	(5) Per capita expenditure (3) ÷ (4)	(6) Number of policeman-teachers	(7) Faculty-pupil ratio
1914	17,063 yen	0 yen	17,063 yen	955	17.8 yen	–	–
1915	17,063	0	17,063	1,260	13.5	–	–
1916	17,063	0	17,063	1,453	11.8	–	–
1917	22,750	0	22,750	1,795	12.6	–	–
1918	24,506	0	24,506	1,904	12.8	–	–
1919	36,862	0	36,862	2,029	18.2	–	–
1920	34,212	0	34,212	2,179	15.8	–	–
1921	51,249	3,600	47,649	2,626	18.2	–	–
1922	52,139	5,400	46,739	3,489	13.4	–	–
1923	51,635	5,400	46,235	4,021	11.5	–	–
1924	57,187	5,400	51,787	4,424	11.8	–	–
1925	54,335	5,400	48,935	4,783	10.2	–	–
1926	49,877	5,400	44,477	4,907	8.9	–	–
1927	75,347	5,400	69,947	5,061	13.6	–	–
1928	79,644	5,400	74,244	5,541	13.4	–	–
1929	84,153	5,390	78,763	6,944	11.3	–	–
1930	81,992	5,391	76,601	6,695	11.5	–	–
1931	71,026	5,390	65,636	7,142	9.2	–	–
1932	66,509	4,851	61,658	7,091	8.7	–	–
1933	71,455	4,851	66,604	7,541	8.8	–	–
1934	75,964	4,839	71,125	7,567	9.4	–	–
1935	75,841	4,839	71,002	8,291	8.6	–	–
1936	75,045[d]	4,839	70,206	8,777	8.0	342	26.8
1937	76,298	4,839	71,459	9,006	7.8	357	25.5
1938	74,092	4,839	69,253	9,392	7.3	358	26.2
1939	70,143	4,839	65,304	9,473	6.9	344	27.2
1940	70,500	4,839	65,661	10,096	6.5	399	29.8

Source: Taiwan sōtokufu, *Takasago zoku no kyōiku*, p. 22.
[a]All the expenses were paid by the central government.
[b]A special fund was set up to send qualified aborigine pupils to postelementary institutions. However, few were able to take advantage of this opportunity.
[c]The figure includes salaries of policeman teachers.
[d]For the years 1936-40, the figure excludes the money spent for the Japanese language training for aborigine adults.

TABLE B.5. Faculty-pupil ratios in primary schools

	(1)	(2)	(3)	(4)	(5)	(6)	
Academic year (April-March)	Number of pupils enrolled	Number of qualified teachers	Faculty-pupil ratio (1) ÷ (2)	All teaching staff including temporary appointments	Faculty-pupil ratio (1) ÷ (4)	Ratio of pupils to school-aged children By sex	Total
1915	12,912	327	39.4	462	29.0	M 94.5%	
						F 93.5	94.0
1916	14,145	346	40.9	527	26.8	95.4	
						94.1	94.8
1917	15,300	364	42.0	553	27.6	95.5	
						94.6	95.0
1918	16,222	397	40.9	578	28.0	95.9	
						94.5	95.2
1919	18,048	431	41.9	598	30.2	96.1	
						95.0	95.6
1920	19,784	501	39.2	598	33.1	97.9	
						97.9	97.9
1921	21,901	545	40.1	674	32.6	97.8	
						97.2	97.6
1922	23,034	599	39.8	718	32.2	98.3	
						97.4	97.8
1923	23,983	615	39.8	715	33.5	99.2	
						98.2	98.8
1924	24,211	657	37.0	751	32.2	98.0	
						97.3	97.6
1925	25,730	669	38.5	764	33.6	98.4	
						98.1	98.3
1926	26,236	674	39.0	768	34.2	98.1	
						97.9	98.0
1927	27,638	700	39.6	787	35.2	98.4	
						98.3	98.4
1928	29,772	698	42.5	819	36.3	98.5	
						98.2	98.3
1929	31,980	719	44.5	851	37.4	98.5	
						98.2	98.3
1930	34,184	748	45.7	868	39.4	98.5	
						98.5	98.5
1931	36,744	809	45.5	924	39.6	99.1	
						98.8	99.0
1932	38,388	823	46.6	930	41.7	99.1	
						98.9	99.0
1933	40,246	843	47.9	944	42.7	99.2	
						99.2	99.2

(continued)

TABLE B.5. (continued)

	(1)	(2)	(3)	(4)	(5)	(6)	
Academic year (April–March)	Number of pupils enrolled	Number of qualified teachers	Faculty-pupil ratio (1) ÷ (2)	All teaching staff including temporary appointments	Faculty-pupil ratio (1) ÷ (4)	Ratio of pupils to school-aged children	
						By sex	Total
1934	41,251	862	48.0	976	42.1	M 99.1% F 99.0	99.0
1935	42,156	903	47.0	1,006	40.0	99.3 99.2	99.2
1936	42,968	929	45.2	1,040	41.2	99.4 99.4	99.4
1937	44,074	995	44.5	1,115	40.0	99.5 99.5	99.5
1938	44,748	1,042	43.0	1,148	39.0	99.5 99.5	99.5
1939	46,877	1,072	43.5	1,190	39.2	99.5 99.5	99.5
1940	48,087	1,133	42.8	1,222	39.5	99.5 99.5	99.5
1941	–	–	–	–	–	99.5 99.6	99.5
1942	50,023	1,230	41.0	1,306	38.5	99.5 99.6	99.6
1943	51,865	1,231	42.0	1,335	38.8	99.6 99.6	99.6
1944	53,797	1,395	39.5	1,493	35.8	99.6 99.6	99.6

Sources: Taiwan jijō, 1920, 1923, 1924, 1926, 1927, 1928, 1930, 1931, 1932, 1934, 1935, 1936, 1937, 1939, 1940, 1942; Taiwan sōtokufu, *Taiwan tōchi gaiyō.*

TABLE B.6. Faculty-pupil ratios in common schools

	(1)	(2)	(3)	(4)	(5)	(6)	
Academic year (April-March)	Number of pupils enrolled	Number of qualified teachers	Faculty-pupil ratio (1) ÷ (2)	All teaching staff including temporary appointments	Faculty-pupil ratio (1) ÷ (4)	Ratio of pupils to school-aged children By sex	Total
1915	66,078	1,076	61.5	1,616	41.0	M 16.0%	
						F 2.2	9.6%
1916	75,545	1,211	62.2	1,805	42.0	18.2	
						2.8	11.0
1917	88,099	1,373	64.0	2,224	39.6	21.4	
						3.7	13.1
1918	107,659	1,537	70.0	2,710	39.6	25.1	
						4.9	15.7
1919	125,135	1,803	69.5	3,315	37.9	32.4	
						7.4	20.7
1920	151,094	2,114	72.0	3,922	39.7	39.1	
						9.4	25.1
1921	185,555	2,102	88.0	4,129	45.0	42.4	
						10.3	27.2
1922	218,211	2,716	80.5	4,772	45.7	43.8	
						12.3	29.2
1923	231,919	3,267	71.0	4,968	46.5	51.8	
						13.6	33.7
1924	240,543	3,808	63.5	5,096	48.0	49.4	
						13.5	32.3
1925	241,985	4,078	59.2	4,957	48.6	44.3	
						13.3	29.5
1926	232,821	4,419	53.0	5,211	44.6	43.3	
						12.7	28.7
1927	231,228	4,506	50.5	5,302	43.5	43.9	
						13.1	29.1
1928	235,164	4,494	52.5	5,249	45.0	44.6	
						13.7	29.8
1929	249,384	4,626	54.0	5,330	46.8	45.6	
						14.7	30.6
1930	257,028	4,663	55.0	5,441	47.5	45.6	
						14.6	30.6
1931	275,207	4,768	57.6	5,522	49.7	49.3	
						17.8	34.1
1932	291,990	4,874	59.9	5,587	52.5	50.7	
						19.1	35.4

(continued)

TABLE B.6. (continued)

Academic year (April-March)	(1) Number of pupils enrolled	(2) Number of qualified teachers	(3) Faculty-pupil ratio (1) ÷ (2)	(4) All teaching staff including temporary appointments	(5) Faculty-pupil ratio (1) ÷ (4)	(6) Ratio of pupils to school-aged children By sex		Total
1933	316,094	5,013	63.0	5,753	55.0	M	52.5%	
1934	344,686	5,078	68.0	5,970	57.8	F	20.6 54.7	37.0
1935	373,892	5,280	70.5	6,255	60.0		23.0 56.8	39.3
1936	407,614	5,518	74.0	6,659	61.5		25.1 59.1	41.4
1937	450,032	5,806	78.0	7,239	62.5		27.3 62.0	43.8
1938	505,545	6,402	79.0	7,888	64.2		30.2 64.5	46.6
1939	557,135	6,954	80.0	8,718	64.0		34.1 67.1	49.8
1940	624,986	7,444	84.0	9,503	65.5		38.1 70.5	53.1
1941	690,670	–	–	–	–		43.4 73.6	57.4
1942	790,676	8,108	97.5	10,770	73.5		48.5 73.6	61.5
1943	745,638	8,591	87.0	11,847	65.0		48.5 76.6	61.5
1944	797,729	9,023	88.5	13,009	61.5		54.1 80.7	65.7
							60.7	71.1

Sources: Taiwan jijō, 1920, 1923, 1924, 1926, 1927, 1928, 1930, 1931, 1932, 1934, 1935, 1936, 1937, 1939, 1940, 1942; Taiwan sōtokufu, *Taiwan tōchi gaiyō.*

Appendix C

Decline of the Shobō

Table C.1

Year	Schools	Teachers	Boys	Girls	Total
1907	873	866	18,236	376	18,612
1908	630	647	14,491	291	14,782
1909	655	669	16,701	400	17,101
1910	567	576	15,374	437	15,811
1911	548	560	15,310	449	15,759
1912	541	555	15,747	555	16,302
1913	576	589	16,729	555	17,284
1914	638	648	18,696	561	19,257
1915	599	609	17,433	567	18,000
1916	584	660	18,562	758	19,320
1917	533	593	16,839	802	17,641
1918	385	452	12,725	589	13,314
1919	302	350	10,347	589	10,936
1920	225	252	7,167	472	7,639
1921	197	221	6,490	472	6,962
1922	94	118	3,229	425	3,664
1923	122	175	4,676	607	5,283
1924	126	180	4,540	625	5,165
1925	129	190	4,491	646	5,137
1930	164	236	5,179	789	5,968
1933	129	185	3,706	788	4,495
1937	33	62	–	–	1,808
1940	17	38	676	320	996

Sources: TKES, pp. 985-986; for 1937, Taiwan sōtokufu, *Taiwan no gakkō kyōiku,* p. 120; for 1940, Taiwan sōtokufu, *Taiwan jijō 1940,* p. 206.

Appendix D

Taiwanese and Japanese Students
Enrolled in Postprimary Educational Institutions

TABLE D.1. Taiwanese and Japanese students in two- and three-year lower level vocational schools, 1922-42[a]

Year	Number of schools	Students[b] Taiwanese	Japanese
1922	8	358	38
1924	10	441	53
1926	24	779	83
1928	31	1,056	90
1930	32	1,273	122
1932	33	1,628	224
1934	35	1,663	348
1936	43	2,197	653
1938	60	4,088	1,541
1940	71[c]	6,869	1,929
1942	83	11,635	1,964

Sources: Taiwan sōtokufu tōkeisho: 1925, pp. 94-95; 1928, pp. 100-101; 1935, pp. 124-125; 1936, pp. 98-99; 1938, pp. 90-91; 1940, pp. 84-85; 1942, p. 390.

[a]These statistics include a number of private schools; there were two private vocational schools in 1925 but by 1944 there were eight private vocational schools. (Taiwan sotō-kufu, *Taiwan tōchi gaiyō,* Taihoku, 1945, p. 40.) These statistics also include a number of women from both ethnic groups. The number of female students grew markedly after 1932 when vocational schools (technical and home economics) for women began to be established. In 1930 vocational school students included 36 Taiwanese and 17 Japanese females; in 1934, 93 Taiwanese and 159 Japanese females; in 1938, 630 Taiwanese and 1,202 Japanese women; in 1942, 4,156 Taiwanese and 1,764 Japanese women.

[b]In addition to the above, there were a very few aborigines studying in two- or three-year vocational schools.

[c]Includes 20 home economics schools.

TABLE D.2. Taiwanese and Japanese students in secondary vocational schools, 1922-44

Year	Agriculture and forestry		Commerce		Industries		Fisheries	
	Taiwanese	Japanese	Taiwanese	Japanese	Taiwanese	Japanese	Taiwanese	Japanese
1922	198	0	196	382	202	245	—	—
1924	224	3	186	436	298	427	—	—
1926	276	48	219	497	197	451	—	—
1928	480	121	311	598	183	434	—	—
1930	882	212	353	700	213	436	—	—
1932	1,025	244	337	778	171	492	—	—
1934	979	276	323	823	163	556	—	—
1936	979	279	322	1,049	213	616	—	—
1938	1,156	472	493	1,517	321	828	—	—
1940	1,667	640	1,281	1,943	732	1,167	—	—
1942	2,236	692	1,963	1,754	1,410	1,518	—	—
1944	3,504	960	2,374	1,893	3,180	2,424	154	90

Source: TWT, pp. 1224-1226.

TABLE D.3. **Taiwanese and Japanese students in Taichū Agriculture and Forestry College**[a] **(Taichū Nōrin Senmon Gakkō), 1919-43**

Year	Taiwanese	Japanese
1919	22	0
1921	113	0
1923	92	35
1925	71	90
1927	8	113
1929	4	89
1931	4	113
1933	7	123
1935	11	121
1937	7	138
1939	5	178
1941	1	160
1943	6	274

Source: TWT, p. 1216.
[a]This was an all-Taiwanese institution before 1922.

TABLE D.4. Taiwanese and Japanese enrolled in common school teacher courses, 1922-40

	Common school teacher trainees			
	Regular course (5 years)		Advanced course (2 years)	
Year	Taiwanese	Japanese	Taiwanese	Japanese
1922	1,384	0	0	64
1924	1,230	58	0	68
1926	774	109	0	70
1928	413	140	198	86
			(7 women)	(27 women)
1930	312	195	76	148
				(26 women)
1932	228	273	78	149
			(3 women)	(28 women)
1934	224	322	41	311
			(4 women)	(55 women)
1936	204	333	51	355
			(3 women)	(57 women)
1938	166	377	42	517
			(2 women)	(73 women)
1940	162	393	112	767
			(1 woman)	(79 women)

Source: Taiwan sōtokufu tōkeisho; 1926, p. 88; 1928, p. 91; 1935, p. 115; 1936, p. 93; 1938, p. 85; 1940, p. 77.

aThere were also Japanese and Taiwanese students of both sexes enrolled in an accelerated course (*kōshu ka*).

TABLE D.5. Taiwanese and Japanese students enrolled in Taiwan's fifteen middle schools in April 1939

School	Year accredited	Students Taiwanese	Japanese
Taihoku 1	1908	28	963
Taihoku 2	1922	508	217
Taihoku 3	1937	49	396
Keelung	1937	114	364
Shinchiku (Hsin-chu)	1922	251	410
Taichū 1	1915	632	88
Taichū 2	1922	27	488
Tainan 1	1914	80	637
Tainan 2	1922	654	87
Kagi (Chia-i)	1924	328	392
Takao	1922	328	608
Heitō (Pingtung)	1938	63	142
Karenkō (Hualien-kang)	1936	89	306
Tamsui Private[a]	1938	421	9
Taihoku Private[a]	1938	545	18

Source: Taiwan sōtokufu bunkyōkyoku, *Taiwan no gakkō kyōiku* (Taihoku, 1940), p. 27.

[a]These private middle schools only received government recognition in 1938 but they had been serving the native population much longer. The Tamsui school for instance dates back to the pre-Japanese days of the Canadian Presbyterian missionary, George Leslie MacKay. A few other private middle schools also existed but because the government general and the Japanese education ministry did not accredit them, their graduates had no official standing.

TABLE D.6. Taiwanese and Japanese students enrolled in Taiwan's fifteen higher girls' schools in April 1939

School	Year accredited	Students Taiwanese	Students Japanese
Taihoku 1	1904	19	871
Taihoku 2	1919	24	866
Taihoku 3[a]	1897	681	82
Keelung	1924	54	367
Ranyō (Lan-yang)	1938	107	92
Shinchiku	1924	148	431
Taichū	1921	33	405
Shōka (Chang-hua)	1919	409	207
Tainan 1	1917	15	450
Tainan 2	1918	431	127
Kagi	1921	178	432
Takao	1924	33	398
Heitō	1932	144	274
Karenkō	1927	28	301
Tamsui Private[b]	1938	237	8

Source: Taiwan sōtokufu bunkyōkyoku, *Taiwan no gakkō kyōiku,* pp. 30-31.
[a]This was Izawa Shūji's first school for Taiwanese girls or at least the "advanced" section of it.
[b]This school also predates Japanese rule although it was only accredited by the Japanese in 1938. In addition to it there were three other well-established but unaccredited private girls' schools for elementary school graduates.

TABLE D.7. Taiwanese and Japanese students in the medical college[a] (Igaku Senmon Gakkō), 1919-35

Year	Taiwanese	Japanese
1919	266	42
1921	343	93
1923	262	122
1925	222	124
1927	176	134
1929	177	169
1931	150	163
1933	203	152
1935[b]	233	170

Source: TWT, p. 1218.

[a]This was founded as a medical school for Taiwanese in 1899, had a special college department for Japanese added in 1918; but with the exception of this department it continued as an institution for Taiwanese until 1922.

[b]The following year, 1936, a medical faculty was opened at Taihoku Imperial University and a medical college department was attached to it. The medical college's student population was divided between the faculty and the college department.

TABLE D.8. Taiwanese and Japanese students in the higher course (Kōtō Ka) of the higher school (Kōtō Gakkō), 1925-43

Year	Taiwanese	Japanese
1925	4	102
1927	53	326
1929	88	355
1931	107	334
1933	109	325
1935	114	306
1937	110	290
1939	87	334
1941	104	363
1943	87	388

Source: TWT, p. 1221.

TABLE D.9. Taiwanese and Japanese students in Taihoku Imperial University, 1928-44

Year	Literature and Political Science		Science[a]		Medicine		Agriculture		Engineering	
	Taiwanese	Japanese	Taiwanese	Japanese	Taiwanese	Japanese	Taiwanese	Japanese	Taiwanese	Japanese
1928	3	16	3	33	—	—	—	—	—	—
1929	6	53	5	49	—	—	—	—	—	—
1930	12	80	8	80	—	—	—	—	—	—
1931	13	83	9	82	—	—	—	—	—	—
1932	14	67	8	87	—	—	—	—	—	—
1933	13	57	12	76	—	—	—	—	—	—
1934	16	49	10	53	—	—	—	—	—	—
1935	13	48	12	41	—	—	—	—	—	—
1936	14	39	11	32	16	24	—	—	—	—
1937	9	49	13	37	37	42	—	—	—	—
1938	11	54	12	36	47	67	—	—	—	—
1939	6	63	9	50	75	78	—	—	—	—
1940	5	81	5	85	75	69	—	—	—	—
1941	3	68	3	95	55	33	—	—	—	—
1942	3	166	2	155	64	67	—	—	—	—
1943[b]	3	164	1	52	64	66	1	102	—	—
1944	2	30	1	42	80	77	0	74	2	47

Source: TWT, pp. 1214-1215.
[a]Science and agriculture were combined in one faculty until agriculture was raised to an independent faculty in 1943.
[b]In this year agriculture separated from the science faculty, taking its students with it.

Notes

Abbreviations Used in the Notes

TKES   *Taiwan kyōiku enkaku shi* (A record of the development of education in Taiwan), ed. Taiwan kyōiku kai. Taihoku, 1939.

TSK   *Taiwan sōtokufu keisatsu enkaku shi* (A history of the Taiwan government-general police), ed. Taiwan sōtokufu. 4 vols. Taihoku, 1933-1941.

TWT   *T'ai-wan-sheng wu-shih-i-nien-lai t'ung-chi t'i-yao* (A statistical summary of the province of Taiwan for the past fifty-one years), ed. T'ai-wan-sheng hsing-cheng-chang-kuan kung-shu t'ung-chi-shih. Taipei, 1946.

1. The Setting

1. Marius B. Jansen, "The Meiji State: 1868-1912," in James B. Crowley, ed., *Modern East Asia: Essays in Interpretation* (New York, 1970), p. 114.

2. Gotō Shimpei, "The Administration of Formosa (Taiwan)," in Ōkuma Shigenobu, ed., *Fifty Years of New Japan* (London, 1910), II, 530. In speeches and writing dealing with Japanese rule in Taiwan, Gotō often referred to Japan's lack of colonial experience. See Tsurumi Yūsuke, ed., *Gotō Shimpei den* (Tokyo, 1937), II, 28-38 and Ide Kiwata, *Taiwan chiseki shi* (Taihoku, 1933), pp. 330-331. Mochiji Rokusaburō, *Taiwan shokumin seisaku* (Tokyo, 1912), and Takekoshi Yosaburō, *Taiwan tōchi shi* (Tokyo, 1905), also evince a keen awareness of Western interest in Japan's first colonial enterprise. Gotō, Mochiji, and Takekoshi may have thought that this interest was greater than it actually was, but their perceptions were not without foundation. A Canadian Presbyterian missionary in Taiwan wrote that "when Formosa was ceded to Japan, the eyes of the world were on the Japanese Government. The Western nations wondered how she would succeed in her new experiment of subjugating and colonizing alien races" (Duncan MacLeod, *The Island Beautiful,* Toronto, 1923, p. 36). Western visitors to Taiwan under Japanese government generally used the institutions of European and American colonies as yardsticks of evaluation. See, for example, Owen Rutter, *Through Formosa: An Account of Japan's Island Colony* (London, 1923); J. Ralston Hayden, "Japan's New Policy in Korea and Formosa," *Foreign Affairs* 2.3:474-487 (March 15, 1924); Harold and Alice Foght, *Unfathomed Japan* (New York, 1928). For a discussion of some Western reactions to Japan's debut as an imperialist see Akira Iriye, "Imperialism in East Asia," in *Modern East Asia: Essays in Interpretation,* esp. pp. 142-147.

3. Harry J. Lamley, "The 1895 Taiwan Republic: A Significant Episode in Modern Chinese History," *Journal of Asian Studies* 27.4:739-762 (August 1968); Harry J. Lamley, "The 1895 Taiwan War of Resistance: Local Chinese Efforts Against a Foreign Power," in Leonard H. D. Gordon, ed., *Taiwan: Studies in Chinese Local History* (New York, 1970), pp. 23-77.

4. On suppression of armed resistance see Ching-chih Chen, "Japanese Socio-political Control in Taiwan, 1895-1945" (Ph.D. diss., Harvard University, 1973), pp. 7-68. For a Western missionary view of the Japanese occupation see Edward Band, *Barclay of Formosa* (Tokyo, 1936), pp. 85-110.

5. Kimura Kyō, "Taiwan no futsū kyōiku" (Ordinary education in Taiwan), *Taiwan kyōiku* (Taiwan education) 28:4 (July 1904), quoted in Ebihara Haruyoshi, *Gendai Nihon kyōiku seisaku shi* (Tokyo, 1965-1967), I, 240.

6. Inō Yoshinori, *Taiwan bunka shi* (Tokyo, 1928), II, 241, 242. Inō, *Taiwan bunka shi* II, 233-242 gives a district-by-district breakdown of Taiwan's population under the Ch'ing, but population figures for Taiwan before the census of 1905 are, at best, educated estimates.

7. Chiao-min Hsieh, *Taiwan, Ilha Formosa: A Geography in Perspective* (Washington, D.C., 1964), pp. 3-6, 44-73.

8. Chiao-min Hsieh, p. 149; Kokubu Naoichi, *Taiwan no minzoku* (Tokyo, 1968), p. 4, estimates that Chinese culture appeared in Taiwan about 1200 A.D.

9. Ō Ikutoku, *Taiwan kumon suru sono rekishi* (Tokyo, 1964), p. 25.

10. Ō, pp. 26-29, 36-37.

11. See Clive Day, *The Policy and Administration of the Dutch in Java* (New York, London, 1904), for details of how the Dutch East India Company procured trading goods in Java. In Java the Dutch, backed by their armed forces, received "contingents" and "forced deliveries," both of which were "supplies of products exacted annually from the native governments of Java as recognition of the supremacy of the Company" (Day, p. 63). The company also collected custom duties, tolls on markets and internal trade, poll taxes, and other levies (Day, p. 79).

12. See James W. Davidson, *The Island of Formosa, Past and Present* (New York, 1903), pp. 9-48, for an account of the Dutch in Taiwan.

13. Chiao-min Hsieh, p. 146.

14. William Campbell, *Formosa under the Dutch* (London, 1903), pp. 63-64; Ō, p. 41.

15. Davidson, pp. 49-62; Shinkichi Etō, "An Outline of Formosan History," in Mark Mancall, ed., *Formosa Today* (New York, 1964), pp. 45-46; Chiao-min Hsieh, pp. 151-152.

16. Harry J. Lamley, "The Taiwan Literati and Early Japanese Rule, 1895-1915" (Ph.D. diss., University of Washington, 1964), pp. 51-63.

17. At first the Ch'ing court had planned to withdraw from maritime affairs and abandon the Chinese settlers and aborigines now that Ming loyalists were no longer a threat. See Ramon H. Myers, "Taiwan under Ch'ing Imperial Rule, 1684-1895: The Traditional Order," *Journal of the Institute of Chinese Studies of the Chinese University of Hong Kong* 4.2:495-520 (1971), p. 496.

18. Ibid., p. 502; Ō, p. 60; Chou Hsien-wen, comp., Ch'ing-tai T'ai-wan ching-chi shih (Taipei, 1957), p. 65.
19. Inō, *Taiwan bunka shi*, I, 751. For information on these rebellions see Inō, *Taiwan bunka shi*, I, 751-787 and Davidson, pp. 63-82, 91-101.
20. Johanna M. Meskill paints a dark portrait of conflict among the Chinese settlers in mid-nineteenth century: "Deep cleavages along ethnic and linguistic lines divided the settlers. Officialdom was unusually venal and indolent, spending a minimum of time in the primitive and malaria-ridden districts of Taiwan. Lacking effective government on the *hsien* level and engaged in chronic armed fighting among each other, the Taiwanese had created a whole series of illegal and semi-legal organizations for self-defense and self-assertion. Secret societies and private armed associations proliferated, as did 'local bullies' who lorded it over strings of villages from their heavily armed, bamboo-palisaded estates in the country" (Johanna M. Meskill, "The Lins of Wufeng: The Rise of a Taiwanese Gentry Family," in Gordon, p. 7).
21. Camphor, gathered in aborigine territory, was a major source of aborigine-Chinese friction. The Chinese method of collecting the gum destroyed the camphor trees. This destruction enraged the tribesmen, who saw their protective forests receding before their eyes.
22. Shi Mei, *Taiwanjin yonhyakunen shi* (Tokyo, 1962), pp. 140-144.
23. Sugar going to north China remained in Chinese hands. See Davidson, pp. 170-206, 444-451.
24. Lamley, "The Taiwan Literati," p. 59.
25. Ō, p. 66, describes an eighteenth-century Chinese farming village which consisted of seventy-nine households containing a total of 257 settlers. Of this number only six individuals were over the age of sixty and none was under sixteen. Only one married couple was among the 257.
26. Edgar B. Wickberg found late nineteenth-century land tenure conditions and tenancy rates in north Taiwan to be rather like their counterparts in south China. See Edgar B. Wickberg, "Late Nineteenth Century Land Tenure in North Taiwan," Gordon, pp. 78-88.
27. Inō, *Taiwan bunka shi*, II, 5-6.
28. For details regarding types of private schools see ibid. II, 21-231, and Lamley, "The Taiwan Literati," pp. 95-101. Until the 1730s residents of Taiwan had to journey to the mainland to sit for the examinations. Only in 1727 did the viceroy of Chekiang and Fukien grant permission to hold examinations in Taiwan.
29. Myers, "Taiwan under Ch'ing Imperial Rule," p. 509.
30. For an analysis of the Chinese gentry class see Chung-li Chang, *The Chinese Gentry* (Seattle, 1955).
31. Inō, *Taiwan bunka shi*, II, 139.
32. In 1885 the Ch'ing court, while maintaining Taiwan within the political unit of Fukien province, created the position of governor of Taiwan and appointed Liu Ming-ch'uan to it. Liu wanted the court to wait five years before it raised Taiwan to provincial status in order to allow the island time to become economically independent of Fukien. However an agreement was worked out under which Fukien supplied an annual subsidy of 440,000 taels for five years. This agreement continued to be honored

after the court decided to make Taiwan a full-fledged province in 1887. See Samuel C. Chu, "Liu Ming-ch'uan and Modernization of Taiwan," *Journal of Asian Studies* 23.1:37-53 (November 1964).

33. See Inō, *Taiwan bunka shi,* II, 63-65 and Chu, "Liu Ming-ch'uan and Modernization of Taiwan."'Liu's choice of Taipei in the north for a capital was probably influenced by his experience during the Sino-French War. It was in the north that the French forces focused much of their attack on the island, and Taipei played a key role in Liu's defense against the French onslaught. See Davidson, pp. 220-242.

34. See Ching-chih Chen, "Japanese Socio-political Control in Taiwan," pp. 7-68.

35. Ibid.; Lamley, "The Taiwan Literati," p. 224.

36. Henceforth the Chinese inhabitants of Taiwan will be referred to as Taiwanese.

37. Officially, civil government began in April 1896.

38. See E. Patricia Tsurumi, "Taiwan under Kodama Gentarō and Gotō Shimpei," in Albert Craig, ed., *Papers on Japan,* 4 (Cambridge, Mass., 1967).

39. Ivan P. Hall, *Mori Arinori* (Cambridge, Mass., 1973), p. 411.

40. Nagai Michio, *Higher Education in Japan: Its Take-off and Crash* (Tokyo, 1971), p. 45.

41. Izawa Shūji may have dreamed of such an eventuality. See Chapter Two.

42. See Ronald P. Dore, *Education in Tokugawa Japan* (Berkeley, 1965), pp. 252-290, for an account of the *tera koya* schools of the Tokugawa Period (1600-1867).

2. The Groundwork

1. Originally from the Takatō domain, Izawa Shūji was appointed by the recently established Ministry of Education to the position of superintendent (*kanji*) of the First Middle School in 1872. The following year he became principal of Aichi Government Normal School (Kanritsu Aichi shihan gakkō) and in 1875 he was sent to study in the United States. Returning to Japan from the Bridgewater Normal School in Massachusetts in 1878, he became principal of Tokyo Normal School, later renamed Tokyo Higher Normal School. During the 1880s he served as superintendent of the Physical Training Institute (Taisō denshū jo), as music examination officer, and as a secretary (*shoki kan*) in the education ministry. When Mori Arinori became education minister in 1885 he made Izawa chief of the ministry's textbook editing bureau. In 1890 Izawa became principal of both the Tokyo School for the Blind and Deaf and the Tokyo Music School. Izawa is credited with introducing Western-style singing into Japanese schools. His interest in gymnastics and music was reflected in the curricula he designed for Taiwan's schools. (Heibonsha, *Dai jimmei jiten,* Tokyo, 1935-1955, I, 171-172; Japanese National Commission for UNESCO, *Development of Modern System of Education in Japan,* Tokyo, 1960, p. 27).

2. Hall, pp. 437-447.

3. Ibid., pp. 447-452.

4. Most of the government's educational outlays were earmarked for Tokyo University and other higher educational facilities.
5. Izawa's society offered what scholarship support it could to children of soldiers who had perished in the Sino-Japanese War. See Kaminuma Hachirō, *Izawa Shūji* (Tokyo, 1962), p. 202.
6. Kaminuma, pp. 198-212.
7. Kabayama was officially appointed governor-general of Taiwan on May 10, 1895. Izawa was a delegate from the Society for State Education in a group that visited the emperor at imperial headquarters in Hiroshima where Kabayama was stationed.
8. The proposals are reproduced in Yoshino Hidekimi, *Taiwan kyōiku shi* (Taihoku, 1927), pp. 11-14.
9. Natives were to be trained in Japanese language institutes, fourteen of which were to be opened immediately while another two were to be established the following year. Japanese who had already been trained as teachers were to be recruited for short-term training programs.
10. The education department was to offer a four-year course in ethics, the Japanese language, pedagogy, Chinese language and literature (*kanbun*), mathematics, bookkeeping, science, music, and gymnastics. The language department's course for natives consisted of three years of ethics, Japanese composition, calligraphy, arithmetic, bookkeeping, science, music, and gymnastics.
11. The normal school course was three years of the subjects taught to natives enrolled in the language department's course plus history and geography.
12. Yoshino, p. 16.
13. The romanization Shisangyan is taken from Kaminuma. This is also how Taiwanese interviewed in 1969 pronounced the name of this hamlet.
14. Kaminuma, pp. 215-217.
15. Kaminuma, p. 127; Ide, *Taiwan chiseki shi*, p. 244. Yoshino, p. 25, claims that the school gained about ten pupils.
16. Yoshino, pp. 16-17.
17. Ide, *Taiwan chiseki shi*, p. 244; Yoshino, p. 25.
18. Taiwan sōtokufu, *Taiwan tōchi sōran* (Taihoku, 1908), p. 456; Taiwan sōtokufu, *Taiwan no gakkō kyōiku* (Taihoku, 1940), p. 6.
19. Kaminuma, pp. 232-233.
20. Kaminuma, pp. 235-236.
21. Yoshino, pp. 103, 106.
22. Ide, *Taiwan chiseki shi*, p. 259.
23. Yoshino, p. 204.
24. Ide, *Taiwan chiseki shi*, p. 260.
25. Mizuno soon followed suit.
26. Miltary expenditures for the Sino-Japanese War amounted to 225,320,000 yen, which was three times the Japanese government revenues of 1894. (E. P. Tsurumi, "Taiwan under Kodama Gentarō and Gotō Shimpei," p. 122).
27. By late 1897 suggestions that Japan should sell Taiwan to another power — perhaps France — were getting louder and louder. See Tsurumi Yūsuke, *Gotō Shimpei den*, II, 22-24.

28. E. P. Tsurumi, "Taiwan under Kodama Gentarō and Gotō Shimpei," p. 122.
29. Takekoshi Yosaburo, *Japanese Rule in Formosa,* tr. George Braithwaite (London, 1907), p. 134.
30. Kaminuma, pp. 250-255.
31. Areas served included the Pescadores. See Yoshino, pp. 103-104.
32. Ide, *Taiwan chiseki shi,* p. 286. There were also at this time ten private schools "founded by or connected with Japanese nationals" in the colony. (Ibid., p. 287.)
33. In Takekoshi, *Japanese Rule in Formosa, kōgakkō* is translated as public school. But common school, which has also been used to designate this institution, is a less confusing appellation of this elementary school.
34. For the common school regulations see Yoshino, pp. 192-193; Tōgō Minoru and Satō Shirō, *Taiwan shokumin hattatsu shi* (Taihoku, 1916), p. 427; *TKES,* pp. 229-238.
35. *TKES,* p. 260. To permit optional subjects to be offered in accordance with local conditions became an official practice in Japanese schools after promulgation of the primary school rescript of 1890. (Mombushō, *Gakusei hyakunen shi,* Tokyo, 1972, II, 90.)
36. *TKES,* pp. 408-409, Yoshino, p. 199, gives 181 schools.
37. Regarding school attendance statistics in South Asian countries the Myrdal study noted: "The major flaw of the enrollment data is that a child who is counted as enrolled does not necessarily go to school for the whole year, or regularly, or at all. Indian enrollment figures, for instance, refer to the end of the school year, March 31, and it is not made clear whether these figures include only pupils who are actually pursuing studies at that date and have done so during the entire year or whether the figures also include children who have been registered but have attended school only briefly or irregularly or have not attended at all. Probably a great number of pupils in the latter category are included, as both teachers and administrators want to meet targets and show results. The few indications we have suggest that the consequent exaggeration may be very substantial. Different practices may be followed in different countries and even in the same country at different times or in different districts. These factors make the enrollment statistics very unreliable, not only for purposes of comparison among countries but also, though probably to a lesser extent, in temporal comparisons" (Gunnar Myrdal, *Asian Drama,* New York, 1968, III, 1715).
38. "Hōzan kōgakkō genkon jōkyō gaiyō" (A survey of the present conditions in Hōzan common school) in *Gotō Shimpei monjo,* pt. 8, no. 107.
39. In the long run, however, the colonial government did intend Japanese to become the language of communication among Japanese, Taiwanese, and aborigines. This was to be achieved gradually, mainly by teaching Japanese in the common schools. As fluency and literacy in Japanese improved, Chinese language studies were to be reduced until they could be discontinued altogether. See Ide, *Taiwan chiseki shi,* p. 331, and Mochiji, p. 295.
40. *TKES,* pp. 232-233.
41. Ching-chih Chen, "Japanese Socio-political Control in Taiwan," pp.

284-287, 292-294; Lamley, "The Taiwan Literati," pp. 360-364. Kodama even went so far as to make a tour of the island in an elegant sedan chair of the kind that was used by officers of the Chinese court. See Tsurumi Yūsuke, *Gotō Shimpei den,* II, 45-46.

42. Lamley, "The Taiwan Literati," pp. 360-364.

43. In the earliest days Japanese was taught by means of side-by-side translations. From about 1899 this gave way to Goudin's method. Perfected by a Frenchman, F. Goudin, this technique stressed the connection between words and action. Pupils were to repeat such phrases as "I go to the door," "I return from the door," "I sit down," "I stand up," while performing the relevant actions. About 1904 or 1905 this method was rejected as putting too much emphasis on rote memorization. Encouraging the remembering of words through the association of ideas became popular. This method was less concerned with the niceties of grammar and syntax. By about 1912 the Japanese language came to be taught chiefly through the medium of Japanese. See Yoshino, pp. 278-283.

44. Although Izawa approved of the basic Confucian classics taught in the traditional Chinese schools, he considered some of the subject matter taught by these schools unsuitable—Sung and Ch'ing learning, for instance. (Kaminuma, p. 244).

45. Kaminuma, pp. 244-245.

46. Izawa's diary quoted in Kaminuma, pp. 244-245; *TKES,* p. 230.

47. Takekoshi, *Japanese Rule in Formosa,* p. 294. I have changed the "Formosan Chinaman" in Braithwaite's translation to "Formosan Chinese."

48. William Campbell, *Sketches from Formosa* (London, 1915), pp. 317-318.

49. Kikuchi Dairoku, *Japanese Education* (London, 1909), pp. 285-287; Mombushō, *Gakusei gojūnen shi* (Tokyo, 1922), pp. 191-193.

50. Yoshino, pp. 103, 206.

51. Yoshino, p. 208; *TKES,* pp. 627-629.

52. Yoshino, pp. 148, 207; *TKES,* p. 626. Officials cited the smaller number of students from the Tainan area enrolled in the Japanese Language School as an illustration of that area's lack of interest in education.

53. Ide, *Taiwan chiseki shi,* pp. 330-331; Mochiji, pp. 282-294; Ōzono Ichizō, *Taiwan shisei yonjūnen shi* (Tokyo, 1935), pp. 482-487.

54. Mochiji, p. 298.

55. Mochiji, pp. 299-300.

56. Yoshino, p. 230.

57. Mochiji, p. 309. Subjects studied during the preparatory year were: zoology, botany, chemistry, mathematics, geography, history, ethics, a foreign language, and gymnastics. Subjects taught in the regular course were: anatomy including laboratory sessions, physiology including laboratory work, physics including laboratory sessions, chemistry with laboratory practice, medical zoology, medical botany, embryology, histology, dermatology, prescription preparation, pharmaceutics with laboratory practice, pharmacology, introductory surgery, pathological anatomy, diagnostics, application of medical dressings (*hōtai gaku*), advanced pathology, advanced surgery, syphilis studies (*baidoku gaku*), pediatrics, medical machinery utilization, surgical techniques, clinical practice in

internal medicine, ophthalmology including laboratory work, obstetrics, surgical clinical practice, legal medicine, gynecology, medical history, hygienics, public health facilities (*eisei seido*), bacteriology, a foreign language, and gymnastics. See Yoshino, pp. 230-231.

58. For example, the educational affairs section in the administration had five different chiefs from 1898 to 1903, when Mochiji Rokusaburō took the post and kept it until 1910. The medical school, as a special project, was not under the jurisdiction of educational affairs.

59. Ide, *Taiwan chiseki shi*, p. 341.

60. During the early 1890s Gotō successfully persuaded the Home Ministry to establish a bureau of sanitation. He also took the initiative in proposing an army quarantine bureau to service soldiers returning from the Sino-Japanese War. When it was established he directed its affairs, working harmoniously with Kodama Gentarō and other military officers. When the war was over he went back to his old post as chief of the Home Ministry's sanitation bureau. There he not only energetically improved the bureau's facilities but also displayed a lively interest in many social and administrative aspects of medicine, including the Taiwan opium problem. See Tsurumi Yūsuke, *Gotō Shimpei den*, I, 878-884.

61. Ide, *Taiwan chiseki shi*, pp. 325-329; Mochiji, pp. 330-340.

62. See Chapter Six.

63. The government hired graduates of the medical school to serve as public physicians in areas that had few medical facilities.

64. George Barclay, *Colonial Development and Population in Taiwan* (Princeton, 1954), pp. 138-139, states that Japanese health measures were qualitatively of a lower grade than "the standards of the more restricted public health work in some of the tropical dependencies of European powers" but that, since the Japanese measures were broadly diffused throughout the whole island, they reaped impressive results.

65. Ide, *Taiwan chiseki shi*, pp. 340-341; Yoshino, pp. 225-229.

66. Ide, *Taiwan chiseki shi*, p. 340; Yoshino, pp. 224-225.

67. Yoshino, p. 340.

68. See Robert H. Van Gulik, *Sexual Life in Ancient China* (Leiden, 1961).

69. Ibid., p. 97.

70. *TKES*, p. 984.

71. See Wakamori Tarō and Yamamoto Fujie, *Nihon no josei shi* (Tokyo, 1965-1966).

72. Dore, *Education in Tokugawa Japan*, p. 66.

73. Ibid., p. 254.

74. Ibid.

75. Ibid.

76. Mombushō, *Gakusei hyakunen shi*, II, 11.

77. Morosawa Yōko, *Onna no rekishi* (Tokyo, 1970), II, 43.

78. The directive continues: "At present, out of one hundred school-aged children, only fifty or so are in school. And only fifteen of the fifty are girls. Therefore, efforts to continue to advise parents and guardians to send their charges to school must be made. At the same time, efforts must be made to increase the practical content of training for girls. For example, sewing is the most necessary skill in a girl's life. Thus, in accord

with local circumstances, it will be necessary to include sewing in the primary school curricula. Where it is difficult to obtain accredited sewing teachers, unaccredited teachers may be substituted temporarily. But the personal character [of the teachers] must be carefully examined before hiring them" (Mombushō, *Gakusei hyakunen shi*, II, 34).

79. Kaigo Tokiomi, *Japanese Education: Its Past and Present* (Tokyo, 1968), p. 65.
80. Yoshino, p. 216.
81. Ōhashi Sutesaburō, "The Attached Girls' School in the Days of the Japanese Language School" (Kokugō gakkō jidai no fuzoku jogakkō) quoted in Yoshino, p. 221.
82. See Lamley, "The Taiwan Literati," pp. 95-100, for an account of Chinese schools in Taiwan during the late Ch'ing period.
83. The fifteen sen was paid in two allotments: ten sen for food and an additional five sen as a general allowance. See Yoshino, p. 104; *TKES*, p. 178.
84. *TKES*, pp. 974-975. During the next few years attempts were made to provide *shobō* with Chinese translations of Japanese books. Translations offered included a commentary on the Imperial Rescript on Education, a history of Japan, and Fukuzawa Yukichi's *Kunmo kyūri zukai* (Elementary science for schoolchildren). But regional authorities reported that the Chinese schoolmasters were unable to teach the contents of these books because they were unable to understand them themselves. See *TKES*, pp. 976-977.
85. *TKES*, pp. 974-975.
86. Lamley, "The Taiwan Literati," p. 430. Without the imperial examination system, many Chinese schools lost the main reason for their existence. See Ch'un-ch'eng, "Jih-chü shih-ch'i chih Chung-wen shu-chü," *T'ai-pei wen-wu* 3.2:131-132 (August 1954).
87. Takeuchi Sadayoshi, *Taiwan kanshū* (Taihoku, 1915), p. 635.
88. Takeuchi's description of *shobō* classes is similar to Dore's account of Chinese studies in Tokugawa Japan. See Dore, *Education in Tokugawa Japan*, pp. 127-136.
89. *TKES*, p. 966, lists additional texts sometimes used in *shobō*.
90. Takeuchi Sadayoshi, *Taiwan kanshū*, pp. 634-641.
91. Lamley, "The Taiwan Literati," pp. 433-436.
92. *TKES*, pp. 984-985.
93. *TKES*, p. 411.
94. *TKES*, pp. 486-488.
95. *TKES*, 988-990.
96. In 1898 schools were established in Taihoku, Keelung, Shinchiku (Hsinchu), and Tainan; in 1899 in Taichū, Giran (I-lan), and Kobi (Hu-wei). Primary school is a standard translation for *shogakkō*, the elementary school established in Japan from the beginning of the Meiji period. Primary schools in Taiwan admitted only Japanese pupils.
97. Yoshino, p. 185; Taiwan sōtokufu, *Taiwan tochi sōran*, p. 461.
98. Ōzono, *Taiwan shisei yonjūnen shi*, p. 490.
99. Quoted in Yoshino, p. 99.
100. Yoshino, pp. 100-101. Textbooks and classroom supplies were scarce in primary schools in Japan during the 1890s too.

101. At least for boys. See *TKES*, p. 419.
102. Tōgō Minoru and Satō Shirō, *Taiwan shokumin hattatsu shi*, p. 422; Ide, *Taiwan chiseki shi*, pp. 332-333.
103. Yoshino, p. 186.
104. Kaigo, *Japanese Education, Its Past and Present*, p. 66.
105. Ibid.; Yoshino, p. 186.
106. To enter middle school Japanese boys had to be primary school graduates over twelve years of age.
107. Yoshino, pp. 210-211; Ide, *Taiwan chiseki shi*, pp. 337-338.
108. The Taihoku Second Primary School was the first primary school founded by the colonial government. It was established in June 1897.
109. From July 1896 to March 1901 a total of 264 recruits graduated from crash training programs held first at Shisangyan and later at other locations. See Ide, *Taiwan chiseki shi*, p. 336.
110. Yoshino, p. 205.
111. Taiwan sōtokufu kokugo gakkō, *Taiwan sōtokufu kokugo gakkō ichiran* (Taihoku, 1917), p. 41. At the same time, the growing numbers of Japanese colonists were creating a demand for primary school teachers. However, there were no facilities in the colony for training Japanese primary school teachers until 1910. See *TKES*, p. 140.
112. Davidson, pp. 604-608.
113. Although the extraordinary Canadian missionary, George Leslie MacKay, showed great respect for Confucian education, most missionaries tended to be more in agreement with Duncan MacLeod, another Canadian missionary in northern Taiwan, who wrote: "In Formosa, in the earlier days, only six in a thousand could read, and the ignorance of the people was appalling. With the establishment of public schools in the island by the Japanese, this has been entirely changed and a condition created much more favorable to the rapid spread of the Christian faith." (MacLeod, *The Island Beautiful*, p. 213.) See William Campbell's generally approving attitude in *Sketches from Formosa*, one of the chapters of which is entitled "Europeans Get Fair-Play Out Here." Many missionaries might have agreed with Davidson's evaluation of traditional Chinese schooling: "There were none of the studies which in Western lands and in Japan are considered necessary for an educated man, and the general tendency of their training was to increase conservativism and love for ancient customs: the greatest stumbling block in the way of Chinese progress. The individual thus educated is conceited, superstitious, and illiberal, and . . . is still ignorant when judged by Western standards." (Davidson, p. 602.) For MacKay's unrepresentative approach see Graeme McDonald, "George Leslie MacKay: Missionary Success in Nineteenth-Century Taiwan," in John K. Fairbank, ed., *Papers on China, 21* (Cambridge, Mass., 1968).
114. Campbell, *Sketches from Formosa*, pp. 317-318.
115. Davidson, p. 607.
116. Ibid.
117. McDonald, "George Leslie MacKay," p. 170. For a description of Oxford College see George L. MacKay, *From Far Formosa* (New York, 1895), pp. 291-296.

118. Campbell, *Sketches from Formosa,* p. 314.
119. The Reverend Thomas Barclay looked to Japanese middle schools for a model for establishment of a missionary middle school in Taiwan. See Band, p. 129. Campbell managed to persuade the government general to take over a school for the blind he had begun in Tainan. See Campbell, *Sketches from Formosa,* p. 256.
120. See Kaigo Tokiomi, ed., *Inoue Kowashi no kyōiku seisaku* (Tokyo, 1968), pp. 975-979, and Nakashima Tarō, *Kindai Nihon kyōiku seido shi* (Tokyo, 1966), pp. 552-556. The 1879 education rescript permitted local authorities to give subsidies to private primary schools if they were serving the public, but private primary schools were expected to be financed by private contributions. A few years later all subsidies were halted. Later, education minister Inoue Kowashi acknowledged private school rights to some support, but made it clear that private schools were only entitled to support when serving as substitutes for government schools. See Mombushō, *Meiji ikō kyōiku seido hattatsu shi* (Tokyo, 1938), II, 151-154; Mombushō, *Gakusei kyūjūnen shi* (Tokyo, 1964), p. 18; Kaigo, *Inoue Kowashi no kyōiku seisaku,* pp. 984-986.
121. Ibid., pp. 969-975.
122. Ibid., pp. 969-987; Nakashima, pp. 557-564.
123. *TKES,* pp. 991-992.
124. *TKES,* pp. 974-975. The guidelines were in a nine-article document entitled "Stipulations concerning shobō and academies" (Shobō gijuku ni kan suru kitei). The document instructed regional officials to see that Japanese language and arithmetic were gradually added to the curricula of *shobō* and academies. It also stated that fixed hours of instruction and textbooks recognized by the governor-general should be used in these schools. Regional authorities were authorized to encourage reform in these schools by providing subsidies to those with outstanding classes, management, and sanitation.
125. Ide, *Taiwan chiseki shi,* p. 351; Lamley, "The Taiwan Literati," p. 364.
126. Ibid.
127. Ide, *Taiwan chiseki shi,* pp. 351-355; Lamley, "The Taiwan Literati," pp. 364-369; Liao Han-ch'en, "Yang-wen hui," *T'ai-pei wen-wu* 2.4:77-82 (January 1954). The itinerary of visits included the central post office, a law court, a pharmaceutical factory where opium was prepared, schools, the police and prison guard training academy, the hospital with its medical school, a warship in the harbor, a camphor factory with modern machinery, and a sawmill in private Japanese hands.
128. Ide, *Taiwan chiseki shi,* pp. 352-355.
129. Gotō Shimpei, "Yōbunkai ni okeru ensetsu" (The speech made at the Cultural Advancement Society), in *Gotō Shimpei monjo,* pt. 8, no. 30.
130. Ibid.
131. Ide, *Taiwan chiseki shi,* pp. 330-331.
132. See Yoshino, pp. 130-150, for early debates over instituting compulsory education.
133. Officially the system had three tracks, the third consisting of aborigine education. But aborigine education was almost nonexistent before 1910.
134. See Taiwan sōtokufu, *Taiwan tōchi sōran,* pp. 4-7, and Okamatsu San-

tarō, *Provisional Report of Investigations of Laws and Customs of the Island of Formosa* (Kobe, 1902), pp. 20-104.

135. Tsurumi Yūsuke, *Gotō Shimpei den,* II, 25-26.

136. See Ching-chih Chen, "The Police and *Hokō* Systems in Taiwan under Japanese Administration (1895-1945)," in Albert Craig, ed., *Papers on Japan,* 4.147-176.

137. See E. P. Tsurumi, "Taiwan under Kodama Gentarō and Gotō Shimpei."

138. Ibid.

139. Proposals to integrate Taiwan within Japan proper were put forward almost before the Treaty of Shimonoseki's ink was dry. See Michael Lubon, "Ryōtō oyobi Taiwan tōchi ni kansuru tōgi" (Questions concerning administration of Taiwan and Liaotung), in Itō Hirobumi, ed., *Taiwan shiryō* (Tokyo, 1936), pp. 399-509.

140. Ide, *Taiwan chiseki shi,* pp. 330-331.

141. Ibid.

142. Yoshino, p. 236. They were paid from national funds (*kokko*) but these in reality were probably funds held by the government general, which, during Izawa's days in Taiwan, was heavily dependent upon subsidies from the home government.

143. Montagne Kirkwood, an English adviser employed by the Japanese government, toured Taiwan in 1897 and made several reports about conditions which contained many policy recommendations. In one of them he urged that Izawa's subsidies to pupils be ended because most of the children attending school belonged to the native upper classes and were not offspring of the lower or laboring classes. See Montagne Kirkwood, "Taiwan oyobi Bōkotō o ite ikko no shokuminchi o sōsetsushi, sōtoku gyōsei-kaigi oyobi rippōin o setchishi, sonota dōshokuminchi no ippan seido ni tsuite kitei suru chokurei sōan (A draft for an edict to establish a government general, legislature, and other colonial structures in Taiwan and the Pescadores), in *Gotō Shimpei monjo,* pt. 8, no. 36, pp. 1-4. Kodama and Gotō took this advice along with other suggestions Kirkwood made. For instance, one of the Kodama-Gotō team's famous early achievements was to send back to Japan 1,080 of the approximately 2,000 unskilled, lower-class Japanese who had poured into the colony during its first three years, hoping to make their fortune. This policy originated with a recommendation made by Kirkwood. See Ibid., pp. 7-8.

144. See E. P. Tsurumi, "Taiwan under Kodama Gentaro and Gotō Shimpei," pp. 122-130.

145. Gotō admired the way the British, as colonial rulers, instilled in native peoples a sense of awe for the British presence. Even when, in speeches and writing, he criticized Western colonialists, he either praised the British or suggested that their faults were less serious than those of other Western colonial powers. See for example his 1903 education speech in Mochiji, pp. 282-293, and in Ide, *Taiwan chiseki shi,* pp. 330-331.

146. Tsurumi Yūsuke, *Gotō Shimpei den,* II, 46. Nitobe Inazō recalled that when a visitor from Japan criticized the "lavish" quarters of the Taiwan administration personnel, Gotō dealt very sharply with him. Ibid., II, 46-48.

147. Kaminuma, p. 235.

148. Izawa's Japanese Language School courses in Japanese for Taiwanese and in native languages for Japanese were proposed more or less on an even footing, similar in length and curricula.
149. Kaminuma, pp. 243-244.
150. Shinano kyōikukai, ed., *Izawa Shūji senshū* (Tokyo, 1958), pp. 582-588.

3. Expansion

1. See Appendix A on aborigine education.
2. In 1902 aborigine education along with all other affairs pertaining to the aborigines was entrusted to the police. See Taiwan sōtokufu keimukyoku, *Takasago zoku no kyōiku* (Taihoku, 1941), p. 1, and *TKES*, p. 460.
3. *TKES*, p. 409. It is doubtful that these schools contained any aborigine pupils. If they did, aborigine pupils must have been very few in number. As late as 1941 the police department reported only four common schools in aborigine territory. The vast majority of aborigine school-goers attended educational centers (*kyōiku sho*), of which there existed 180 in 1941. See Taiwan sōtokufu keimukyoku, *Takasago zoku no kyōiku*, pp. 96, 98.
4. *TKES*, p. 409. Whether or not aborigines are included in these "native" percentages is not entirely clear. However, aborigines formed such a small percentage of the colony's population that their exclusion or inclusion would not significantly change such percentages. In 1907 aborigines formed 2.44 percent of the colony's population while Japanese formed 2.45 percent, Taiwanese 94.75 percent, and foreigners 0.36 percent. In 1918 aborigines made up 2.35 percent of the population while Japanese made up 4.06 percent, Taiwanese 93.01 percent, and foreigners 0.58 percent. (Taiwan sōtokufu, *Taiwan sōtokufu dai sanjū [1925] tōkeisho;* Taihoku, 1928), p. 29.
5. Yoshino, pp. 236, 354. Julean H. Arnold, the American consul in Taiwan in 1908, observed: "Native pupils are selected from among the middle and wealthier classes, for only the children of those who are in a position to contribute toward the support of a school are admitted. In addition to the tax levied upon the property of the parents, each child in attendance at the public schools must pay a tuition fee which averages about 35 cents a year." Julean H. Arnold, *Education in Formosa* (Washington, D.C., 1908), p. 39.
6. Yoshino, p. 236.
7. Taiwanese wincing from the financial strain common schools brought to their communities were experiencing a sting long familiar to local taxpayers in Japan. Although, during the first decade of Meiji, primary schools were often subsidized by the central treasury, as the costs of such subsidies mounted — the subsidies began in 1873 with 240,000 yen and three years later amounted to 600,000 yen — officials worried about the cost of a growing elementary school system to a government with so many financial obligations. (Kaigo, *Inoue Kowashi no kyōiku seido*, p. 120). Thus in 1879 the subsidies were limited to payments for primary teachers' salaries and for books, equipment, and school improvements. The following year they were abolished completely. Until 1896 when subsidies were partially restored, the administrations of cities, towns, and villages

had to struggle constantly to pay for elementary education in their jurisdictions, and parents were forced to pay formidable tuition fees.

The drastic governmental budget cutbacks after 1880 were part of
Matsukata Masayoshi's financial policy of economic retrenchment and
deflation. Like so many aspects of this policy the cutbacks brought much
hardship to the poorer sections of the nation's population. During the
1880s private donations were an important source of primary school
revenues but tuition fees paid by parents were even more important. By
1889 tuition fees provided about one quarter of government primary
schools' revenues (ibid., p. 122). Soaring tuition fees seriously hindered
the government's campaign to increase the percentage of Japanese boys
and girls attending school (ibid., pp. 101-102). Consequently the education ministry tried not only to cut costs but also to increase the city, town,
and village governments' financial obligations to schools. Cost-cutting
measures included discontinuation of such "luxuries" as school hats and
athletic meets (ibid., pp. 113-117). Attempts to use school facilities more
intensively—school buildings were occupied in turn by two shifts of pupils
—were also made (ibid., pp. 106-107). During the 1890s, directives from
prefectural governments urged hard-pressed communities to seek new
ways to raise school fees. Tree planting, raising chickens for their eggs,
collecting "donations" when marriages and births occurred, taxing
household possessions, collecting fees from salaried individuals, and
using revenue from ferry and bridge tolls were all suggested projects (Ebihara, I, pp. 154-155). By 1894 local governments were providing more
than 60 percent of the funds spent on public primary schools and five
years later these contributions amounted to 70 percent. See Naka Arata,
Nihon kindai kyōiku shi (Tokyo, 1973), pp. 1-165; Ebihara, I, 154-155;
Kaigo, *Inoue Kowashi no kyōiku seido,* pp. 97-163; Mombusho, *Gakusei
hyakunen shi,* I, 292.

In Taiwan elementary schooling began with full subsidies from the
Japanese government. Even when Gotō and Kodama shifted the financial
burden to local taxpayers, teachers' salaries continued to be paid by the
colony's central administration—something not achieved in Japan until
1900 and then only partially (Ebihara, I, 163; Naka, pp. 162-164).

8. See for instance Mochiji, pp. 292-300, and Komori Tokuji, *Akashi Motojirō* (Taihoku, 1928), II, 131-133.

9. Takekoshi Yosaburō, "Kanjin kyōiku ni tsuite no byūken" (Mistaken notions about the education of Koreans), *Kyōiku jiron* (Views on education)
746:16 (January 5, 1906), quoted in Ebihara, I, 241.

10. Mochiji spoke to members of the Taiwan Education Society (Taiwan
kyōikukai), an organization founded in 1901 by educational affairs officers and teachers. It published a monthly organ which acted as a forum
for colonial educators' opinions and policy recommendations. See Yoshino, pp. 154-155.

11. Mochiji's speech to the Taiwan Education Society is reproduced in Mochiji, pp. 525-574.

12. Tōgō Minoru, "Hi-dōka ron," *Taiwan jihō* 23:16-21 (June 1911).

13. Ibid., p. 17.

14. Ibid., pp. 18-19.

15. Ibid., p. 20.
16. *TSK,* IV, 182.
17. *TKES,* pp. 278-279.
18. *TKES,* pp. 288-324.
19. *TKES,* pp. 319-321. Regional officials were told to keep an eye on school facilities to see that they met local needs. Vocational departments were to be encouraged but not to the extent that unrealistic burdens were placed upon local funding (*TKES,* p. 322). The accent was upon motivating teachers to do their best within the boundaries of existing financing. Elementary school teachers were urged to take active parts in community affairs even though this would entail heavy extracurricular responsibilities.
20. *TKES,* pp. 398-400.
21. *TKES,* p. 288.
22. Kaigo, *Inoue Kowashi no kyōiku seisaku,* pp. 120-158.
23. Ibid., pp. 85-92.
24. From 1899 to 1925 government-general subsidies to the sugar industry amounted to 12,700,000 yen. In addition to this, the government distributed sugar and provided nursery plants free of charge (Yanaihara Tadao, "Teikokushugika no Taiwan," in his *Yanaihara Tadao zensū,* Tokyo, 1963, II, 323. This book was first published in 1929).
25. Samuel P. S. Ho, "The Development Policy of the Japanese Colonial Government in Taiwan, 1895-1945," in Gustav Ranis, ed., *Government and Economic Development* (New Haven, 1971), p. 314.
26. Yanaihara Tadao, "Teikokushugika no Taiwan," p. 344. This study is very well known among Taiwanese who received postelementary school training in Taiwan during the Japanese colonial period. In 1969 nearly every Taiwanese interviewed who had completed middle school or had received other secondary schooling mentioned this book. Yanaihara's model of a colony seems to have been British India. The pattern he observed in Taiwan and found "unlike that of other colonies," filling even lower echelons of nontraditional occupations with colonists from the ruling country, was in actuality quite similar to what was practiced in French Indochina. See Myrdal, III, 1643-1644; Virginia Thompson, *French Indochina* (London, 1937); Thomas E. Ennis, *French Policy and Developments in Indochina* (Chicago, 1936).
27. *Taiwan sōtokufu dai sanjū [1925] tōkeisho,* p. 28.
28. Ho, p. 307.
29. Japanese National Commission for UNESCO, *Development of Modern System of Education in Japan,* p. 44.
30. See Chapter Six.
31. At the same time, these attitudes and habits were fostered outside the school system by the police force and its native auxiliaries, the *hokō.* Police and *hokō* activity was especially important in enforcement of the rigorous measures taken to control the spread of infectious diseases like plague, cholera, dysentery, and smallpox, which had ravaged the island's populace since the days of Ch'ing rule.
32. *TKES,* p. 320. At this time sole use of Japanese above the first grade would probably have been difficult to enforce.

33. *TKES,* p. 323. Chinese, it should be remembered, was usually taught by a native scholar.
34. *TKES,* pp. 409, 984. In 1912 there were 49,554 pupils attending common school. (*TKES,* p. 409).
35. *TKES,* pp. 322-323.
36. *TKES,* p. 323.
37. Ibid.
38. Arnold, p. 37, suggests that parents were less excited than children about music and physical education: "The Chinese parent finds it difficult to understand the usefulness of music and physical culture in the school curriculum, and if he had his way he would have more Chinese and less music and gymnastics."
39. Arnold, p. 40.
40. Arnold, p. 37.
41. *TKES,* p. 978.
42. *TKES,* p. 979.
43. Ide, *Taiwan chiseki shi,* pp. 468-473.
44. Arnold, p. 39.
45. This distressed administrators greatly and caused them to reluctantly continue common school Chinese language courses.
46. See Taiwan sōtokufu, *Kōgakkō shūshinsho maki ichi: kyōshi yō* (Taihoku, 1913).
47. Arnold, p. 39.
48. See Table 27 in Chapter Seven.
49. Even in postcolonial Taiwan, daughters—at least in peasant families—continued to be more useful at home from an earlier age than boys. See Margery Wolf, *Women and the Family in Rural Taiwan* (Stanford, Calif., 1972).
50. Table 6 gives the percentages of common school pupils who left school before graduation. Unfortunately, however, no data were available regarding the grade-by-grade dropout rates of common school pupils.
51. Yoshino, p. 326.
52. *TWT,* p. 1218.
53. *Taiwan jihō* 16:112-113 (May 1909).
54. *TWT,* p. 1249.
55. Arnold, pp. 34, 44.
56. Arnold, p. 34; *TKES,* pp. 563, 600.
57. Arnold, p. 41.
58. Yoshino, p. 247.
59. Taiwanese middle school graduates who were interviewed in Taiwan in 1969 repeatedly made this point.
60. Harry J. Lamley, "Assimilation Efforts in Colonial Taiwan: The Fate of the 1914 Movement," *Monumenta Serica* 29:496-520 (1970-71), p. 504.
61. Itagaki Morimasa, *Itagaki Taisuke zenshū* (Tokyo, 1969), pp. 395-412.
62. Lamley, "Assimilation Efforts in Colonial Taiwan," p. 509.
63. *Taiwan nichi nichi shimpō* (November 23, 1914), p. 3, cited in Lamley, "Assimilation Efforts in Colonial Taiwan," p. 512. Gotō's meeting with Itagaki was ironic in more ways than one. It had been Itagaki's introduction that originally got Gotō started on his career as an administrator.

For their first meeting see Tsurumi Yūsuke, *Gotō Shimpei den*, II, 229-247.

64. Kan Te-chung, "Hsien-t'ang hsien-sheng yü T'ung-hua-hui" (Lin Hsien-t'ang and the Assimilation Society), in Yeh Jung-chung, comp., *Lin Hsien-t'ang hsien-sheng chi-nien chi* (Taichung, 1960), chuan 3, 31b.
65. Lamley, "Assimilation Efforts in Colonial Taiwan," p. 512.
66. *TSK*, III, 22.
67. *TSK*, III, 23.
68. Lamley, "Assimilation Efforts in Colonial Taiwan," p. 516.
69. Ō, p. 115.
70. Yoshino, pp. 247-248.
71. Ō, p. 114.
72. *TKES*, p. 745.
73. Ibid. Complaints about the unworthiness of Taiwanese for higher education date back to the days of the three normal schools for Taiwanese. See *TKES*, p. 627, for the normal school teachers' denunciation of their students' behavior.
74. *TKES*, p. 744.
75. Yoshino, p. 248.
76. Yoshino, p. 330; *TKES*, pp. 820-826. A separate education department to train teachers of general academic subjects was also planned but never materialized.
77. See Kikuchi. Arnold, p. 34, claims that in his day Japanese women teachers were "paid from $10 to $20 a month" while Taiwanese women teachers were paid "from $3 to $10 a month." He reports that Japanese male teachers received "upon an average, a salary of $300 a year in addition to living quarters" while Taiwanese male teachers earned "about $8 a month."
78. Yoshino, p. 332.
79. Arnold, p. 44, reported that as of 1908, out of fifty graduates, thirty had been engaged as teachers of public schools.
80. See the biographies of Taiwanese women in Chang Tzu-hui, ed., *T'ai-wan shih-jen chih* (Taipei, 1946).
81. Band, p. 129, states that Thomas Barclay "had encouraged promising Formosan boys to go to Japan to complete their studies, in some cases even paying their expenses out of his own pocket." Girls received less encouragement, but there existed in Japan a number of Christian schools which they could enter.
82. Karasawa Tomitarō, *Gakusei no rekishi* (Tokyo, 1955), pp. 134-140.
83. Tsurumi Yūsuke, *Gotō Shimpei den*, II, 46.
84. Ibid., II, 46-48.
85. Gotō Shimpei, "Our Colonization Policy of Formosa," *Gotō Shimpei monjo*, pt. 8, no. 23. Goto called the hospital the "Vatican" because he maintained that while other colonizers had given conquered peoples Christianity the Japanese had given the people they ruled sanitation and medicine instead.
86. Arnold, p. 52.
87. Satō Genji, *Taiwan kyōiku no shinten* (Taihoku, 1943), p. 95; Yoshino, p. 264.

88. Satō Genji, *Taiwan kyōiku no shinten,* p. 95.
89. *TKES,* p. 441.
90. Yoshino, pp. 335-336.
91. Yoshino, pp. 338.
92. *Gotō Shimpei monjo,* pt. 8, contains many reports on conditions in neighboring Asian colonies. These reports include information on religion, finance, defense, administration, minority problems, etc. Pt. 8, no. 9, for instance, is a report on Ceylon, Sumatra, Celebes, Borneo, and Hong Kong—all under British rule.
93. *Gotō Shimpei monjo,* pt. 8, no. 105.
94. See Gotō Shimpei, "Our Colonization Policy of Formosa."
95. Philip Mason, *Patterns of Dominance* (London, 1970), analyzes differences in the way the British ruled different parts of their empire during different periods of history. These differences may have escaped Gotō.
96. As he saw it, "The education of Japanese statesmen themselves in the matter of colonial politics [is] even more urgent than the education of the Formosan people." ("Our Colonization Policy of Formosa.")
97. Tsurumi Yūsuke, *Gotō Shimpei den,* II, 375.
98. For example, one of his subordinates, Nitobe Inazō (1862-1933), who was simultaneously chief of two bureaus in the Taiwan administration, did not possess the educational requirements that would have admitted him to the administrative elite in Japan. Because of this Nitobe officially remained an acting or temporary bureau chief, but Gotō made sure Nitobe's salary equaled that of a permanent bureau chief. See ibid., II, 58.
99. Gotō outlined the purpose of the school in "Kōtō gakkō shisetsubi kyōiku ni kan suru iken" (An opinion regarding educational facilities for higher schooling), *Gotō Shimpei monjo,* pt. 8, no. 32.
100. See ibid.
101. Ibid.
102. Ibid.; *TKES,* p. 737.
103. Gotō Shimpei, "Kōtō gakkō shisetsubi kyōiku"; *TKES,* pp. 737-738.
104. Tsurumi Yūsuke, *Gotō Shimpei den,* II, 377; Arnold, pp. 55-56.
105. *TKES,* p. 739.
106. Ibid.
107. Gotō apparently took his defeat philosophically, with a remark that Tolstoy had also failed when he attempted to set up an ideal school (Tsurumi Yūsuke, *Gotō Shimpei den,* II, 378).
108. For instance, in 1917 when the governor-general granted permission to establish a private school of commerce and engineering authorized to train both Japanese and Taiwanese, the institution was immediately swamped with Taiwanese applications. In 1917 there were 279 applicants to the commerce department; eighteen Japanese and twenty-nine Taiwanese students were accepted. For the engineering department there were 106 applicants; twenty-eight Japanese and five Taiwanese were selected. The large majority of applicants to both departments must have been Taiwanese. See *Taiwan jihō* 105:2-6 (June 1918).

4. Systematization and Integration

1. Actually point four of Wilson's famous fourteen points was not a declara-

tion of a right of self-determination for subject peoples. It simply gave equal weight to the claims of rulers and ruled.

2. The Japanese were very aware that this slogan appealed to colonized peoples, including those under Japanese government. See *TSK*, III, 5; Mombushō, *Meiji ikō kyōiku seido hattatsu shi*, XI, 1068.

3. See Peter Duus, *Party Rivalry and Political Change in Taishō Japan* (Cambridge, Mass., 1968), and Tetsuo Najita, *Hara Kei in the Politics of Compromise, 1905-1915* (Cambridge, Mass., 1967).

4. John K. Fairbank, Edwin O. Reischauer, and Albert Craig, *East Asia: The Modern Transformation* (Boston, 1965), p. 556.

5. Duus, p. 129.

6. See Duus and Najita, *Hara Kei in the Politics of Compromise.*

7. Located between Russia and Japan, Korea was considered to be of enormous strategic importance to the defense of Japan. Thus, military officers continued to head the Korean administration.

8. See Chapter Three.

9. Tsurumi Yūsuke, *Gotō Shimpei den*, II, 38.

10. See E. P. Tsurumi, "Taiwan under Kodama Gentarō and Gotō Shimpei," pp. 107-109.

11. Tōgō Minoru, "Hi-dōka ron," p. 19.

12. Nihon rekishi daijiten henshū iinkai, *Nihon rekishi daijiten* (Tokyo, 1969), VI, 449.

13. Takekoshi Yosaburō, "Japan's Colonial Policy," *Oriental Review* 3.2:102-103 (December 1912), p. 102.

14. Takekoshi not only published articles in English-language periodicals. He also took the trouble to have his book on the Kodama-Gotō administration of Taiwan, *Taiwan tōchi shi*, translated into English. See Takekoshi, *Japanese Rule in Formosa.*

15. Takekoshi, "Japan's Colonial Policy," pp. 102-103.

16. See Edward I-te Chen, "Japanese Colonialism in Korea and Formosa: A Comparison of its Effects upon the Development of Nationalism" (Ph.D. diss., University of Pennsylvania, 1968), pp. 241-244; Yanaihara Tadao, "Teikokushugika no Taiwan," pp. 259-292; Ching-chih Chen, "Japanese Socio-political Control in Taiwan," pp. 216-241.

17. Komori, I, 86. In Russia when Akashi's superior rebuked him for studying too much, Akashi replied that a soldier had to be able to rule a colony once he had conquered it (Komori, I, 86). Akashi's Korean experiences were, however, more important influences upon him. From 1907 to 1908 he served as commander of the Japanese gendarmerie. In 1908 he was appointed director of police affairs for the regency general. Akashi helped Governor-General Terauchi Masatake (who arrived in Korea in July of 1910) turn the entire Korean peninsula into a military camp.

18. Chong-sik Lee, *The Politics of Korean Nationalism* (Berkeley, 1963) comments fairly on the Akashi-Terauchi campaign against anti-Japanese thought and action. Lee concludes that "the suppressive policy of Terauchi and Akashi can be accurately described as hysterical" (Lee, p. 90). One of Lee's examples of the implementation of this policy was the 1911 torture of 123 Korean Christian leaders who were selected from a total of 700 Koreans arrested on a fabricated charge that they had attempted to

assassinate Terauchi (Lee, pp. 92-93). Lee documents his restrained account of Akashi's Korean activities largely from Japanese sources, including official reports of the colonial administration and Akashi's biography.

19. Komori, II, 68-69.
20. Koromi, II, 335.
21. Komori, II, 68-69.
22. Sakuma Samata and his director of civil administration, Uchida Kakichi, had been less reluctant than Kodama and Gotō to speak of assimilation as a policy goal. Nevertheless they had emphasized gradualism. For Sakuma's attitude see *TSK,* IV, 116-117, 125, 163; for Uchida's see *TSK,* IV, 128.
23. Komori, II, 50-51. The subordinates were not all solidly in agreement with Akashi. After those who had held that assimilation was impossible were silenced, they began to argue that from an economic point of view, the benefits to be gained from assimilation were few (ibid.).
24. Komori, II, 50-59.
25. Komori, II, 133.
26. *TKES,* pp. 91-99.
27. *TKES,* p. 915.
28. *TKES,* pp. 992-993.
29. *TKES,* p. 93.
30. *TKES,* pp. 96, 756-757.
31. Both Gotō Shimpei and Mochiji Rokusaburō had used economic arguments against vocational education for natives, stressing that employment opportunities would not be made available to islanders so trained.
32. The vigorous opposition of Akashi's bureau and department heads clearly represented the judgment of the policy makers of earlier administrations. However, employers were finding fewer and fewer skilled Japanese workers available for employment. World War I, which stimulated the Japanese economy immensely, created a great demand for skilled workers in Japanese industries. Thus there were fewer of them available for employment in the colonial economy, which also had surged ahead during the war. Because of this scarcity of skilled workers, a need for new vocational educational facilities was felt in Japan, and some of this concern also spilled over to the island colony. See Yanihara, "Teikokushugika no Taiwan," p. 344.
33. *TKES,* p. 960. During the same year there were 330 Taiwanese studying in the medical college (*TKES,* p. 962).
34. Komori, II, 335.
35. Komori, II, 334.
36. This was an extremely important motive. Because the army general and populist politician agreed on this point they actually held a great deal in common.
37. However, when the rescript was replaced by a new one in 1922, the man who had been Akashi's education chief resigned because he felt that his work had been undone (Komori, II, 138).
38. *TKES,* p. 93.
39. Because it was so financially rewarding the demand for medical educa-

tion in colonial Taiwan was always great. Colonial education is often discussed in terms of what kind of schools the colonial rulers chose to provide. However, in *Education and Social Change in Ghana* (Chicago, 1965), Philip Foster argues that British colonial education in Africa was shaped to a greater degree than is usually realized by native demands. Of course in Africa and elsewhere colonial policy makers helped create demands for education.

40. Yoshino, pp. 247-248.
41. Kuroda Kōshirō, ed., *Den Kenjirō den* (Tokyo, 1932), pp. 90-99, 377; Itō Hirobumi, *Taiwan shiryō,* pp. 32-34.
42. Hara Kei, *Hara Kei nikki* (Tokyo, 1950-1951), VIII, 216-217, 243-244, 284, 287; Shinobu Seizaburō, *Taishō seiji shi,* III, 846-847.
43. Yamagata Aritomo and Terauchi Masakata objected to replacing the military governor-general of Korea with a civil one, but Tanaka Giichi, Hara's army minister, proposed a compromise. He suggested formally opening the post to civil as well as military candidates but in practice appointing Admiral Saitō Makoto. As a result of this compromise, Yamagata felt he could support Hara's proposed reform. It became effective on August 18, 1918, and Hara appointed Saitō Makoto governor-general of Korea. The same reform made civilians eligible for the governor-generalship of Taiwan (Hara, *Hara Kei nikki,* VIII, 292-293).
44. I am indebted to Ching-chih Chen for pointing this out.
45. If the first civilian governor-general was a Yamagata man, Hara could be assured that he would not have to run interference from that quarter (Hara, *Hara Kei nikki,* VIII, 368).
46. See Najita, *Hara Kei in the Politics of Compromise,* for Hara's pork-barrel style of political appointments.
47. Kuroda, *Den Kenjirō den,* pp. 377-378.
48. He visited Yamagata before accepting the post (*Den Kenjirō nikki,* October 28, 1919). Visits to Yamagata after becoming governor-general are recorded in *Den Kenjirō nikki,* January 27, 1921, January 28, 1921, and April 6, 1921.
49. See Ching-chih Chen, "Japanese Socio-political Control in Taiwan," pp. 349-350.
50. Kuroda, *Den Kenjirō den,* pp. 390-404.
51. Ibid., p. 383.
52. *Kyōka* means education in the sense of enlightenment or edification or evangelization.
53. Ibid., pp. 390-404; Den Kenjirō, "Taiwan shisei kunji," *Taiwan jihō* 106:11-26 (December 1919).
54. When the governor-general became a civilian, his chief subordinate's title was changed from *minseichōkan* to *chōkan.* Presumably the post would accordingly become a less powerful one, but even civilian governors-general had to spend a great deal of time in Tokyo.
55. Kuroda, *Den Kenjirō den,* pp. 405-406; Ide, *Taiwan chiseki shi,* p. 628.
56. Ibid., p. 652.
57. *TKES,* pp. 351-352.
58. *TKES,* pp. 352-354.
59. *TKES,* p. 352.

60. *TKES,* pp. 457, 409 respectively.
61. Yoshino, pp. 247-248. A large number of Taiwanese applicants to primary schools appear to have been rejected. Hirano Shōichi, "Taiwan no kyōgaku ni tsuite," *Taiwan jihō* (February 1920), pp. 6-9, noted in an article praising integrated education that very few Taiwanese were getting into the primary schools. He suggested that this was either because examinations for entrance were too strict or because Taiwanese children were unqualified. He did not mention the fact that schools could reject applicants on a number of nonacademic grounds.
62. *TKES,* p. 354-355.
63. Hirano Shōichi declared that the cultural level of the Taiwanese people equaled that of the Japanese people fifty years previously ("Taiwan no kyōgaku ni tsuite," p. 9).
64. *TKES,* p. 355.
65. Taiwan sōtokufu, *Taiwan ni okeru gakkō jidō ni kan suru kenkyū* (Taihoku, 1923), p. 26.
66. Ibid., p. 27.
67. Ibid., pp. 28-29.
68. Ibid., p. 29.
69. For insights on this question I am especially indebted to discussions with Margaret Henderson of the New School, Vancouver, British Columbia.
70. *TKES,* p. 409, and Yoshino, p. 494, respectively.
71. See Appendix B.
72. The boys in this population represented more than 43 percent of school-aged Taiwanese boys.
73. This work was clearly marked "not for sale."
74. At this point in time it is not easy to judge how much the decision was caused by emotional factors and how much it was a result of budgetary considerations. Certainly fear of an ethnic group different from one's own is a common enough phenomenon. However, compared to hostilities and fears that other ethnic groups in other settings have expressed, the anti-Taiwanese feelings of the Japanese in Taiwan appear rather mild. See for example Mason, *Patterns of Dominance,* and W. Peter Ward, "The Oriental Immigrant and Canada's Protestant Clergy, 1858-1925," *B.C. Studies* 22:40-55 (Summer 1974).
75. *TKES,* p. 349.
76. Ibid.
77. *TKES,* p. 350.
78. *TKES,* p. 110.
79. *TKES,* p. 993.
80. Satō Genji, *Taiwan kyōiku no shinten,* p. 125.
81. Quoted in Yoshino, p. 467. See Yoshino, pp. 466-468, for comments on the 1922 rescript made by other officials.
82. Quoted in Yoshino, pp. 467-468. The education bureau chief also stated that in Taiwan removal of educational discrimination had gone much further than in Korea.
83. Shibata Ren, *Taiwan dōka saku ron* (Taihoku, 1923), p. 81, reported that Taiwanese parents, in the south especially, objected strenuously when Chinese language studies were dropped.

84. In 1925 there were thirty-three schools with four-year courses and 489 schools with six-year courses (*Taiwan sōtokufu dai sanjū* [*1925*] *tōkeisho*, p. 102).

85. For regulations regarding history and geography see *TKES*, pp. 365-366; for regulations regarding Chinese see *TKES*, p. 369. As late as 1921 common school regulations contained injunctions to teach Chinese readings of island place names and proper names. See *TKES*, p. 336.

86. Satō Genji, *Taiwan kyōiku no shinten*, p. 124. The *Kōtō ka* was an advanced course for graduates of the regular primary school course who wanted a few years' additional schooling but did not necessarily intend to go on to secondary school. The *hoshu ka* was a course of review and enrichment for primary school graduates who may have hoped to enter middle school or higher girls' school.

87. *TKES*, pp. 356-357.

88. Ching-chih Chen, "Japanese Socio-political Control in Taiwan," p. 368.

89. See Ide, *Taiwan chiseki shi*, pp. 637-639.

90. Ching-chih Chen, "Japanese Socio-political Control in Taiwan," pp. 372-373. See Ide, *Taiwan chiseki shi*, p. 639, for what was discussed at the three sessions.

91. Satō Genji, *Taiwan kyōiku no shinten*, pp. 164-165.

92. *TKES*, p. 409.

93. This is perhaps the most important difference between Akashi's rescript and Den's rescript, at least as far as the least affluent of the academically ambitious Taiwanese were concerned. Under Akashi's rescript the wealthiest island families could still send their children to superior schools in Japan; thus they were not severely hampered by Akashi's segregated education system. For those who could not go to Japan Den offered superior schools for a few of their number, but Akashi brought postelementary schooling to a much larger number.

94. Taiwan sōtokufu bunkyōkyoku, *Gakuji nijūgonen hō* as reproduced in Hsieh Ch'un-mu, *Taiwanjin wa kaku miru* (Taihoku, 1930), pp. 60-61.

95. Ibid.

96. *TWT*, p. 1216.

97. Ibid.

98. See Yanaihara Tadao, "Teikokushugika no Taiwan," p. 248, and Hseih Ch'un-mu, *Taiwanjin wa kaku miru*, pp. 55-60.

99. Higher girls' school provided what was usually terminal education.

100. In 1915 there were 137,229 Japanese, 3,327,812 Taiwanese, and 86,576 aborigines in Taiwan; in 1925 there were 189,630 Japanese, 3,838,636 Taiwanese, and 85,938 aborigines (*Taiwan sōtokufu dai sanjūni* [*1928*] *tōkeisho*, p. 28).

101. Yanaihara Tadao, "Teikokushugika no Taiwan," p. 248; Hsieh Ch'un-mu, *Taiwanjin wa kaku miru*, p. 60.

102. See Kuroda, *Den Kenjirō den*, pp. 444-485. Den argued his policies before Japanese government officials and elected representatives with energy and enthusiasm. On January 20, 1920, for instance, he answered questions in the Diet about Taiwan, while the prime minister had to answer for Korean policies because the governor-general of Korea, Saitō Makoto, was not present. Den spoke on the peaceful state of the island's

people, production increases, Taiwanese and Japanese joint management enterprises, and other matters. He ventured opinions regarding appointing Taiwanese to high offices, recognizing Taiwanese and Japanese intermarriages, introducing integrated education (*kyōgaku*), and carrying out regional government reforms.

103. Ching-chih Chen, "Japanese Socio-political Control in Taiwan," p. 350.
104. Tsurumi Yūsuke, *Gotō Shimpei den,* II, 580-581; Itō Kinjirō, *Shinryōchi Kaitaku to Goto Shimpei* (Tokyo, 1942), pp. 257-258.
105. See Ching-chih Chen, "Japanese Socio-political Control in Taiwan."
106. Den Kenjirō, "Assimilation Keynote of Taiwan Policy," *Trans-Pacific* 8:2.3 (February-March 1923), p. 46.
107. The *Trans-Pacific* was an English-language monthly published in Tokyo. Although not officially a government publication it often featured articles favorably publicizing the activities of Japanese government and business.

5. After the Integration Rescript

1. Ching-chih Chen, "Japanese Socio-political Control in Taiwan," pp. 326-327. See also Izawa Takio denki hensan iinkai, *Izawa Takio* (Tokyo, 1951), p. 150, and Kō Se-kai, *Nihon tōchika no Taiwan* (Tokyo, 1972), p. 231.
2. See his Taiwan policy speech in *Izawa Takio,* pp. 149-150, and Ide, *Taiwan chiseki shi,* pp. 722-723.
3. Kamiyama kun kinen jigyōkai, *Kamiyama Mitsunoshin* (Tokyo, 1941), I, 323-330, 378-380. Kamiyama talked about the fusion of three peoples: Japanese, Taiwanese, and aborigines. The latter he called Takasago people (Takasago was another name for Taiwan) instead of the pejorative terms *seiban* (savages) or *banjin* (savages) in common usage.
4. Ibid., I, 324-328.
5. Katō Haruki, "Taiwan no kyōkasho hensan ni tsuite" (Regarding the editing of Taiwan textbooks), in Ōtsuka Kiyotoshi, ed., *Yakushin Taiwan daikan (tsuzuki)* (Tokyo, 1939), p. 75. In 1929 Yanaihara Tadao pointed out that, in spite of all the talk about hastening integration, a Taiwanese-Japanese dictionary had yet to be published. Since the scholars working on one were financed by a private association and not by the government general, Yanaihara thought this indicated that the administration was not entirely serious when it claimed that integration of Taiwanese and Japanese was one of its most important policies ("Teikokushugika no Taiwan," p. 351).
6. This was an old idea. Katsura Tarō, one of the colony's first governors-general, had been an advocate of it. See Tokutomi Iichirō, ed., *Koshaku Katsura Tarō den* (Tokyo, 1917), I, 706-710.
7. See Chapter Six. In 1939 the army sent military inspectors to the ministry of education and the navy dispatched officers to fill the "navy chairs" (*kaigun kōza*) established in all normal schools (Karasawa Tomitarō, *Kyōshi no rekishi,* Tokyo, 1955, p. 202). Military drill was increasingly encouraged in the schools. From about 1930 the interschool drill competitions of middle schools became heavily military in character. In girls' schools military drill as well as Red Cross training was introduced. See Ebihara, II, 169-170.

8. Kawamura Takeji, *Taiwan no ichinen* (Tokyo, 1930), p. 6.
9. *TKES*, p. 667. See Naka, *Nihon kindai kyōiku shi*, pp. 298-304, for background information on this ordinance.
10. Ibid., p. 302, lists the courses these military instructors taught. See Peng Ming-min, *A Taste of Freedom: Memoirs of a Formosan Independence Leader* (New York, 1972), p. 28, for a case of a military instructor—in a higher school in Japan—trying to prevent a Taiwanese student from graduating because, although the student possessed a brilliant academic record, he did not do well in military drill.
11. In administrators' eyes, the schools were already doing a good job of Japanization. The problem was how to get more Taiwanese into them.
12. See Barclay, pp. 117-125.
13. *TWT*, p. 1232. Previously, the two years with the largest number of Japanese in common schools had been 1936 with fifty-nine Japanese among 398,983 common school pupils and 1930 with forty-eight Japanese out of a total common school population of 248,478 (*TWT*, p. 1232).
14. In 1922 there were 533 Taiwanese in primary schools; in 1932 there were 2,097 Taiwanese in primary schools; in 1942 there were 4,800 in primary schools (*TWT*, p. 1229.)
15. Only in 1942, when there were 5,356 Taiwanese primary school pupils out of a total of 53,219 primary schoolers, did Taiwanese slightly exceed 10 percent of the primary school population (*TWT*, p. 1229).
16. According to Taiwanese interviewed in 1969.
17. *TKES*, p. 386.
18. In 1933 there were thirty-two four-year common schools and 736 six-year common schools (*Taiwan sōtokufu dai sanjūkyū [1935] tōkeisho*, p. 136). In 1926 handicrafts, drawing, and vocational studies had been made compulsory for students in the two-year advanced courses of Japanese primary schools because the advanced courses were regarded as terminal. These subjects were not made mandatory in the regular six-year primary school course. Mombushō, *Gakusei no hyakunen shi*, I, 467. The distinction between academic preparatory studies stressed in the regular primary school course and terminal schooling provided by the advanced course was maintained when the Primary School Rescript was revised in 1941. See ibid., II, 112.
19. *TKES*, p. 389; *Taiwan sōtokufu dai yonjūsan [1939] tōkeisho*, p. 100. Taiwan sōtokufu, *Taiwan no gakkō kyōiku*, p. 120, claims that in 1936 there were 84 *shobō* with 3,404 pupils.
20. *TKES*, p. 338.
21. Satō Genji, *Taiwan kyōiku no shinten*, pp. 160-163.
22. Ibid., pp. 164-167.
23. Ibid.
24. Ibid.
25. *TKES*, pp. 984-986.
26. *Taiwan sōtokufu dai yonjūsan [1939] tōkeisho*, p. 100, lists seventeen remaining *shobō;* Taiwan sotokufu, *Taiwan jijō [1939]* (Taihoku, 1939), p. 198, lists eighteen remaining *shobō*.
27. *Taiwan sōtokufu dai sanjūroku [1935] tōkeisho*, pp. 124-125; *Taiwan sōtokufu dai yonjūichi [1940] tōkeisho*, pp. 84-85.
28. Officially one needed only to be a graduate of a primary school in order

to apply to the normal school program that trained primary school teachers. See Satō Genji, *Taiwan kyōiku no shinten*, p. 134.

29. The *Taiwan sōtokufu tōkeisho* for various years reveal that during the 1930s a large number of elementary school teachers who lacked the qualifications provided by teachers' training programs were employed in common schools in particular.

30. Two new normal schools were established in 1940, one in Shinchiku and one in Heitō (Pingtung). See Satō Genji, *Taiwan kyōiku no shinten*, p. 134.

31. The integration rescript established five years of regular studies and one year of specialized studies for a total of six years of normal school for elementary school graduates. In 1933 specialized studies were expanded to two years, just as the specialized study program in Japanese normal schools had been lengthened two years earlier. *TKES*, pp. 642-673; Mombushō, *Gakusei hyakunen shi*, I, 502; Naka, *Nihon kindai kyōiku shi*, pp. 348-349; Taiwan sōtokufu, *Taiwan tōchi gaiyō*, p. 40.

32. Male students received three hours a week of drill. See *TKES*, p. 666.

33. *TKES*, pp. 665-666.

34. *TKES*, pp. 672-673, 688-704.

35. Satō Genji, *Taiwan kyōiku no shinten*, p. 134; Naka, *Nihon kindai kyōiku shi*, pp. 348-349.

36. See Katsuda Shuichi and Nakauchi Toshio, *Nihon no gakkō* (Tokyo, 1965), pp. 77-84, for one account of the competition to gain entrance to secondary schools in Japan.

37. Wyndham, pp. 154-155.

38. Officials' complacency regarding Japanese educational "gifts" to the Taiwanese lasted longer than Japanese rule in Taiwan. See Gaimushō, *Nihon tōchika gojūnen no Taiwan* (Tokyo, 1964), p. 276.

39. Taiwanese interviewed in 1969 repeatedly testified to this.

40. *TKES*, p. 788.

41. *TKES*, p. 790.

42. *TKES*, pp. 788-791.

43. In 1920 there were 166,621 Japanese in the colony; in 1925 there were 189,630 Japanese in Taiwan; in 1930, 232,299; in 1935, 269,798; in 1940, 346,663 (*Taiwan sōtokufu dai sanjūni [1928] tōkeisho*, p. 28; *Taiwan sōtokufu dai yonjūroku [1942] tōkeisho*, p. 18).

44. See Hsieh Ch'un-mu, *Taiwanjin wa kaku miru*, pp. 60-61.

45. Taiwan sōtokufu, *Taiwan no gakkō kyōiku*, p. 93.

46. Many of the women who taught were unaccredited teachers. Some teachers were also recruited from among women who had gone through vocational schools studying such subjects as home economics.

47. See, for example, Chang Tzu-hui, *T'ai-wan shih-jen-chih*, p. 43, and Chin Miao-chiang, *Buraku kyōka no jissai* (Taichū, 1940), p. 256.

48. Lin Ching-ming, *Shirarezaru Taiwan: Taiwan dokuritsu undōka no sakebi* (Tokyo, 1970), p. 77.

49. *TKES*, p. 111.

50. See Hokkaidō daigaku, *Hokkaidō daigaku sōki hachijūnen shi* (Sapporo, 1965) and Tōhoku daigaku, *Tōhoku daigaku gojūnen shi* (Sendai, 1932).

51. Lee, pp. 240-242; Ōno Ken'ichi, *Chosen kyōiku mondai kanken* (Keijō, 1936), p. 141.

52. *TKES,* p. 955; Yoshino, pp. 452-453.
53. See Ide, *Taiwan chiseki shi,* pp. 696-697; Taiwan sōtokufu, *Taiwan jijō (1940)* (Taihoku, 1940), pp. 765-775; Okamatsu, *Provisional Report.*
54. Ide, *Taiwan chiseki shi,* pp. 779-780.
55. Taiwan sōtokufu, *Taiwan jijō (1936)* (Taihoku, 1936), p. 178.
56. Testimony of Taiwanese interviewed in 1969.
57. Yanaihara, "Teikokushugika no Taiwan," p. 347.
58. Kinebuchi Yoshifusa, *Taiwan shakai jigyō shi* (Taihoku, 1940), pp. 1208-1209.
59. Interviews with Taiwanese who attended these schools.
60. Lin Ching-ming, p. 74.
61. Taiwan sōtokufu, *Taiwan jijō (1937)* (Taihoku, 1937), p. 171; Taiwan tsūshin sha, *Taiwan nenka (1939)* (Taihoku, 1939), pp. 103-104, 131-132; *Taiwan nenkan (1942)* (Taihoku, 1942), pp. 189, 191; *Taiwan nenkan (1944)* (Taihoku, 1944), pp. 239-240.
62. Lin Ching-ming, p. 74.
63. Yanaihara, "Teikokushugika no Taiwan," p. 357; Taiwanese interviewed in 1969.
64. Yanaihara, "Teikokushugika no Taiwan," p. 354. Taiwan sōtokufu naimukyoku gakumuka, *Taiwan gaku jijō (1919)* (Taihoku, 1919), p. 137, states that such Christian institutions as Dōshisha University and Meiji Gakuin were among the earliest Japanese educational institutions attended by Taiwanese.
65. *Taiwan nenkan* (1942), p. 240; *Taiwan nenkan* (1944), p. 507.
66. Taiwanese interviewed stressed this point.
67. See the biographies of educated Taiwanese in Taiwan shinminpō sha, ed., *Taiwan jinshi kan* (Taihoku, 1937).
68. See Peng Ming-min.
69. Chang Tzu-hui, *T'ai-wan shih-jen chih,* pp. 219, 223.
70. *TSK,* III, 23-24. The supervision was intended to be very close, involving frequent meetings with students and regular reports on their progress in school, behavior, and accomplishments. See Taiwan sōtokufu naimukyoku gakumuka, *Taiwan gaku jijō,* p. 135.
71. See Taiwan sōtokufu, *Taiwan no gakkō kyōiku,* p. 121, for the estimate of less than 700; *TSK,* III, 24, for the confidential police estimate.
72. *Taiwan sōtokufu daiyonjūroku [1942] tōkeisho,* pp. 18-19. These figures appear to include a small number of aborigines.
73. Testimony of Taiwanese interviewed in 1969.
74. Lin Ching-ming, p. 85.
75. Satō Genji, *Taiwan kyōiku no shinten,* p. 176. Exactly what the society did is unclear.
76. Ibid.; Peng Ming-min, p. 32; Lin Ching-ming, p. 86.
77. Peng Ming-min, p. 32.
78. Satō Genji, *Taiwan kyōiku no shinten,* pp. 182-186.
79. Ibid., p. 186.
80. Taiwanese interviewed in 1969.
81. A small number of "assimilated" Taiwanese families received the better class of ration ticket. Some of those who did reported that their families avoided the ill feeling of less lucky neighbors by sharing with them.
82. *Taiwan sōtokufu yonjūroku [1942] tōkeisho,* p. 18.

6. Japanization in the Common Schools

1. Arithmetic was also considered an essential subject. Manual arts and physical education were considered fairly important. Science, history, and geography were regarded as desirable but nonessential.
2. Taiwan sōtokufu, *Kokugo kyōjusho ichi* (Taihoku, 1941), p. 5.
3. Taiwan sōtokufu, *Kogakkō shūshinsho, maki ichi: kyōshi yō* (Taihoku, 1913), pp. 1-2.
4. Taiwan sōtokufu, *Kokugo kyōjusho ichi* (1941), pp. 5-7.
5. See Ide, *Taiwan chiseki shi,* pp. 330-331; Mochiji, pp. 282-293.
6. Before 1903 there was some governmental control of textbook writing and publishing, but in this year the Ministry of Education introduced a new system of state-compiled textbooks under which all textbook compilation, production, and distribution came under the ministry's control.
7. See Karasawa Tomitarō, *Kyōkasho no rekishi* (Tokyo, 1956).
8. Ibid., pp. 253-255.
9. Ibid., pp. 228, 237-253.
10. Ibid., pp. 270-329.
11. Ibid., pp. 330-430.
12. Ibid., p. 453.
13. Ibid., pp. 431-480.
14. Ibid., p. 515.
15. My independent examination of the ethics textbooks produced conclusions close to Karasawa's, although I found the ethics texts of the second (1910-18) and third (1918-33) periods to be very similar.
16. Karasawa, *Kyōkasho no rekishi,* pp. 515-516.
17. See Mombushō, *Yomikata 2* (Osaka, 1941).
18. Karasawa, *Kyōkasho no rekishi,* p. 515.
19. Mombushō, *Yomikata 3* (Osaka, 1941); *Yomikata 4* (Osaka, 1941).
20. See Kaigo Tokiomi and Naka Arata, eds., *Nihon kyōkasho taikei: kindai hen* (Tokyo, 1961-1967). See the bibliography for a list of the individual readers examined.
21. See Kaigo and Naka, *Nihon kyokasho taikei: kindai hen* and the ethics books in the bibliography.
22. See John Caiger, "The Aims and Content of School Courses in Japanese History, 1872-1945," in Edmund Skrzypckak, ed., *Japan's Modern Century* (Tokyo, 1969), pp. 51-81.

    Even during the last two periods, however, ultranationalist, ethnocentric content in Japanese primary school textbooks appears to have been less than such content in nineteenth-century American textbooks. See Ruth Miller Elson, *Guardians of Tradition: American Schoolbooks of the Nineteenth Century* (Lincoln, Nebraska, 1964). Elson found nineteenth-century American elementary school textbooks to contain an interesting amalgam of antiforeignism, religious bigotry, and racial prejudice as well as support for economic liberalism, political republicanism, and equality of opportunity as a social value. Her study suggests that nineteenth-century American schoolbooks were intended to perform a function very much like that assigned to the Japanese textbooks. "Most nineteenth-century schoolbooks include specific descriptions of the American character, but in a larger sense everything they teach the American child is part of this attempt to find out what the American is and should be. Whatever is good in ideas, behavior, and institutions they identify with the United States and its citizens. By selecting what they consider most essential to preserve in America, nineteenth-century schoolbooks offered to the broadest and most impressionable American audience an image of themselves as a guide to the future" (Elson, p. 342).

23. A series of arithmetic texts was begun in 1909. See *TKES,* pp. 342-408, for textbooks published up to 1939.

24. I found no trace of any post-1934 set. However, Kōshōkai yomikata kenkyūbu, *Kōgakkō yō kokugo tokuhon kyōju saimonkuhen ni kyōzai kenkyū* (Taihoku, 1938), p. 15, suggests that by the end of the 1930s preparation for a new set of language readers was under way.

25. Ts'ai P'ei-huo, *Nihon honkokumin ni atō* (Tokyo, 1928), p. 47.

26. Ibid., p. 48.

27. See Taiwan sōtokufu, *Kōgakkō kokugo kyōjusho, dai ichinen yō* (Taihoku, 1913); *Kōgakkō kokugo kyōjusho, dai ninen yō* (Taihoku, 1914); *Kōgakkō kokugo kyōjusho, dai sannen yō* (Taihoku, 1915).

28. Taiwan sōtokufu, *Kōgakkō shūshinsho, kyōshi yō, maki ichi* (Taihoku, 1913), pp. 1-6.

29. Taiwan sōtokufu, *Kōgakkō shūshinsho, kyōshi yō, maki ichi* (1913).

30. See the bibliography for the Taiwan readers of this period and for the education ministry readers which were examined. See also Kaigo and Naka, *Nihon kyōkasho taikei: kindai hen.*

31. See ibid.; the government-general readers; and the education ministry readers in the bibliography.

32. See Kaigo and Naka, *Nihon kyōkasho taikei: kindai hen,* and the government-general readers and the education ministry readers in the bibliography.

33. For instance, a comparison of the second and third readers in each set reveals the following: there is one historical story in each of the two Japanese readers, but none in either of the two Taiwanese readers. Similarly, examination of the fourth readers of both sets reveals that although the Japanese reader has one historical tale which takes up two lessons, there are no historical stories in the Taiwanese reader. In the fifth Japanese reader there are five lessons concerning Japanese history: one in which a samurai father teaches solidarity to his sons, a story about the Great Buddha in Nara, a story about Chihisagobe, and two lessons about the Genji-Heike War. In the fifth Taiwanese reader there is only one "historical" lesson, about the Japanese storm god's activities in Japan's prehistorical, mythical, heroic "age of the gods." See the following Taiwan sōtokufu readers: *Kōgakkō yō kokugo tokuhon, maki ni* (Taihoku, 1923, ninth printing: 1931); *Kōgakkō yō kokugo tokuhon, maki san* (Taihoku, 1923, ninth printing: 1931); *Kōgakkō yō kokugo tokuhon, maki yon* (Taihoku, 1923, ninth printing: 1931); *Kōgakkō yō kokugo tokuhon, maki go* (Taihoku, 1924, eighth printing: 1930). See the following corresponding Mombusho readers: *Jinjō shōgakkō tōkuhon, maki ni* (1926); *Jinjō shōgakkō tokuhon, maki san* (1923); *Jinjō shogakkō tokuhon, maki yon* (1919); *Jinjō shōgakkō tokuhon, maki go* (1920).

34. See Taiwan sōtokufu, *Kōgakkō yō kokugo tokuhon, maki jūni* (1931), and Mombushō, *Jinjō shōgakkō tokuhon, maki jūni* (1926). The former

contains two stories which draw upon Chinese history, one about Ko-dama Gentarō with heavy emphasis upon his activities in Taiwan, and one about Kinbara Meizen (1830-1923) and his encouragement of agricultural enterprises. The latter, in addition to a lesson on Confucius, contains several lessons related to Japanese history.

35. See Taiwan sōtokufu, *Kōgakkō yō kokugo tokuhon, maki jūni* (1931), and Mombushō, *Jinjō shōgakkō tokuhon, maki jūni* (1926).
36. See Taiwan sōtokufu, *Kōgakkō yō kokugo tokuhon, maki jūichi* (1931).
37. See Taiwan sōtokufu, *Kōgakkō yō kokugo tokuhon, maki go* (1924, eighth printing: 1930).
38. Ibid.
39. See Taiwan sōtokufu, *Kōgakkō yō kokugo tokuhon, maki yon* (1923, ninth printing: 1931).
40. See all the readers for this period listed in the bibliography.
41. See Mombushō, *Jinjō shōgakkō tokuhon, maki roku* (1915) and Taiwan sōtokufu, *Kōgakkō yō kokugo tokuhon, maki roku* (1924, ninth printing: 1931).
42. See ibid.
43. See Taiwan sōtokufu, *Kōgakkō yō kokugo tokuhon, maki go* (1924, eighth printing: 1930).
44. See the Taiwanese ethics textbooks in the bibliography.
45. See Mombushō, *Jinjō shōgakkō shūshinsho, maki ni* (1919), and Taiwan sōtokufu, *Kōgakkō shūshinsho, maki ni, jidō yō* (1931).
46. See Taiwan sōtokufu, *Kōgakkō shūshinsho, maki yon, jidō yō* (1931). A lesson in this book that would have been particularly at home in a primary school text was entitled "The Duties of Males and the Duties of Females." Its message was that although boys and girls were equally humans and citizens they were born with different bodies and natures and hence assigned different responsibilities. Males guarded their families and worked for the sake of society; females managed family affairs and brought up children. If each sex strove harmoniously in his or her respective field of endeavor, family life would flourish and the country would prosper.
47. Unfortunately I was able to find only a copy of a common school first-grade Japanese language reader (equal to the former first and second readers) and a copy of a common school first-grade ethics textbook. Both were published in 1941. Librarians and others in Taiwan, when asked about these books in 1969, said they believed such textbooks to have been destroyed in 1945. Some individuals said that formerly they possessed such books, but that after the war the books became useless and thus they had used them to light fires.
48. Taiwan sōtokufu, *Kokugo kyōkasho ichi* (Taihoku, 1941), p. 239.
49. See Taiwan sōtokufu, *Kokugo kyōkasho ichi* (1941).
50. Unfortunately, inability to obtain copies of the textbooks used in later grades prevented me from learning if this trend continued throughout all the grades. It seems logical to assume that it did.
51. See Taiwan sōtokufu, *Kōgakkō shūshinsho, maki ni jidō yō* (1941), and Mombushō, *Jinjō shōgakkō shūshinsho, maki ni* (1941).
52. See Taiwan sōtokufu, *Kōgakkō kōtō ka shūshinsho, maki ichi kyōshi yō* (1933). The lesson was similar to lesson nine in Taiwan sōtokufu, *Kō-*

gakkō shūshinsho, maki roku jidō yō (1931), which told children in their last year of common school that they should follow their parents' occupations. If one was forced to take up a new occupation, it counselled, work should not be chosen without first giving a great deal of thought to whether or not one was equipped for this kind of work in terms of one's health, finances, and interests. One should also consult extensively with parents and elders before branching out on a new career.

53. See Taiwan sōtokufu, *Kōgakkō yō kokugo tokuhon, maki hachi* (1924, eighth printing: 1931).
54. See ibid.

7. Japanese Education and Taiwanese Life

1. There was a vast difference between the village school described by Norma J. Diamond, "K'un Shen: A Taiwanese Fishing Village" (Ph.D. diss., Cornell University, 1966), p. 171, and the common schools Western visitors to Taihoku were taken to see. See Harold and Alice Foght, pp. 374-379.
2. The school Diamond described appeared to have been completely outside of the main stream of village life. During the Japanese period it was furnished by the government and patronized by a few of the richer residents.
3. This situation closely resembled elementary school attendance patterns of early Meiji Japan. See Chapter Two.
4. Taiwan sōtokufu, *Taiwan no kyōiku* (Taihoku, 1930), p. 18.
5. Ibid.
6. In 1930 almost 42 percent of the girls in Taihoku city were in school. Ibid.
7. Margery Wolf has described vividly girls' school attendance at a rural school during the postcolonial period. See Wolf, pp. 80-94. Norma Diamond observed the children of K'un Shen dropping out of school because what it taught was not relevant to their working lives.
8. Mao Yeh-hsin and Lin Ch'ao-ching, *Taiwan no kosaku mondai* (Taihoku, 1933), p. 164.
9. Nakagoe Eiji, *Taiwan no shakai kyōiku* (Taihoku, 1936), pp. 10-11.
10. Nakagoe, pp. 64-66.
11. Nakagoe, p. 67; Satō Genji, *Taiwan no kyōiku no shinten,* p. 140.
12. Nakagoe, p. 216.
13. Nakagoe, pp. 215-216.
14. The use of hamlet for *buraku* is taken from Ronald P. Dore, *Land Reform in Japan* (London, 1959).
15. See Chin Miao-chang, *Buraku kyōka no jissai* and Taiwan sōtokufu, *Taiwan ni okeru yūryō buraku shisetsu gaikyō* (Taihoku, 1940).
16. Ibid. contains accounts of only twenty-six hamlets.
17. See Chin Miao-ching.
18. Chin Miao-ching, pp. 38-42.
19. Chin Miao-ching, pp. 42-52.
20. Chin Miao-ching, pp. 39-42.
21. For biographies of leaders of San-shih-chang-li's betterment movement see Chin Miao-ching, pp. 242-261, which describe the backgrounds of two women and sixteen men.
22. Chin Miao-ching, p. 6.

23. Chin Miao-ching, pp. 21, 95-96. As of 1939 there were also twelve privately owned radios, eighteen subscribers to newspapers, and fifteen subscribers to magazines in this hamlet.
24. For information regarding hamlet meeting houses see Nakagoe, pp. 240-242, 245-246.
25. See Taiwan sōtokufu, *Taiwan shakai kyōiku gaiyō* (Taihoku, 1935), pp. 47-48, for this description.
26. Nakagoe, pp. 151-152.
27. Nakagoe, p. 152.
28. For information on the boys' groups especially, see Nakagoe, pp. 151-170.
29. Nakagoe, pp. 169-170.
30. Nakagoe, pp. 170-172. In addition, by 1935 about 20,000 boys between the ages of eleven and eighteen were enrolled in the boy scout troops which were affiliated with boy scouts in thirty-nine other countries. In 1935 there existed but one troop of sea scouts (Nakagoe, pp. 283-287).
31. Literacy is measured in so many ways that it is difficult to judge from statistics on literacy. In Pakistan, for instance, the 1951 census showed only 19.1 percent of the total population to be literate, that is "able to read print." The census of 1961 upgraded the definition of literacy to "the ability to read with understanding" and the literacy percentage of the population consequently fell to 15.9 (T. W. T. Miller, ed., *Education in South-East Asia,* Sydney, 1968), p. 40.
32. Myrdal, III, 1681-1682.
33. Arithmetic textbooks for teachers were published even before complete sets of textbooks began appearing after 1912. See Taiwan sōtokufu, *Kōgakkō sanjutsuka kyōzai, maki ichi* (Taihoku, 1909); *Kōgakkō sanjutsuka kyōzai, maki ni* (Taihoku, 1910); *Kōgakkō sanjutsuka kyōzai, maki yon* (Taihoku, 1911).
34. Interviews in 1969. Some who attended evening courses reported that after working all day they were tired and found it hard to study. Some said they enjoyed the music and the company. A few stated that these courses were very valuable for those who were intelligent but too poor to be able to go to regular school.
35. There is no way of knowing exactly what Japanese survey takers meant by the definition "able to understand Japanese." Did all survey takers maintain the same standards? Obviously Ts'ai P'ei-huo and Hasuda Zenmei, mentioned below, had different standards for fluency in Japanese.
36. The vernacular script employed a syllabary consisting of twenty-four symbols with seven kinds of stress marks. The symbols, which Ts'ai and others referred to as roman letters, were really abbreviations of Chinese characters. In 1924 and 1935 the Japanese refused to permit use of this script. See Ts'ai P'ei-huo, "Taiwan ni okeru kokuji mondai," *Kyōiku* 4.8:1233-1238 (August 1936).
37. Ibid., p. 1234.
38. Hasuda Zenmei, "Taiwan no kokugo kyōiku," *Kyōiku* 6.8:1233-1236 (August 1938).
39. Mao Yeh-hsin and Lin Ch'ao-ching, pp. 164-166.
40. Interviews in Taiwan during 1969.

41. Bernard Gallin, *Hsin Hsing, Taiwan: A Chinese Village in Change* (Berkeley, 1966), pp. 2, 19-20, suggests otherwise. He is surely correct in concluding that the Japanese influence never reached the heart of cultural and social life in Taiwanese agricultural villages, but I think he greatly underestimated the amount of contact many rural Taiwanese had with the Japanese, the extent of Japanese language penetration in the countryside, and the general Japanese influence in rural areas. He is completely mistaken regarding the common schools. According to those who attended them and to those who taught in them they did not teach in local dialects as Gallin states (p. 19). Japanese, incidentally, was one of the working languages of his research in Hsin Hsing village during 1957-1958 (p. 285).

42. Interviews in Taiwan during 1969.

43. An interview in a village in Pingtung prefecture during 1969. The man, who was twenty years old when the Japanese period ended, said that in 1945 he had to begin learning Mandarin Chinese so he could teach in the new school system. In 1969 he was a part-time farmer as well as a teacher.

44. Ching-chih Chen, "Japanese Socio-political Control in Taiwan," pp. 239-240. Chapter Four of this work contains an excellent account of the *hokō* system. See also Ching-chih Chen, "The Police and the *Hokō* Systems in Taiwan under Japanese Administration (1895-1945)."

45. Ide, *Taiwan chiseki shi,* pp. 471-472.

46. An interview in Taipei, July 1969.

47. A conversation in Taipei, August 1969. As Richard W. Wilson has pointed out in *Learning to be Chinese: The Political Socialization of Children in Taiwan* (Cambridge, Mass., 1970), to blame the Japanese influence for everything that is considered "wrong" about the Taiwanese is common among mainlanders. See ibid., p. 158, note.

48. Interviews in Taipei, Taichung, Tsao-tun, Hu-wei, and Yun-lin in 1969.

49. An interview in Taipei, June 1969.

50. An interview in Taipei, July 1969.

51. Interviews in Taipei and Taichung in 1969.

52. An interview with a junior executive in a Japanese-Taiwanese company in Taipei, June 1969.

53. Interviews in Taipei, Taichung, Tsao-tun, I-lan, Taitung, and Tainan in 1969.

54. An interview in Taipei, June 1969.

55. In 1969 this man was in the import-export business in Taipei.

56. One informant, a medical doctor, who had attended Taihoku Imperial University during the 1930s, bitterly described the Japanese professors' unkind treatment of Taiwanese students in the medical faculty. He remembered that several of his Taiwanese classmates had been arrested for "thought crimes," but he said he knew nothing of the details because he had concentrated on minding his own business and finishing his studies.

57. An interview in Taipei, July 1969. The informant was a graduate of a prestigious Japanese university. I met middle school graduates who expressed feelings of bitterness and frustration regarding their inability to go on to higher school. They resented not only the education authorities

who had discriminated against Taiwanese applicants to schools but also the wealthy Taiwanese who could afford to go to Japan to study.

58. Since the Japanese controlled most of the industrial concerns as well as the administration, there was little Taiwanese could do about this. Almost no Taiwanese ever became high-ranking bureaucrats. See Yanaihara Tadao, "Teikokushugika no Taiwan," pp. 279-293.
59. An interview in Taipei, June 1969.
60. This comment was repeated over and over again.
61. See Etō Shinkichi, "An Outline of Formosan History," p. 57.
62. An interview in Taipei, July 1969.
63. See Edward I-te Chen, "Japanese Colonialism in Korea and Formosa."
64. Mombushō, *Meiji ikō kyōiku seido hattatsu shi*, X, 577-578, XI, 1045.
65. See Ōno, pp. 19-28, for Gotō's address on education to Japanese officials in Korea in 1903.
66. The two volumes of *Meiji ikō kyōiku seido hattsu shi* devoted to education in Korea and Taiwan (X and XI) clearly reveal this.
67. See Hirano Ken'ichirō, "Manchu ni okeru Nihon no kyōiku seisaku, 1901-1931," *Ajïya kenkyū* 15.3:24-52.
68. Ōno, p. 246. See also C. I. Eugene Kim, "Japan's Colonial Education and Korea's Nation Building," in C. I. Eugene Kim, ed., *A Pattern of Political Development: Korea* (Korea Research and Publication, Inc., 1964), p. 6.
69. Hyung-chan Kim, "A Study of North Korean Education under Communism since 1945" (Ed.D. diss., George Peabody College for Teachers, 1969), I, 150.
70. See James Earnest Fischer, *Democracy and Mission Education in Korea* (New York, 1928; reprint: Seoul, 1970), p. 38.
71. A missionary who came later argued: "The logical conclusion of this attitude [mission education for the converted only] is that to teach a boy to make a good honest living is a fine thing to do, providing the boy is a Christian; a very dangerous and wicked thing to do if the boy happens to be a Buddhist. Or, respect for and emancipation of women should be taught and encouraged among orthodox Christians, but such noble traits of character and social reform should never be taught to nonbelievers" (Fischer, p. 97).
72. By 1901 Pyongyang city and its suburbs contained five hundred mission primary schools (H. Kim, I, 152).
73. See H. Kim, I, 154-157.
74. H. Kim, I, 154.
75. H. Kim, I, 156-160.
76. Lee, p. 97; Pak Kyŏng-sik, *Nihon teikokushugi no Chōsen shihai* (Tokyo, 1973), I, 145.
77. Elementary school books published by the Yi government in 1896 contained much information about the West as well as about Korea. See "The Kukmin Sohak Tokpon," *Korean Repository* 4:356-357 (September 1897) for a description of the textbook *Kukmin Sohak Tokpon* (National elementary reader) written in mixed script which used Chinese characters as well as *ŏnmun,* the Korean syllabary.
78. Lee, p. 60.

79. Ibid. states that Jaisohn's use of the *ŏnmun* in his newspaper probably alienated the *yangban* and thus contributed to the failure of his reform movement. Missionaries used the *ŏnmun* in their publications and taught it in their schools.
80. Pak, I, 145.
81. Pak, I, 147.
82. See Ōno, p. 31, for Terauchi's policy statement.
83. Kang Tŏk-sang, "Kenpei seijika no Chōsen" (Korea under the government of the military police), in *Rekishi gaku kenkyū* (Historical studies), no. 321, quoted in Pak, I, 158. See also Yuge Kōtarō, *Chōsen no kyōiku* (Tokyo, 1923), pp. 73-80.
84. Generally Christian secondary and higher schools were operated directly by missionaries, while Christian elementary schools were run by native churches. Native churches, however, could be controlled by missionaries and foreign churches.
85. In his outline of educational policy, Terauchi mentioned that private schools run by foreign missionaries must be handled very carefully because "although supervisory authority belongs fundamentally to the government, historically under the name of extraterritoriality these schools have been left alone." However he stressed that "religion and politics must not be mixed" and ordered his officials to see that schools did not mix religion and politics. But again he cautioned that for the time being missionaries were to be treated with care because "in Korea abolition of extraterritoriality over various facilities has not yet been completely achieved" (Ōno, p. 32).
86. Shibata Yoshisaburō, "Bunka seiji to gakusei kaikaku" (Civil politics and revision of the education system), in Chōsen shimbunsha, ed., *Chōsen tōchi no kaiko to hihan* (Keijō, 1936), p. 215; Yuge, pp. 77-80.
87. Ōno, p. 12. Some women did become scholars in premodern Korea. Queen Insu, mother of Sŏngjong, the ninth king of the Yi dynasty, was a great educator and scholar. She translated classical works into Korean script, thus making them available to large numbers of Korean women who knew no Chinese (Chung Tae-shi, " 'Yesterday' of Korean Education," *Korea Journal* 3.4:16-19, April 1, 1963, p. 18).
88. Ōno, p. 32.
89. Yuge, p. 184.
90. Yuge, pp. 195-196.
91. See Frank Baldwin, "Missionaries and the March First Movement: Can Moral Men be Neutral?" in Andrew C. Nahm, ed., *Korea under Japanese Colonial Rule* (Western Michigan University, 1973), pp. 193-219.
92. Yuge, pp. 193-200.
93. Ōno, p. 246. The 1918 regulations stipulated that Japanese language and arithmetic were to be added to *sŏdang* curricula "according to local conditions." The 1929 reform required (1) government permission to establish or dissolve a *sŏdang;* (2) that government-general textbooks for Japanese, Korean, and arithmetic classes be used; (3) that pupils be taught Japanese ethics, including loyalty to the emperor (Wi Jo Kang, "Japanese Rule and Korean Confucianism," in Nahm, p. 70).
94. C. I. Eugene Kim, "Japan's Colonial Education and Korea's Nation

Building," p. 7. See also Ōno, pp. 245-246. Wi Jo Kang, "Japanese Rule and Korean Confucianism," describes the government's overtures to Confucian institutions. The government also sought to maintain the *hyanggyo* in each county and its adjoining temple and to set up a new Confucian academy "to carry on the study of the Confucian classics, hold religious services for Chinese sages, and aid in the promotion of the moral culture of the people" (ibid., p. 68).

95. Chōsen sōtokufu, *Chōsen sōtokufu tōkei nenpō,* cited in C. I. E. Kim, "Japan's Colonial Education and Korea's Nation Building," p. 7.

96. Yuge, pp. 139-140.

97. Pak, II, 65, 71. However, the majority of the government schools stopped teaching Korean after the 1938 revision (Pak, II, 71).

98. Ebihara, I, 244-245; C. I. Eugene Kim, "Japanese Colonial Education and Korea's Nation Building," pp. 7-8; Chung Tae-shi, " 'Yesterday' of Korean Education," p. 18.

99. In 1920 there were twenty-one academic secondary schools in Korea (fourteen for boys, seven for girls); by 1930 thirty-four (twenty-four for boys, ten for girls) existed (Wonmon Dong, "Assimilation and Social Mobilization in Korea," in Nahm, p. 158).

100. For instance, Chōsun Christian College (the present Yonsei University) was not founded until 1915. It was founded as a college with a broad base of studies which included agricultural, industrial, professional, and cultural subjects. It received *senmon gakkō* recognition in 1917. See H. Kim, I, 159-160.

101. Dong, "Assimilation and Social Mobilization in Korea," p. 161. The 580 Koreans in government *senmon gakkō* made up only 26.9 percent of the government *senmon gakkō* population.

102. Fischer, pp. 5-10, 65-93.

103. Unfortunately I know much less about these schools. Christians were a numerically large group. In 1919, according to missionary sources, there were 318,708 Korean Christians out of a Korean population of 16,900,000. Of the 318,708, 219,220 were Protestant and 99,688 were Roman Catholic or Greek Orthodox (Arthur Judson Brown, *The Mastery of the Far East,* New York, 1919, p. 514). However, other important religious groups also operated schools. The Ch'ondogyo, a religious body that emerged from the Tonghak rebel movement of the 1890s, managed schools (Lee, p. 106).

104. Baldwin, "Missionaries and the March First Movement: Can Moral Men be Neutral?" p. 209.

105. Chōsen sōtokufu, *Showa jūgonen sōtokufu tōkei nenpō* (Keijō, 1942), p. 34. The total Korean elementary school population during this year was 1,385,944 (Dong, "Assimilation and Social Mobilization in Korea," p. 157).

106. Interview in I-lan, July 1969.

107. Takemura Toyotoshi, ed., *Taiwan taiiku enkakushi* (Taihoku, 1933), p. 5.

108. Takemura, pp. 5-6.

109. Not all these games were played at elementary schools. See Takemura for sports played by schools and the public at large.

110. Takemura, p. 6.
111. Ibid.
112. Fischer, p. 95.
113. Chiu-sam Tsang, *Nationalism in School Education in China* (Hongkong, 1933), p. 82.
114. Dong, "Assimilation and Social Mobilization in Korea," p. 158. C. I. Eugene Kim has pointed out that "Japanese educational efforts were indeed note-worthy for the Korean school age children and they could be favorably compared numerically with those of their own school age children in modern Japan. In 1890, twenty-three years after the Meiji Restoration, 55.4 percent of the Japanese school age children were enrolled in school as compared with 50.5 percent of the Korean school age children in school in 1942, thirty-two years after the Japanese annexation of Korea in 1910" (C.I. Eugene Kim, "Japan's Colonial Education and Korea's National Building," pp. 5-6).
115. See Chong-sik Lee's excellent study, *The Politics of Korean Nationalism.*
116. The participation of women in the March First Movement of 1919 was historic. In traditional Korea, women's place had been at home out of sight. They were not supposed to appear in public.
117. Lee, p. 120.
118. Lee, p. 242; Chung Tae-shi, " 'Yesterday' of Korean Education," p. 19.
119. Ibid.
120. Lee, p. 253.
121. Foreign Affairs Association of Japan, *Japan Year Book 1943-1944* (Tokyo, 1944), p. 913.
122. Lee, p. 124.
123. Lamley, "The Taiwan Literati," pp. 234-252.
124. Lee, p. 96.
125. See Donald Keene, "The Sino-Japanese War of 1894-95 and Its Cultural Effects in Japan," in Donald Shively, ed., *Tradition and Modernization in Japanese Culture* (Princeton, 1971), pp. 121-175.
126. This kind of argument was not uncommon among prominent Taiwanese collaborators. In 1911 a Taiwanese society to encourage queue-cutting was organized. The society's leader said during his inaugural address: "Law-abiding citizens must realize that after the Meiji Restoration all Japanese, including the Emperor himself, cut off their long locks. We Taiwanese bound our hair during the Ming dynasty and adopted the pigtail during the Ch'ing dynasty. But Taiwan is now part of Japan. It should therefore adopt Japanese customs" (quoted in Howard S. Levy, *Chinese Footbinding: The History of a Curious Erotic Custom,* New York, 1967, p. 96). See also Ō, pp. 120-121, for the argument of the famous collaborator, Ku Hsien-jung. Ku claimed that although previously he was loyal to the Ch'ing, after 1895 he owed all allegiance to the Japanese empire.
127. See Edward I-te Chen, "Japanese Colonialism in Korea and Formosa," for a description of differences in the economic impact of Japanese rule in the two countries.
128. Lee, pp. 93-95.
129. Lee, p. 95.

130. Edward I-te Chen, "Japanese Colonialism in Korea and Formosa," pp. 211-213. Chen also points out that sugar exports for Taiwan "served as an economic cushion" with which to balance trade with Japan without exporting large amounts of rice (*ibid.,* p. 217).
131. Ibid., pp. 238-240.
132. Ibid., p. 242. Chen cites the differential wage scales of dyers, joiners, sawyers, furniture makers, sugar refinery workers, compositors, and tailors.
133. Ibid., pp. 242-243.
134. Ibid., p. 240-241.
135. In 1937 Japanese occupied 6.5 percent of the jobs available in Korea; in 1936 Japanese occupied 4.9 percent of the jobs available in Taiwan (ibid., p. 241).

8. Japanese Education, Taiwanese Intellectuals, and Political Activism

1. Ō, p. 134, mentions Taiwanese writers who became masters of the Japanese language.
2. After the end of the Second World War, Ō Ikutoku became deeply involved in Taiwanese nationalist activities. He has served as editor of *Taiwan seinen* (Taiwanese youth), the postwar organ of organized Taiwanese nationalists in Japan.
3. Ō, p. 133.
4. Ō, pp. 133-134.
5. Literally *minponshugi* may be translated as "[government] based on the people." Although Yoshino rejected the natural-right theory of popular sovereignty as incompatible with the Meiji Constitution, his *minponshugi* did stand for "democracy within constitutional monarchy, in which the people had the right to select leaders and render ultimate judgement over governmental policy" (Tetsuo Najita, "Some Reflections on Idealism in the Political Thought of Yoshino Sakuzō," in Bernard S. S. Silberman and H. D. Harootunian, eds., *Japan in Crisis: Essays on Taishō Democracy,* Princeton, 1974, p. 39).
6. See Gail Bernstein, "Kawakami Hajime: A Japanese Marxist in Search of the Way," in Silberman and Harootunian, pp. 86-109.
7. Ching-chih Chen, "Japanese Socio-political Control in Taiwan," p. 416.
8. *TSK,* III, 38. For background on the Shinjinkai see Henry D. Smith, *Japan's First Student Radicals* (Cambridge, Mass., 1972). Smith does not describe Taiwanese participation in the Shinjinkai nor does he discuss the Taiwanese radical group which, according to police reports, was organized by Tokyo Imperial University's Shinjinkai.
9. For instance, about 1920 a Taiwanese student at Sofia University (a private Roman Catholic institution) named Fan Pen-liang got to know Osugi Sakae, a veteran of the Meiji socialist movement. Fan soon became an anarchist. About the same time, a Taiwanese student at Meiji University (also private), P'eng Hua-ying, was working with Sakai Toshihiko and Yamakawa Hitoshi, pioneers in the founding of Japan's first Communist Party. P'eng joined the off-campus student-worker group known as the Gyominkai (Dawn of the People Society). See Kō Se-kai, p. 264.
10. Yoshino Sakuzō had especially close ties with Chinese students. Yoshino

helped bring a delegation of student leaders of the May Fourth Movement from Peking to do a speaking tour of Japan during the spring of 1920. See Matsuo Takayoshi, *Taishō demokurashii no kenkyū* (Tokyo, 1966), pp. 297-303.

11. How much the Taiwanese students' interest in contemporary China was stimulated by an awareness of their own Chinese origins is not easy to gauge. Presumably at least some of their elders would have passed on to them memories of Taiwan under Ch'ing rule. They certainly admired Chinese efforts at national reform and unification but so did other East Asians. The independence-minded Koreans who established exile communities in China, and the Vietnamese opponents of French colonial rule who sought aid from Chinese reformers and revolutionaries, also took inspiration from the Chinese. See Lee and David Marr, *Vietnamese Anti-Colonialism, 1885-1925* (Berkeley, 1971).

12. Ching-chih Chen, "Japanese Socio-political Control in Taiwan," pp. 414-415. See also Ts'ai P'ei-huo et al., eds., *T'ai-wan min-tsu yün-tung shih* (Taipei, 1971), pp. 77-78, and Shi Mei, *Taiwanjin yonhyakunen shi,* pp. 334-336.

13. Supervision in the dormitory did not prevent Taiwanese students from organizing for political purposes.

14. Here the two wings of Taiwanese anticolonialism are found to be conservative and radical largely in relation to each other rather than in measurement against some abstract criteria for conservatism or radicalism.

15. Lin had been a leader in Itagaki's Assimilation Society of 1914-15, but at least as early as 1907 he had been actively seeking ways to free Taiwan from its colonial status. In that year he sought aid from the Chinese reformer Liang Ch'i-ch'ao, and in 1913 he visited Peking to seek help from other Chinese leaders.

16. Largely through Lin's initiative Taiwanese students had established an all-student society in Tokyo in 1918. This was dissolved the following year to permit nonstudents to join the Shinminkai which welcomed all interested Taiwanese in Japan (Edward I-te Chen, "Formosan Political Movements Under Japanese Colonial Rule, 1914-1937," *Journal of Asian Studies* 31.3:477-497 [May 1972], p. 481; *TSK,* III, 25; Kō Se-kai, pp. 182-183). "A term taken from the Confucian classic, the *Greater Learning,* the 'new people' (*shinmin*) denoted the society's expressed objective —the transformation of the Taiwanese people" (Ching-chih Chen, "Japanese Socio-political Control in Taiwan," p. 418).

17. Ching-chih Chen, "Japanese Socio-political Control in Taiwan," p. 419.

18. *TSK,* III, 25. The society's regulations spelled out two specific aims for the organization: study of "all matters connected with Taiwan that need to be reformed" and advancement of Taiwan's culture. In March 1920 a three-point platform was approved: launching of a political reform movement to promote the happiness of the Taiwanese people; publishing a journal to disseminate the society's ideas among Taiwanese; furthering liaison with Chinese comrades (*TSK,* III, 27).

19. In 1920 Den Kenjirō went to the Diet and asked that a new fundamental law be passed which would in principle apply the laws of Japan to Taiwan but in practice allow the governor-general of the colony to continue to

exercise enormous discretionary power. See *TSK,* I, 242-244, and *Den Kenjirō nikki,* Oct. 20, Nov. 15-20, Dec. 3-8, 1920.

20. Edward I-te Chen, "Formosan Political Movements," p. 482.

21. Ts'ai stated this in his preface to the book. See Ts'ai P'ei-huo, *Nihon honkokumin ni atō,* pp. 23-27.

22. See Yanaihara's preface, pp. 9-21, of Ts'ai P'ei-huo, *Nihon honkokumin ni atō.* Yanaihara pointed out that although the Japanese people displayed considerable interest in international affairs and foreign lands they possessed little knowledge of their own colonies. He urged the Japanese people who were electing their own national legislature on a franchise wider than ever before (universal male suffrage came in 1925), not to leave the eighteen million Koreans and four million Taiwanese under the authority of the colonial governments alone.

23. See Ts'ai P'ei-huo, *Nihon honkokumin ni atō.*

24. Ibid., pp. 39-44.

25. Ibid., p. 43.

26. Ibid., pp. 52-53.

27. According to Japanese mythology, the Japanese state was founded in 660 B.C. in the Yamato plain, inland from the present city of Osaka. This date of 660 B.C. was supposedly selected in about 601 A.D. by counting back 1260 years, 1260 years being, according to Chinese historical counting, a major cycle of history. Although there is no archaeological evidence to support this early date, before the end of World War II Japanese schoolchildren were taught to remember 660 B.C. as the date Japan was founded. Ts'ai, then, was ridiculing an official myth that everyone was supposed to acknowledge (or at least not to contradict). This myth provided an especially convenient excuse for Japanese in Taiwan to continue to maintain their privileges. Government-general officials repeatedly mentioned this "three-thousand-year history" in their explanations of differences between Japanese and Taiwanese. They did not dwell upon the long history of the Chinese ancestors of the residents of Taiwan.

28. Ibid., pp. 148-152.

29. Ibid., pp. 157-158.

30. See Ts'ai P'ei-huo, *Nihon honkokumin ni atō,* and ̣sieh Ch'un-mu, *Taiwanjin wa kaku miru.* The latter is a collection of Hs'ieh's newspaper articles and essays dealing mainly with Taiwanese demands.

31. Kanda Masao, *Ugoki yuku Taiwan* (Tokyo, 1930), pp. 247-248, presents these complaints in this book which was written on behalf of the conservative political reformers.

32. See Hsieh Ch'un-mu's article in *Taiwan minpō* (Oct. 12, 1924) reproduced in Hsieh Ch'un-mu, *Taiwanjin wa kaku miru,* pp. 52-74.

33. Ts'ai P'ei-huo, *Nihon honkokumin ni atō,* pp. 59-60.

34. The birth date for Lin Ch'eng-lu given here is the one in Taiwan shinminpō, *Taiwan jinshi kan* (1937), p. 459. Ts'ai P'ei-huo et al., *T'ai-wan min-tsu yün-tung shih,* p. 290, states that Lin was born in 1890. See Edward I-te Chen, "Formosan Political Movements," p. 482; *TSK,* III, 312-313; Kō Se-kai, pp. 193-194. Lin cited Professor Yamamoto Miono, a distinguished authority on colonial policy at Kyoto Imperial University who advocated self-rule for the colonies. See Yamamoto Miono, *Shokuminchi seisaku kenkyū* (Tokyo, 1920).

35. Taiwan shinminpō, *Taiwan jinshi kan* (1937), pp. 459-460.
36. Edward I-te Chen, "Formosan Political Movements," p. 483.
37. *TSK*, III, 23-24, suggests that Korean students in Japan had become interested in social and political problems earlier than had Taiwanese students. The authors of this work claimed that only gradually, under the influence of an atmosphere created by ideas associated with "the self-determination of peoples," the Korean independence movement, and the Chinese revolution, did some Taiwanese begin to advocate Taiwan for the Taiwanese.
38. Ō, p. 116.
39. Ts'ai P'ei-huo et al., *T'ai-wan min-tsu yün-tung shih*, pp. 119-120. Signatures of ten Taiwanese in Taiwan (including Lin Hsien-t'ang) were included in the 178 (ibid., pp. 119-120; *TSK*, III, 340).
40. The petition with its entire preface is reproduced in *TSK*, III, 340-341.
41. *TSK*, III, 342.
42. Before 1925 petitioners signed a joint petition form that was circulated among them. Consequently, it took a long time for the petition form to pass from one supporter to another. In 1925 individual petition forms to be signed separately by each supporter were prepared. Thousands of these were distributed to sympathizers. Frequently they were handed out to members of audiences at Cultural Association lectures and collected with signatures upon them at the end of the lectures. The new petition form helped increase the number of signatures collected, which rose from 782 in 1925 to 1,990 in 1926 (Ching-chih Chen, "Japanese Socio-political Control in Taiwan," pp. 430-432).
43. Distinguished liberal politicians and academics were implored to throw their weight behind the activists' cause. There was no hesitation about approaching persons of national stature—Sakatani Yoshirō, Seki Naohiko, Uzawa Fusaaki, Ōtake Kan'ichi, Takada Shuhan, Nagai Ryutarō, Ozaki Yukio, Tagawa Daikichirō, Kiyose Ichirō, Yoshino Sakuzō, Abe Isoo, Uemura Masahisa, Izumi Tetsu, Shimada Saburō, and Ebara Soroku were all visited by petition leaders. See *TSK*, III, 343.
44. Most of the men mentioned in note 43 willingly gave support during the 1920s. Abe (Social Democratic Party), Tagawa (Labor-Farmer Party), and Kiyose (a distinguished lawyer) were active in the House of Representatives on behalf of the petition; Ebara (Seiyūkai) and Sakatani (a famous criminal lawyer) gave support in the House of Peers. Other politicians, like Shimada (Kenseikai) and Uzawa (Seiyūkai), were also ready to assist the Taiwanese. Professors like Takada and Nagai of Waseda and Yoshino and Ozaki of Tokyo Imperial were outspoken advocates of a Taiwanese parliament. And of course the greatest champion of home rule for Taiwan was the colonial expert, Yanaihara Tadao. The Japanese press was wooed also. Some of the men mentioned above were well-established journalists, and they and others sympathetic to the cause had ample contacts with newspapers and journals. Editorials in such dailies as *Tokyo mainichi* and *Ōsaka mainichi* supported the Taiwanese demand. See Edward I-te Chen, "Formosan Political Movements," p. 486; *TSK*, III, 343; Izumi Masakichi, *Taiwan no minzoku undō* (Taichū, 1928), pp. 56-59.
45. Because many of those who signed were prestigious and educated some

have suggested that those who signed represented a much larger number of Taiwanese than their mere numbers suggest. See Edward I-te Chen, "Formosan Political Movements," p. 485.

46. *TSK*, III, 343. The conservative activists soon discerned precisely who made up the consistent proportion of their fellow islanders in Japan who signed each petition. Approximately the same number of Taiwanese in Japan signed each petition. See Ching-chih Chen, "Japanese Socio-political Control in Taiwan," p. 430.

47. *Den Kenjirō nikki*, Dec. 25, 1922. Den himself unsuccessfully tried friendly persuasion in Tokyo in February of 1921. At that time he summoned four of the initiators of the first petition to the government general's Tokyo office. There he told the four about his plans for broadening the membership of the colonial consultative council (*hyōgikai*), hinting that if they dropped their petition some of them might be appointed to the revised council (*TSK*, III, 342-343). Later he tried to persuade Taiwanese home-rule leaders to exchange their campaign for one aimed at achieving Taiwanese representation in the Imperial Diet (*Den Kenjirō nikki*, Sept. 29, 1922).

48. *TSK*, III, 353.

49. *TSK*, III, 916; Kō Se-kai, pp. 214-215.

50. Ching-chih Chen, "Japanese Socio-political Control in Taiwan," p. 452. See also Ts'ai P'ei-huo et al., *T'ai-wan min-tsu yün-tung shih*, p. 167, and Kō se-kai, p. 215.

51. Ts'ai P'ei-huo et al., *T'ai-wan min-tsu yün-tung shih*, pp. 167-168.

52. Ching-chih Chen, "Japanese Socio-political Control in Taiwan," p. 452. Local police officers were especially efficient harassers of petition supporters. Individuals would be detained for short periods on the pretense that they had violated some police regulation. One effective method was to have a police officer spend a day sitting in a petitioner's house, shop, or office. In the latter two cases the presence of the colonial policeman, a figure avoided by most Taiwanese when at all possible, could be very bad for business. See Ts'ai P'ei-huo et al., *T'ai-wan min-tsu yün-tung shih*, p. 168. Such "preventive measures," which were particularly strictly enforced in Taichū province, the heartland of petition activity, helped reduce the number of signatures from 512 in 1922 to 278 on the 1923 petition (*TSK*, III, 327).

53. In November Uchida told his regional government chiefs: "Generally the people on this island seem to be quiet and peaceful . . . However, we will on no account be lenient with any ideas that are basically misguided — no matter how peaceful their outward appearance is. If this toying about with radical talk confuses the people and seduces the masses, then this is disturbing the peace and we will take resolute measures" (Kō Se-kai, pp. 222-223). Den had worried less about the petition movement. Not only had it been in its infant stages during his tenure, but he judged the political expectations of the Taiwanese to be low. See *Den Kenjirō nikki*, Jan. 29, 1923.

54. *Ōsaka asahi shimbun* (March 16, 1924), cited in Kō Se-kai, p. 223.

55. Ts'ai P'ei-huo et al., *T'ai-wan min-tsu yün-tung shih*, p. 201. A Taiwanese student group in Shanghai which held a conference to condemn the

police action stated that "more than sixty were arrested" (Kō Se-kai, p. 228). Kanda, pp. 279-280, also mentions that more than sixty were arrested.

56. *TSK,* III, 359.
57. Ibid.
58. Kō Se-kai, p. 226.
59. Kō Se-kai, pp. 227-228; *TSK,* III, 69, 93-96.
60. Kō Se-kai, pp. 226-227.
61. Kō Se-kai, pp. 223-226. Watanabe was the defense lawyer for the first trial; Kiyose for the appeal; and Hanai for the final appeal.
62. They came at different times. Kanda had been to Taiwan in 1921 as an *Asahi shimbun* reporter (Kanda, p. 3).
63. Ibid., p. 280.
64. During the first trial the prosecutor dwelt so much upon the motives and "real desires" he attributed to the defendants that the presiding justice was moved to point out that "the procurator's political discourse has little connection with the crime in question" (*Dai ichiban kōhan tokubetsu go,* p. 13, cited in Kō Se-kai, p. 225).
65. *TSK,* III, 360-361.
66. As Lin Ch'eng-lu, who received a three-month prison sentence, recollected later, " 'After the raging storm has passed, the mountains and rivers remain the same; while trees and grass gain even more abundant life.' We not only survived our year and a half ordeal in the courts; we also learned much from it. What this true-life experience taught us best of all was how to use the government's power to push our own cause" (quoted in Kō Se-kai, p. 228). One might conclude from the court records of the appeal against the first trial that second time round the defendants were unlucky enough to get a hostile presiding judge. See ibid., p. 225.
67. Ts'ai P'ei-huo et al., *T'ai-wan min-tsu yün-tung shih,* p. 195; Ching-chih Chen, "Japanese Socio-political Control in Taiwan," pp. 457-459. Several Taiwanese interviewed in 1969 compared the police of the colonial period favorably with the police in 1969. Two Taiwanese who reported that they had often attended public meetings during the colonial period remarked that the Japanese police warned speakers at such meetings that they would be arrested if they continued speaking. According to these informants, only when speakers disregarded these warnings were arrests made.
68. *TSK,* III, 328.
69. Under the conservatives, the Taiwan Popular Party demanded that Taiwanese be given access to power and privileges monopolized by colonial Japanese and be allowed some room to fulfill their own cultural needs. Much of the Popular Party's platform was familiar: Taiwanese participation in popular elections at all governmental levels, permission for Taiwanese to publish newspapers and journals and to hold meetings freely, compulsory elementary education for all island children, the Taiwanese language used along with Japanese as a language of classroom instruction in common schools, written Chinese taught in the common schools, equal educational opportunities for Taiwanese and Japanese, abolition of the

hokō system, reform of the police system, judicial reforms, and an end to the discriminatory procedure that required Taiwanese but not Japanese to obtain passports before traveling to China. The economic reforms the party demanded were piecemeal and in some cases rather vague. Details of reforms proposed for the government's fiscal and monopoly institutions were not spelled out, but economic measures did include establishment of financial institutions for farmers and laborers and legislation to protect tenants. Social policy tended to be the most general of all. The two planks in the social platform were: "(1) Support for farm and labor movements and for 'social groups' (*she-hui t'uan-t'i*); (2) confirmation of the principle of equality between the sexes, support for the women's rights movement, and opposition to slave trading" (Ts'ai P'ei-huo et al., *T'ai-wan min-tsu yün-tung shih,* p. 368). For the party's platform see ibid., pp. 366-368.

70. See *TSK,* III, 523-582, for details of the league's activities.
71. Ts'ai P'ei-huo et al., *T'ai-wan min-tsu yün-tung shih,* p. 475.
72. Ching-chih Chen, "Japanese Socio-political Control in Taiwan," p. 441.
73. Ibid., pp. 438-439.
74. Ts'ai P'ei-huo et al., *T'ai-wan min-tsu yün-tung shih,* pp. 445-446.
75. See ibid.; Ching-chih Chen, "Japanese Socio-political Control in Taiwan"; Edward I-te Chen, "Formosan Political Movements."
76. See Lee.
77. See Marr. The Taiwanese anticolonialists might have found it ironic that Meiji Japan was a model for early anti-French activists in Vietnam who sought aid from Japanese authorities as well as from Chinese nationalists.
78. Of course other Vietnamese political reformers took a very different position: they favored use of the colonizer as a model for modernizing their own society before seeking independence. However, this position led its proponents perilously close to unconditional collaboration with the regime. It usually meant more acceptance of colonial rule than was displayed by even the most conservative of the Taiwanese home rule leaders. Vietnamese scholar-gentry activists as described by Marr, in their class backgrounds at least, appear close to the conservative-activists of Taiwan. They did not have international communist or socialist connections or a Marxist orientation as some of Taiwan's radical anticolonialists did, so in this respect too they seem like Taiwan's conservative-activists. Their anticolonial stance, however, was much more militant than that of Taiwan's conservative opponents of Japanese rule.
79. In this novel, the mysterious and violent Simoun, who is dedicated to inciting Filipinos to rise against their Spanish rulers, argues with a young Filipino who is organizing to improve the educational opportunities of his compatriots: "You ask parity of rights, the Spanish way of life, and you do not realize that what you are asking is death, the destruction of your national identity, the disappearance of your homeland, the ratification of tyranny. What is to become of you? A people without a soul, a nation without freedom; everything in you will be borrowed, even your very defects" (José Rizal, *El Filibusterismo,* trans. Leon M. Guerrero as *The Subversive,* New York, 1968, p. 49). Simoun asks the young man he is addressing to join him in armed insurrection but the youth is unmoved.

Simoun then continues to try to persuade him that piecemeal reform is hopeless: "These stupid yearnings for Spain and the Spanish way of life, for equality of rights . . . will only lead at best toward becoming a poor imitation and our people should aim higher. It is folly to try to influence the thinking of those who rule us; they have their own plans and their eyes are closed to anything else . . . What you should do is to take advantage of the prejudices of our rulers. So they refuse to integrate you into the Spanish nation. So much the better! Take the lead in forming your own individuality, try to lay the foundations of a Filipino nation. They give you no hopes. All the better! Hope only in yourselves and your own efforts. They deny you representation in the Spanish parliament. Good for you! Even if you were able to elect representatives of your own choosing, what could you do there but be drowned among so many voices, yet sanction by your presence the abuses and wrongs which may afterwards be committed?" (Rizal, *The Subversive,* p. 51).

The Taiwanese conservative-activists might have agreed with Simoun (and Rizal) regarding the importance of preserving a people's identity and traditions. Their home-rule movement and the platform of the Taiwan Popular Party stressed the importance of doing so. But they would have rejected any denunciation of all reformist measures short of an armed rising. (Rizal himself called for reformist improvements in Spanish rule of the Philippines during the 1880s. See Enarnacion Alzona, "Rizal and the Reformists," in Leopoldo Y. Yabes, ed., *José Rizal on his Centenary* (Quezon City, 1963), pp. 109-123, and José Rizal, *Political and Historical Writings,* VII [1872-1896] (Manila, 1964). It would be interesting to know if the Taiwanese activists knew of Rizal and his writings.

80. Ts'ai P'ei-huo et al., *T'ai-wan min-tsu yün-tung shih* is a good example of such rejection. See the preface to this book.
81. See ibid.
82. Ching-chih Chen makes this point. See "Japanese Socio-political Control in Taiwan," p. 450.
83. Kō Se-kai, p. 229.
84. See Kō Se-kai, pp. 234-235, for other conservative-activists who leaned toward China.
85. In 1907 Lin Hsien-t'ang encountered by chance the famous Chinese reformer, Liang Ch'i-chiao, in Nara, Japan. Lin asked Liang how the Taiwanese might best resist their Japanese rulers. The reply he got was a warning "not to indulge in any notion that Formosans might expect help from China. 'China will not have such ability at least in the next thirty years.' Liang advised Lin that the aid of some liberal Japanese in the central government be enlisted to restrain the governor-general from overly oppressing the Formosans" (Edward I-te Chen, "Formosan Political Movements," p. 479). About two years earlier Liang had given similar advice to the Vietnamese nationalist, Phan Boi Chau (1867-1940), who had come to Liang seeking Chinese assistance to overthrow the French who ruled his country. "Liang advised Phan to put his real emphasis on educating and awakening his own people to the multifold challenges of the modern world. Only when this had born fruit, he counseled, would external assistance prove meaningful" (Marr, p. 109). Incidentally both

Lin and Phan communicated with Liang largely through "brush conver-
sations"—by using their writing brushes to write classical Chinese, the
only language all three shared (Ō, 115 and Marr, 109). Lin, Phan, and
other Taiwanese and Vietnamese also contacted other Chinese nationalists but received little encouragement.

86. Ō, p. 119, states that Taiwanese activists had a tendency to look at China
through rose-colored glasses.

87. Lin's only son, as a graduate of Tokyo Imperial University's law faculty,
had received the most prestigious Japanese education of all. As of 1937
Lin's son was employed in the government general's department of finance (kin'yū-ka). Lin's five younger children were attending elite colonial public schools (primary school and higher girls' school). His wife was
a graduate of Tokyo School of Fine Arts (Tokyo bijutsu gakkō). Taiwan
shinminpō sha, Taiwan jinshi kan (1937), pp. 459-460.

88. See Teodoro A. Agoncillo and Oscar M. Alfonso, History of the Filipino
People (Quezon City, 1967); Usha Mahajani, Philippine Nationalism:
External Challenge and Filipino Response, 1565-1946 (St. Lucia, Queens-
land, 1971); D. C. Williams, The United States and the Philippines (New
York, 1924); Grayson L. Kirk, Philippine Independence, Motives, Prob-
lems, and Prospects (New York, 1936).

89. See V. P. S. Raghuvanshi, Indian Nationalist Movement and Thought
(Agra, 1959), and Bernhard Dahm, History of Indonesia in the Twentieth Century (London, 1971).

90. The paternalism of Dutch administrators in Indonesia tolerated much
more agitation and organization than officials in Taiwan would have
considered wise. But only a small fraction of the Indonesian population
was in any way literate or "educated." This probably gave administrators
confidence. See Dahm.

91. Lee, p. 243. Koreans had between 1920 and 1940 three newspapers and a
few magazines in their own language. Strict censorship was enforced, but
the very existence of these periodicals greatly helped keep national consciousness alive (Gregory Henderson, Korea and the Politics of the Vortex, Cambridge, Mass., 1968, p. 93).

92. See Bruce McCully, English Education and the Origins of Indian Nationalism (New York, 1940; reprint: Gloucester, Mass., 1966); Richard Butwell, U Nu of Burma (Stanford, 1963); William R. Roff, The Origins of
Malay Nationalism (New Haven, 1967); Marr; Robert Van Niel, The
Emergence of the Modern Indonesian Elite (The Hague and Bandung,
1960).

93. The League for the Attainment of Local Autonomy was at one point in
1931 planning to urge noncooperation with the government general.
However, after a Japanese member of the league opposed such a policy
they dropped this stance. See Ching-chih Chen, "Japanese Socio-political
Control in Taiwan," pp. 442-443. Taiwanese conservative-activists' economic nationalism was much more inclined to be expressed in denunciations of the economic favors Japanese firms received, and demands that
Taiwanese businessmen be allowed to participate fully and equally in the
colony's economic development.

Rather than counsel islanders to withdraw from the education system, they urged compulsory governmental schooling for Taiwanese children and less restricted Taiwanese entry to the higher ranks of the public education system. By contrast, Burmese anticolonial intellectuals opened their own poorly equipped schools and sent their children to them instead of to better-established British ones. They did this knowing full well that such action might cost their children secure and remunerative careers. See Richard Butwell, *U Nu of Burma*, pp. 7-10. Ts'ai P'ei-huo and others attacked the government-general opposition to Taiwanese students studying in Japan. But in Burma young U Nu, a key figure in the anti-British strikes at the University of Rangoon, refused a British offer of a scholarship to study in Britain. According to his close friend U Thant, U Nu's father wanted him to accept but Nu refused, claiming that he would not be bribed by the colonial authorities. Ibid., p. 20.

94. Ts'ai P'ei-huo et al., *T'ai-wan min-tsu yün-tung shih*, pp. 286-287.
95. See Ching-chih Chen, "Japanese Socio-political Control in Taiwan," p. 424.
96. Reproduced in Hsieh Ch'un-mu, *Taiwanjin no yōkyū* (Taihoku, 1931), pp. 16-17.
97. See Kō Se-kai, esp. pp. 234, 265, for Chiang's admiration of the Chinese nationalists.
98. Hsieh Ch'un-mu, *Taiwanjin no yōkyū*, pp. 14-15.
99. After noting that Chiang's declaration voiced Itagaki Taisuke's hope that the Taiwanese would act as a bridge between Japan and China, Edward I-te Chen concluded: "It was not that Chiang shared Itagaki's idea of forming a Sino-Japanese alliance against white imperialism. Rather Sino-Japanese friendship was the only plausible excuse under which the Association could devote itself to the development of native culture at a time when the Japanese colonial authorities were making an all-out effort for the cultural assimilation of Formosans. Actually, the real aim of the Association was said to be the awakening of Formosan national consciousness and the development of a political atmosphere favorable to the ultimate enforcement of the principle of self-determination" ("Formosan Political Movements," p. 490).
100. Ts'ai P'ei-huo et al., *T'ai-wan min-tsu yün-tung shih*, pp. 306-308.
101. See Ts'ai P'ei-huo, "Taiwan ni okeru kokuji mondai."
102. Miyagawa Jirō, *Taiwan no seiji undō* (Taihoku, 1931), p. 124.
103. See Ching-chih Chen, "Japanese Socio-political Control in Taiwan," pp. 421-422, for an excellent analysis of the educational backgrounds of association members. See also Ts'ai P'ei-huo et al., *T'ai-wan min-tsu yün-tung shih*, pp. 289-292. Regarding student members see ibid., p. 323.
104. Hsieh Ch'un-mu, *Taiwanjin no yōkyū*, pp. 14-15, describes Taiwanese students doing this at normal school in Taihoku.
105. The interest in the Cultural Association that young Taiwanese studying at Taihoku Normal School displayed especially worried the government. Taihoku Normal was supposed to produce Taiwanese common school teachers dedicated to government values and goals. However, through the influence of men like Hsieh Ch'un-mu, an alumnus of the school, and Ts'ai P'ei-huo, who had also been trained as a common school teacher, students at Taihoku Normal had become familiar with Taiwan Cultural

Association activities. In the authorities' minds, at least, incidents involving student unrest at the normal school during 1922 and 1924 removed any doubt about the association's "dangerous" influence among education students.

In February 1922 police officers visited Taihoku Normal to investigate student provocation of traffic policemen on duty at two nearby police boxes. When they arrived at the school the officers were pelted with stones by about six hundred students. Forty-five students were arrested and it was discovered that most of them belonged to the Taiwan Cultural Association.

Late in 1924 unrest again shook Taihoku Normal. This time it was directed toward the school authorities. Taiwanese students staged a strike in support of their demand that the school staff immediately redress thirty-six grievances. Some of the grievances concerned rules that restricted Japanese and Taiwanese students alike: objections to the ban against strolls in the vicinity of the school gate and to the school's censorship of all student reading materials are two examples. However most of the grievances dealt with the school's blatant favoritism of Japanese members of the student body.

According to the protesting Taiwanese students, this favoritism permeated all school life. In the dormitories, incoming Japanese were provided with new bedding while Taiwanese newcomers were given old bedding. Japanese parents visiting the school were entertained in better quarters than Taiwanese parents. The staff usually took the Japanese pupil's side in a dispute between a Taiwanese and Japanese student. A Japanese would be made class captain even when Taiwanese classmates achieved higher grades than he did. Japanese students got to do their practice teaching in first-rate schools under highly trained teachers while Taiwanese were sent to unqualified, less skilled professionals for practice teaching experience (Yamakawa Hitoshi, "Shokumin seisakuka no Taiwan," in Yamakawa Hitoshi, *Yamakawa Hitoshi zenshū,* Tokyo, 1966, VII, 287-288).

Anti-Japanese resentment is clearly embodied in the Taiwanese students' list of grievances — which they gave to the government general and to the news media as well as to their school authorities. Yet it is not clear how much of their resentment was directed at Japanese classmates. Some grievances protested specific school policies which hindered close association of the two ethnic groups. For example, one complaint accused the school of "forgetting the spirit of integrated education" because while the two races were together in the classroom, they were segregated in dormitory accommodations (ibid., p. 287). This and others like it suggest that the anti-Japanese sentiments of the striking students did not necessarily include a total rejection of assimilation.

Taihoku Normal authorities were only able to break this strike after they had expelled thirty-eight Taiwanese students. Significantly, most of those expelled soon left for China or Tokyo to continue their studies in environments conducive to gaining experience as anticolonial activists. In later years they took part in antigovernmental campaigns within the colony (*TSK,* III, 173). Taiwanese students at other schools soon became involved in incidents that worried the colonial government enough to impose a ban on student membership in the Cultural Association (*TSK*, III, 173-174).

106. See Ching-chih Chen, "Japanese Socio-political Control in Taiwan," pp. 425-426, for estimates of the number of Taiwanese who attended the meetings.

107. At least to my knowledge no such work has been published. The excellent critical bibliography at the end of Kō Se-kai's *Nihon tōchika no Taiwan*, which contains an exhaustive survey of material on this topic available up to about 1972, does not mention such a work.

108. These members began to bring their newly developing political concerns into the Youth Association. Serious discussion of political and social questions became a popular pastime. According to police observers: "This did not stop at advocacy of self-determination of peoples. Spurred on by the trends of the time some were drawn toward anarchism and some became believers in communism. Thus within the Taiwan Youth Association, ideological polarization was steadily increasing. In addition, there was a tendency for various factions with orientations different from the Taiwan Youth Association to be formed [within the Association]" (*TSK*, III, 33). Some of these factions evinced an ideological coloration that, as those masters of understatement, the police reporters, put it, "went beyond simple friendly relations and mutual aid" (*TSK*, III, 33).

109. *TSK*, III, 27.

110. Kō Se-kai, p. 264. Kō cites a 1927 article by Lien Wên-ch'ing for this judgment. See Lien Wên-Ch'ing, "Kako Taiwan no shakai undō" (Socialist movements in Taiwan in the past), *Taiwan minpō*, no. 138 (Jan. 2, 1927), pp. 12-13.

111. Korean students in Japan also spoke out against Japanese rule under YMCA auspices. See Lee, p. 99.

112. Kō Se-kai, p. 264. P'eng apparently eventually joined the conservative stream of anticolonialism. See Taiwan shinminpō, *Taiwan jinshi kan* (1937), p. 336.

113. *TSK*, III, 38.

114. *TSK*, III, 37-41.

115. See Tse-tung Chow, *The May Fourth Movement: Intellectual Movement in Modern China* (Cambridge, Mass., 1960).

116. *TSK*, III, 174.

117. Ibid.

118. *TSK*, III, 79.

119. For groups and organizations involving Taiwanese students in China see *TSK*, III, 68-133.

120. The police seem to have been extraordinarily well informed. Police information was eventually published in *TSK*, the monumental history of the Japanese police in Taiwan which is a main source for information about antigovernment-general activity.

121. See Van Niel, p. 121.

122. For background information on Yamaguchi Koshizu see *TSK*, III, 183, and Miyagawa Jirō, *Taiwan no seiji undō*, pp. 280-283.

123. See Yamakawa Hitoshi, "Shokumin seisakuka no Taiwan," pp. 258-292.

This work was originally published in 1926 by Purebusu shupansha. From internal evidence it appears to have been begun in 1925. See the rest of this chapter for Lien's role in the Taiwanese anticolonial movement.

124. *TSK*, III, 887.

125. Kō Se-kai, p. 265; *TSK*, III, 184-185.

126. The would-be founders of the Cultural Association youth group switched their plans when the police prevented them from going ahead with their original intention. They created two organizations called Taihoku Young People's Physical Education Society (Taihoku seinen taiiku kai) and Taihoku Young People's Reading Society (Taihoku seinen dokusho kai). As police observers sourly noted, these two clubs were not interested in sports or nonpolitical reading but in anarchist and communist politics (*TSK*, III, 884). Budding young Taiwanese leftists did not differentiate sharply between anarchism and communism but welcomed all kinds of left-wing influences. When Lien Wên-ch'ing returned to Taiwan after his Esperanto conference, he brought back with him copies of Japanese left-wing periodicals. These were eagerly bought by members of these clubs and by other young Taiwanese—all of whom were being drawn into the anarchist groups which began to emerge from about the middle of 1925. In 1925 a group called the Lenin Memorial Society (Rēnin tsuitō kai) planned a May Day celebration but were thwarted by the police. The following year anarchists tried to hold a political lecture on the anniversary of the founding of the Japanese state, and as a result Lien Wên-ch'ing and four others were arrested and fined (*TSK*, III, 883-884; Kō Se-kai, p. 268).

127. In 1926 anarchist youths (including Lien Wên-ch'ing) met with Taiwan Cultural Association executive members (including Lin Hsien-t'ang, Ts'ai P'ei-huo, and Hsieh Ch'un-mu) and told them that they opposed the petition movement because it had little chance of success and even if it should succeed its tolerance of capitalism and imperialism was unacceptable (*TSK*, III, 885).

128. *TSK*, III, 158.

129. Any association youth groups suspected of being leftist were quickly broken up, but a handful of clubs for the young—including two organizations for women—functioned for several years in different localities (*TSK*, III, 166-167).

130. Kō Se-kai, pp. 253-254.

131. *TSK*, III, 1028.

132. In addition, the Japanese Farmer-Labor Party (Nihon rōdō nōmintō) sent a leading activist of the Japanese labor movement, Aso Hisashi, to Taiwan to serve as a defense lawyer in the case (*TSK*, III, 1026-1029; Kō Se-kai, pp. 256-257). Some of the accused received mild sentences which were appealed. The president of the Federation of Japan Peasant Unions (Nihon nōmin kumiai rengo) came to act as defense lawyer during the appeal (Kō Se-kai, p. 257).

133. Ko Se-kai, p. 258.

134. The Lin Pen-yuan Sugar Corporation, for instance, was owned by the wealthy Lin Hsiung-cheng, whose fortunes had been furthered by collaboration.

135. See Yamakawa Hitoshi, "Shokumin seisakuka no Taiwan," pp. 258-292.
136. Lien Wên-ch'ing, "Kako Taiwan no shakai undō," pp. 12-13, quoted in Kō Se-kai, p. 279.
137. For a description and analysis of the takeover see Kō Se-kai, pp. 274-292. See also Hsieh Ch'un-mu, *Taiwanjin no yōkyū,* pp. 50-68.
138. Kō Se-kai, p. 283.
139. *TSK,* III, 203-204; Ts'ai P'ei-huo et al., *T'ai-wan min-tsu yün-tung shih,* pp. 349-350.
140. Kō Se-kai, pp. 287-288.
141. Kō Se-kai, p. 290.
142. Kō Se-kai, pp. 292-293.
143. For information on the Taiwan Communist Party see Kō Se-kai, pp. 327-341, 358-375, and Ō, pp. 126-129.
144. Kō Se-kai, p. 377.
145. This is illustrated by the mixed educational backgrounds of individuals arrested in "communist incidents." See Kō Se-Kai, pp. 359-360, 367-369.
146. Ō, pp. 126-129. Hsieh received a thirteen-year prison sentence in 1931, but she was released in 1939 because she was gravely ill. Upon her release she opened a wine shop in Taichū and continued to do underground work even though the party had been destroyed by the massive arrests in 1931. Despite her illness she outlived the colonial government, surviving to play an important role in political events which occurred immediately after Japanese rule ended. In 1949 she went to Peking (Lin Ching-ming, pp. 83-84; Ō, p. 147).
147. Kō Se-kai, pp. 328, 333.
148. For a while one such lawyer, Furuya Sadao, a veteran of peasant movement activities in Japan from the Japan Labor-Farmer Party, opened a permanent office in Taichū from which he acted as a consultant to the Taiwan Peasant Union (Taiwan nōmin kumiai). See Kō Se-kai, pp. 287-288.
149. Yanaihara Tadao, "Teikokushugika no Taiwan," pp. 371-388.
150. Yamabe Kentarō, ed., *Gendai shi shiryō: Taiwan I* (Tokyo, 1971), XXI, 426-428, analyzes tenant disputes in Taiwan during the years 1927, 1928, and 1929. Many of the disputes during these years involved corporations owned by Taiwanese or individual landlords who were Taiwanese. See also Asada Kyōji, *Nihon teikokushugika no minzoku kakumei undō* (Tokyo, 1973), p. 61.

9. Conclusion

1. See Gotō Shimpei, "The Administration of Formosa (Taiwan)," pp. 530-553.
2. Pre-Meiji nationalism was largely a ruling-class phenomenon. Among commoners especially regional ties were strong.
3. Kaminuma, pp. 221-222.
4. D. D. Chelliah, *A History of Educational Policy of the Straits Settlements* (Kuala Lumpur, 1947), p. 145.
5. T. W. G. Miller, p. 79.
6. It was the few Japanese who made it to the nation's higher schools and universities who acquired the leisure and access to a wide variety of ideas that they needed to begin to think for themselves. As a result, many of

Japan's rebels came from the ranks of this educated elite. See Smith.

7. Charles E. Trevelyan, *On the Education of the People of India* (London, 1838), pp. 191-192.

8. J. S. Furnivall, *Colonial Policy and Practice: A Comparative Study of Burma and Netherlands India* (New York, 1956), p. 203.

9. This appears to have been so in the case of the school in the fishing village described so vividly by Norma J. Diamond, "K'un Shen: A Taiwanese Fishing Village," esp. pp. 171-187.

10. Wyndham, p. 42, mentions that in Ceylon in mid-nineteenth century, the Colebroke Commission concluded that, since girls did not go to school, boys did not speak their school language at home. The problem of literacy and skill retention existed in postcolonial Taiwan too. See Gallin, p. 197.

11. This occurred for a variety of complex reasons. See McCully, esp. p. 391.

12. McCully, p. 389.

13. See for example the complicated colonial school system in early twentieth-century Indonesia, as described in Dahm, pp. 16-19.

14. See ibid.

15. Western visitors to Taiwan, both sympathizers and critics of Japanese colonial rule, observed that life in the colony was in many ways very like life in the home islands. See Poultney Bigelow, *Japan and Her Colonies* (London, 1923); Harold and Alice Foght; Janet B. M. McGovern, *Among the Head-Hunters of Formosa* (London, 1922); J. Ralston Hayden, "Japan's New Policy in Korea and Formosa"; Andrew J. Grajdanzev, *Formosa Today: An Analysis of Economic Development and Strategic Importance of Japan's Tropical Colony* (New York, 1942).

16. See Albert Memmi, *The Colonizer and the Colonized* (Boston, 1967), for a poignant expression of this anguish.

17. Japanese primary school textbooks from the beginning of the Meiji period on also contain a surprising amount of nonsexist content. Although male and female spheres of endeavor are clearly delineated, many moral injunctions are addressed equally to children of both sexes. The frequent use of neuter pronouns characteristic of the Japanese language also helps these books appear relatively free from sexist bias. See Kaigo and Naka, *Nihon kyōkasho taikei: kindai hen.*

18. Levy, p. 102.

19. Quoted in Levy, p. 100.

20. Levy, pp. 102-103. For discussions of Japanese support of the Taiwanese antifootbinding movement see Levy, pp. 95-103, and Ide, *Taiwan chiseki shi,* pp. 355-358. As among women on the mainland, those who undid their bindings suffered greatly. Originally they had been forced to endure binding in order that a husband could be found to marry them. In changing times, husbands became ashamed of their wives' "backward" bound feet and forced them to unbind them, a painful process for those who had originally been crippled many years earlier.

21. *TWT,* pp. 763-766. In 1941, 36.6 percent of male factory workers had received no schooling whereas 67.4 percent of female factory workers had never been to school. In 1942 the percentages of unschooled workers were 33 for men and 57 for women. In 1943 these percentages were 30.8 and

53.7 respectively (*TWT,* pp. 838-840). Interestingly, out of the more than 5,000 women employed in mining during these three years, over 81 percent had received no education. Their lack of education suggests that they were employed in arduous, unskilled, low-status work. Thus although females made up a small percentage of the total mining labor force (never more than 14 percent) several thousand women were laboring in Taiwan's mines during the last years of the colonial period (see *TWT,* p. 838).

22. *TWT,* pp. 840-841. Of the 2,285 who had been to school 116 are listed under "other education." It is highly likely that some of these had some postelementary schooling too.

23. Unfortunately, the *TWT* statistics referred to above do not tell how many of the workers were Japanese and how many were Taiwanese. *Tōkeisho* year-by-year statistics on occupational divisions of the colony's population, however, do show that a majority of the females employed in the island's various industries were Taiwanese. One can surmise that, in shops as in factories, Taiwanese women probably vastly outnumbered Japanese.

24. The subject is P'eng Ts'ai-a-hsin (1899-?), wife of P'eng Hua-ying, the left-wing activist who later became actually or ostensibly a conservative participant in the Taiwan Popular Party and the colonial business world. P'eng Ts'ai-a-hsin was a distinguished physician who had qualified in Japan and had done postgraduate work in gynecology and obstetrics there. She returned to Taiwan both to open her own obstetrics clinic and obstetrics training institute and to become a leader in island medical circles. She was particularly renowned for her contributions to improvements in obstetrics and prenatal health (Taiwan shinminpō, *Taiwan jinshi kan* [1937], p. 336).

25. See for example the entries on Taiwanese women in Chang Tzu-hui, *T'ai-wan shih-jen chih.*

26. By 1937 seventy women had studied at government universities (Rekishi kyōiku kenkyū kai, ed., *Joshi shi kenkyū,* Tokyo, 1937, p. 343).

27. Ibid., pp. 343-344.

28. Ibid., p. 343.

29. Taiwan sōtokufu, *Taiwan no gakkō kyōiku,* p. 121; *Taiwan nenkan 1944,* p. 505.

30. Rekishi kyōiku kenkyū kai, *Joshi shi kenkyū,* pp. 347-348.

31. The kinds of conflicts they must have faced would have been much like some of the problems that a young Indonesian woman with a colonial education wrote about at the turn of the century. See Raden Adjeng Kartini, *Letters of a Javanese Princess* (New York, 1964).

32. Royama Masamichi and Takeuchi Tatsuji, *The Philippine Polity: A Japanese View* (New Haven, 1967), p. 126.

33. Ibid., p. 127.

34. Myrdal, III, 1635.

35. Furnivall, *Educational Progress in Southeastern Asia* (New York, 1943), p. 111.

36. John P. Halstead, *Rebirth of a Nation: The Origins and Rise of Moroccan Nationalism, 1912-1944* (Cambridge, Mass., 1969), p. 113.

37. Virginia Thompson and Richard Adloff, *Cultural Institutions and Educational Policy in Southeast Asia* (New York, 1948), p. 82.
38. For the case of India see McCully, pp. 74, 38, 98-100.
39. For instance, the British supported private Chinese schools in Malaya. See Furnivall, *Educational Progress in Southeastern Asia,* p. 67.
40. See McCully and Foster.
41. Myrdal, III, 1633-1634. See also William B. Freer, *The Philippine Experiences of an American Teacher* (New York, 1906).
42. See Charles Edward Russell, *The Outlook for the Philippines* (New York, 1923) and Carl H. Lande, "The Philippines," in James S. Coleman, ed., *Education and Political Development* (Princeton, 1965), pp. 313-349.
43. Furnivall, *Colonial Policy and Practice,* p. 211.
44. Furnivall, *Educational Progress in Southeastern Asia,* pp. 118-119.
45. The curricula of Philippine schools were as American as Taiwan's were Japanese. The same care was taken to remodel American studies to suit the perceived needs of the Filipinos. See Freer; Russell, pp. 220-264; J. Ralston Hayden, *The Philippines: A Study in National Development* (New York, 1942), pp. 463-533.
46. Mahajani, p. 306.
47. The Board of Educational Survey, *A Survey of the Educational System of the Philippine Islands* (Manila, 1925), p. 13.
48. Ibid., esp. pp. 32, 199-218.
49. Antonio Isidro, *The Philippine Educational System* (Manila, 1949), pp. 102-103.
50. With American rule, English replaced Spanish as the language of government and ruling-class society. Thus the native Spanish-educated and Spanish-speaking elite lost an advantage. This encouraged greater equalitarianism and mobility among Filipinos.
51. Dahm, pp. 15-19.
52. Roff, esp. pp. 23-29.
53. See the case of the family of Peng Ming-min in Peng Ming-min, pp. 9-11.
54. Gaimushō, *Nihon tōchika gojūnen no Taiwan,* p. 276.
55. See Hayden, "Japan's New Policy in Korea and Formosa."
56. It also gave them some drawbacks. In *Learning to be Chinese,* Wilson found that the foundations for the mindless indoctrination present in postcolonial Nationalist Chinese education in Taiwan were laid by Japanese education in the island. Clearly, both Japanese and Nationalist Chinese elementary education subjected and in the latter case continues to subject Taiwanese children to such instruction. However it is much easier to discern what the children think they are supposed to believe as a result of these lessons than it is to discern what the children actually, perhaps privately, believe. See Robert Coles, "What Children Know about Politics," *New York Review of Books* 22.2:22-24 (Feb. 20, 1975); "The Politics of Middle Class Children," *New York Review of Books* 22.3:13-16 (March 6, 1975); "Children and Politics: Outsiders," *New York Review of Books* 22.4:29-30 (March 20, 1975).
57. Thompson and Adloff, p. 85; Myrdal, III, 1644; Furnivall, *Educational Progress in Southeastern Asia,* p. 116.
58. Myrdal, III, 1646.
59. Myrdal, III, 1764.

Appendix A

1. McGovern, p. 90.
2. See Government of Formosa, *Report on the Control of the Aborigines* (Taihoku, 1911), pp. 4-10.
3. Ibid., p. 5.
4. *TKES,* pp. 481-482.
5. Taiwan sōtokufu keimukyoku, *Takasago zoku no kyōiku* (Taihoku, 1941), p. 11; *TKES,* pp. 498-500.
6. Taiwan sōtokufu keimukyoku, *Takasago zoku no kyōiku,* p. 11.
7. *TKES,* pp. 467-469.
8. Taiwan sōtokufu keimukyoku, *Riban shikō* (Taihoku, 1932), pp. 400-404.
9. *TKES,* pp. 480-481, 503-504; Yoshino, p. 405-406.
10. *TKES,* pp. 483-506.
11. Taiwan sōtokufu keimukyoku, *Takasago zoku no kyōiku,* p. 7.
12. Studies were, however, published from the surveys' data collections. Some of these are: Taiwan sōtokufu, *Riban gaiyō* (Taihoku, 1913); Taiwan sōtokufu, *Taiwan banjin jijō* (Taihoku, 1910); Rinji Taiwan kyūkan chōsa kai, *Taiwan banzoku zufu* (Tokyo, 1921); Suzuki Sakutarō, *Taiwan no banzoku kenkyū* (Taihoku, 1932); Taihoku teikoku daigaku dozoku jinrui gaku kenkyushitsu chōsa, *Taiwan takasago zoku keitō shozoku no kenkyū* (Taihoku, 1935); Iwaki Kamehiko, *Taiwan no banchi kaihatsu to banjin* (Taihoku, 1936).
13. See McGovern and Rutters.
14. *TKES,* pp. 466-467.
15. Taiwan sōtokufu keimukyoku, *Takasago zoku no kyōiku,* p. 12.
16. See ibid., esp. the colored chart before p. 1. This chart omits the largest aborigine group, the Ami.
17. Interviews in Pingtung prefecture during 1969.
18. Ibid.
19. Taiwan sōtokufu keimukyoku, *Takasago zoku no kyōiku,* p. 14; Taiwan sōtokufu, *Taiwan tōchi gaiyō,* pp. 46-49. By 1940 aborigine graduates of secondary level schools consisted of two from the medical school, six from normal school, one from middle school, six from agricultural and forestry school. See ibid.
20. Taiwan sōtokufu keimukyoku, *Takasago zoku no kyōiku,* p. 14.
21. In 1969 this man was a teacher in a secondary agricultural school for aborigines in Pingtung prefecture.

Bibliography

Abe Akiyoshi 安倍明義, comp. *Taiwan chimei kenkyū* 臺灣地名研究 (A study of Taiwanese place names). Taihoku, Bango kenkyūkai, 1938.

Agoncillo, Teodoro A., and Oscar M. Alfonso. *History of the Filipino People.* Quezon City, Malay Books, 1967.

Arnold, Julean H. *Education in Formosa.* Washington, D.C., United States Bureau of Education, 1908.

Asada Kyōji 浅田喬二. *Nihon teikokushugika no minzoku kakumei undō* 日本帝國主義下の民族革命運動 (Revolutionary movements of people under Japanese imperialism). Tokyo, Miraisha, 1973.

Band, Edward. *Barclay of Formosa.* Tokyo, Christian Literature Society, 1936.

Barclay, George W. *Colonial Development and Population in Taiwan.* Princeton, Princeton University Press, 1954.

Bigelow, Poultney. *Japan and Her Colonies.* London, Edward Arnold, 1923.

Board of Educational Survey. *A Survey of the Educational System of the Philippine Islands.* Manila, 1925.

Brown, Arthur Judson. *The Mastery of the Far East.* New York, Charles Scribner's Sons, 1919.

Butwell, Richard. *U Nu of Burma.* Stanford, Stanford University Press, 1963.

Caiger, John. "The Aims and Content of School Courses in Japanese History, 1872–1945." In Edmund Skrzypczak, ed., *Japan's Modern Century.* Tokyo, Sophia University, 1968.

Campbell, William. *Formosa under the Dutch.* London, Kegan, Paul, Trench, Trubner, 1903.

————*Sketches from Formosa.* London, Marshall Brothers, 1915.

Chang Chung-li. *The Chinese Gentry: Studies on Their Role in Nineteenth Century Chinese Society.* Seattle, University of Washington Press, 1955.

Chang Tzu-hui 章子惠, ed. *T'ai-wan shih-jen chih* 臺灣時人誌 (A who's who of Taiwan). Taipei, Kuo-kuang ch'u-pan she, 1946.

Chai Chen-kang. *Taiwan Aborigines: A Genetic Study of Tribal Variations.* Cambridge, Mass., Harvard University Press, 1967.

Chelliah, D. D. *A History of the Educational Policy of the Straits Settlements.* Kuala Lumpur, The Government Press, 1947.

Chen Ching-chih. "The Police and the *Hokō* Systems in Taiwan under Japanese Administration (1895–1945)." In Albert Craig, ed. *Papers on Japan*, 4. Cambridge, Mass., Harvard East Asian Research Center, 1967.

————"Japanese Socio-political Control in Taiwan, 1895–1945." Ph.D. diss. Harvard University, 1973.

Chen, Edward I-te. "Japanese Colonialism in Korea and Formosa: A Comparison of its Effects upon the Development of Nationalism." Ph.D. diss. University of Pennsylvania, 1968.

————"Formosan Political Movements under Japanese Colonial Rule, 1914–1937." *Journal of Asian Studies* 31.3: 477–497 (May 1972).

Chen K'un-shu 陳崑樹. *Taiwan tōchi mondai* 臺灣統治問題 (Problems in ruling Taiwan). Taihoku, Hōbundō shoten, 1931.

Chin Miao-chiang 邱森鏘. *Buraku kyōka no jissai* 部落教化の實際 (The practical side of hamlet education). Taichū, San-shih-chang-li buraku shinkōkai, 1940.

Chōsen shimbunsha 朝鮮新聞社, ed. *Chōsen tōchi kaiko to hihan* 朝鮮統治回顧と批判 (Recollections and criticisms of the administration in Korea). Keijō, 1936.

Chōsen sōtokufu 朝鮮総督府. *Shōwa jūgonen sōtokufu tōkei nenpō* 昭和十五年総督府統計年報 (Government-general statistical year book for Showa 15 [1940]). Keijō, 1942.

Chou Hsien-wen 周憲文, comp. *Ch'ing-tai T'-ai-wan ching-chi shih* 清代台湾経済史 (An economic history of Taiwan during the Ch'ing period). Taipei, T'ai-wan yin-hsing, 1957.

Chow Tse-tung. *The May Fourth Movement: Intellectual Movement in Modern China.* Cambridge, Mass., Harvard University Press, 1960.

Chu, Samuel C. "Liu Ming-ch'uan and Modernization of Taiwan." *Journal of Asian Studies* 23.1: 37–53 (November 1964).

Ch'un-ch'eng 著丞. "Jih-chü shih-ch'i chih Chung-wen shu-chü" 日據時期之中文書局 (Chinese bookshops during the Japanese Period). *T'ai-pei wen wu* 台北文物 (Taipei cultural matters) 3.2: 131–132 (August 1954).

Chung Tae-shi. "'Yesterday' of Korean Education." *Korea Journal* 3.4: 16–19 (April 1, 1963).

Clark, J. D. *Formosa.* Shanghai, Shanghai Mercury Office, 1896.

Coleman, James S. *Education and Political Development.* Princeton, Princeton University Press, 1965.

Coles, Robert. "What Children know about Politics." *New York Review of Books* 22.2: 22–24 (Feb. 20, 1975).

———"The Politics of Middle Class Children." *New York Review of Books* 22.3: 13–16 (March 6, 1975).

———"Children and Politics: Outsiders," *New York Review of Books* 22.4: 29–30 (March 20, 1975).

Cowan, L. Gray, James O'Connell, and David G. Scanlon, eds. *Education and Nation-Building in Africa.* New York, Praeger, 1965.

Croizier, Ralph C. "Cheng Ch'eng-kung's Conquest of Taiwan: Intent, Event, and Legacy," Ms., 1972.

Crowley, James B., ed. *Modern East Asia: Essays in Interpretation.* New York, Harcourt, Brace and World, 1970.

Davidson, James W. *The Island of Formosa, Past and Present.* New York, Book World, 1903.

Dahm, Bernhard. *History of Indonesia in the Twentieth Century.* London, Pall Mall, 1971.

Day, Clive. *The Policy and Administration of the Dutch in Java.* New York, London, Macmillan, 1904.

Den Kenjirō 田健治郎. "Taiwan shisei kunji" 臺灣施政訓示 (Speech on the administration of Taiwan). *Taiwan jihō* 臺灣時報 (Taiwan times) 106: 11–26 (December 1919).

———"Assimilation Keynote of Taiwan Policy." *Trans-Pacific* 8.2–3: 45–47 (February–March 1923).

Den Kenjirō nikki 田健治郎日記 (The diary of Den Kenjirō). In the National

Diet Library, Tokyo.

Diamond, Norma J. "K'un Shen: A Taiwanese Fishing Village," Ph.D. diss. Cornell University, 1966.

Dodd, John. *Journal of a Blockaded Resident in North Formosa during the Franco-Chinese War, 1884–5.* Hongkong, printed for private circulation, 1888.

Dore, Ronald P. *Land Reform in Japan.* London, Oxford University Press, 1959.

————*Education in Tokugawa Japan.* Berkeley, University of California Press, 1965.

Duus, Peter. *Party Rivalry and Political Change in Taishō Japan.* Cambridge, Mass., Harvard University Press, 1968.

Ebihara Haruyoshi 海老原治善. *Gendai Nihon kyōiku seisaku* 現代日本教育政策 (Education policy in modern Japan). 2 vols. Tokyo, Sanichi shobō, 1965–1967.

Elson, Ruth Miller. *Guardians of Tradition: American Schoolbooks of the Nineteenth Century.* Lincoln, University of Nebraska Press, 1964.

Ennis, Thomas E. *French Policy and Developments in Indochina.* Chicago, University of Chicago Press, 1936.

Fairbank, John K., Edwin O. Reischauer, and Albert Craig. *East Asia: The Modern Transformation.* Boston, Houghton Mifflin, 1965.

Fischer, James Earnest. *Democracy and Mission Education in Korea.* New York, Bureau of Publications, Teachers' College, Columbia University, 1928; reprint: Seoul, Yonsei University Press, 1970.

Foght, Harold, and Alice Foght. *Unfathomed Japan.* New York, Macmillan, 1928.

Foreign Affairs Association of Japan. *Japan Year Book 1943–44.* Tokyo, 1944.

Foster, Phillip. *Education and Social Change in Ghana.* Chicago, University of Chicago Press, 1965.

Freer, William B. *The Philippine Experiences of an American Teacher.* New York, Charles Scribners, 1906.

Furnivall, J. S. *Educational Progress in Southeastern Asia.* New York, Institute of Pacific Relations, 1943.

————*Colonial Policy and Practice: A Comparative Study of Burma and Netherlands India.* New York, New York University Press, 1956.

Gaimushō 外務省. *Nihon tōchika gojūnen no Taiwan* 日本統治下五十年の台湾 (Taiwan under fifty years of Japanese rule). Tokyo, 1964.

Gallin, Bernard. *Hsin Hsing Taiwan: A Chinese Village in Change.* Berkeley, University of California Press, 1966.

Gordon, Leonard H. D. *Taiwan, Studies in Chinese Local History.* New York, Columbia University Press, 1970.

Gotō Shimpei 後藤新平. "Formosa under Japanese Administration." *Independent* 54: 1578–1589 (July 1902).

———— "The Administration of Formosa (Taiwan)." In Ōkuma Shigenobu, ed., *Fifty Years of New Japan.* London, Longmans, 1910.

————*Nihon shokumin seisaku ippan; Nihon bōchō ron* 日本植民政策一斑・日本膨脹論 (An outline of Japan's colonial policies and a study of Japan's population expansion). Tokyo, Nihon hyōronsha, 1944.

Gotō Shimpei monjo 後藤新平文書 (The papers of Gotō Shimpei). In the National Diet Library, Tokyo.

Government of Formosa. *Report on the Control of Aborigines in Formosa.* Taihoku, 1911.

Grajdanzev, Andrew. *Formosa Today: An Analysis of Economic Development and Strategic Importance of Japan's Tropical Colony.* New York, Institute of Pacific Relations, 1942.

Gray, Herbert Branston. *The Public School and the Empire.* London, Williams and Norgate, 1913.

Hall, Ivan P. *Mori Arinori.* Cambridge, Mass., Harvard University Press, 1973.

Halstead, John P. *Rebirth of a Nation: The Origins and Rise of Moroccan Nationalism, 1912–1944.* Cambridge, Mass., Harvard University Press, 1969.

Hara Kei 原敬. *Hara Kei nikki* 原敬日記 (The diary of Hara Kei). 9 vols. Tokyo, Kangensha, 1950–1951.

Hashimoto Hakusui 橋本白水. *Taiwan no kanmin* 台湾之官民 (Officials of Taiwan). Taihoku, Nankoku shuppan kyōkai, 1919.

Hasuda Zenmei 蓮田善明. "Taiwan no kokugo kyōiku" 臺灣の國語教育 (Japanese language education in Taiwan). *Kyōiku* 教育 (Education). 6.8: 1233–1236 (August 1938).

Hayden, J. Ralyston. "Japan's New Policy in Korea and Formosa." *Foreign Affairs* 2.3: 474–487 (March 1924).

———*The Philippines: A Study in National Development.* New York, Macmillan, 1942.

Heibonsha 平凡社. *Dai jimmei jiten* 大人名辞典 (Great biographical dictionary). 10 vols. Tokyo, 1935–1955.

Henderson, Gregory. *Korea and the Politics of the Vortex.* Cambridge, Mass., Harvard University Press, 1968.

Hirano Ken'ichirō 平野謙一郎. "Manshū ni okeru Nihon no kyōiku seisaku, 1906–1931" 満洲に於る日本の教育政策, 1906–1931. (Japanese educational policy in Manchuria, 1906–1931). *Ajiya kenkyū* アジア研究 (Asian research) 15.3: 24–52 (October 1968).

Hirano Shōichi 平野象一. "Taiwan no kyōgaku ni tsuite" 台湾の共学について (Integration in Taiwan's schools). *Taiwan jihō* (February 1920).

Hishida Seiji. "Formosa: Japan's First Colony." *Political Science Quarterly* 22.2: 267–281 (June 1907).

Ho, Samuel P. S. "The Development Policy of the Japanese Colonial Government in Taiwan, 1895–1945." In Gustav Ranis, ed., *Government and Economic Development.* New Haven, Yale University Press, 1971.

Hokkaidō daigaku 北海道大学. *Hoddaidō daigaku sōki hachijūnen shi* 北海道大學創期八十年史 (The first eighty years of Hokkaidō University). Sapporo, 1965.

Hosono Akio 細野昭雄 et al. *Taiwan no hyōjō* 台湾の表情 (The face of Taiwan). Tokyo, Kokon shoin, 1963.

Hsieh Chiao-min. *Taiwan, Ilha Formosa: A Geography in Perspective.* Washington, D.C., Butterworths, 1964.

Hsieh Ch'un-mu 謝春木. *Taiwanjin wa kaku miru* 台湾人はかく見る (The Taiwanese see it this way). Taihoku, Taiwan minpōsha, 1930.

———*Taiwanjin no yōkyū* 台湾人の要求 (The demands of the Taiwanese). Taihoku, Taiwan shinminpōsha, 1931.

Ide Kiwata 井出李和田. *Taiwan chiseki shi* 臺灣治績史 (The administrative record in Taiwan). Taihoku, Taiwan nichi nichi shimpōsha, 1933.

———*Nanshin Taiwan shi kō* 南進台湾史攻 (Southward Advancement from Taiwan). Tokyo, Seibi shokaku, 1943.

Inō Yoshinori 伊能嘉矩. *Taiwan junbu to shite no Ryū Mei-den* 台湾巡撫として

の劉銘傳 (Liu Ming-ch'uan as governor of Taiwan). Taihoku, Keibunsha, 1905.

——*Taiwan bunka shi* 台湾文化史 (A record of Taiwan's cultural history). 3 vols. Tokyo, Tōkō shoin, 1928.

Isidro, Antonio. *The Philippine Educational System.* Manila, Bookman, 1949.

Ishiguro Hidehiko 石黒英彦. "Taiwan no kyōiku" 台湾の教育 (Education in Taiwan). *Jiyu tsūshin* (Independent News) 2: 16–17 (June 1929).

Itagaki Morimasa 板垣守正, ed. *Itagaki Taisuke zenshū* 板垣退助全集 (Collected works of Itagaki Taisuke). Tokyo, Hara shobō, 1969.

Itō Hirobumi 伊藤博文. *Taiwan shiryō* 臺灣資料 (Documents concerning Taiwan). Tokyo, Hissho ruisan kankōkai, 1936.

Itō Kinjirō 伊藤金次郎. *Shinryochi kaitaku to Gotō Shimpei* 新領地開拓と後藤新平 (Gotō Shimpei and the opening up of new territory). Tokyo, 1942.

Iwaki Kamehiko 岩城亀彦. *Taiwan no banchi kaihatsu to banjin* 台湾の蕃地開発と蕃人 (Aborigines and the opening up of aborigine lands). Taihoku, Riban no tomo, 1936.

Izawa Takio denki hensan iinkai 伊澤多喜男傳記編纂委員会. *Izawa Takio* 伊澤多喜男. Tokyo, 1951.

Izumi Masakichi 泉政吉. *Taiwan no minzoku undō* 台湾の民族運動 (The Taiwanese people's movement). Taihoku, Taiwan toshoinsatsu gōshi kaisha, 1928.

"Japan as a Colonizing Power." *Spectator* 98: 447–448 (March 23, 1907).

Japanese National Commission for UNESCO. *Development of Modern System of Education in Japan.* Tokyo, 1960.

Kaigo Tokiomi 海後宗臣 and Naka Arata 仲新, eds. *Nihon kyōkasho taikei: kindai hen* 日本教科書体系近代編 (An outline of Japanese textbooks: the modern period). 27 vols. Tokyo, Kōdansha, 1961–1967.

Kaigo Tokiomi. *Japanese Education: Its Past and Present.* Tokyo, Kokusai Bunka Shinkokai, 1965.

——, ed. *Inoue Kowashi no kyōiku seisaku* 井上毅の教育政策 (Inoue Kowashi's education policy). Tokyo, Tokyo daigaku shuppankai, 1968.

Kaminuma Hachirō 上沼八郎. *Izawa Shūji* 伊沢修二. Tokyo, Yoshikawa kōbunkan, 1962.

Kamiyama kun kinen jigyōkai 上山君記念事業会. *Kamiyama Mitsunoshin* 上山満之進. Tokyo, 1941.

Kanda Masao 神田正雄. *Ugoki yuku Taiwan* 動きゆく台湾 (Uneasy Taiwan). Tokyo, Kaigaisha, 1930.

Karasawa Tomitarō 唐澤富太郎. *Gakusei no rekishi* 学生の歴史 (A history of students). Tokyo, Sōbunsha, 1955.

——*Kyōshi no rekishi* 教師の歴史 (A history of teachers). Tokyo, Sōbunsha, 1955.

——*Kyōkasho no rekishi* 教科書の歴史 (A history of textbooks). Tokyo, Sōbunsha, 1956.

Kartini, Raden Adjeng. *Letters of a Javanese Princess.* Trans. Agnes Louise Symmers. New York, W. W. Norton, 1964.

Katsuda Shuichi 勝田守一 and Nakauchi Toshio 中内敏夫. *Nihon no gakkō* 日本の学校 (Schools in Japan). Tokyo, Iwanami shinsho, 1964

Kawamura Takeji 川村竹治. *Taiwan no ichinen* 台湾の一年 (A year in Taiwan). Tokyo, Jiji kenkyūkai, 1930.

Keene, Donald. "The Sino–Japanese War of 1894–95 and Its Cultural Effects in Japan." In Donald Shively, ed., *Tradition and Modernization in Japanese Culture*. Princeton, Princeton University Press, 1971.

Keenleyside, Hugh L. and A. F. Thomas. *History of Japanese Education and Present Educational System*. Tokyo, Hokuseido Press, 1937.

Kerr, George. *Formosa Betrayed*. Boston, Houghton Mifflin, 1965.

Kim, C. I. Eugene, ed. *A Pattern of Political Development: Korea*. Korea Research and Publication, 1964.

Kim Hyung-chan. "A Study of North Korean Education Under Communism since 1945." Ed.D diss. George Peabody College for Teachers, 1969.

Kinebuchi Yoshifusa 杵淵義房. *Taiwan shakai jigyō shi* 台湾社会事業史 (A history of philanthropy in Taiwan). Taihoku, Tokyūkai, 1940.

Kikuchi Dairoku. *Japanese Education*. London, Longmans, 1909.

Kirk, Grayson L. *Philippine Independence: Motives, Problems, and Prospects*. New York, Farrar and Rinehart, 1936.

Kō Se-kai 許世楷. *Nihon tōchika no Taiwan* 日本統治下の台湾 (Taiwan under Japanese rule). Tokyo, Tokyo daigaku shuppankai, 1972.

Kokubu Naoichi 國分直一. *Taiwan no minzoku* 台湾の民俗 (The customs of Taiwan). Tokyo, Iwasaki bijutsusha, 1968.

Komori Tokuji 小森徳治. *Akashi Motojirō* 明石元二郎. 2 vols. Taihoku, Taiwan nichi nichi shimpōsha, 1928.

Kōnan shimbunsha 興南新聞社. ed. *Taiwan jinshi kan* 台湾人士鑑 (A who's who of Taiwan). Taihoku, 1943.

Kondō Toshikiyo 近藤俊清. *Taiwan no unmei* 台湾の運命 (Taiwan's fate). Tokyo, Misuzu shobō, 1961.

Kōshōkai yomikata kenkyūbu 光昭会讀方研究会. *Kōgakkō yō kokugo tokuhon kyōju saimoku hen ni kyōzai kenkyū* 公學校用國語讀本教授細目編に教材研究 (Research on teaching materials for common school readers). Taihoku, 1938.

Kublin, Hyman. "The Evolution of Japanese Colonialism." *Comparative Studies in Society and History* 2: 67–84 (1959).

"The Kukmin Sohak Tokpon." *Korean Repository* 4: 356–357 (September 1897).

Kuo T'ing-i 郭廷以. *T'ai-wan shih-shih kai-shuo* 台湾史事概説 (A survey of Taiwanese history). Taipei, Cheng-chung shu-chü, 1954.

Kuroda Ken'ichi 黒田謙一. *Nihon shokumin shisō shi* 日本植民思想史 (A history of colonial ideology in Japan). Tokyo, Kōbundō, 1942.

Kuroda Kōshirō 黒田甲子郎, ed. *Den Kenjirō den* 田健治郎伝 (A Life of Den Kenjirō). Tokyo, Den Kenjirō denki hensankai, 1932.

Lamley, Harry J. "The Taiwan Literati and Early Japanese Rule, 1895–1915." Ph.D. diss. University of Washington, 1964.

———"The 1895 Taiwan Republic." *Journal of Asian Studies* 27.4: 739–362 (August 1968).

———"Assimilation Efforts in Colonial Taiwan: The Fate of the 1914 Movement." *Monumenta Serica* 29: 496–520 (1970–71).

Levy, Howard S. *Chinese Footbinding: The History of a Curious Erotic Custom*. New York, Bell, 1967.

Lee Chong-sik. *The Politics of Korean Nationalism*. Berkeley, University of California Press, 1963.

Liao Han-ch'en 廖漢臣. "Yang-wen hui" (Yōbunkai) 揚文会 (Cultural advancement society). *T'ai-pei wen-wu* 2.4: 77: 82 (January 1954).

Lien Ya-tang 連雅堂. *T'ai-wan t'ung shih* 台湾通史 (A history of Taiwan). 3 vols. Taihoku, T'ai-wan-t'ung-shih-she, 1920–21.

Lin Chin-fa 林進発. *Taiwan tōchi shi* 台湾統治史 (A history of the Taiwan administration). Taihoku, Minshū kōronsha, 1935.

———*Taiwan hattatsu shi* 台湾発達史 (A history of Taiwan's development). Taihoku, Minshū kōronsha, 1936.

Lin Ching-ming 林景明. *Shirarezaru Taiwan: Taiwan dokuritsu undōka no sakebi* 知られざる台湾: 台湾独立運動下の叫び (The Taiwan yet to be known: the cry of Taiwanese independence activists). Tokyo, Sanshōdō 1970.

Lin Hsiung-hsiang 林熊祥. "T'ai-wan chien-sheng yü Liu Ming-ch'uan" 台湾建省與劉銘傳 (Taiwan's establishment as a province and Liu Ming-ch'uan). In Lin Hsiung-hsiang, ed., *T'ai-wan wen-hua lun-chi* 台湾文化論集 (Collected essays on the culture of Taiwan). Vol. 1. Taipei, Chung-hua-wen-hua-ch'un-pan-shih-yeh-yuan-hui, 1954.

McCully, Bruce T. *English Education and the Origins of Indian Nationalism.* New York, Columbia University Press, 1940; reprint: Gloucester, Mass., Peter Smith, 1966.

McDonald, Graeme. "George Leslie MacKay: Missionary Success in Nineteenth-Century Taiwan." In John K. Fairbank, ed., *Papers on China,* 21. Cambridge, Mass., Harvard East Asian Research Center, 1968.

McGovern, Janet B. M. *Among the Head-Hunters of Formosa.* London, T. Fisher Unwin, 1922.

MacKay, George Leslie. *From Far Formosa.* New York, Fleming H. Revell, 1895.

MacLeod, Duncan. *The Island Beautiful: The Story of Fifty Years in North Formosa.* Toronto, Board of Foreign Missions of the Presbyterian Church in Canada, 1923.

Mahajani, Usha. *Philippine Nationalism: External Challenge and Filipino Response, 1565–1946.* St. Lucia, Queensland, University of Queensland Press, 1971.

Mancall, Mark, ed. *Formosa Today.* New York, Praeger, 1964.

Mao Yeh-hsin 茂野信 and Lin Ch'ao-ching 林朝卿. *Taiwan no kosaku mondai* 台湾の小作問題 (Problems of tenant farmers in Taiwan). Taihoku, Yoshimura shōkai shuppansha, 1933.

Marr, David. *Vietnamese Anti-Colonialism, 1885–1925.* Berkeley, University of California Press, 1971.

Mason, Philip. *Patterns of Dominance.* London, Oxford University Press, 1959.

Matsuo Takayoshi 松尾尊兊. *Taishō demokurashii no kenkyū* 大正デモクラシーの研究 (Studies in Taishō democracy). Tokyo, Aoki shoten, 1966.

Memmi, Albert. *The Colonizer and the Colonized.* Boston, Beacon, 1967.

Miller, T. W. G. *Education in South-East Asia.* Sydney, Ian Novak, 1968.

Miyagawa Jirō 宮川次郎. *Taiwan no nōmin undō* 台湾の農民運動 (The farmers' movement in Taiwan). Taihoku, Takushoku tsūshinsha shisha, 1927.

———*Taiwan no shakai undō* 台湾の社会運動 (Social movements in Taiwan). Taihoku, Taiwan jitsugyōkaisha, 1929.

———*Taiwan no seiji undō* 台湾の政治運動 (Political movements in Taiwan). Taihoku, Taiwan jitsugyōkaisha, 1931.

Miyasaka Kōsaku 宮坂広作. *Kindai Nihon shakai kyōiku seisaku* 近代日本社会教育政策 (Modern Japan's social education policy). Tokyo, Kokudosha, 1966.

Mochiji Rokusaburō 持地六三郎. *Taiwan shokumin seisaku* 台湾植民政策 (The colonial policy of Taiwan). Tokyo, Fuzanbō, 1912.

Mombushō 文部省. *Gakusei gojūnen shi* 學制五十年史 (A fifty-year history of the education system). Tokyo, 1922.

————*Meiji ikō kyōiku seido hattatsu shi* 明治以降教育制度発達史 (A history of the devlopment of the education system from Meiji on). 12 vols. Tokyo, 1938.

————*Gakusei kyūjūnen shi* 學制九十年史 (A ninety-year history of the education system). Tokyo, 1964.

————*Gakusei hyakunen shi* 學制百年史 (A hundred-year history of the education system). 2 vols. Tokyo, 1972.

————*Jinjō shōgakkō tokuhon, maki ni* 尋常小學讀本卷二 (Ordinary primary school reader, number two). Tokyo, 1913.

————*Jinjō shōgakkō tokuhon, maki ni.* Tokyo, 1926.

————*Jinjō shōgakkō tokuhon, maki san* (Ordinary primary school reader, number three). Tokyo, 1912.

————*Jinjō shōgakkō tokuhon, maki san.* Tokyo, 1923.

————*Jinjō shōgakkō tokuhon, maki yon* (Ordinary . . . four). Tokyo, 1913.

————*Jinjō shōgakkō tokuhon, maki yon.* Tokyo, 1919.

————*Jinjō shōgakkō tokuhon, maki go.* (Ordinary . . . five). Tokyo, 1914.

————*Jinjō shōgakkō tokuhon, maki go.* Tokyo, 1920.

————*Jinjō shogakkō tokuhon, maki roku* (Ordinary . . . six). Tokyo, 1915.

————*Jinjō shōgakkō tokuhon, maki shichi* (Ordinary . . . seven). Tokyo, 1914.

————*Jinjō shōgakkō tokuhon, maki shichi.* Tokyo, 1920, 1930.

————*Jinjō shōgakkō tokuhon, maki hachi* (Ordinary . . . eight). Tokyo, 1913.

————*Jinjō shōgakkō tokuhon, maki hachi.* Tokyo, 1926.

————*Jinjō shōgakkō tokuhon, maki kyū* (Ordinary . . . nine). Tokyo, 1912.

————*Jinjō shōgakkō tokuhon, maki jūichi* (Ordinary . . . eleven). Tokyo, 1914.

————*Jinjō shōgakkō tokuhon, maki jūni* (Ordinary . . . twelve). Tokyo, 1926.

————*Jinjō shōgakkō shūshinsho, maki ni* 尋常小學修身書卷二 (Ordinary primary school ethics textbook, number two). Tokyo, 1919.

————*Jinjō shōgakkō shūshinsho, maki san* (Ordinary . . . three). Tokyo, 1930.

————*Jinjō shōgakkō shūshinsho, maki yon* (Ordinary . . . four). Tokyo, 1927.

————*Jinjō shōgakkō shūshinsho, maki go* (Ordinary . . . five). Tokyo, 1930.

————*Jinjo shōgakkō shūshinsho, maki roku* (Ordinary . . . six). Tokyo, 1930.

————*Yomikata 1* ヨミカター (How to read, 1). Osaka, 1941.

————*Yomikata 2.* Osaka, 1941.

————*Yomikata 3.* Osaka, 1941.

————*Yomikata 4.* Osaka, 1941.

Moody, Campbell N. *The Heathen Heart: An Account of the Reception of the Gospel among the Chinese of Formosa.* Edinburgh, Oliphant, Anderson, Ferrier, 1907.

Mori Ushinosuke 森丑之助. *Taiwan banzoku zufu* 台湾蕃俗図布 (Illustrations of aboriginal customs in Taiwan). Taihoku, Rinji Taiwan kyūkan chōsakai, 1915.

————*Taiwan banzoku shi* 台湾蕃俗史 (A history of the aborigines of Taiwan). Taihoku, Rinji Taiwan kyūkan chōsakai, 1917.

Morosawa Yōko 両沢葉子. *Onna no rekishi* 女の歴史 (A history of women). 2 vols. Tokyo, Miraisha, 1970.

Munakata Seiya 宗像誠也. *Kyōiku to kyōiku seisaku* 教育と教育政策 (Education and education policy). Tokyo, Iwanami shinsho, 1961.

————and Kokubu Ichitarō 國分一太郎. *Nihon no kyōiku* 日本の教育 (Education in Japan). Tokyo, Iwanami shinsho, 1962.

Myers, Ramon H. "Taiwan under Ch'ing Imperial Rule, 1684–1895: The Traditional Order," *Journal of the Institute of Chinese Studies of the Chinese*

University of Hongkong 4.2: 495–520 (1971).

Myrdal, Gunnar. *Asian Drama: An Inquiry into the Poverty of Nations.* New York, Pantheon, 1968.

Naito Hideo, ed. *Taiwan: A Unique Colonial Record, 1937–1938.* Tokyo, Kokusai Nippon kyōkai, 1938.

Najita Tetsuo. *Hara Kei in the Politics of Compromise, 1905–1915.* Cambridge, Mass., Harvard University Press, 1967.

Naka Arata 仲新. *Nihon kindai kyōiku shi* 日本近代教育史 (A history of modern education in Japan). Tokyo, Kōdansha, 1973.

Nakagoe Eiji 中越榮二. *Taiwan no shakai kyōiku* 台湾の社会教育 (Social education in Taiwan). Taihoku, Taiwan no shakai kyōiku kankōsho, 1936.

Nakamura Tetsu 中村哲. *Shokuminchi tōchihō no konpon mondai* 植民地統治法の根本問題 (Fundamental problems of colonial administration). Tokyo, Nihon hyōronsha, 1943.

Nakanishi Inosuke 中西伊之助. *Taiwan kenbunki* 台湾見聞記 (Notes from a trip to Taiwan). Tokyo, Jissensha, 1937.

Nakajima Tarō 中島太郎. *Kindai Nihon kyōiku seido shi* 近代日本教育制度史 (A history of the education system in modern Japan). Tokyo, Yamasaki shoten, 1966.

Nihon rekishi daijiten henshū iinkai 日本歴史大辞典編集委員会. *Nihon rekishi daijiten* 日本歴史大辞典 (Dictionary of Japanese history). 10 vols. Tokyo, Kawade shobōshinsha, 1968–1970.

Nitobe Inazō 新渡戸稲造. *Shokumin seisaku kōgi oyobi ronbunshū* 植民政策講義及び論文集 (Collected lectures and essays on colonial policy). Tokyo, Iwanami shoten, 1943.

Nu, U. *Burma under the Japanese.* London, MacMillan, 1954.

Ō Ikutoku 王育徳. *Taiwan: kumon suru sono rekishi* 台湾: 苦悶するその歴史 (Taiwan: Her agony and her history). Tokyo, Kobundō, 1964.

Okamatsu Santarō. *Provisional Report of Investigations of Laws and Customs of the Island of Formosa.* Kobe. 1902.

Ōno Ken'ichi 大野謙一. *Chōsen kyōiku mondai kanken* 朝鮮教育問題管見 (Views on the problems of education in Korea). Keijō, Chōsen kyōiku kai, 1936.

Osborne, Milton E. *The French Presence in Cochinchina and Cambodia.* Ithaca, Cornell University Press, 1969.

Ōtsuka Kiyotoshi 大塚清賢, ed. *Yakushin Taiwan daikan (tsuzuki)* 躍進台湾大觀 (續) (A survey of progressive Taiwan [continued]). Tokyo, Chūgai mainichi shimbun, 1939.

Ozawa Yūsaku 小沢有作. *Minzoku kyōiku ron* 民族教育論 (On people's education). Tokyo, Meiji tosho, 1966.

Ōzono Ichizō 大園市藏, ed. *Taiwan jimbutsu shi* 台湾人物史 (A who's who of Taiwan). Taihoku, 1916.

———*Taiwan shisei yonjūnen shi* 台湾始政四十年史 (A forty-year history of Taiwan's administration). Tokyo, Nihon shokuminchi hihansha, 1935.

Pak Kyŏng-sik 朴慶植. *Nihon teikokushugi no Chōsen shihai* 日本帝國主義の朝鮮支配 (Rule of Korea under Japanese imperialism). 2 vols. Tokyo, Aoki shoten, 1973.

Peng Ming-min. *A Taste of Freedom: Memoirs of a Formosan Independence Leader.* New York, Holt, Rinehart, Winston, 1972.

Raghuvanshi, V. P. S. *Indian Nationalist Movement and Thought.* Agra, Lakshmi Narain Agarwal Educational Publishers, 1959.

Rekishi kyōiku kenkyūkai 歴史教育研究会. *Joshi shi kenkyū* 女子史研究 (Studies in women's history). Tokyo, Shikai Shobō, 1937.

Riban no tomo 理蕃の友. *Taiwan bankai tenbō* 台湾蕃界展望 (The world of Taiwan's aborigines). Taihoku, 1915.

Rizal, José. *Political and Historical Writings*. Trans. Encarnacion Alzona. 7 vols. Manila, National Heroes Commission, 1964.

——— *The Subversive*. Trans. León M. Guerrero. New York, W. W. Norton, 1968.

Roff, William R. *The Origins of Malay Nationalism*. New Haven, Yale University Press, 1967.

Royama Masamichi and Takeuchi Tatsuji. *The Philippine Polity: A Japanese View*. New Haven, Yale University Southeast Asia Studies, 1967.

Russell, Charles Edward. *The Outlook for the Philippines*. New York, Century, 1922.

Rutter, Owen. *Through Formosa: An Account of Japan's Island Colony*. New York, Institute of Pacific Relations, 1948.

Satō Genji 佐藤源治. *Taiwan kōmin rensei kōwa* 台湾皇民練成講話 (Lectures on training the imperial people of Taiwan). Taihoku, Niitakadō shoten, 1941.

——— *Taiwan kyōiku no shinten* 台湾教育の進展 (Progress of education in Taiwan). Taihoku, Taiwan shuppan bunka kabushiki kaisha, 1943.

Satō Masakura 佐藤政藏. *Kaireɨ yonjūnen no Taiwan* 改隷四十年の台湾 (Taiwan's forty years as a dependency). Taihoku, Taiwan kankōkai, 1935.

Shi Mei 史明. *Taiwanjin yonhyakunen shi* 台湾人四百年史 (Four hundred years of Taiwanese history). Tokyo, Otoba shobō, 1962.

——— *Taiwan—sono genzai to shōrai* 台湾・その現在と將来 (Taiwan: The present and the future). Tokyo, Shūhō shuppan, 1965.

Shibata Ren 柴田廉. *Taiwan dōkasaku ron* 台湾同化策論 (On Taiwan's assimilation policy). Taihoku, kōbunkan, 1923.

Shinano kyōikukai 信濃教育会. *Izawa Shūji senshū* 伊沢修二選集 (Selected works of Izawa Shūji). Tokyo, 1958.

Shinobu Seizaburō 信夫清三郎. *Gotō Shimpei—kagakuteki seijika no shōgai* 後藤新平—科学的政治家の生涯 (Gotō Shimpei: the career of a scientific statesman). Tokyo, Hakubunkan, 1941.

——— *Taishō seiji shi* 大正政治史 (A political history of Taishō). 4 vols. Tokyo, Kawade shobō, 1952.

Shinchiku shū 新竹州. *Kyōiku ronbunshū* 教育論文集 (Collected essays on education). Taichū, Taiwan shimbun, 1922.

Silberman, Bernard S., and H. D. Harootunian, eds. *Japan in Crisis: Essays on Taishō Democracy*. Princeton, Princeton University Press, 1974.

Sugiyama Yasunori 杉山靖憲. *Taiwan rekidai sōtoku no chiseki* 台湾歴代総督の治績 (Successive administrations of the governors-general of Taiwan). Tokyo, Teikoku chihō gyōsei gakkai, 1922.

Suzuki Sakutarō 鈴木作太郎. *Taiwan no banzoku kenkyū* 台湾の蕃族研究 (Studies of the aborigines of Taiwan). Taihoku, Kita Taiwan shiseki kankōkai, 1932.

Taihoku teikoku daigaku dozoku jinrui gaku kenkyūshitsu chōsa 台北帝國大學土族人類學研究室調査. *Taiwan takasago zoku keitō shozoku no kenkyū* 台湾高砂族系統所屬の研究 (The Taiwan aborigines: A genealogy and classificatory study). 2 vols. Taihoku, 1935.

Taiwan jihō

Taiwan kyōiku enkaku shi 台湾教育沿革史 (A record of the development of education in Taiwan). Taiwan kyōiku kai, ed. Taihoku, 1939.

Taiwan nichi nichi shimpō 台湾日日新報 (Taiwan daily news). Taiwan nichi nichi shimpōsha. *Taiwan ichiran* 台湾一覧 (An outline of Taiwan). Taihoku, 1912.

T'ai-wan-sheng wu-shih-i-nien-lai t'ung-chi t'i-yao 臺灣省五十一年来統計提要 (A statistical summary of the province of Taiwan for the past fifty-one years). ed. T'ai-wan sheng hsing-cheng-chang-kuan kung-shu t'ung-chi-shih. Taipei, 1946.

Taiwan shimpō 台湾新報 (Taiwan news). Taiwan shimpōsha, ed. *Taiwan jinshi kan* 台湾人士鑑 (A who's who of Taiwan). Taihoku, 1934.

————*Taiwan jinshi kan* (A who's who of Taiwan). Taihoku, 1937.

Taiwan sōtokufu 臺灣総督府. *Kōgakkō chirisho, maki ni* 公学校地理書卷二 (Common school geography textbook, number two). Taihoku, 1921.

————*Kōgakkō kokugo kyōjusho, dai ichinen yō* 公学校國語教授書第一年用 (Common school Japanese language teaching manual for grade one). Taihoku, 1913.

————*Kōgakkō kokugo kyōjusho, dai ninen yō* (Common school Japanese language teaching manual for grade two). Taihoku, 1914.

————*Kōgakkō kokugo kyōjusho, dai sannen yō* (Common school Japanese language teaching manual for grade three). Taihoku, 1915.

————*Kōgakkō yō kokugo tokuhon, maki ni* 公学校用國語讀本卷二 (Common school reader, number two). Taihoku, 1923, 1931.

————*Kōgakkō yō kokugo tokuhon, maki san* (Common school reader, number three). Taihoku, 1923, 1931.

————*Kōgakkō yō kokugo tokuhon, maki yon* (Common . . . four). Taihoku, 1923, 1931.

————*Kōgakkō yō kokugo tokuhon, maki go* (Common . . . five). Taihoku, 1924, 1930.

————*Kōgakkō yō kokugo tokuhon, maki roku* (Common . . . six). Taihoku, 1924, 1931.

————*Kōgakkō yō kokugo tokuhon, maki shichi* (Common . . . seven). Taihoku, 1924, 1931.

————*Kōgakkō yō kokugo tokuhon, maki hachi* (Common . . . eight). Taihoku, 1924, 1931.

————*Kōgakkō yō kokugo tokuhon, maki kyū* (Common . . . nine). Taihoku, 1925, 1931.

————*Kōgakkō yō kokugo tokuhon, maki jū* (Common . . . ten). Taihoku, 1925, 1931.

————*Kōgakkō yō kokugo tokuhon, maki jūichi* (Common . . . eleven). Taihoku, 1925, 1931.

————*Kōgakkō yō kokugo tokuhon, maki jūni* (Common . . . twelve). Taihoku, 1925, 1931.

————*Kōgakkō nōgyō kyōjusho, dai rokunen yō* 公学校農業教授書第六年用 (Common school agriculture teaching manual for grade six). Taihoku, 1915.

————*Kōgakkō rikasho, maki san* 公学校理科書卷三 (Common school science textbook, number three). Taihoku, 1924.

————*Kōgakkō sanjutsuka kyōzai, maki ichi* 公学校算術科教材卷一 (Common school arithmetic teaching materials, book one). Taihoku, 1909.

————*Kōgakkō sanjutsuka kyōzai, maki ni* (Common school arithmetic teaching materials, book two). Taihoku, 1910.

————*Kōgakkō sanjutsuka kyōzai, maki san* (Common school arithmetic teaching materials, book three). Taihoku, 1911.

————*Kōgakkō shūshinsho, maki ichi, kyōshi yō* 公学校修身書卷一教師用 (Common school ethics textbook, number one, teacher's version). Taihoku, 1913.

————*Kōgakkō shūshinsho, maki ichi, kyōshi yō.* Taihoku, 1928.

————*Kōgakkō shūshinsho, maki ichi, kyōshi yō.* Taihoku, 1930.

————*Kōgakkō kōtō ka shūshinsho, maki ichi, kyōshi yō* 公学校高等科修身書卷一教師用 (Common school advanced course ethics textbook, number one, teacher's version). Taihoku, 1933.

————*Kōgakkō shūshinsho, maki ni, jidō yō* 公学校修身書卷二児童用 (Common school ethics textbook, number two, pupil's version). Taihoku, 1930.

————*Kōgakkō shūshinsho, maki ni, jidō yō.* Taihoku, 1931.

————*Kōgakkō shūshinsho, maki ni, jidō yō.* Taihoku, 1941.

————*Kōgakkō shūshinsho, maki yon, jidō yō* (Common school ethics . . . four, pupil's version). Taihoku, 1931.

————*Kōgakkō shūshinsho, maki roku, jidō yō* (Common school ethics . . . six, pupil's version). Taihoku, 1931.

————*Kokugo kyōkasho ichi* 國語教科書一 (Japanese language textbook one). Taihoku, 1941.

————*Riban gaiyō* 理蕃概要 (A survey of aborigine control). Taihoku, 1913.

————*Taiwan banjin jijō* 台湾蕃人事情 (Conditions of Taiwan aborigines). Taihoku, 1900.

————*Taiwan bansei shi* 台湾蕃政史 (History of the administration of Taiwan aborigines). Taihoku, 1904.

————*Taiwan jijō* 台湾事情 (Conditions in Taiwan). Taihoku, 1916–1942.

————*Taiwan ni okeru gakkō jidō ni kansuru kenkyū* 台湾に於る學校児童に関する研究 (A study of schoolchildren in Taiwan). Taihoku, 1923.

————*Taiwan ni okeru yūryō buraku shisetsu gaikyō* 台湾に於る優良部落施設概況 (A survey of outstanding village facilities in Taiwan). Taihoku, 1940.

————*Taiwan no gakkō kyōiku* 台湾の学校教育 (School education in Taiwan). Taihoku, 1940.

————*Taiwan no kyōiku* 台湾の教育 (Education in Taiwan). Taihoku, 1930.

————*Taiwan shakai jigyō yōran* 台湾社会事業要覧 (A summary of the social services of Taiwan). Taihoku, 1935, 1939.

————*Taiwan shakai kyōiku gaiyō* 台湾社会教育概要 (A survey of social education in Taiwan). Taihoku, 1935.

————*Taiwan sōtokufu gakuji dai jūninen* 台湾総督府学事第十二年 (Twelve years of schools in Taiwan). Taihoku, 1913.

————*Taiwan sōtokufu kampō* 台湾総督府官報 (Official bulletin of the government general of Taiwan). Taihoku, 1943.

————*Taiwan tōchi gaiyō* 台湾統治概要 (A summary of the administration of Taiwan). Taihoku, 1945.

————*Taiwan tōchi sōran* 台湾統治總覧 (A general survey of the administration in Taiwan). Taihoku, 1908.

————*Taiwan sōtokufu tōkeisho* 台湾総督府統計書 (Statistical yearbooks of the government general of Taiwan). Taihoku, 1899–1944.

Taiwan sōtokufu banmukyoku 台湾総督府蕃務局. *Riban shikō* 理蕃誌稿 (Aborigines of Taiwan). Taihoku, 1932.

Taiwan sōtokufu banzoku chōsakai 台湾総督府蕃族調査会. *Taiwan banzoku kanshū kenkyū* 台湾蕃族慣習研究 (A study of the customs of Taiwan aborigines). 18 vols. Taihoku, 1921.

Taiwan sōtokufu keimukyoku 台湾総督府警務局. *Takasago zoku no kyōiku* 高砂族の教育 (Education of the aborigines of Taiwan). Taihoku, 1941.

Taiwan sōtokufu keisatsu enkaku shi 台湾総督府警察沿革史 (A history of the Taiwan government-general police). Taiwan sōtokufu. 4 vols. Taihoku, 1933–41.

Taiwan sōtokufu kokugo gakkō 台湾総督府國語学校. *Taiwan sōtokufu kokugo gakkō ichiran* 台湾総督府國語学校一覧 (Prospectus of the Japanese Language School). Taihoku, 1917.

Taiwan sōtokufu naimukyoku gakumuka 台湾総督府内務局学務課. *Taiwan gaku jijō (1919)* 台湾学事情 (Taiwan school affairs, 1919). Taihoku, 1919.

Taiwan taikansha 台湾大観社. *Saikin no nanbu Taiwan* 最近の南部台湾 (Southern Taiwan in recent times). Taihoku, 1923.

Taiwan tsūshinsha 台湾通信社. *Taiwan nenkan* 台湾年鑑 (Taiwan year book). Taihoku, 1925–1944.

Takekoshi Yosaburō 竹越與三郎. *Taiwan tōchi shi* 台湾統治史 (A history of the administration of Taiwan). Tokyo, Hakubunkan, 1905.

———*Japanese Rule in Formosa*. Trans. George Braithwaite. London, Longmans, 1907.

———"Japan's Colonial Policy." *Oriental Review* 3.2: 102–103 (December 1912).

Takemura Toyotoshi 竹村豊俊, ed. *Taiwan taiiku shi* 台湾体育史 (A history of physical education in Taiwan). Taihoku, Taiwan taiiku kyōkai, 1933.

Takeuchi Sadayoshi 武内貞義. *Taiwan kanshū* 台湾慣習 (Customs of Taiwan). Taihoku, Taiwan nichi nichi shimpōsha, 1915.

———*Taiwan* 台湾. Taihoku, Taiwan nichi nichi shimpōsha, 1928.

Thompson, Virginia. *French Indo-China*. London, Allen and Unwin, 1937.

———and Richard Adloff. *Cultural Institutions and Educational Policy in South East Asia*. New York, Institute of Pacific Relations, 1948.

Tōgō Minoru 東鄉實. "Hidōka ron" 非同化論 (In opposition to integration). *Taiwan jihō* 23: 16–21 (June 1911).

———and Satō Shirō 佐藤四郎. *Taiwan shokumin hattatsu shi* 台湾植民発達史 (A history of Taiwan's colonial development). Taihoku, Kōbunkan, 1916.

Tōhoku daigaku 東北大學. *Tōhoku daigaku gojūnen shi* 東北大學五十年史 (A fifty-year history of Tōhoku University). Sendai, 1932.

Tokutomi Iichirō 德富猪一郎. *Kōshaku Katsura Tarō den* 公爵桂太郎傳 (A life of Prince Katsura). 2 vols. Tokyo, Katsura kōshaku kinen jigyōkai, 1917.

Trevelyan, Charles E. *On the Education of the People of India*. London, Longman, Orme, Brown, Green, Longmans, 1938.

Ts'ai P'ei-huo 蔡培火. *Nihon honkokumin ni atō* 日本國民に與ふ (Attention, homeland Japanese!). Tokyo, Taiwan mondai kenkyūkai, 1928.

———"Taiwan ni okeru kokuji mondai" 台湾に於る國字問題 (The problem of written Japanese in Taiwan), *Kyōiku* 4.8: 1233–1238 (August 1938).

———et al., eds. *T'ai-wan min-tsu yün-tung shih* 台湾民族運動史 (A history of the Taiwanese nationalist movement). Taipei, Tsu-li-wan-pao-ts'ung-shu-pien-chi-wei-yuan-hui, 1971.

Tsang Chiu-sam. *Nationalism in School Education in China*. Hongkong, Progressive Publishers, 1933.

Tsurumi, E. Patricia. "Taiwan under Kodama Gentarō and Gotō Shimpei." In Albert Craig, ed., *Papers on Japan,* 4. Harvard East Asian Research Center, Cambridge, Mass., 1967.

Tsurumi Yūsuke 鶴見祐輔, ed. *Gotō Shimpei den* 後藤新平傳 (A life of Gotō Shimpei). 4 vols. Tokyo, Gotō Shimpei denki hensankai, 1937–1938.

Van Gulik, Robert H. *Sexual Life in Ancient China.* Leiden, Brill, 1961.

Van Niel, Robert. *The Emergence of the Modern Indonesian Elite.* The Hague and Bandung, W. Van Hoeve, 1960.

Wakamori Tarō 和歌森太郎 and Yamamoto Fujie 山本藤枝. *Nihon no josei shi* 日本の女性史 (A history of Japanese women). 4 vols. Tokyo, Shukyōsha, 1965–1966.

Ward, W. Peter. "The Oriental Immigrant and Canada's Protestant Clergy, 1858–1925." *B.C. Studies* 22: 40–55 (Summer 1974).

Wilson, Richard W. *Learning to be Chinese: The Political Socialization of Children in Taiwan.* Cambridge, Mass., M.I.T. Press, 1970.

Wolf, Margery. *Women and the Family in Rural Taiwan.* Stanford, Stanford University Press, 1972.

Wyndham, H. A. *Native Education: Ceylon, Java, Formosa, Philippines, French Indo-China, and British Malaya.* London, Royal Institute of International Affairs, 1933.

Yabes, Leopoldo Y., ed. *José Rizal on His Centenary.* Quezon City, Office of Research Coordination, University of the Philippines, 1963.

Yamabe Kentarō 山辺健太郎, ed. *Gendai shi shiryō: Taiwan I* 現代史資料: 台湾 I; *Gendai shi shiryō: Taiwan II* (Modern historical documents: Taiwan I; Modern historical documents: Taiwan II). 45 vols. Tokyo, Misuzu shobō, 1962–1973.

————*Nihon tōchika no Chōsen* 日本統治下の朝鮮 (Korea under Japanese administration). Tokyo, Iwanami shoten, 1971.

Yamakawa Hitoshi 山川均. *Shokumin seisakuka no Taiwan* 植民政策下の台湾 (Taiwan under colonial policy). Tokyo, Purebusu shuppansha, 1926.

————*Yamakawa Hitoshi zenshū* 山川均全集 (Collected works of Yamakawa Hitoshi). 20 vols. Tokyo, Keisō shobō, 1966.

Yamamoto Miono 山本美越乃. *Shokuminchi seisaku kenkyū* 植民地政策研究 (Studies in colonial policy). Tokyo, Kōbun shobō, 1920.

Yamazaki Tanshō 山崎丹照. *Gaichi tōchi kikō no kenkyū* 外地統治機構の研究 (A study of the structures of overseas administrations). Tokyo, Takayama shoin, 1943.

Yanaihara Tadao 矢内原忠雄. *Teikokushugika no Taiwan* 帝國主義下の台湾 (Taiwan under imperialism). Tokyo, Iwanami shoten, 1934.

————*Yanaihara Tadao zenshū* 矢内原忠雄全集 (Collected works of Yanaihara Tadao). 29 vols. Tokyo, Iwanami shinsho, 1963–1965.

Yeh Jung-chung 葉榮鐘, comp. *Lin Hsien-t'ang hsien-sheng chi-nien chi* 林獻堂先生紀念集 (Collected essays in commemoration of Lin Hsien-t'ang). 3 vols. Taichung, Lin Hsien-tang hsien-sheng chi-nien pien-tsuan-wei-yüan-hui, 1960.

Yoshino Hidekimi 吉野秀公. *Taiwan kyōiku shi* 台湾教育史. Taiwan nichi nichi shimpōsha, 1927.

Yuge Kōtarō 弓削幸太郎. *Chōsen no kyōiku* 朝鮮の教育 (Education in Korea). Tokyo, Jiyū tōkyūsha, 1923.

Glossary

Abe Isoo 安部磯雄
Amoy 厦門
Andō Sadayoshi 安東貞美
Asahi shimbun 朝日新聞
Asō Hisashi 麻生久
baidoku gaku 梅(黴)毒學
banjin 蕃人
Banjin tokuhon 蕃人讀本
Bimbō monogatari 貧乏物語
bungo 文語
"Bunka seiji to gakusei kaikaku"
　文化政治と学制改革
buraku 部落
changoro チャンゴロ
Chekiang 浙江
Cheng Ch'eng-kung 鄭成功
Chian keisatsuhō 治安警察法
Chiang Kai-shek 蔣介石
Chiang Wei-shui 蔣渭水
Chihisagobe 小子部
chōkan 長官
daigaku igaku senmon bu 大學医學
　専門部
Dai Nihon heiwa kyōkai 大日本平和
　協会
dekasegi 出稼ぎ
dōka 同化
Dōshisha 同志社
Ebara Soroku 江原素六
eisei seido 衛生制度
Erh-lin 二林
eta 穢多
Fan Pen-liang 范本梁
Feng-shan 鳳山
Fukuzawa Yukichi 福澤諭吉
Furuya Sadao 古屋貞雄
gakkō kyōiku 學校教育
gakubu san'yo kan 學部参与官
gakumon 學問
gakumu bu 學務部
gakusei 学制
Genji 源氏

Giran (I-lan) 宜蘭
goyō shinshi 御用紳士
Gyōminkai 曉民會
Hanai Takuzō 花井卓藏
heichi min 平地民
Heike 平家
Heitō (Pingtung) 屏東
hokō (pao-chia) 保甲
Horiuchi Tsuguo 堀内次雄
hoshū ka 補習科
hōtai gaku 繃帶學
Hsieh Hsüeh-hung 謝雪紅
hsien 縣
"Hsien-t'ang hsien-sheng yü T'ung-
　hua wei" 献堂先生與同化会
Hsü Nai-chang 許乃昌
Huang Yü-chieh 黃玉階
hyanggyo 鄉校
hyōgikai 評議会
igaku senmon gakkō 医学専門学校
i-hsüeh 義學
ine kari 稲刈
Inoue Den 井上伝
Inoue Kaoru 井上薫
Insu 仁粹
ippan jinrui 一般人類
isei 医生
Ishizuka Eizō 石塚英藏
Itō Jinsai 伊藤仁斉
Izumi Tetsu 泉哲
Izumo 出雲
jitsuka kōtō jogakkō 實科高等女學校
Kabayama Sukenori 樺山資紀
Kagi (Chia-i) 嘉義
Kaigun kōza 海軍講座
"Kako Taiwan no shakai undō" 過去
　台湾の社会運動
Kan Te-chung 甘得中
kanbun 漢文
Kanda 神田
Kang Tŏk-sang 姜德相
kan'i kōgyō 簡易工業
kanji 監事

"Kanjin kyōiku ni tsuite no byūken" 韓人教育についての謬見

Kanritsu Aichi shihan gakkō 官立愛知師範學校

Karenkō (Hualien-kang) 花蓮江

Katō Haruki 加藤春城

Kawakami Hajime 河上肇

Keelung 基隆

keimō undō 啓蒙運動

kendō 剣道

kenkyū ka 研究科

Kigen setsu 紀元節

Kimura Kyō 木村匡

"kenpei seijika no Chōsen" 憲兵政治下の朝鮮

Kinbara Meizen 金原明善

kinrō 勤労

kin'yu-ka 金融課

Kiyose Ichirō 清瀬一郎

Kobi (Hu-wei) 扈尾

Kodama Gentarō 児玉源太郎

kōgakkō 公学校

kōgyō 工業

Kokka kyōiku sha 國家教育社

kokko 國庫

"Kokugo gakkō jidai no fuzoku jo-gakkō" 國語學校時代の附屬女學校

Kokugo nōgyō tokuhon 國語農業讀本

kokumin gakkō 國民學校

kokumin seishin 國民精神

kokumintaru no seikaku 國民たるの性格

Kokushoku seinen renmei 黒色青年連盟

kokutai 國体

kōmin 皇民

Kōmin hōkō kai 皇民奉公会

kōminka 皇民化

kōshūsho 講習所

kōtō ka 高等科

Ku Hsien-jung 辜顯榮

Kunmō kyūri zukai 訓蒙窮理図解

Kuomintang 國民党

Kurume 久留米

Kwangju 光州

Kwangtung 廣東

kyōgaku 共学

Kyoiku 教育

Kyōiku jiron 教育時論

kyōiku sho 教育所

kyōka 教化

kyōkan 教官

Kyūshū 九州

Liang Ch'i-ch'ao 梁啓超

lien-chuang 聯荘

Lien Wên-ch'ing 連温卿

Lin Ch'eng-lu 林呈祿

Lin Hsiung-cheng 林熊徵

Lin Pen-yuan 林本源

ling-sheng 廩生

Matsukata Masayoshi 松方正義

Meiji Gakuin 明治學院

Minobe Tatsukichi 美濃部達吉

minponshugi 民本主義

minseibu 民政部

minseichōkan 民政長官

minsei kyoku 民政局

minzoku yūwa 民族融和

Mitsubishi 三菱

miso 味噌

Mizuno Jun 水野遵

Mori Arinori 森有礼

myŏn 面

Nagai Ryutarō 永井柳太郎

naimu kyoku 内務局

Nihon nōmin kumiai rengō 日本農民組合連合

Nihon no ryōmin 日本の良民

Nihon rōdō nōmintō 日本労働農民党

Ninomiya Sontoku 二宮尊徳

Nogi Maresuke 乃木稀典

Ogyū Sorai 荻生祖來

Ōhashi Sutesaburō 大橋捨三郎

ŏnmun 言文

on o wasureruna 恩を忘れるな

Ōsaka asahi shimbun 大阪朝日新聞

Ōsaka mainichi 大阪毎日

Ōsugi Sakae 大杉栄

Ōtake Kan'ichi 大竹貫一

Ozaki Yukio 尾崎行雄

Ozawa Hajime 小沢一

P'eng Hua-ying 彭華英

P'eng T'sai-a-hsin 彭蔡阿信

Rēnin tsuitō kai レーニン追悼会

rinji kyōiku kaigi 臨時教育会議

Rōgakkai 労學会

"Ryōtō oyobi Taiwan tōchi ni kansuru tōgi" 遼東及び台湾統治に関する討議

saibai 栽培

saikei rei 最敬礼
Saitō Makoto 斉藤實
Sakai Toshihiko 堺利彦
Sakatani Yoshirō 坂谷芳郎
Sakuma Samata 佐久門左馬太
seiban 生蕃
Seiyūkai 政友会
Sejong 世宗王
Seki Naohiko 関直彦
senmon gakkō 専門学校
she-hui t'uan-t'i 社会團体
Shibata Yoshisaburō 柴田善三郎
Shidehara Hiroshi 幣原坦
shidō kantoku 指導監督
Shimada Saburō 島田三郎
shin 眞
Shinchiku (Hsin-chu) 新竹
Shinjinkai 新人会
Shinminkai 新民会
shiritsu shihan gakkō 私立師範學校
Shisangyan (Chih-san-yen) 芝山巖
shobō (shu-fang) 書房
"shobō gijuku ni kan suru kitei" 書房
　義塾に関する規程
shōgakkō 小學校
shōgakkō kyōin no kokoroe 小学校教
　員の心得
shoki kan 書記官
shūmitsu 周密
Sŏ Choe-p'il 徐載弼
sŏdang 書堂
Sŏngjong 成宗王
Tagawa Daikichirō 田川大吉郎
Taichū (Taichung) 台中
Taihoku (Taipei) 台北
Taihoku joshi kōtō gakuin 台北女子
　高等學院
Taihoku seinen dokusho kai 台北青年
　讀書会
Taihoku seinen taiiku kai 台北青年体
　育会
Tainan 台南
Taisō denshū jo 体操伝習所
Taitō (Taitung) 台東
Taiwan bunka kyōkai 台湾文化協会
Taiwan chihōjichi renmei 台湾地方
　自治聯盟
Taiwan dōka kai 台湾同化会
Taiwan gikai kisei dōmeikai 台湾議会
　期成同盟会

Taiwan jimu kyoku 台湾事務局
Taiwan kyōiku 台湾教育
Taiwan kyōikukai 台湾教育会
Taiwan minshu tō 台湾民主党
"Taiwan no futsū kyōiku" 台湾の普
　通教育
"Taiwan no kyōkasho hensan ni
　tsuite" 台湾の教科書編纂について
Taiwan nōmin kumiai 台湾農民組合
Taiwan seinen 台湾青年
Taiwan seinenkai 台湾青年会
Takada Shuhan 高田早苗
Takagi Tomoeda 高木友枝
Takao (Kaohsiung) 高雄
Tamsui 淡水
Tanaka Giichi 田中義一
tera koya 寺子屋
Terauchi Masatake 寺内正毅
T'ien Wei 田尾
t'ing 廳
Tokyo bijutsu gakkō 東京美術学校
Tokyo joshi kōtō shihan gakkō 東京
　女子高等師範学校
Tokyo kōtō shihan gakkō 東京高等
　師範学校
Tokyo mainichi 東京毎日
Tongnip shinmun 独立新聞
tori ire 取入れ
Tsao-tun 草屯
tsuzurikata 綴方
t'uan-lien 團練
Uchida Kakichi 内田嘉吉
Uchimura Kanzō 内村鑑三
Uemura Masahisa 植村正久
Uzawa Fusaaki 鵜澤聰明
Wang Min-ch'uan 王敏川
Watanabe Noboru 渡邊暢
Yamakawa Kikue 山川菊栄
Yamagata Aritomo 山縣有朋
Yamaguchi Koshizu 山口小静
Yamashina Nobutsugu 山科宣次
Yamato 大和
yangban 両班
"Yōbunkai ni okeru ensetsu" 揚文会
　における演説
Yoshino Sakuzō 吉野作造
yukata 浴衣
Yun-lin 雲林

Index

Aborigines, 2, 3, 4-5; 9; supervision of, by Ch'ing officials, 6; attempts to educate, 45

Absenteeism, in common schools, 19-20, 61-62

Activists, *see* Conservative activists; Radical activists

Agresseau, Henri-François d', 134

Aims and achievements, of Japanese education in Taiwan, 38-44, 215-217

Akashi Motojirō, 95, 97, 103, 107, 131, 216; assimilation policy of, 80, 81-91, 92; and education rescript, 99, 102

Algeria, 48

Andō Sadayoshi, 45

Aoki Konyō, 143

Arnold, Julean H., 60, 61

Assimilation (*dōka*), 66-68; Tōgō Minoru's opposition to, 48, 81; policy of, 79, 80; Akashi Motojirō's concept of, 81-91, 92; and Den Kenjirō's integration rescript, 91-106

Assimilation Society, *see* Taiwan Assimilation Society

Austria, 162

Bimbō monogatari (Tales of the poor), 178

Boarding school experiment, 74-77

Bridgewater (Massachusetts) Normal School, 13

Burma, 225

Campbell, William, 22, 35, 124

Cheng Ch'eng-kung (Koxinga), 4, 5-6, 7

Chiang Kai-shek, 201

Chiang Wei-shui, 193, 195, 197-198, 203; and Taiwan Cultural Association, 206, 207

China, radical Taiwanese students in, 200-201

Chinese immigration, to Taiwan, 3, 4, 7

Ch'ing empire: Taiwan as outpost of, 6-8; examination system of, 38; collective security organizations of, 40-41

Chong-sik Lee, 172

Cities and towns, Japanese influence in, 156-159

Classical Chinese, teaching of, abolished from common schools, 111-112

Classics: teaching of, in common schools, 20; teaching of, in Shobō, 31, 38

Colonial rulers, Japanese compared to other, 224-228

Common School Regulations: (1898), 18; (1907), 50, 51; (1912), 50-51, 59

Common schools, 18-22, 30, 31; opportunities available to graduates of, 22-26; language institutes within, 32; percentage of Taiwanese school-aged children in, 40, 45-46; revision in curriculum of, 49-52; and vocational training, 52-53, 58; design of curriculum of, 59-60; absenteeism at, 61-62; female attendance at, 62-63; dropouts, 63-64; entry of graduates of, into medicine and teaching, 64-65; graduates of, studying in Japan, 65-66; Japanese enrollment in, 110; abolishing of classical Chinese from, 111-112; Japanese and Taiwanese teachers in, 112; renaming

HARVARD EAST ASIAN SERIES